SERIF IN USE

A C LECT OF
SERIF
PEFACE

OM A T Z

6 PAGES
YPEFACE
PROJECT

ISBN
978 988 76844-3-5
VICTIONARY.COM

Published and distributed by
viction:workshop ltd

viction:ary™

viction:workshop ltd
Unit C, 7/F, Seabright Plaza,
9-23 Shell Street,
North Point, Hong Kong
Url: www.victionary.com
Email: we@victionary.com

@victionworkshop
@victionworkshop
@victionary
@victionary

Edited and produced by viction workshop ltd
Creative direction: Victor Cheung
Art direction and design: Ben Lee@BD85BD85
Editorial: Ynes Filleul, YL Lim
Coordination: Katherine Wong, Jeanie Choy
Production: Bryan Leung
Typefaces: Fraktion Mono, Orbikular

Second Edition

ISBN 978-988-76844-3-5
Printed and bound in China

"WHY NOT?" NOTES ON (SERIF) TYPE DESIGN BY FABIAN HARB

AT DINAMO, WE INITIALLY CAME TO TYPE VIA GRAPHIC DESIGN AND HAD NO FORMAL EDUCATION. IN FACT, MOST OF OUR EARLIEST TYPEFACES WERE JUST CREATED FOR OUR OWN WORK: FOR POSTERS PROMOTING OUR FRIENDS' CLUB NIGHTS, BOOKS ACCOMPANYING AN EXHIBITION OR A WEBSITE FOR AN ACQUAINTED PHOTOGRAPHER AND SUCH. WE'VE ALWAYS BEEN DRAWN TO CREATING STRAIGHT-FORWARD, READY-TO-USE TOOLS THAT HAVE RECOGNISABLE TWEAKS; SOMETHING FUNCTIONAL BUT SPECIAL THAT CAN SHINE IN MULTIPLE USAGES AND CONTEXTS.

IN OUR EARLY DAYS, DESIGNING A SANS FELT THE MOST NATURAL AND PRACTICAL TO US. ASIDE FROM NEVER HAVING RECEIVED MANY GRAPHIC DESIGN COMMISSIONS THAT ASKED FOR A SERIF, I ALSO PERSONALLY ALWAYS FOUND THEM MORE INTIMIDATING TO TACKLE FROM A TYPE DESIGN PERSPECTIVE - NOT ONLY DUE TO THE SERIFS THEMSELVES, WHICH CAN COME IN LOTS OF DIFFERENT SHAPES, BUT ALSO THE TRANSITIONS INTO THE STEMS OR TERMINALS, WHICH HAVE TO BE DEFINED AND KEPT CONSISTENT IN SO MANY DIFFERENT LETTERS AND SITUATIONS.

WHILE WE STILL MADE SOME CONCEPTUAL AND GRAPHIC FORAYS INTO THE GENRE WITH PARETO AND LAICA, THE SERIF WORLD ITSELF HAS SUCH A RICH HISTORY AND THEORETICAL UNPINNING — THEREFORE, IT ALWAYS FELT A BIT MORE AWE-INSPIRING AND CHALLENGING TO US THAN CREATING A SANS. TODAY, AFTER PUBLISHING AND DESIGNING TYPEFACES FOR MORE THAN 10 YEARS, THE SERIF-GAP IN OUR LIBRARY HAS BECOME A GROWING MOTIVATION TO LOOK MORE INTO THE GENRE. AS OF WRITING THIS, THREE OUT OF OUR FIVE NEXT RELEASES WILL BE SERIFS. AND LIKE OUR SANS', OUR SERIFS ARE GENERALIST TOOLS WITH A DISTINCT FEATURE OR IDEA ADDED TO THEM; NEUTRAL-ISH TOOLS WITHOUT TOO MUCH DATE-STAMPED SHAPE VOCABULARY. IN A WAY, NO MATTER WHAT THE GENRE, OUR ETHOS REMAINS: WE LOOK FOR SOMETHING SPECIAL THAT PREVENTS THE DESIGN FROM BEING “ANOTHER ONE” OF WHAT IS ALREADY OUT THERE. “WHAT IF?” AND “WHY NOT?” HAVE ALWAYS BEEN THE IMPULSES GUIDING OUR TYPE DESIGN PRACTICE.

COMPENDIUMS LIKE THE ONE YOU HOLD IN YOUR HANDS HAVE ALWAYS BEEN DEAR AND IMPORTANT TO US — NOT ONLY TO SEE AND TEST YOUR OWN DESIGNS NEXT TO THOSE OF OTHERS, BUT ALSO TO SEE WHAT ELSE HAS BEEN - OR ACTUALLY HAS NOT BEEN — DONE YET. FROM A FOUNDRY PERSPECTIVE, THESE COLLECTIONS CAN ALSO BE A GREAT PLACE TO LEARN ABOUT NEW ARTISTS AND FIND POSSIBLE FUTURE RELEASES. FOR TYPE DESIGNERS THEMSELVES, IT CAN BECOME A NICE DIRECTORY OF LIKEMINDS AND POTENTIAL CONVERSATION PARTNERS OR PROJECT COLLABORATORS.

AFTER ALL, DESIGN WORK IS, ULTIMATELY, TEAM WORK. SO WHY NOT START CONNECTING A FEW DOTS TODAY?

CONTENTS

TYPE CHECK

		HAIRLINE	THIN	EXTRA LIGHT	LIGHT	BOOK	REGULAR	MEDIUM
A	ADORNO						•	
	AFFAIRS						•	
	ALDGATE SERIF	•	•		•		•	•
	ALIZEH						•	
	GT ALPINA		•		•		•	•
	ANTIQUA ROMAN						•	
	APOC	•			•		•	
	ABC ARIZONA		•		•		•	•
	ARTUSI			•	•		•	•
B	BEASTLY							
	F37 BELLA		•		•		•	
	F37 BOBBY				•		•	
C	CAKO		•				•	
	CANILARI						•	•
	CARDINAL						•	•
	CARDINAL TECH				•		•	
	CIGARS		•	•	•		•	•
	COFO CINEMA 1909						•	
	CX80				•		•	
E	ELIZETH		•	•	•		•	•
	EMILIO		•	•	•		•	
	ERNST		•	•	•		•	•
	TT ESPINA		•		•		•	
	EXPOSURE						•	
F	FANSAN				•		•	•
	OHNO FATFACE							
	FRAGEN		•	•	•		•	•
G	ABC GAISYR		•		•	•	•	•
	GAMUTH COLLECTION			•	•		•	•
	GESTURA		•	•	•		•	
	GLASGOW						•	•
	TT GLOBS			•	•		•	
	GREENSTONE						•	
I	INFERI	•	•	•	•	•	•	•
	INKA						•	•
	ITEMS		•		•		•	•
J	JAZZIER						•	
	JOANE PRO		•	•	•		•	•
	JUGENDREISEN							
	JÄGER						•	
K	KERNEVEL					•	•	
	KESSLER						•	
L	ABC LAICA				•	•	•	•
	LARKEN VARIABLE		•		•		•	•
	OR LEMMEN		•		•		•	•
	TT LIVRET				•		•	•
	LOUIZE DISPLAY						•	•
	LUCIFER						•	•
	FAIRE LUMA						•	•
M	MAGNO SERIF		•	•	•		•	•
	MARBLE ARCH	•	•		•		•	•
	ABC MARIST					•	•	•
	MESSER				•		•	
	COFO METEOR							
	MINOTAUR				•		•	
	MOLEN						•	
	MORION		•	•	•		•	

SEMIBOLD	BOLD	EXTRA BOLD	BLACK	EXTRA BLACK	ITALIC	OTHERS	CONDENSED	MONO	EXTENDED	PAGE
						●				012
					●	●		●		016
●	●	●	●		●	●	●		●	020
										024
	●				●	●	●		●	028
										032
	●	●	●		●	●				036
	●				●	●				042
	●	●	●		●	●				046
						●				050
	●				●	●				054
	●				●					058
			●		●					062
	●			●	●	●				068
●	●				●	●				074
	●				●	●				078
●	●		●	●						082
										086
	●					●				090
	●	●			●	●	●			096
●	●		●		●					100
	●	●			●	●				106
●	●		●			●				110
						●				114
●	●				●	●				120
						●				126
	●	●	●		●					130
	●		●		●	●		●		134
	●		●		●	●				138
●	●		●		●	●				142
	●		●		●					148
						●				152
					●					156
●	●	●	●		●					160
	●		●		●	●				166
	●		●		●	●	●	●	●	170
										174
●	●	●	●		●	●				178
						●				184
	●					●				188
	●		●		●					194
					●	●				198
	●				●	●		●		202
	●	●	●		●					206
	●				●	●	●	●		212
●	●				●	●				216
	●				●					220
●	●				●	●				224
	●		●			●				230
	●	●	●		●	●				234
●	●	●	●		●	●				238
●	●		●		●					242
	●				●	●	●			246
●										250
	●				●	●				254
										258
●	●				●	●				262

TYPE CHECK		HAIRLINE	THIN	EXTRA LIGHT	LIGHT	BOOK	REGULAR	MEDIUM
N	NEUMOND						●	
	NOE		●		●		●	●
	NUANCES		●	●	●		●	●
O	FAIRE OCTAVE						●	●
	OGG		●		●	●	●	●
	ORBIKULAR			●	●		●	
R	RABBIT HOLE DISPLAY						●	
	TT RICORDI TODI						●	
	COFO ROBERT				●	●	●	●
	ROMEK		●	●	●		●	●
S	SAINTE COLOMBE			●	●		●	●
	FT SAKRAL						●	●
	SALTER						●	
	SAMZARA						●	
	GT SECTRA				●	●	●	●
	SIGURD				●		●	
	SIMULA					●		
	SLACK LIGHT				●			
	FAIRE SPRIG	●	●		●		●	●
	STELLAGE						●	
	GT SUPER				●	●	●	●
	SWEAR		●		●		●	●
T	TARTUFFO		●		●		●	●
	TECHNIK SERIF							
	TESSERACT			●	●		●	
	FT THESAURUS						●	●
	TOBIAS		●		●		●	●
	TT TRICKS				●		●	
V	KOMETA VICTOR SERIF	●	●		●		●	●
	VISCONTE							
W	F37 WICKLOW				●		●	●
	WULKAN				●		●	●
Z	ZIN SERIF				●		●	●
	ZNVT23						●	

SEMIBOLD	BOLD	EXTRA BOLD	BLACK	EXTRA BLACK	ITALIC	OTHERS	CONDENSED	MONO	EXTENDED	PAGE
						●	●			268
●	●		●		●	●				272
●	●		●		●	●	●		●	276
	●		●							282
	●				●					288
●	●	●			●	●				292
										296
										300
	●	●	●		●					304
●	●				●	●				308
	●				●					312
	●		●		●	●				316
					●					320
					●					324
	●		●		●	●				328
	●	●	●		●	●				332
					●					338
										342
	●		●	●	●	●				346
					●	●				352
	●		●	●	●	●				356
	●		●		●	●				360
	●				●					364
						●				370
	●		●		●	●				374
	●		●		●	●				378
●	●	●	●		●	●				382
●	●	●	●		●	●				388
●	●		●		●					392
			●							396
	●	●	●		●	●				400
●	●		●		●					404
	●		●		●	●	●		●	408
										412

CH1. TYPEFACES A–Z

TYPEFACE	:	ADORNO
DESIGNER	:	W TYPE FOUNDRY
LOCATION	:	SANTIAGO, CHILE; BARCELONA, SPAIN; LONDON, UK

PUBLISHED BY	:	W TYPE FOUNDRY
CHRONOLOGY	:	2020
RELEASED IN	:	2020

LINK	:	HTTPS://WTYPEFOUNDRY.COM/TYPEFACES/ADORNO
STYLES	:	REGULAR, BORDERS

THE ADORNO TYPEFACE AROSE FROM THE DESIRE TO EXPLORE NEW FORMS IN THE DEVELOPMENT OF DIGITAL FONTS. EXPERIMENTAL, PURPOSEFUL, AND FREE TO DOWNLOAD, IT TAKES GLYPHIC TYPEFACES AS AN INITIAL REFERENCE, THEN TURNS TOWARDS UNCIAL AND GAELIC TYPEFACES. IT MIXES A HUMANISTIC SANS SERIF SKELETON WITH CLASSIC 15TH CENTURY FONT FEATURES, AS WELL AS A COPPERPLATE TOUCH.

adorno

REGULAR – 50PT

The quick brow
It would be th
It's a lovely da
and the punge
promise of a su

REGULAR – 14PT

The quick brown fox jumps over a lazy dog. He didn't
It would be the cheeky thing to do. After all, he had
It's a lovely day in the neighbourhood, with the sun
and the pungent aroma of fresh rubbish bins waftin
promise of a sumptuous meal. The sprightly fox ru
thinking about the delicious treasures he's about to
The lazy dog remains unperturbed. With her long sn
long black fur fluttering in the breeze, she is in a dr
the mountains are made of beefy treats, the valley
and the puddles are just the right temperature. Why
It's a dog's life, after all.

REGULAR – 8PT

The quick brown fox jumps over a lazy dog. He didn't have to, but he thought
it would be the cheeky thing to do. After all, he had a reputation to maintain.
It's a lovely day in the neighbourhood, with the sun shining, the birds chirping,
and the pungent aroma of fresh rubbish bins wafting through the air - the
promise of a sumptuous meal. The sprightly fox rubs his paws together in glee,
thinking about the delicious treasures he's about to dig into. Still in her spot,
the lazy dog remains unperturbed. With her long snout, droopy jowls, and
long black fur fluttering in the breeze, she is in a dreamland far away - where
the mountains are made of beefy treats, the valleys are filled with tennis balls,
and the puddles are just the right temperature. Why be in the rat race?
It's a dog's life, after all.

ECCE
HOMO

aabBcdD

eeffGhHI

JjkKLLm

nopPqq

RSTZuUV

wWXyy

Z012345

6789¢&

($1

TYPEFACE	:	AFFAIRS
DESIGNER	:	SM FOUNDRY
LOCATION	:	APELDOORN, THE NETHERLANDS

16

PUBLISHED BY	:	SM FOUNDRY
CHRONOLOGY	:	2019 - 2021
RELEASED IN	:	2021

LINK	:	HTTP://S-M.NU/TYPEFACES/AFFAIRS
STYLES	:	REGULAR, ITALIC, MONOSPACE

AFFAIRS IS A COMPACT BUT VERSATILE SERIF TYPE FAMILY. ITS GEOMETRIC STRUCTURE AND SLEEK CURVES GIVE IT A FUNCTIONAL BUT SOFT CHARACTER, ALLOWING IT TO BE APPLIED IN BOTH FORMAL AND INFORMAL SETTINGS. AFFAIRS HAS CHARACTERISTICS AND PROPORTIONS THAT ARE SIMILAR TO EVERYONE'S FAVOURITE NEO-GROTESQUE, WHICH MAKES IT A GREAT COMPANION FOR SANS SERIF TYPEFACES.

CAP HEIGHT

REGULAR – 290PT

X-HEIGHT

Aa

BASELINE

Affairs

REGULAR – 40PT

THE QUICK BROWN F
IT WOULD BE THE CH
IT'S A LOVELY DAY IN
AND THE PUNGENT A
PROMISE OF A SUMPT
THINKING ABOUT TH
THE LAZY DOG REMA
LONG BLACK FUR FL
THE MOUNTAINS AR
AND THE PUDDLES A

REGULAR – 10PT

The quick brown fox jumps over a lazy dog. He didn't have to, but he thought it would be the cheeky thing to do. After all, he had a reputation to maintain. It's a lovely day in the neighbourhood, with the sun shining, the birds chirping, and the pungent aroma of fresh rubbish bins wafting through the air - the promise of a sumptuous meal. The sprightly fox rubs his paws together in glee, thinking about the delicious treasures he's about to dig into. Still in her spot, the lazy dog remains unperturbed. With her long snout, droopy jowls, and long black fur fluttering in the breeze, she is in a dreamland far away - where the mountains are made of beefy treats, the valleys are filled with tennis balls, and the puddles are just the right temperature. Why be in the rat race? It's a dog's life, after all.

Affairs FAMILY

AM

Affairs

1 Regular 2 *Italic*

3 Monospace

Ff z

!?

@Æ

TYPEFACE	:	ALDGATE SERIF
DESIGNER	:	DALTON MAAG
LOCATION	:	LONDON, UK

20

PUBLISHED BY	:	DALTON MAAG
CHRONOLOGY	:	2023
RELEASED IN	:	2023

LINK	:	HTTPS://WWW.DALTONMAAG.COM/PORTFOLIO/FONT-LIBRARY/ALDGATE-SERIF.HTML
STYLES	:	MULTI-AXIS VARIABLE FONTS + STATIC FONTS IN WEIGHTS & STYLES RANGING FROM XCONDENSED HAIR TO XEXTENDED BLACK

ALDGATE SERIF IS A CONTEMPORARY SERIF TYPEFACE DESIGNED TO SUPPORT AND COMPLEMENT ITS SANS COUSIN. ITS OPEN LETTER SHAPES ENSURE LEGIBILITY WITH A WARM AND DIGNIFIED TONE, AND ITS VARIABLE FONT OFFERS EXTENSIVE WEIGHT, WIDTH, AND ITALIC AXES FOR EXCEPTIONAL VERSATILITY.

CAP HEIGHT

REGULAR – 290PT

X-HEIGHT

Aa

BASELINE

Aldgate Serif

REGULAR – 55PT

THE QUICK BRO
IT WOULD BE T
IT'S A LOVELY I
AND THE PUNG
PROMISE OF A S
THINKING ABO
THE LAZY DOG

REGULAR – 16PT

The quick brown fox jumps over a lazy dog. He didn't ha
it would be the cheeky thing to do. After all, he had a re
It's a lovely day in the neighbourhood, with the sun shin
and the pungent aroma of fresh rubbish bins wafting th
promise of a sumptuous meal. The sprightly fox rubs his
thinking about the delicious treasures he's about to dig
the lazy dog remains unperturbed. With her long snout,
long black fur fluttering in the breeze, she is in a dreaml
the mountains are made of beefy treats, the valleys are

Aldgate *Serif*

Aa Aa

XCd XE

Aa Aa

A
fox
ran
down
Maple
Street

a *a* a *a* a *a* a *a* a *a* a *a*
a *a* a *a* a *a* a *a* a *a* a *a*
a *a* a *a* a *a* a *a* a *a* a *a*
a *a* a *a* a *a* a *a* a *a* a *a*
a *a* a *a* a *a* a *a* a *a* a *a*
a *a* a *a* a *a* a *a* a *a* a *a*
a *a* a *a* a *a* a *a* a *a* a *a*
a *a* a *a* a *a* a *a* a *a* a *a*
a *a* a *a* a *a* a *a* a *a* a *a*

N E W

Gateway	Forge	Flag	King	Dart	Wren	Emblem
Markets	Glens	Fish	Moor	Pool	Cake	Archive
Butcher	Shard	Lake	Arch	Kite	Teas	Barrage
Taverns	Baker	Pint	Bell	Ales	Lady	Tenants
Templar	Canal	Hawk	Dock	Beef	Time	Ancient
Lantern	Rugby	Lord	Bard	Peas	Oath	Tunnels
Bastion	Manor	Gent	Duke	Kent	Gale	Charter
History	Tudor	Tree	Rose	York	Play	Aldgate
Culture	Lakes	Chip	Pies	Gray	Tide	Streets

TYPEFACE : ALIZEH
DESIGNER : THEYTYPE
LOCATION : MONTREAL, CANADA; SARATOGA, US

PUBLISHED BY : THEYTYPE
CHRONOLOGY : PRESENT
RELEASED IN : 2022

LINK : HTTPS://THEYTYPE.COM/
STYLES : REGULAR

ALIZEH IS A REVIVAL AND ODE TO ITS ORIGINAL SOURCE OF LEIPZIG-BASED FOUNDRY SCHELTER & GIESECKE'S 1819 SPECIMEN CATALOGUE. IT HONOURS THE CONDENSED PROFILE AND DISTINCT CONTRAST OF ITS EARLY "EGYPTIENNE" SOURCE, CREATING A FORM OF BOTH GRACEFULNESS AND STABILITY. ITS PLAYFUL BALL TERMINALS AND DELICATE CURVES GIVE ALIZEH A DISTINCT COMBINATION OF ELEGANCE AND COMMAND PERFECT FOR DISPLAY APPLICATIONS. THE DEVELOPING CHARACTER SET INCLUDES EXTENDED LATIN LANGUAGE SUPPORT, BASIC PUNCTUATION AND SYMBOLS.

CAP HEIGHT

REGULAR – 290PT

X-HEIGHT

Aa

BASELINE

Alizeh

REGULAR – 40PT

THE QUICK BROWN FOX JU
IT WOULD BE THE CHEEKY
IT'S A LOVELY DAY IN THE
AND THE PUNGENT AROM
PROMISE OF A SUMPTUOU
THINKING ABOUT THE DE

REGULAR – 16PT

The quick brown fox jumps over a lazy dog. He didn't have to, but he th
it would be the cheeky thing to do. After all, he had a reputation to mai
It's a lovely day in the neighbourhood, with the sun shining, the birds c
and the pungent aroma of fresh rubbish bins wafting through the air - t
promise of a sumptuous meal. The sprightly fox rubs his paws together
thinking about the delicious treasures he's about to dig into. Still in her
the lazy dog remains unperturbed. With her long snout, droopy jowls, a
long black fur fluttering in the breeze, she is in a dreamland far away -
the mountains are made of beefy treats, the valleys are filled with tenn
and the puddles are just the right temperature. Why be in the rat race?
It's a dog's life, after all.

REGULAR – 8PT

The quick brown fox jumps over a lazy dog. He didn't have to, but he thought it would be the cheeky thing to do. After all, he had a reputation to maintain. It's a lovely day in the neighbourhood, with the sun shining, the birds chirping, and the pungent aroma of fresh rubbish bins wafting through the air - the promise of a sumptuous meal. The sprightly fox rubs his paws together in glee, thinking about the delicious treasures he's about to dig into. Still in her spot, the lazy dog remains unperturbed. With her long snout, droopy jowls, and long black fur fluttering in the breeze, she is in a dreamland far away - where the mountains are made of beefy treats, the valleys are filled with tennis balls, and the puddles are just the right temperature. Why be in the rat race? It's a dog's life, after all.

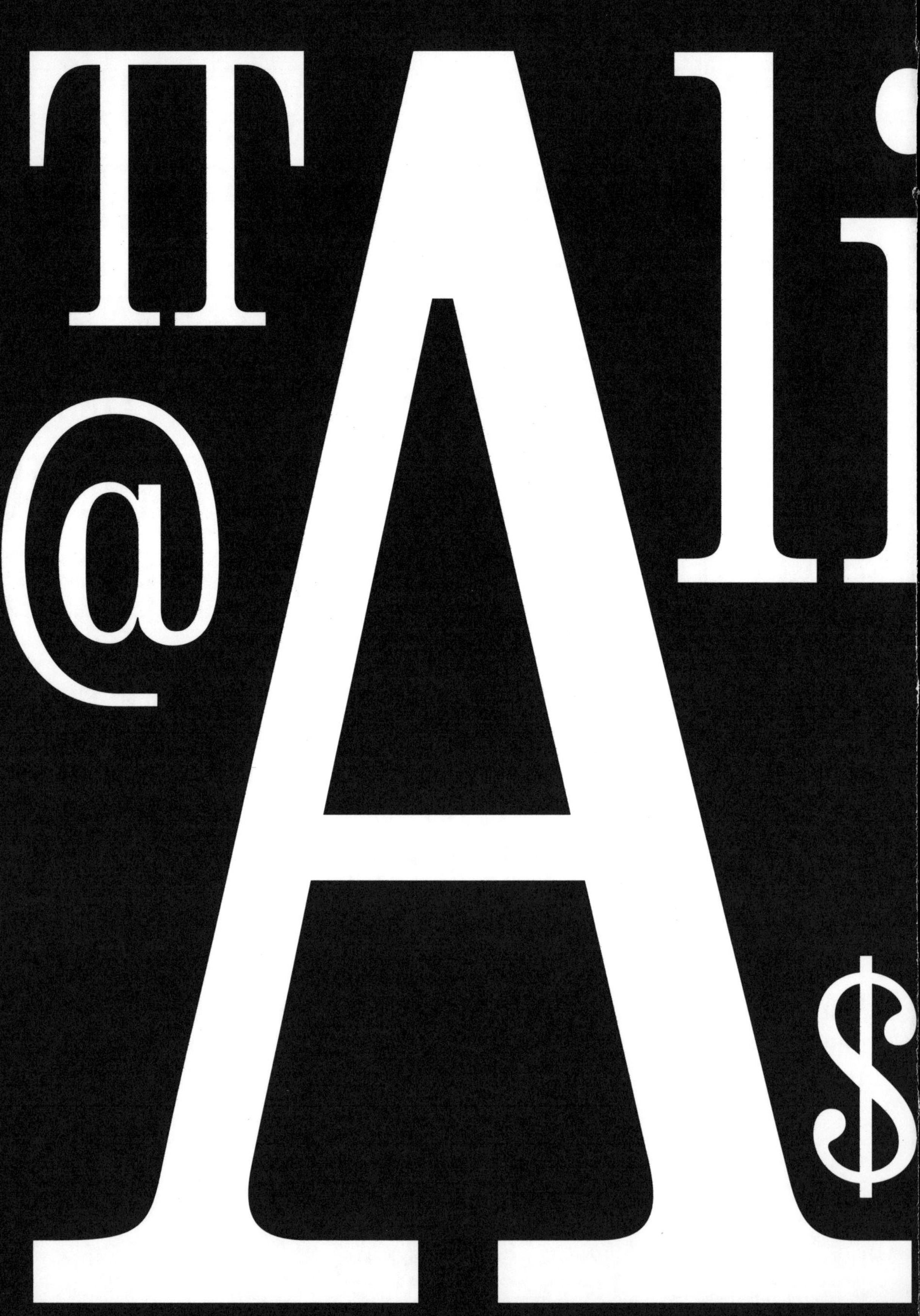

Z & www. eh

TYPEFACE	:	GT ALPINA
DESIGNER	:	GRILLI TYPE
LOCATION	:	LUCERNE, SWITZERLAND; NEW YORK, US

PUBLISHED BY	:	GRILLI TYPE
CHRONOLOGY	:	N/A
RELEASED IN	:	2020

LINK	:	HTTPS://WWW.GT-ALPINA.COM/
STYLES	:	70
CREDITS	:	RETO MOSER (DESIGN)

GT ALPINA PROUDLY CALLS ITSELF A WORKHORSE SERIF, BUT DELIGHTS IN PLAYING WITH THE VERY MEANING OF THAT CONCEPT. IT REACHES INTO THE GRAB BAG OF TYPOGRAPHIC HISTORY TO RESURRECT SHAPES SOME MAY FALSELY SEE AS TOO EXPRESSIVE, RESULTING IN A METICULOUS FAMILY THAT MELDS THESE DISTINCT SHAPES WITH PRAGMATIC EXECUTION. THE RESULT IS A COMPREHENSIVE FAMILY OF SEVENTY FONTS COVERING A WIDE RANGE OF WIDTHS, WEIGHTS, CONTRASTS, AND PROPORTIONALITY. GT ALPINA ALSO INCLUDES PLAYFUL ICONS AND EMOJIS TO COMPLEMENT THE TYPE.

CAP HEIGHT

REGULAR – 290PT

X-HEIGHT

Aa

BASELINE

GT Alpina

REGULAR – 36PT

THE QUICK BROWN FOX
IT WOULD BE THE CHEE
IT'S A LOVELY DAY IN TH
AND THE PUNGENT ARO
PROMISE OF A SUMPTUO
THINKING ABOUT THE D
THE LAZY DOG REMAIN

REGULAR – 18PT

The quick brown fox jumps over a lazy dog. He didn't hav
it would be the cheeky thing to do. After all, he had a rep
It's a lovely day in the neighbourhood, with the sun shinin
and the pungent aroma of fresh rubbish bins wafting thro
promise of a sumptuous meal. The sprightly fox rubs his
thinking about the delicious treasures he's about to dig in
the lazy dog remains unperturbed. With her long snout, d
long black fur fluttering in the breeze, she is in a dreamla

REGULAR – 8PT

The quick brown fox jumps over a lazy dog. He didn't have to, but he thought it would be the cheeky thing to do. After all, he had a reputation to maintain. It's a lovely day in the neighbourhood, with the sun shining, the birds chirping, and the pungent aroma of fresh rubbish bins wafting through the air - the promise of a sumptuous meal. The sprightly fox rubs his paws together in glee, thinking about the delicious treasures he's about to dig into. Still in her spot, the lazy dog remains unperturbed. With her long snout, droopy jowls, and long black fur fluttering in the breeze, she is in a dreamland far away - where the mountains are made of beefy treats, the valleys are filled with tennis balls, and the puddles are just the right temperature. Why be in the rat race? It's a dog's life, after all.

W *Swiss Alps*

Wo *Swiss Alp*

Wor *Swiss Al*

World *Swiss A*

World *Swiss*

Worldw *Swis*

Worldwi *Swi*

Worldwid *Sw*

Worldwide *S*

S Worldwide

Sw Worldwid

Swi Worldwi

Swis Worldw

Swiss World

Swiss A Worl

Swiss Al Wor

Swiss Alp Wo

Swiss Alps W

TYPEFACE : ANTIQUA ROMAN
DESIGNER : YUANCHEN JIANG
LOCATION : CALIFORNIA, US

PUBLISHED BY : MYFONT.COM
CHRONOLOGY : N/A
RELEASED IN : 2017

LINK : HTTPS://YUANCHENJIANG.CARGO.SITE/ANTIQUA-ROMAN-TYPEFACE
STYLES : REGULAR
CREDITS : TOBIAS FRÈRE-JONES

THE MOST DISTINCT FEATURE OF THE ANTIQUA ROMAN TYPEFACE IS THAT EACH LETTER CONTAINS A VERY THIN STROKE. ITS DESIGN IS BASED ON THE ORIGINAL HAND-WRITING OF FRITZ HELMUTH EHMCKE IN 1907.

CAP HEIGHT

REGULAR – 290PT

Aa

X-HEIGHT

BASELINE

Antiqua Roman

THE QUICK BROWN FO
IT WOULD BE THE CHE
IT'S A LOVELY DAY IN TH
AND THE PUNGENT AR
PROMISE OF A SUMPTU
THINKING ABOUT THE
THE LAZY DOG REMAI
LONG BLACK FUR FLUT
THE MOUNTAINS ARE M
AND THE PUDDLES ARE
IT'S A DOG'S LIFE, AFTE

Bb Cc Dd Ee Ff

Mm Nn Oo Pp

Tt Uu Vv Ww Xx

1/5 2/5 3/5 4/5 1/6 5/6

SO, HOW DO YOU SEE A FACE?

TYPEFACE : APOC
DESIGNER : BLAZE TYPE
LOCATION : MARSEILLE, FRANCE

PUBLISHED BY : BLAZE TYPE
CHRONOLOGY : 2018, 2019, 2020, 2023
RELEASED IN : 2018

LINK : HTTPS://BLAZETYPE.EU/TYPEFACES/APOC
STYLES : SERIF, SANS, DISPLAY, TEXT, UPRIGHT, ITALIC

APOC(ALYPSE) EMBODIES THE BATTLE BETWEEN LIGHT AND DARK. ITS SHARP CHARACTER SET AND ALTERNATES WERE RELEASED IN 2018 AND UPDATED IN 2020 THEN 2022 BY MATTHIEU SALVAGGIO. ITS CRYILLIC LANGUAGES WERE DESIGNED BY ILYA RUDERMAN OF TOMORROW TYPE. DEFINED BY DESIGNERS AS THE MOST POPULAR TYPEFACE FOR STANDOUT CONTEMPORARY INDEPENDENT DESIGN, APOC IS AN ELEGANT, SHARP, AND EXPRESSIVE FONT FAMILY PERFECT FOR BOLD STANDOUT DISPLAYS FOCUSING ON HEAVY FONT USES. IT IS WELL SUITED FOR SHARPENING WEBSITE HEADLINES, ART EXHIBITION POSTERS AND ALBUM COVERS.

CAP HEIGHT

REGULAR – 290PT

X-HEIGHT

Aa

BASELINE

Apoc

THE QUIC
IT WOULD
IT'S A LOV
AND THE
PROMISE
THINKING

MONOTHEISTS
APPLICABILITY
CONGRUENCY
DISSOCIATING
SOUNDPROOF
RECAPITULATE
TECHNICALITY
ETHOLOGICAL
PROCEEDINGS
TRANSLUCENT
UNDERLININGS
JUDGEMENTAL
INVIGORATING

OVERT
DISCO
DIVERT
CULT
BIVOU
PRED
DISIN
IMAG
HARV
ABSO
BACKG
MISAN
EXTINC

IMPROVEMENT

CAMPAIGNERS

ROWS BEHAVIOURIST

NECTS HAMMERHEAD

CULAR ANTAGONISED

ATION APPLICABILITY

ACKED INDUSTRIALISE

TIONS COLONIALISTS

CTING CENTRALISING

ATION DECREMENTAL

STING SANDCASTLES

UTION UNREASONING

OUND DEMORALISED

HROPY

UISHED

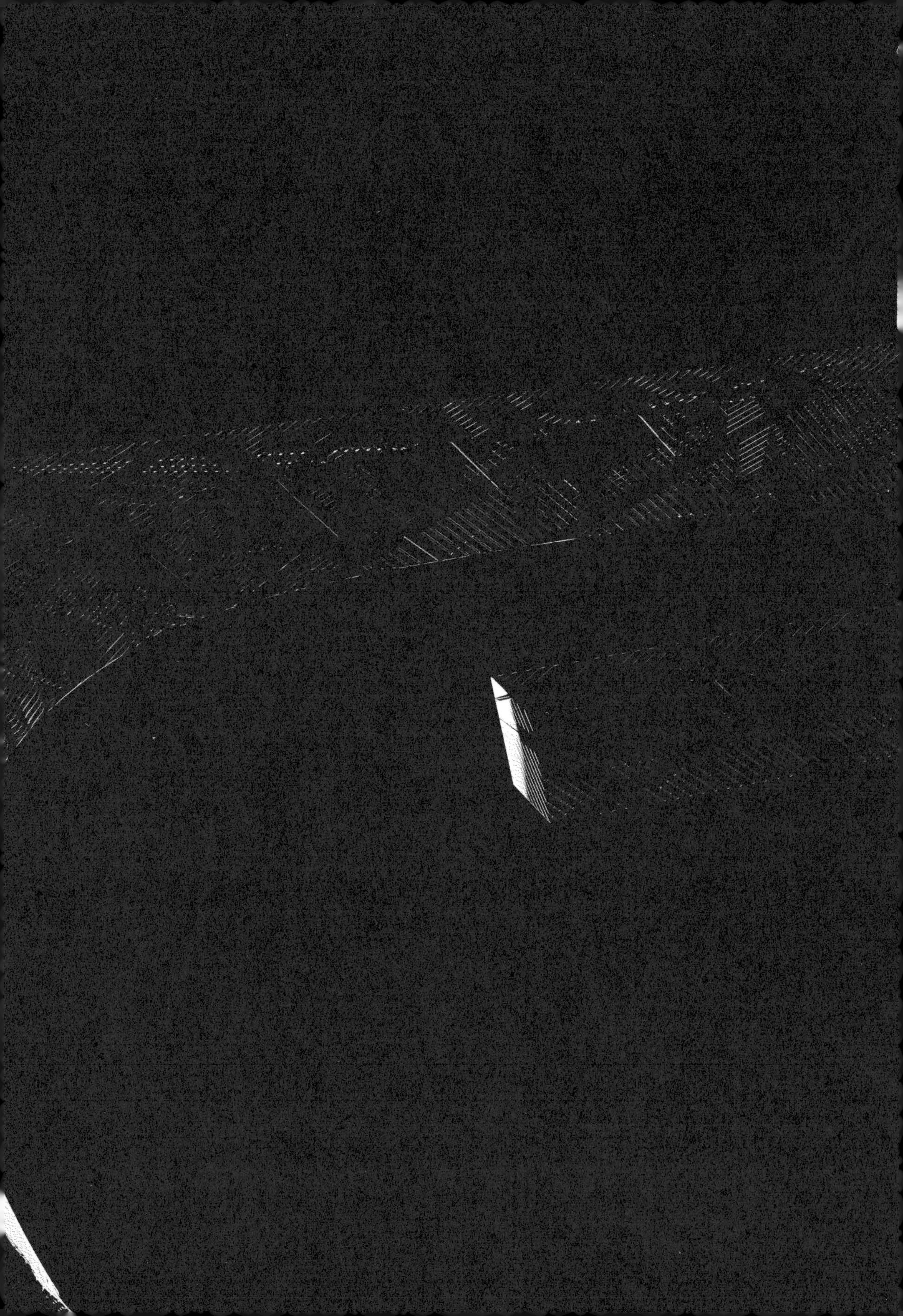

TYPEFACE : ABC ARIZONA
DESIGNER : DINAMO
LOCATION : BERLIN, GERMANY

PUBLISHED BY : DINAMO
CHRONOLOGY : N/A
RELEASED IN : 2021

LINK : HTTPS://ABCDINAMO.COM/TYPEFACES/ARIZONA
STYLES : 5 FAMILIES, 50 STYLES
CREDITS : ELIAS HANZER (DESIGN), IGINO MARINI (SPACING & KERNING), ROBERT JANES/DINAMO (PRODUCTION)

ABC ARIZONA IS THE FIRST-EVER SANS TO SERIF “SUPERFAMILY” THAT PACKAGES ITS FIVE LOOKS — SERIF, TEXT, MIX, FLARE, AND SANS — INTO ONE SINGLE FONT FILE. IN OTHER WORDS, IT IS A SLIM, ALL-GENRES-IN-ONE FONT HAPPY-MEAL, VERSATILE AND ADJUSTABLE FOR ANY CONTEXT. ARIZONA HAS FIVE DISTINCTIVE YET CONNECTED SUBFAMILIES. ARIZONA SERIF IS A HIGH CONTRAST, POINTY SERIF WITH A MODERN-MEETS-RENAISSANCE FRESHNESS, AND ON THE OTHER SIDE OF THE SPECTRUM, ARIZONA SANS IS A STRAIGHT-FORWARD GROTESQUE WITH A HUMANISTIC TOUCH. IN BETWEEN LIE OTHER SPECIES, SUCH AS THE NEARLY-BUT-NOT SANS ARIZONA FLARE. ARIZONA MIX IS CHUNKIER AND LOW-CONTRAST, WHILE ARIZONA TEXT IS A CLASSIC TEXT SERIF TYPEFACE THAT IS WELL SUITED FOR READING. STRETCHING FROM ITS HEADLINE TO SMALL TEXT POSSIBILITIES, AN ENTIRE LIBRARY CAN BE TYPESET WITH JUST THIS ONE TYPEFACE.

CAP HEIGHT

REGULAR - 290PT

X-HEIGHT

Aa

BASELINE

ABC Arizona

REGULAR – 36PT

THE QUICK BROWN FOX
IT WOULD BE THE CHEE
IT'S A LOVELY DAY IN TH
AND THE PUNGENT ARO
PROMISE OF A SUMPTUO
THINKING ABOUT THE D
THE LAZY DOG REMAIN

REGULAR – 18PT

The quick brown fox jumps over a lazy dog. He didn't ha
it would be the cheeky thing to do. After all, he had a rep
It's a lovely day in the neighbourhood, with the sun shin
and the pungent aroma of fresh rubbish bins wafting thr
promise of a sumptuous meal. The sprightly fox rubs his
thinking about the delicious treasures he's about to dig i
the lazy dog remains unperturbed. With her long snout,
long black fur fluttering in the breeze, she is in a dreaml

REGULAR – 8PT

The quick brown fox jumps over a lazy dog. He didn't have to, but he thought it would be the cheeky thing to do. After all, he had a reputation to maintain. It's a lovely day in the neighbourhood, with the sun shining, the birds chirping, and the pungent aroma of fresh rubbish bins wafting through the air - the promise of a sumptuous meal. The sprightly fox rubs his paws together in glee, thinking about the delicious treasures he's about to dig into. Still in her spot, the lazy dog remains unperturbed. With her long snout, droopy jowls, and long black fur fluttering in the breeze, she is in a dreamland far away - where the mountains are made of beefy treats, the valleys are filled with tennis balls, and the puddles are just the right temperature. Why be in the rat race? It's a dog's life, after all.

a A

Affirm › Affirm

0123456789
0123456789

g g g

Morning
Hello World
How Are You?

TYPEFACE : ARTUSI
DESIGNER : ZETAFONTS TYPE FOUNDRY
LOCATION : FLORENCE, ITALY

PUBLISHED BY : ZETAFONTS TYPE FOUNDRY
CHRONOLOGY : 2023
RELEASED IN : 2023

LINK : HTTPS://ZETAFONTS.COM/ARTUSI
STYLES : 28 STYLES + 2 VARIABLES INCLUDING 8 WEIGHTS + ITALICS X 2 STYLES

TAKING INSPIRATION FROM PELLIGRINO ARTUSI AND HIS LEGACY, THE ARTUSI TYPEFACE REPRESENTS A TYPOGRAPHIC HOMAGE TO THE DELICACY AND FINESSE OF ITALIAN TRADITIONAL CUISINE. IT IS AN ENCHANTING COMBINATION OF TRADITIONAL ITALIAN STYLE, CONTEMPORARY REFINEMENT AND A PLAYFUL TOUCH OF INNOVATION. IT IS ALSO A TRANSITIONAL SERIF TYPEFACE WITH BOTH TEXT (ARTUSI ROMAN) AND DISPLAY (ARTUSI GRANDE) VERSIONS, DEVELOPED ON A WIDE RANGE OF SEVEN WEIGHTS AND INCLUDING A HUGE RANGE OF ALTERNATES, OPENTYPE FEATURES AND LIGATURES. FROM PACKAGING TO WEB PAGES, THE ARTUSI TYPEFACE WILL BRING A FEELING OF TRADITION, CRAFT AND QUALITY TO ANY PROJECT.

CAP HEIGHT

REGULAR - 290PT

X-HEIGHT

Aa

BASELINE

Artusi

REGULAR – 60PT

THE QUICK BRO
IT WOULD BE TI
IT'S A LOVELY D
AND THE PUNG
PROMISE OF A S
THINKING ABOU
THE LAZY DOG

REGULAR – 8PT

The quick brown fox jumps over a lazy dog. He didn't have to, but he thought it would be the cheeky thing to do. After all, he had a reputation to maintain. It's a lovely day in the neighbourhood, with the sun shining, the birds chirping, and the pungent aroma of fresh rubbish bins wafting through the air - the promise of a sumptuous meal. The sprightly fox rubs his paws together in glee, thinking about the delicious treasures he's about to dig into. Still in her spot, the lazy dog remains unperturbed. With her long snout, droopy jowls, and long black fur fluttering in the breeze, she is in a dreamland far away - where the mountains are made of beefy treats, the valleys are filled with tennis balls, and the puddles are just the right temperature. Why be in the rat race? It's a dog's life, after all.

b
A
w
i
*
m
3

iii gg

£ ¾

My

TYPEFACE : BEASTLY
DESIGNER : OH NO TYPE CO.
LOCATION : CALIFORNIA, US

PUBLISHED BY : OH NO TYPE CO.
CHRONOLOGY : N/A
RELEASED IN : 2018

LINK : HTTPS://OHNOTYPE.CO/FONTS/BEASTLY
STYLES : 9 OPTICAL STYLES + 1 BEASTLY RULES STYLE

A RIFF ON LUBALIN-ERA TYPOGRAPHY, BEASTLY IS A REVERSED CONTRAST SLAB SERIF DESIGN THAT CAME ABOUT WHILE ITS DESIGNERS WERE WORKING ON THE LOGOTYPE FOR LUBALIN 100. IT IS A COMPLETELY NEW DESIGN THAT IMBUES QUALITIES OF HERB LUBALIN'S TEAM OF LETTERING ARTISTS' SIGNATURE STYLES.

Beastly

REGULAR – 36PT

THE QUICK BROWN FOX
IT WOULD BE THE CHEE
IT'S A LOVELY DAY IN TH
AND THE PUNGENT ARO
PROMISE OF A SUMPTU
THINKING ABOUT THE D
THE LAZY DOG REMAINS
LONG BLACK FUR FLUTT
THE MOUNTAINS ARE M
AND THE PUDDLES ARE
IT'S A DOG'S LIFE, AFTE

REGULAR – 10PT

The quick brown fox jumps over a lazy dog. He didn't have to, but he thought it would be the cheeky thing to do. After all, he had a reputation to maintain. It's a lovely day in the neighbourhood, with the sun shining, the birds chirping, and the pungent aroma of fresh rubbish bins wafting through the air - the promise of a sumptuous meal. The sprightly fox rubs his paws together in glee, thinking about the delicious treasures he's about to dig into. Still in her spot, the lazy dog remains unperturbed. With her long snout, droopy jowls, and long black fur fluttering in the breeze, she is in a dreamland far away - where the mountains are made of beefy treats, the valleys are filled with tennis balls, and the puddles are just the right temperature. Why be in the rat race? It's a dog's life, after all.

Hey
Boy

Hey Girl

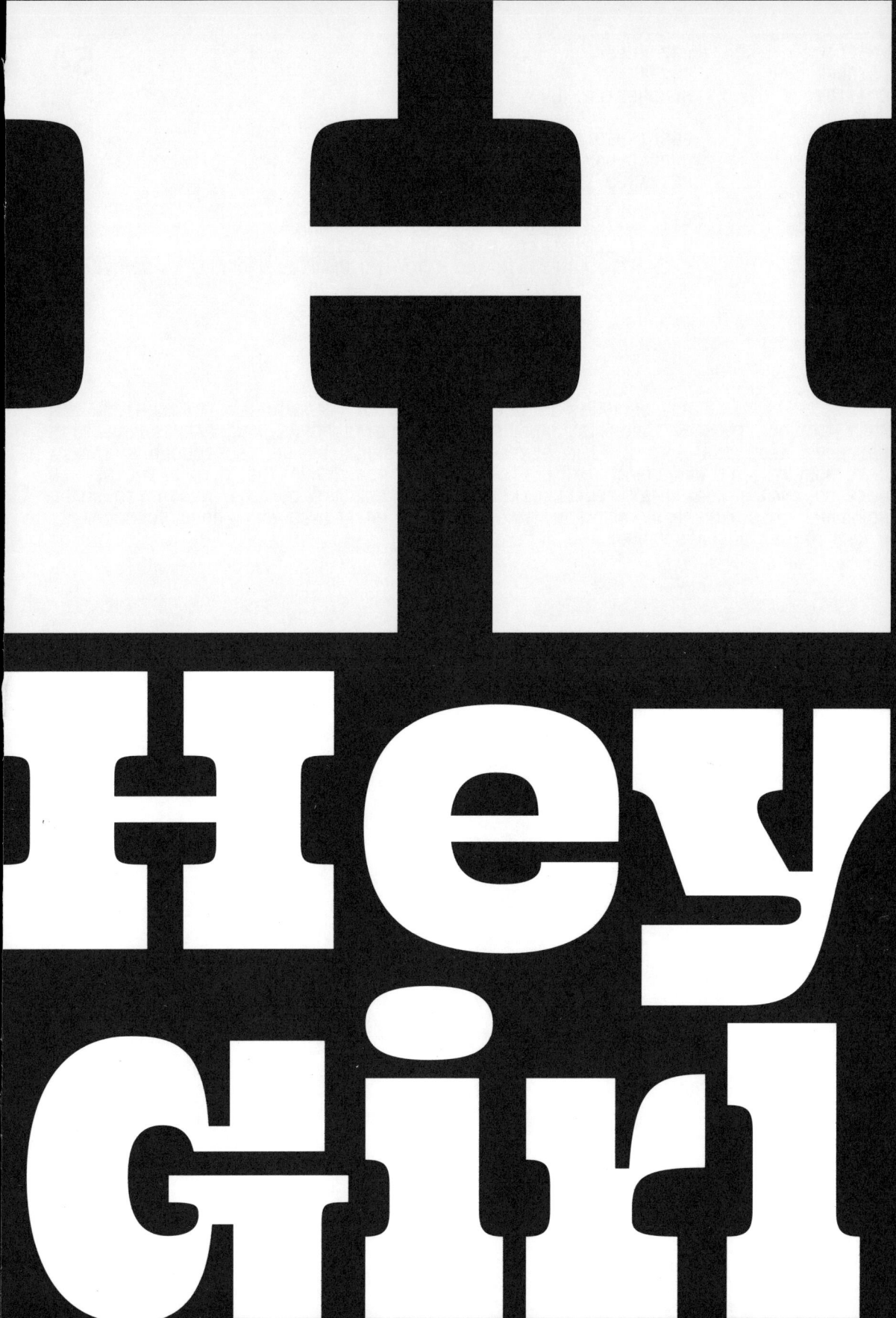

TYPEFACE : F37 BELLA
DESIGNER : F37®
LOCATION : MANCHESTER, UK

PUBLISHED BY : F37®
CHRONOLOGY : 2011 - 2021
RELEASED IN : 2011

LINK : HTTPS://F37FOUNDRY.COM/FONTS/F37-BELLA
STYLES : 4 FAMILIES: TEXT, DISPLAY, HEADLINE, STENCIL.
EACH WITH 4 WEIGHTS AND MATCHING ITALICS, TOTALLING 32 STYLES.

F37 BELLA IS INFLUENCED BY SWISS TYPOGRAPHER JAN TSCHICHOLD'S EARLY EXPLORATIONS OF GEOMETRY AND SHAPE IN LETTERFORMS. IN PARTICULAR, ITS DESIGNERS WERE INSPIRED BY THE PERFECT BALL TERMINALS OF TSCHICHOLD'S SASKIA FONT. HOWEVER, IT WAS JOHN PISTILLI'S PISTILLI ROMAN AND THE THIN HAIRLINES IN LOUIS DORFMAN'S WORK THAT FINALLY INSPIRED F37 BELLA'S OVERALL AESTHETIC SHAPE AND FORM. THIS INTERPLAY BETWEEN FRACTURE-THIN HAIRLINES AND PRONOUNCED CURVES IS KEY TO F37 BELLA'S CHARM AND APPEAL.

F37 Bella

REGULAR – 36PT

THE QUICK BROWN FOX J

IT WOULD BE THE CHEEK

IT'S A LOVELY DAY IN THE

AND THE PUNGENT AROM

PROMISE OF A SUMPTUOU

THINKING ABOUT THE DE

THE LAZY DOG REMAINS

LONG BLACK FUR FLUTTE

THE MOUNTAINS ARE MAD

AND THE PUDDLES ARE J

IT'S A DOG'S LIFE, AFTER

REGULAR – 10PT

The quick brown fox jumps over a lazy dog. He didn't have to, but he thought it would be the cheeky thing to do. After all, he had a reputation to maintain. It's a lovely day in the neighbourhood, with the sun shining, the birds chirping, and the pungent aroma of fresh rubbish bins wafting through the air – the promise of a sumptuous meal. The sprightly fox rubs his paws together in glee, thinking about the delicious treasures he's about to dig into. Still in her spot, the lazy dog remains unperturbed. With her long snout, droopy jowls, and long black fur fluttering in the breeze, she is in a dreamland far away – where the mountains are made of beefy treats, the valleys are filled with tennis balls, and the puddles are just the right temperature. Why be in the rat race? It's a dog's life, after all.

Text

Bella

Text Italic

Bella

Display

Bella

Display Italic

Bella

Headline

Bella

Headline Italic

Bella

Stencil

Bella

Bella

TYPEFACE : F37 BOBBY
DESIGNER : F37®
LOCATION : MANCHESTER, UK

PUBLISHED BY : F37®
CHRONOLOGY : 2018 - 2023
RELEASED IN : 2018

LINK : HTTPS://F37FOUNDRY.COM/FONTS/F37-BOBBY
STYLES : 3 WEIGHTS WITH MATCHING TRUE ITALICS, TOTALLING 6 STYLES

F37 BOBBY IS A CONTEMPORARY GEOMETRIC SERIF. ITS DESIGN WAS INFLUENCED BY THE WARM SERIFS THAT WERE POPULAR BACK IN THE 1970'S. ITS DESIGNERS TOOK INSPIRATION FROM THE ROUNDED, FRIENDLY FEEL OF FONTS LIKE SOUVENIR, WINDSOR AND COOPER BLACK.

CAP HEIGHT

REGULAR – 290PT

X-HEIGHT

Bb

BASELINE

F37Bobby

REGULAR - 48PT

THE QUICK BROWN
IT WOULD BE THE
IT'S A LOVELY DAY
AND THE PUNGENT
PROMISE OF A SUM

REGULAR - 14PT

The quick brown fox jumps over a lazy dog. He didn't have to, but
it would be the cheeky thing to do. After all, he had a reputation t
It's a lovely day in the neighbourhood, with the sun shining, the bi
and the pungent aroma of fresh rubbish bins wafting through the
promise of a sumptuous meal. The sprightly fox rubs his paws tog
thinking about the delicious treasures he's about to dig into. Still i
the lazy dog remains unperturbed. With her long snout, droopy jo
long black fur fluttering in the breeze, she is in a dreamland far av
the mountains are made of beefy treats, the valleys are filled with
and the puddles are just the right temperature. Why be in the rat r

REGULAR - 10PT

The quick brown fox jumps over a lazy dog. He didn't have to, but he thought it would be the cheeky thing to do. After all, he had a reputation to maintain. It's a lovely day in the neighbourhood, with the sun shining, the birds chirping, and the pungent aroma of fresh rubbish bins wafting through the air - the promise of a sumptuous meal. The sprightly fox rubs his paws together in glee, thinking about the delicious treasures he's about to dig into. Still in her spot, the lazy dog remains unperturbed. With her long snout, droopy jowls, and long black fur fluttering in the breeze, she is in a dreamland far away - where the mountains are made of beefy treats, the valleys are filled with tennis balls, and the puddles are just the right temperature. Why be in the rat race? It's a dog's life, after all.

Bobby Light

Ken

Bobby Light Italic

Rol

Bobby Regular

Cha

Bobby Regular Italic

Da

Bobby Bold

Fis

Bobby Bold Italic

Gill

edy

(20 November 1925 – 6 June 1968)

son

(18 February 1933 – 31 July 2009)

lton

(Born 11 October 1937)

rin

(14 May 1936 – December 20 1973)

her

(9 March 1943 – 17 January 2008)

spie

(Born 22 June 1961)

TYPEFACE : CAKO
DESIGNER : VIOLAINE & JÉRÉMY
LOCATION : PARIS, FRANCE

PUBLISHED BY : VIOLAINE & JÉRÉMY
CHRONOLOGY : N/A
RELEASED IN : 2019

LINK : HTTPS://VJ-TYPE.COM/7-CAKO
STYLES : BLACK, REGULAR, THIN, BLACK ITALIC, REGULAR ITALIC, THIN ITALIC

WHAT MAKES CAKO UNIQUE IS ITS VERY GRAPHIC SHAPES OF LETTERS AND SERIFS AS WELL AS ITS NUMEROUS STYLISTIC ALTERNATES – GIVING THE TYPEFACE A GREAT RHYTHM. CAKO HAS THREE CONTRASTED WEIGHTS – BLACK, REGULAR AND THIN – OFFERING SEVERAL DEGREES OF IMPACT. THE DRAWING OF CAKO BLACK IS CHARACTERISED BY BIG CONTRASTS BETWEEN THICKS AND THINS, FINE DETAILS AND SPIKY TERMINALS.

CAP HEIGHT

REGULAR – 290PT

X-HEI

Cc

BASELINE

Cako

REGULAR – 48PT

THE QUICK BROW
IT WOULD BE THE
IT'S A LOVELY DAY
AND THE PUNGENT
PROMISE OF A SU
THINKING ABOUT
THE LAZY DOG RE
LONG BLACK FUR
THE MOUNTAINS A

REGULAR – 8PT

The quick brown fox jumps over a lazy dog. He didn't have to, but he thought it would be the cheeky thing to do. After all, he had a reputation to maintain. It's a lovely day in the neighbourhood, with the sun shining, the birds chirping, and the pungent aroma of fresh rubbish bins wafting through the air - the promise of a sumptuous meal. The sprightly fox rubs his paws together in glee, thinking about the delicious treasures he's about to dig into. Still in her spot, the lazy dog remains unperturbed. With her long snout, droopy jowls, and long black fur fluttering in the breeze, she is in a dreamland far away - where the mountains are made of beefy treats, the valleys are filled with tennis balls, and the puddles are just the right temperature. Why be in the rat race? It's a dog's life, after all.

01*|2

4|56

78|9

3

Lake Erie
Life
Karma
Rythmic

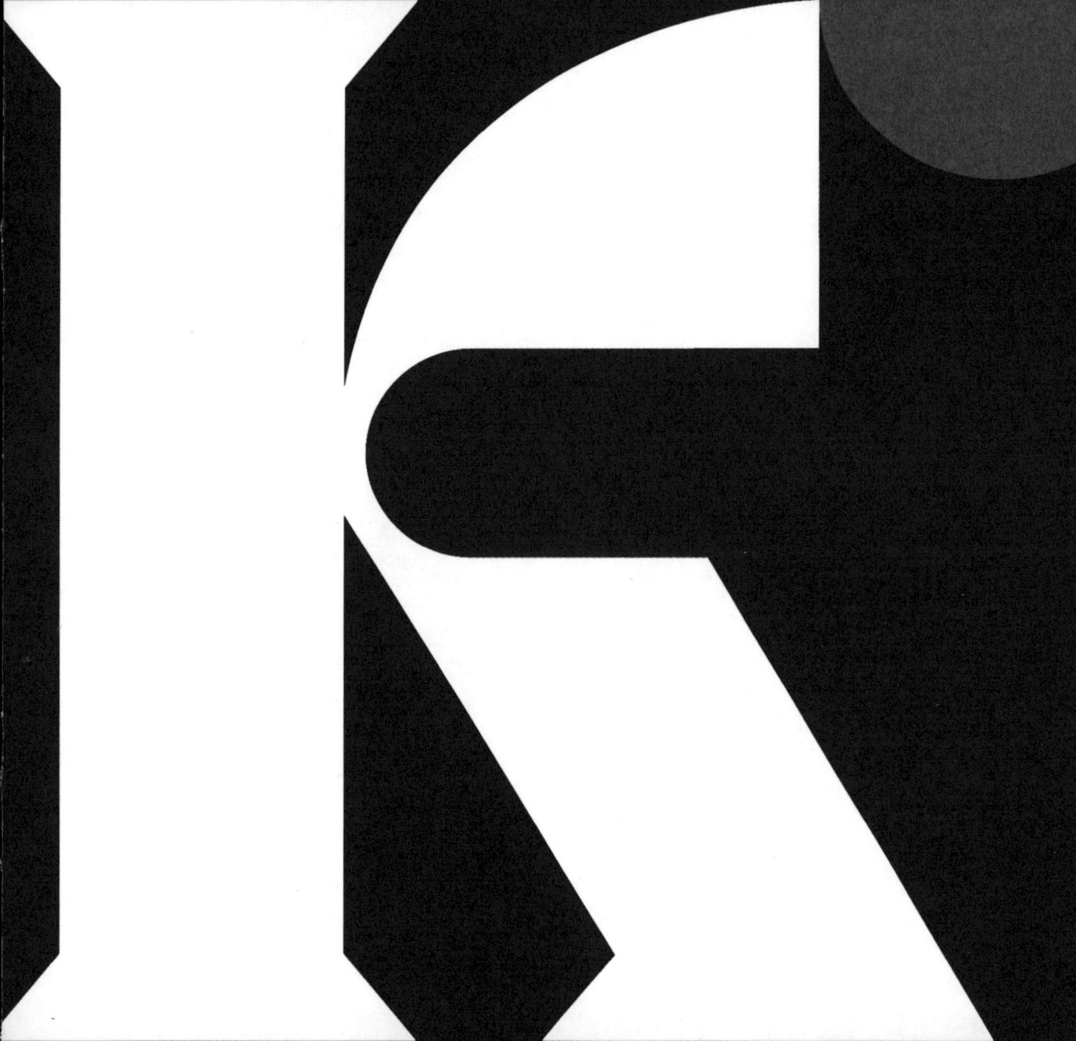

g

THE SATURN CIRCLE & THE FIRMAMENT

fief

TYPEFACE : CANILARI
DESIGNER : W TYPE FOUNDRY
LOCATION : SANTIAGO, CHILE; BARCELONA, SPAIN; LONDON, UK

PUBLISHED BY : PATRICIO TRUENOS
CHRONOLOGY : N/A
RELEASED IN : 2014

LINK : HTTPS://WTYPEFOUNDRY.COM/TYPEFACES/CANILARI
STYLES : REGULAR, MEDIUM, BOLD, HEAVY, ITALIC, MEDIUM ITALIC, BOLD ITALIC, HEAVY ITALIC, ORNAMENTS

CANILARI, A POST-MODERN TYPE INSPIRED BY DIAGUITA POTTERY AND CONTEMPORARY SERIFS, REFLECTS THE DIAGUITA CULTURE OF CHILE AND ARGENTINA. WITH ROOTS FROM THE 10TH TO 16TH CENTURY A.D., THE DIAGUITA HAD SETTLED IN PRESENT-DAY NORTH CHILE AND NORTHWEST ARGENTINA, LEAVING BEHIND LIMITED POTTERY EXPRESSIONS. A BOLD IDENTITY "SCREAM", THE TYPEFACE ITSELF MERGES NATIVE AMERICAN ELEMENTS INTO A DISTINCTIVE TONE. ITS INTENSE PERSONALITY SUITS VARIOUS USES, FROM CHALLENGING TEXT ENVIRONMENTS TO IMPACTFUL HEADLINES. IDEAL FOR PUBLISHING AND EYE-CATCHING DESIGNS LIKE POSTERS AND LOGOS, IT OFFERS 4 WEIGHTS + ITALICS WITH 710 CHARACTERS EACH. IT ALSO INCLUDES ORNAMENTS AND ILLUMINATED CAPS.

CAP HEIGHT

REGULAR – 290PT

X-HEIGHT

Cc

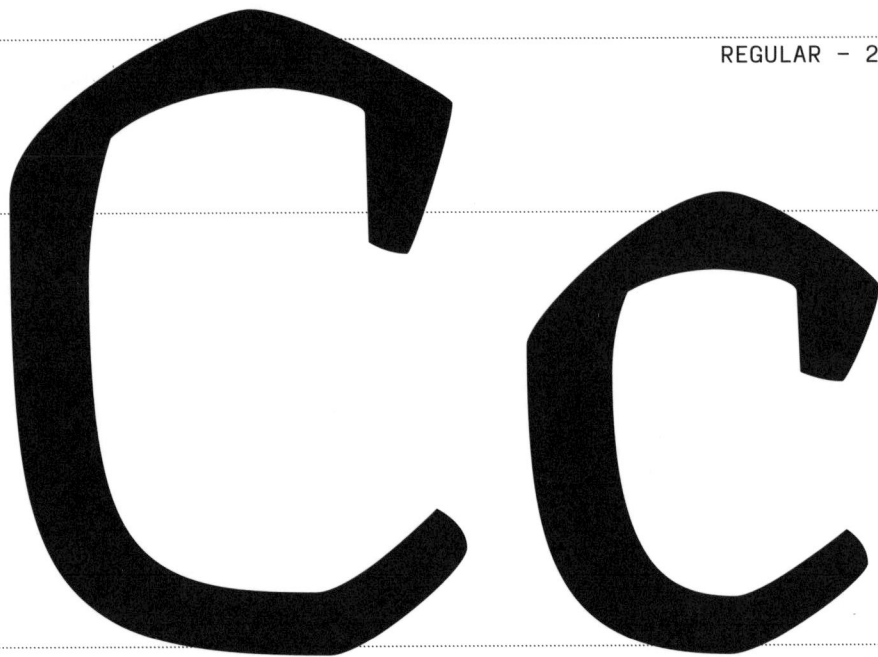

BASELINE

Canilari

THE QUICK BROW

IT WOULD BE THE

IT'S A LOVELY DA

AND THE PUNGE

PROMISE OF A SU

THINKING ABOU

THE LAZY DOG R

LONG BLACK FUR

THE MOUNTAINS

CANILARI

Regular

Italic

Medium

Medium Italic

Bold

Bold Italic

Heavy

Heavy Italic

Sol Estrella Sangre
Desierto Viento
Venus Lluvia
Tierra Norte Sur
Mineral Hierro Oro
Plata Sal Lechuza
Pequén Tucúquere
Guanaco Vicuña
Zorro Flamenco
Atacama Chakay
Llulliallaco Rojo
Negro Blanco Luna

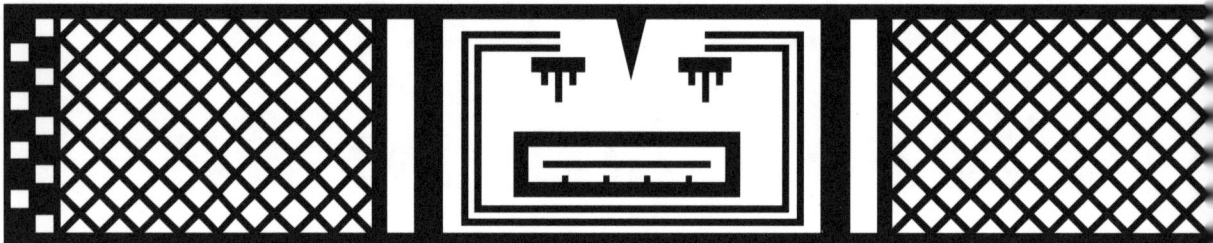

VIENTO

SANGRE

TYPEFACE : CARDINAL
DESIGNER : PRODUCTION TYPE
LOCATION : PARIS, FRANCE; SHANGHAI, CHINA

PUBLISHED BY : PRODUCTION TYPE
CHRONOLOGY : 2018 - 2020
RELEASED IN : 2018 - 2020

LINK : HTTPS://WWW.PRODUCTIONTYPE.COM/COLLECTION/CARDINAL_COLLECTION
STYLES : 5 FAMILIES WITH 40 STYLES, 3 X-HEIGHTS, 4 WEIGHTS, 2 WIDTHS + ROMAN & ITALIC
CREDITS : JEAN-BAPTISTE LEVÉE, YOANN MINET, QUENTIN SCHMERBER (DESIGN)

CARDINAL IS A TYPE DESIGN EXPLORATION BRIDGING CLASSIC TEXT FONTS WITH CONTEMPORARY DIGITAL TYPOGRAPHY. IT EMBODIES TRAITS OF GARAMOND AND GRANJON WHILE EXUDING ITS OWN DRYNESS AND RIGIDITY. REMINISCENT OF EARLY DIGITAL TYPEFACES, CARDINAL EVOKES A SENSE OF NOSTALGIA FOR THE OLD COMPUTING DAYS. ITS SYSTEM INCLUDES CARDINAL CLASSIC SHORT, MID, AND LONG, WITH ADJUSTABLE X-HEIGHTS BASED ON BODY COPY AND LINE LENGTH. CARDINAL FRUIT OFFERS A UNIQUE CONDENSED FLAVOUR, WITH ITALICS THAT DELIVER SHARPNESS AND ACCURACY WHILE CARDINAL PHOTO BOASTS A HEIGHTENED CONTRAST AND OH-SO-TIGHT SPACING FOR BOLD HEADLINES AND ADDED IMPACT.

CAP HEIGHT

REGULAR – 290PT

X-HEIGHT

Cc

BASELINE

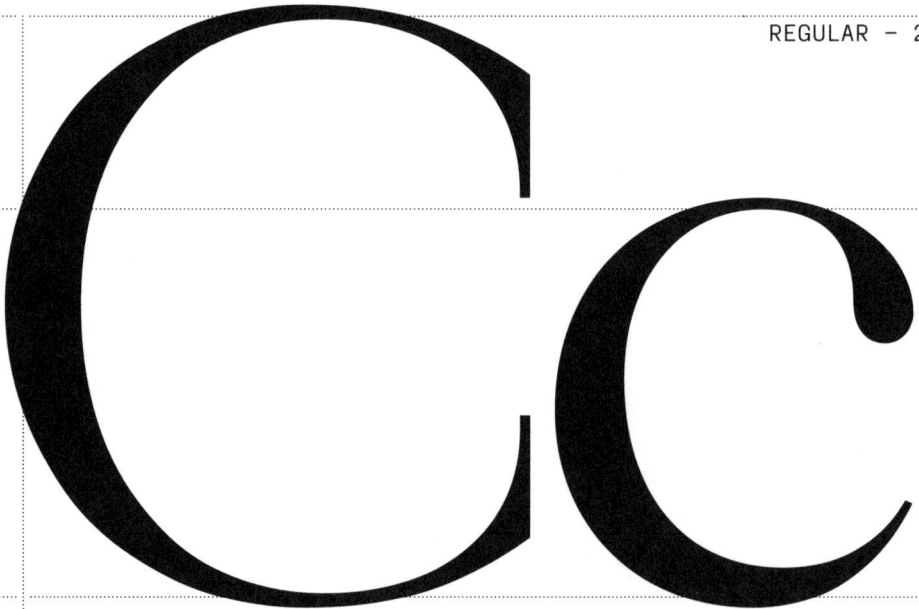

Cardinal

REGULAR – 36PT

THE QUICK BROWN FOX JU
IT WOULD BE THE CHEEK
IT'S A LOVELY DAY IN THE
AND THE PUNGENT AROM
PROMISE OF A SUMPTUOU
THINKING ABOUT THE DE
THE LAZY DOG REMAINS
LONG BLACK FUR FLUTTE
THE MOUNTAINS ARE MAD
AND THE PUDDLES ARE JU

REGULAR – 14PT

The quick brown fox jumps over a lazy dog. He didn't have to, but he thought it would be the cheeky thing to do. After all, he had a reputation to maintain. It's a lovely day in the neighbourhood, with the sun shining, the birds chirping, and the pungent aroma of fresh rubbish bins wafting through the air - the promise of a sumptuous meal. The sprightly fox rubs his paws together in glee, thinking about the delicious treasures he's about to dig into. Still in her spot, the lazy dog remains unperturbed. With her long snout, droopy jowls, and long black fur fluttering in the breeze, she is in a dreamland far away - where the mountains are made of beefy treats, the valleys are filled with tennis balls, and the puddles are just the right temperature. Why be in the rat race?
It's a dog's life, after all.

2896°

(+48°52' 7.6434")

P§a

[£ }

ct

TYPEFACE : CARDINAL TECH
DESIGNER : PRODUCTION TYPE
LOCATION : PARIS, FRANCE; SHANGHAI, CHINA

PUBLISHED BY : PRODUCTION TYPE
CHRONOLOGY : 2015 - 2023
RELEASED IN : UNRELEASED - BETA

LINK : HTTPS://WWW.PRODUCTIONTYPE.COM/COLLECTION/CARDINAL_COLLECTION (UPCOMING RELEASE)
STYLES : 6 STYLES, ROMAN & ITALIC

CARDINAL TECH IS AN IMMERSION IN A WORLD WHERE TYPOGRAPHY IS FILTERED THROUGH GRITTY AND CHAOTIC AESTHETICS. EMBODYING JAGGED CONTOURS AND INTRICATE DETAILS EMBLEMATIC OF A TECHNOLOGICALLY ADVANCED UNIVERSE, IT EVOKES REBELLION AND DEFIANCE. THE TYPEFACE IS READY FOR EXPERIMENTS WITH GLITCH EFFECTS, DISTORTED TEXTURES, AND AUGMENTED REALITY OVERLAYS. IT IS AIMED AT IMMERSIVE VISUAL EXPERIENCES, INSPIRED BY FLICKERING HOLOGRAPHIC BILLBOARDS, DECAYING NEON SIGNS, AND THE PULSATING ENERGY OF THE URBAN UNDERBELLY.

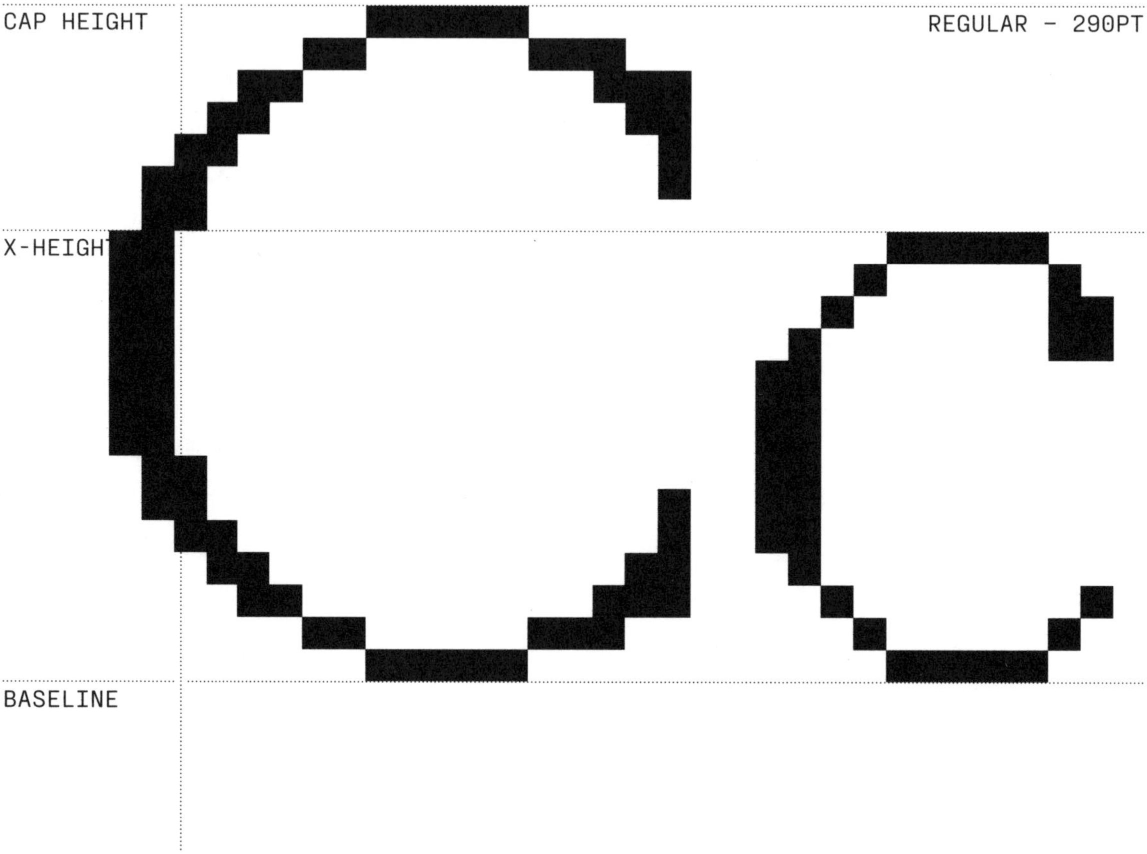

Cardinal Tech

REGULAR – 48PT

THE QUICK BRO
IT WOULD BE T
IT'S A LOVELY
AND THE PUNC
PROMISE OF A S
THINKING ABO
THE LAZY DOG

REGULAR – 16PT

The quick brown fox jumps over a lazy dog. He didn't ha
it would be the cheeky thing to do. After all, he had a rep
It's a lovely day in the neighbourhood, with the sun shini
and the pungent aroma of fresh rubbish bins wafting thro
promise of a sumptuous meal. The sprightly fox rubs his
thinking about the delicious treasures he's about to dig i
the lazy dog remains unperturbed. With her long snout,
long black fur fluttering in the breeze, she is in a dreamla
the mountains are made of beefy treats, the valleys are fil
and the puddles are just the right temperature. Why be i
It's a dog's life, after all.

FIRES OF
LLANA O
2010: ODE
WILLIAM
THECAVE
GUSTAVU
SCIENCEF

AZEROTH
GATHOL
SEY TWO
SANDERS
SOFSTELL
S W.POPE
CTIONAL

TYPEFACE : CIGARS
DESIGNER : HEAVYWEIGHT DIGITAL TYPE FOUNDRY
LOCATION : PRAGUE, CZECH REPUBLIC

PUBLISHED BY : HEAVYWEIGHT DIGITAL TYPE FOUNDRY
CHRONOLOGY : N/A
RELEASED IN : 2021

LINK : HTTPS://HEAVYWEIGHT-TYPE.COM/FONTS/CIGARS/DETAIL
STYLES : SUPERSLIM, SLIM, LIGHT, REGULAR, MEDIUM, SEMIBOLD, BOLD, BLACK, STRONG

IN THE CHRONOLOGY OF HEAVYWEIGHT'S WORK, THE CIGARS FONT IS ONE OF ITS FIRST ATTEMPTS AT A SERIF FONT, UNDERTAKEN IN SPITE OF FEAR OF ITS DIFFICULTY; HOWEVER, THE CHALLENGE WAS ALSO SEEN AS AN IMPORTANT STEP IN THE DEVELOPMENT OF THE TYPE FOUNDRY. THE TYPEFACE'S NAME WAS INSPIRED BY OLD MARLBORO TOBACCO BRAND POSTERS THAT FEATURED THE VERY POPULAR CENTURY TYPEFACE DESIGNED BY AMERICAN TYPE FOUNDERS. MOST OF HEAVYWEIGHT'S FONTS ARE CREATED FOR A SPECIFIC PURPOSE MANIFESTED IN DETAILS, NOT IN DESIGN. FOR CIGARS, REFERENCE TO CALLIGRAPHIC TOOLS IS EVIDENT, PARTICULARLY IN THE LETTERS "C", "F", "R" AND OTHERS, WHERE THE LETTER DOES NOT END WITH A CLASSIC TERMINAL, BUT RATHER, A PERPENDICULAR CUT.

CAP HEIGHT

REGULAR – 290PT

X-HEIGHT

Cc

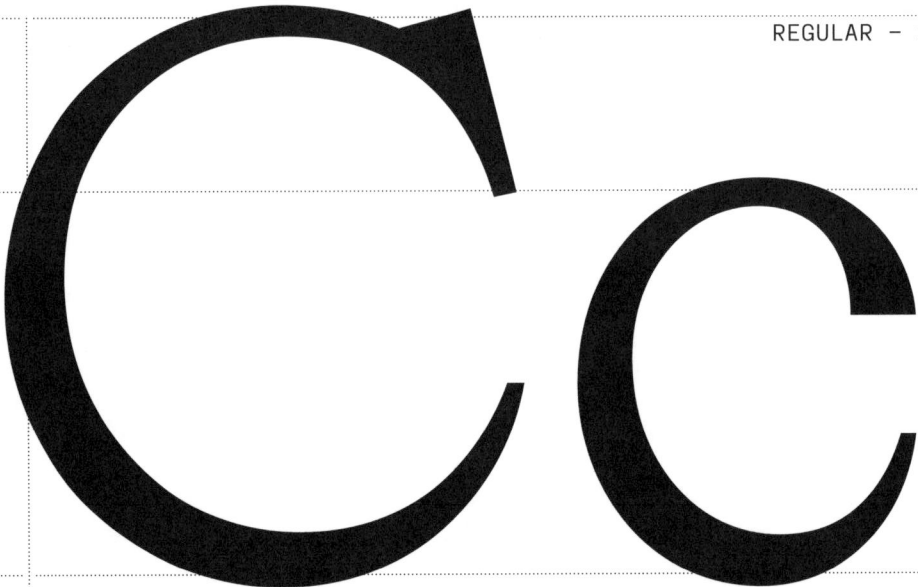

BASELINE

Cigars

REGULAR - 40PT

THE QUICK BROWN F
IT WOULD BE THE CH
ITS A LOVELY DAY IN
AND THE PUNGENT A
PROMISE OF A SUMPT
THINKING ABOUT TH
THE LAZY DOG REMA
LONG BLACK FUR FLU
THE MOUNTAINS ARE
AND THE PUDDLES AI

REGULAR - 10PT

The quick brown fox jumps over a lazy dog. He didnt have to, but he thought it would be the cheeky thing to do. After all, he had a reputation to maintain. Its a lovely day in the neighbourhood, with the sun shining, the birds chirping, and the pungent aroma of fresh rubbish bins wafting through the air - the promise of a sumptuous meal. The sprightly fox rubs his paws together in glee, thinking about the delicious treasures hes about to dig into. Still in her spot, the lazy dog remains unperturbed. With her long snout, droopy jowls, and long black fur fluttering in the breeze, she is in a dreamland far away - where the mountains are made of beefy treats, the valleys are filled with tennis balls, and the puddles are just the right temperature. Why be in the rat race? Its a dogs life, after all.

T

CONTEMPORARY
SERIF
TYPEFACE

9 1 2

8

7 2

6 0 3

4 5

TYPEFACE : COFO CINEMA 1909
DESIGNER : CONTRAST FOUNDRY
LOCATION : CALIFORNIA, US

PUBLISHED BY : CONTRAST FOUNDRY
CHRONOLOGY : 2018 - 2022
RELEASED IN : 2022

LINK : HTTPS://CONTRASTFOUNDRY.COM/TYPEFACE/COFO-CINEMA1909
STYLES : REGULAR
CREDITS : TASYA PETELINA

WITH CINEMA 1909, THE DESIGN TEAM CREATED ITS OWN CINEMATIC UNIVERSE – ONE IN WHICH OLD-FASHIONED ELEGANCE EXISTS IN DIGITAL FORM, WHERE THE TRADITIONAL AND THE CONTEMPORARY WORK IN UNISON. ALTHOUGH ITS NAME INCLUDES A DATE, THE TYPEFACE EXISTS OUTSIDE OF A PARTICULAR TIME AND SPACE. ITS PROPORTIONS ARE UNUSUAL, NEITHER NARROW NOR WIDE BUT INTENTIONALLY DYNAMIC – PLAYING WITH THE READER'S PERCEPTION AND CONTRIBUTING TO THE STRONG RHYTHM. THIS LINEAR PATTERN IS FURTHER EMPHASISED BY THE COMPACT SERIFS AND TERMINALS, AND THE CAREFULLY CONSIDERED BALANCE BETWEEN THICK AND THIN STROKES.

CAP HEIGHT

REGULAR – 290PT

CC

X-HEIGHT

BASELINE

COFO CINEMA 1909

REGULAR – 38PT

THE QUICK BROWN FOX JUMPS OVER

IT WOULD BE THE CHEEKY THING TO

IT'S A LOVELY DAY IN THE NEIGHBOU

AND THE PUNGENT AROMA OF FRES

PROMISE OF A SUMPTUOUS MEAL. T

THINKING ABOUT THE DELICIOUS TR

THE LAZY DOG REMAINS UNPERTUR

LONG BLACK FUR FLUTTERING IN TH

THE MOUNTAINS ARE MADE OF BEEF

AND THE PUDDLES ARE JUST THE RI

REGULAR – 12PT

THE QUICK BROWN FOX JUMPS OVER A LAZY DOG. HE DIDN'T HAVE TO, BUT HE THOUGHT IT WOULD BE THE CHEEKY THING TO DO. AFTER ALL, HE HAD A REPUTATION TO MAINTAIN. IT'S A LOVELY DAY IN THE NEIGHBOURHOOD, WITH THE SUN SHINING, THE BIRDS CHIRPING, AND THE PUNGENT AROMA OF FRESH RUBBISH BINS WAFTING THROUGH THE AIR - THE PROMISE OF A SUMPTUOUS MEAL. THE SPRIGHTLY FOX RUBS HIS PAWS TOGETHER IN GLEE, THINKING ABOUT THE DELICIOUS TREASURES HE'S ABOUT TO DIG INTO. STILL IN HER SPOT, THE LAZY DOG REMAINS UNPERTURBED. WITH HER LONG SNOUT, DROOPY JOWLS, AND LONG BLACK FUR FLUTTERING IN THE BREEZE, SHE IS IN A DREAMLAND FAR AWAY - WHERE THE MOUNTAINS ARE MADE OF BEEFY TREATS, THE VALLEYS ARE FILLED WITH TENNIS BALLS, AND THE PUDDLES ARE JUST THE RIGHT TEMPERATURE. WHY BE IN THE RAT RACE? IT'S A DOG'S LIFE, AFTER ALL.

A CINEMATIC UNIVERSE

TYPEFACE FOR AN OLDEST CINEMA

FOUNDED IN 1909

THE KHUDOZHESTVENNY CINEMA BECAME

1ST MOVIE THEATER

В ХУДОЖЕСТВЕННОМ ПРОХОДИЛИ ПРЕМЬЕРЫ
«БРОНЕНОСЕЦ ПОТЁМКИН» С. ЭЙЗЕНШТЕЙНА

OPENING

TYPEFACE	:	CX80
DESIGNER	:	DAMIEN GAUTIER
LOCATION	:	LYON, FRANCE

PUBLISHED BY	:	205TF
CHRONOLOGY	:	2022
RELEASED IN	:	2022

LINK	:	HTTPS://WWW.205.TF/CX80
STYLES	:	LIGHT, REGULAR, BOLD, 0 LIGHT, 0 REGULAR, 0 BOLD, 1 LIGHT, 1 REGULAR, 1 BOLD, 2 LIGHT, 2 REGULAR, 2 BOLD, 3 LIGHT, 3 REGULAR, 3 BOLD
CREDITS	:	DAMIEN GAUTIER

THE CX80 TYPEFACE IS A "MACHINE" AS RUDIMENTARY AS IT IS ATYPICAL. FOUR KINDS OF SERIFS ARE COMBINED IN THE SAME FONT: SANS SERIFS, TRIANGULAR SERIFS, SHARP RECTANGULAR SERIFS, AND SMOOTH RECTANGULAR SERIFS. EACH LETTER CAN EXHAUST ALL POSSIBLE COMBINATIONS: UP TO 256 VARIATIONS FOR ANY ONE SIGN! THE USER IS FREE TO PLAY WITH THE POSSIBILITIES PROVIDED BY THE TYPEFACE – THEY CAN EITHER CHOOSE TO BE AN ICONOCLAST BY ASSOCIATING DIFFERENT SERIFS (SIMPLY BY USING THEIR KEYBOARD), OR THEY MAY PREFER ONE OF THE FOUR BASIC STYLES THAT CORRESPOND TO EACH OF THE SERIFS.

CAP HEIGHT

REGULAR – 290PT

CC

BASELINE

THE QUICK BROW
IT WOULD BE THE
IT'S A LOVELY DA
AND THE PUNGEN
PROMISE OF A SU
THINKING ABOUT
THE LAZY DOG RE
LONG BLACK FUR
THE MOUNTAINS

MINT

FRENCH
MARTINI

FEW DROPS
OF EGG WHITE

THE ORIGIN OF
THE WORD "RUM"
IS UNCLEAR

CX80 1 BOLD

MINT

FRENCH
MARTINI

FEW DROPS
OF EGG WHITE

THE ORIGIN OF
THE WORD "RUM"
IS UNCLEAR

CX80 2 LIGHT

DRY M
PINE
MARA
FREN

RTINI
APPLE
CHINO
CH 75

TYPEFACE : ELIZETH
DESIGNER : DANIEL SABINO
LOCATION : SÃO PAULO, BRAZIL

PUBLISHED BY : BLACKLETRA TYPE FOUNDRY
CHRONOLOGY : 2020
RELEASED IN : 2020

LINK : HTTPS://BLACKLETRA.COM/TYPEFACES/ELIZETH
STYLES : NORMAL & CONDENSED: THIN, THIN ITALIC, EXTRALIGHT, EXTRALIGHT ITALIC, LIGHT, LIGHT ITALIC, REGULAR, ITALIC, MEDIUM, MEDIUM ITALIC, BOLD, BOLD ITALIC, EXTRABOLD, EXTRABOLD ITALIC

ELIZETH IS THE SERIF COUNTERPART TO OFELIA. IT IS A VERY VERSATILE TYPEFACE IN TWO WIDTHS AND SEVEN WEIGHTS, TO BE USED IN A GREAT VARIETY OF SITUATIONS. ITS NORMAL WIDTH IS A GEOMETRIC SLAB WHICH EVOKES EARLY XX CENTURY RATIONALISM — ESTABLISHING A DIALOGUE WITH TYPEFACES SUCH AS ROCKWELL — HOWEVER USING BRACKETED SERIFS. IT ALSO OFFERS TRUE ITALICS, BROAD LANGUAGE SUPPORT AND OPENTYPE FEATURES SUCH AS SMALL CAPITALS AS WELL AS OLD STYLE AND TABULAR FIGURES.

CAP HEIGHT

REGULAR – 290PT

X-HEIGHT

Ee

BASELINE

Elizeth

THE QUICK BR

IT WOULD BE T

IT'S A LOVELY D

AND THE PUNC

PROMISE OF A

THINKING ABO

THE LAZY DOG

LONG BLACK F

THE MOUNTAI

KOHLEFLÖZ

FIELDWORK

POTÊNCIAS

RECUEILLÎT

GÂDILĂTURĂ

PRIVILÉGIUM

BEËINDIGING

arbeitersöhne

zaokrętować

riorganizzerà

hljóðstafrófið

nyåndelige

fotossíntese

bedoeïenen

100

TYPEFACE	:	EMILIO
DESIGNER	:	NARROW TYPE
LOCATION	:	CZECH REPUBLIC

PUBLISHED BY	:	NARROW TYPE
CHRONOLOGY	:	2022
RELEASED IN	:	2023

LINK	:	HTTPS://WWW.NARROWTYPE.COM
STYLES	:	THIN, THIN ITALIC, EXTRALIGHT, EXTRALIGHT ITALIC, LIGHT, LIGHT ITALIC, REGULAR, REGULAR ITALIC, SEMIBOLD, SEMIBOLD ITALIC, BOLD, BOLD ITALIC, BLACK, BLACK ITALIC

EMILIO IS A CONTEMPORARY SERIF FAMILY AVAILABLE IN 14 STYLES. IT IS AN ELEGANT TYPEFACE WITH A FRIENDLY AND WARM PERSONALITY WHICH SEEKS A BALANCE BETWEEN THE TRADITIONAL AND THE MODERN. THE TYPEFACE OFFERS SEVERAL STYLISTIC SETS, STANDARD AND DISCRETIONARY LIGATURES, AS WELL AS MANY OTHER OPENTYPE FEATURES. IT ALSO SUPPORTS MOST LATIN LANGUAGES. THE BIG HEADLINES AND TITLES ARE WHERE EMILIO SHINES THE MOST, BUT DUE TO ITS LARGE X-HEIGHT AND SUBTLE CONTRAST, IT WILL WORK FOR SMALLER TEXT AS WELL. IT IS THE IDEAL TYPEFACE FOR EDITORIAL DESIGN, POSTERS, COVERS, AND BRANDING.

CAP HEIGHT

REGULAR - 290PT

X-HEIGHT

Ee

BASELINE

Emilio

REGULAR – 48PT

THE QUICK BROWN
IT WOULD BE THE
IT'S A LOVELY DAY
AND THE PUNGENT
PROMISE OF A SUM

REGULAR – 14PT

The quick brown fox jumps over a lazy dog. He didn't have to, but h
it would be the cheeky thing to do. After all, he had a reputation to r
It's a lovely day in the neighbourhood, with the sun shining, the bir
and the pungent aroma of fresh rubbish bins wafting through the ai
promise of a sumptuous meal. The sprightly fox rubs his paws toget
thinking about the delicious treasures he's about to dig into. Still in
the lazy dog remains unperturbed. With her long snout, droopy jow
long black fur fluttering in the breeze, she is in a dreamland far awa
the mountains are made of beefy treats, the valleys are filled with te
and the puddles are just the right temperature. Why be in the rat ra
It's a dog's life, after all.

REGULAR – 10PT

The quick brown fox jumps over a lazy dog. He didn't have to, but he thought it would be the cheeky thing to do. After all, he had a reputation to maintain. It's a lovely day in the neighbourhood, with the sun shining, the birds chirping, and the pungent aroma of fresh rubbish bins wafting through the air – the promise of a sumptuous meal. The sprightly fox rubs his paws together in glee, thinking about the delicious treasures he's about to dig into. Still in her spot, the lazy dog remains unperturbed. With her long snout, droopy jowls, and long black fur fluttering in the breeze, she is in a dreamland far away – where the mountains are made of beefy treats, the valleys are filled with tennis balls, and the puddles are just the right temperature. Why be in the rat race? It's a dog's life, after all.

CHECK
MODE
RES
MANUAL
DEPTH
RATE
ULTRA
STANDARD
GATE
/PAN
MIN
MAX
MIN
MAX
MIN
MAX
MOMENTARY
SET TEMPO: PRESS & HOLD (>2 sec.)
OUTPUT B
OUTPUT A
GUITAR IN
BASS IN
Flanger
AF-5

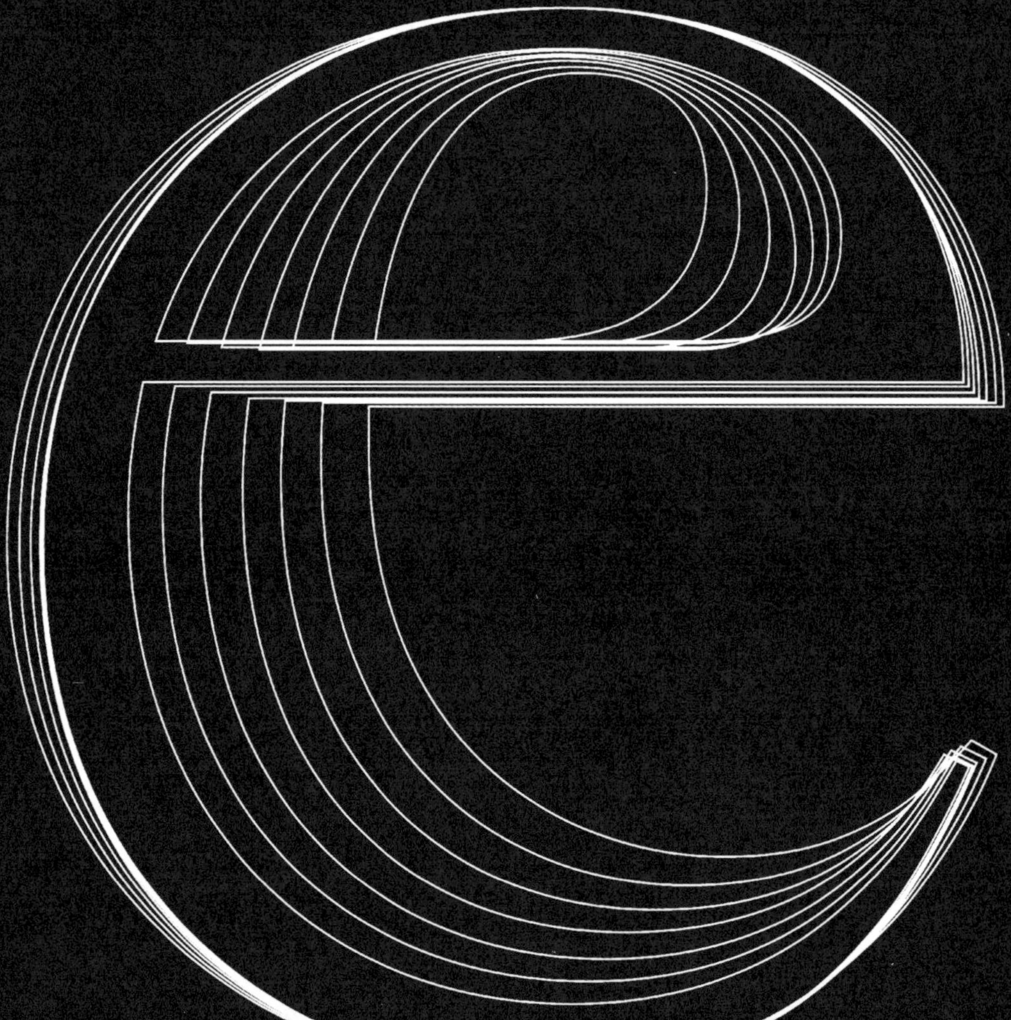

Ten
RR

Current
«Artists»
Elegant?
@1976—
2028†

TYPEFACE : ERNST
DESIGNER : LÉON HUGUES
LOCATION : PARIS, FRANCE

PUBLISHED BY : CAST TYPE FOUNDRY
CHRONOLOGY : 2021
RELEASED IN : 2023

LINK : HTTPS://WWW.C-A-S-T.COM/TYPEFACES/ERNST/
STYLES : 14 STYLES, 7 WEIGHTS + ROMAN & ITALIC

ERNST IS AN ELEGANT BUT PLAYFUL SLAB SERIF WHICH EVOKES THE PECULIAR TYPEFACES OF THE EARLY 20TH CENTURY AND RESPONDS TO CONTEMPORARY DEMANDS BY OFFERING A WIDE RANGE OF APPLICATIONS. IT BLENDS TOGETHER TYPE DETAILS FROM AVANT-GARDE FACES SUCH AS ERNST DEUTSCH-DRYDEN'S TANGO AND GEORG BELWE'S BELWE ANTIQUA. ITS PRONOUNCED AND FRISKY DETAILS MAKE IT IDEAL FOR DISPLAY PURPOSES, WHILE THE BIG X-HEIGHT, THE RIGOUR OF ITS DESIGN AND THE CONSISTENCY OF ITS PROPORTIONS ALSO MAKE IT SUITABLE FOR LONG TEXTS. ITS NAME PAYS HOMAGE TO ERNST HIMSELF, AN AUSTRIAN DESIGNER WHO IN HIS YOUTH CREATED PECULIAR LETTERING BESIDES THE AFOREMENTIONED TANGO TYPEFACE. IN GERMAN, "ERNST" ALSO MEANS "SERIOUS", BUT THE TYPEFACE IS ANYTHING BUT; NOTABLY, ITS WHIMSICAL ITALIC RECALLS THE LETTERING OF EARLY 20TH CENTURY PARISIAN STREET THEATRES AND SILENT MOVIES. ERNST AND ITS ITALIC COME IN A RANGE OF 7 WEIGHTS, FROM THIN TO EXTRABOLD, AND FEATURE OLD STYLE FIGURES, SMALL CAPS AND SOME ALTERNATIVE LETTERS.

CAP HEIGHT

REGULAR – 290PT

X-HEIGHT

BASELINE

Èe

Ernst

REGULAR – 50PT

THE QUICK BROW
IT WOULD BE THE
IT'S A LOVELY DAY
AND THE PUNGE
PROMISE OF A SU
THINKING ABOUT
THE LAZY DOG R
LONG BLACK FUR
THE MOUNTAINS

REGULAR – 8PT

The quick brown fox jumps over a lazy dog. He didn't have to, but he thought it would be the cheeky thing to do. After all, he had a reputation to maintain. It's a lovely day in the neighbourhood, with the sun shining, the birds chirping, and the pungent aroma of fresh rubbish bins wafting through the air - the promise of a sumptuous meal. The sprightly fox rubs his paws together in glee, thinking about the delicious treasures he's about to dig into. Still in her spot, the lazy dog remains unperturbed. With her long snout, droopy jowls, and long black fur fluttering in the breeze, she is in a dreamland far away - where the mountains are made of beefy treats, the valleys are filled with tennis balls, and the puddles are just the right temperature. Why be in the rat race? It's a dog's life, after all.

*Æ d
g
%
@
st¥

3

Three

TYPEFACE : TT ESPINA
DESIGNER : TYPETYPE.ORG
LOCATION : SAINT PETERSBURG, RUSSIA

PUBLISHED BY : TYPETYPE.ORG
CHRONOLOGY : N/A
RELEASED IN : 2022

LINK : HTTPS://TYPETYPE.ORG/FONTS/TT-ESPINA/
STYLES : 7 STYLES + A VARIABLE FONT

TT ESPINA IS AN EXPRESSIVE DISPLAY ANTIQUA WITH A VIBRANT CHARACTER. THE CREATIVE IDEA BEHIND IT WAS TO MAKE A HIGHLY ATTRACTIVE AND RECOGNISABLE DISPLAY SERIF THAT WOULD BE PRACTICAL AND MODERN. INSPIRED BY A HISTORICAL REFERENCE, THE TYPEFACE HAS CONTRASTING CHARACTERS, LARGE SERIFS, AND IMPRESSIVE PROPORTIONS. IT CAN ADD A TOUCH OF ELEGANCE AND LUXURY TO ANY DESIGN, WHILE ITS SET OF CHARMING ICONS WILL MAKE A PROJECT EVEN MORE SPECIAL.

CAP HEIGHT

REGULAR – 290PT

X-HEIGHT

Ee

BASELINE

TT Espina

REGULAR – 80PT

THE QUICK BROWN FOX JU

IT WOULD BE THE CHEEKY

IT'S A LOVELY DAY IN THE

AND THE PUNGENT AROMA

REGULAR – 30PT

THE QUICK BROWN FOX JUMPS OVER A LAZY DOG. HE DIDN'T HAVE TO,
IT WOULD BE THE CHEEKY THING TO DO. AFTER ALL, HE HAD A REPUTA
IT'S A LOVELY DAY IN THE NEIGHBOURHOOD, WITH THE SUN SHINING, T
AND THE PUNGENT AROMA OF FRESH RUBBISH BINS WAFTING THROUGH
PROMISE OF A SUMPTUOUS MEAL. THE SPRIGHTLY FOX RUBS HIS PAWS
THINKING ABOUT THE DELICIOUS TREASURES HE'S ABOUT TO DIG INTO.
THE LAZY DOG REMAINS UNPERTURBED. WITH HER LONG SNOUT, DROO
LONG BLACK FUR FLUTTERING IN THE BREEZE, SHE IS IN A DREAMLAN

TT Espina
TypeType

TT Espina
Display antiqua

TYPEFACE : EXPOSURE
DESIGNER : FEDERICO PARRA BARRIOS
LOCATION : LYON, FRANCE

PUBLISHED BY : 205TF
CHRONOLOGY : 2019 - 2022
RELEASED IN : 2022

LINK : HTTPS://WWW.205.TF/EXPOSURE
STYLES : ROMAN
-100, -90, -80, -70, -60, -50, -40, -30, -20, -10, 0 , +10, +20, +30, +40, +50, +60, +70, +80, +90, +100
ITALIC
-100, -90, -80, -70, -60, -50, -40, -30, -20, -10, 0 , +10, +20, +30, +40, +50, +60, +70, +80, +90, +100
CREDITS : FEDERICO PARRA BARRIOS

EXPOSURE BORROWS THE EPONYMOUS PRINCIPLE FROM PHOTOGRAPHY, USING IT TO QUESTION THE POSSIBILITIES OFFERED BY VARIABLE FONTS IN A COMPLETELY ORIGINAL WAY. ITS AXIS OF VARIATION RANGES FROM −100 TO +100, AND GIVES A FEELING OF ADJUSTING THE INTENSITY OF THE LIGHT TO WHICH THE TYPEFACE IS EXPOSED, THUS AFFECTING ITS OUTLINE. AT ZERO, THE TYPEFACE IS SHARP AND CRISP. AS THE INDEX DECREASES, THE FONT BECOMES INCREASINGLY UNDEREXPOSED – MAKING IT SEEM TO DEFORM AND BECOME OVERWHELMINGLY BLACK WHILE THE COUNTERFORMS ARE FILLED ALMOST TO THE POINT OF ILLEGIBILITY.

CAP HEIGHT

REGULAR – 290PT

X-HEIGHT

Ee

BASELINE

Exposure

REGULAR – 45PT

THE QUICK BROWN
IT WOULD BE THE
IT'S A LOVELY DAY
AND THE PUNGENT
PROMISE OF A SUM
THINKING ABOUT

REGULAR – 12PT

The quick brown fox jumps over a lazy dog. He didn't have to, but he thought it would be the cheeky thing to do. After all, he had a reputation to maintain. It's a lovely day in the neighbourhood, with the sun shining, the birds chirping and the pungent aroma of fresh rubbish bins wafting through the air - the promise of a sumptuous meal. The sprightly fox rubs his paws together in gle thinking about the delicious treasures he's about to dig into. Still in her spot, the lazy dog remains unperturbed. With her long snout, droopy jowls, and long black fur fluttering in the breeze, she is in a dreamland far away - where the mountains are made of beefy treats, the valleys are filled with tennis balls, and the puddles are just the right temperature. Why be in the rat race? It's a dog's life, after all.

REGULAR – 8PT

The quick brown fox jumps over a lazy dog. He didn't have to, but he thought it would be the cheeky thing to do. After all, he had a reputation to maintain. It's a lovely day in the neighbourhood, with the sun shining, the birds chirping, and the pungent aroma of fresh rubbish bins wafting through the air - the promise of a sumptuous meal. The sprightly fox rubs his paws together in glee, thinking about the delicious treasures he's about to dig into. Still in her spot, the lazy dog remains unperturbed. With her long snout, droopy jowls, and long black fur fluttering in the breeze, she is in a dreamland far away - where the mountains are made of beefy treats, the valleys are filled with tennis balls, and the puddles are just the right temperature. Why be in the rat race? It's a dog's life, after all.

IN PHOTO

EXPOSU

AMOUNT

PER UN

THE IMAG

ILLUMINA

THE EXPO

GRAPHY,
E IS THE
OF LIGHT
T AREA
GE PLANE
CE TIMES
SURE TIME

EXPOSURE PHOTOGRAPH

illuminance	-100
illuminance	-80
illuminance	-60
illuminance	-40
illuminance	-20
illuminance	0
illuminance	20
illuminance	40
illuminance	60
illuminance	80
illuminance	100

TYPEFACE : FANSAN
DESIGNER : W TYPE FOUNDRY
LOCATION : SANTIAGO, CHILE; BARCELONA, SPAIN; LONDON, UK

PUBLISHED BY : W TYPE FOUNDRY
CHRONOLOGY : 2022
RELEASED IN : 2022

LINK : HTTPS://WTYPEFOUNDRY.COM/TYPEFACES/FANSAN
STYLES : LIGHT, REGULAR, MEDIUM, SEMIBOLD, BOLD, LIGHT ITALIC, ITALIC, MEDIUM ITALIC, SEMIBOLD ITALIC, BOLD ITALIC, DISPLAY LIGHT, DISPLAY, DISPLAY MEDIUM, DISPLAY SEMIBOLD, DISPLAY BOLD, DISPLAY LIGHT ITALIC, DISPLAY ITALIC, DISPLAY MEDIUM ITALIC, DISPLAY SEMIBOLD ITALIC, DISPLAY BOLD ITALIC

ORGANIC AND SUBLIME, FANSAN IS AN ART NOUVEAU TYPE FAMILY THAT INCLUDES ROMAN, ITALIC, AND OPTICAL SIZES. ITS ROOTS CAN BE FOUND IN FAMOUS WORKS SUCH AS BENGUIAT, WINDSOR, AND MELBOURNE — WORLDWIDE TYPOGRAPHIC REFERENCES WHICH ALL HAVE A SENSE OF BEING IMPERFECTLY APPEALING.

CAP HEIGHT

REGULAR - 290PT

Ff

X-HEIGHT

BASELINE

REGULAR – 36PT

THE QUICK BROWN FO
THOUGHT IT WOULD B
TO MAINTAIN. IT'S A LC
THE BIRDS CHIRPING, A
THROUGH THE AIR - TH
HIS PAWS TOGETHER I
ABOUT TO DIG INTO. S

REGULAR – 14PT

The quick brown fox jumps over a lazy dog. He didn't have tc
it would be the cheeky thing to do. After all, he had a reputat
It's a lovely day in the neighbourhood, with the sun shining,
and the pungent aroma of fresh rubbish bins wafting throug
promise of a sumptuous meal. The sprightly fox rubs his pa
thinking about the delicious treasures he's about to dig into.
the lazy dog remains unperturbed. With her long snout, droc
long black fur fluttering in the breeze, she is in a dreamland
the mountains are made of beefy treats, the valleys are filled
and the puddles are just the right temperature. Why be in th
It's a dog's life, after all.

REGULAR – 8PT

The quick brown fox jumps over a lazy dog. He didn't have to, but he thought it would be the cheeky thing to do. After all, he had a reputation to maintain. It's a lovely day in the neighbourhood, with the sun shining, the birds chirping, and the pungent aroma of fresh rubbish bins wafting through the air - the promise of a sumptuous meal. The sprightly fox rubs his paws together in glee, thinking about the delicious treasures he's about to dig into. Still in her spot, the lazy dog remains unperturbed. With her long snout, droopy jowls, and long black fur fluttering in the breeze, she is in a dreamland far away - where the mountains are made of beefy treats, the valleys are filled with tennis balls, and the puddles are just the right temperature. Why be in the rat race? It's a dog's life, after all.

SUM
IS HI
2024

MER
ERE

→

Fansan

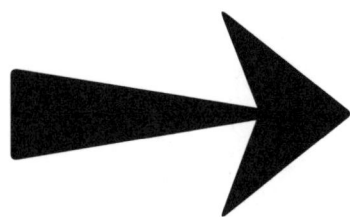

AN OPEN SEASON

ABCDEFGHIJ
KLMNOPQRS
TUVWXYZ
abcdefghijkl
mnopqrstuv
wxyz012345
6789!?*&

TYPEFACE : OHNO FATFACE
DESIGNER : OH NO TYPE CO.
LOCATION : CALIFORNIA, US

PUBLISHED BY : OH NO TYPE CO.
CHRONOLOGY : N/A
RELEASED IN : 2020

LINK : HTTPS://OHNOTYPE.CO/FONTS/FATFACE
STYLES : 9 OPTICAL SIZES FROM 12PT TO 72PT

THE 11TH FAMILY RELEASED BY OH NO TYPE CO., OHNO FATFACE IS ONE OF THE MORE CLASSICALLY-INFORMED MEMBERS OF THE LIBRARY. IT IS AN ODE TO THE 1800'S THROUGH THE LENS OF THE 1970'S THAT STARTED WITH THE LETTERING THAT JAMES EDMONDSON DID FOR THE TYPOGRAPHICS 2017 CONFERENCE LOGO, WHICH ITSELF WAS BASED ON THE FAMOUS "OH!" AND "AH!" LETTERING BY TOM CARNASE.

CAP HEIGHT

T) - 290PT

X-HEIGHT

Ff

BASELINE

OHNO Fatface

(12PT) - 36PT

THE QUICK BROWN FOX
IT WOULD BE THE CHEE
ITS A LOVELY DAY IN TH
AND THE PUNGENT ARO
PROMISE OF A SUMPTU
THINKING ABOUT THE D
THE LAZY DOG REMAINS
LONG BLACK FUR FLUTT
THE MOUNTAINS ARE M
AND THE PUDDLES ARE
ITS A DOGS LIFE, AFTER

(12PT) - 10PT

The quick brown fox jumps over a lazy dog. He didnt have to, but he thought it would be the cheeky thing to do. After all, he had a reputation to maintain. Its a lovely day in the neighbourhood, with the sun shining, the birds chirping, and the pungent aroma of fresh rubbish bins wafting through the air the promise of a sumptuous meal. The sprightly fox rubs his paws together in glee, thinking about the delicious treasures hes about to dig into. Still in her spot, the lazy dog remains unperturbed. With her long snout, droopy jowls, and long black fur fluttering in the breeze, she is in a dreamland far away where the mountains are made of beefy treats, the valleys are filled with tennis balls, and the puddles are just the right temperature. Why be in the rat race
Its a dogs life, after all.

Beginning in the early 1800s, the Fann Street foundry in London produced a few designs in the brand new genre of fatfaces. They were intended for short words to be printed HUGE, and for this purpose, they worked quite well

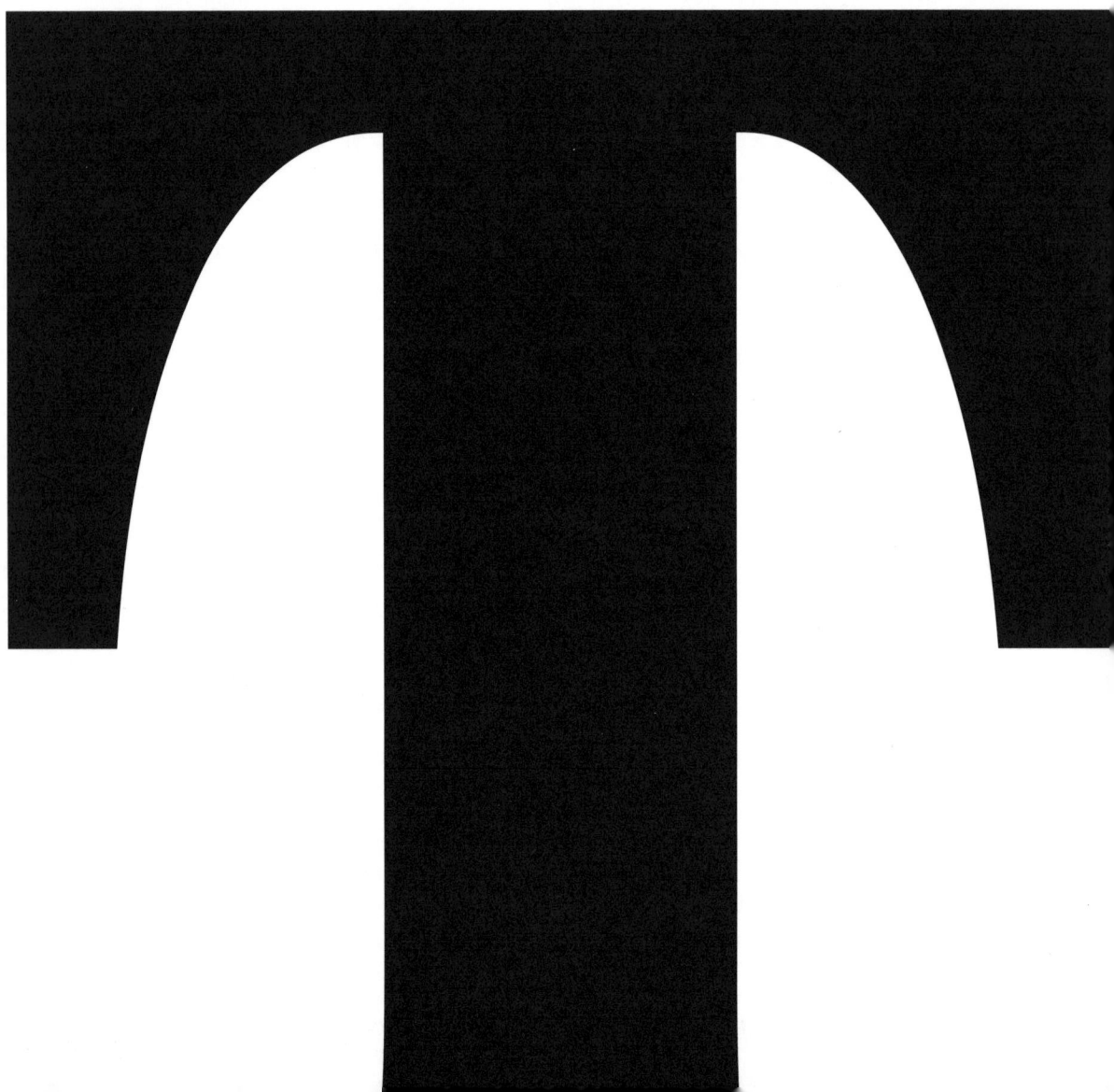

T

Fatface
Happyface
Ohnoface
Sadface
Cryingface
Slimface

TYPEFACE	:	FRAGEN
DESIGNER	:	THE DESIGNERS FOUNDRY
LOCATION	:	NEW ZEALAND

PUBLISHED BY	:	THE DESIGNERS FOUNDRY
CHRONOLOGY	:	N/A
RELEASED IN	:	2019

LINK	:	HTTPS://THEDESIGNERSFOUNDRY.COM/FRAGEN
STYLES	:	16
CREDITS	:	LUCAS DESCROIX (DESIGN)

FRAGEN IS A TEXT-DISPLAY HYBRID WITH A STRONG SLAB FLAVOUR AND SPIRITED ITALICS. AVAILABLE IN 16 STYLES, IT BALANCES DIVERSE AND SOMETIMES CONTRADICTORY ELEMENTS INTO ONE COHESIVE AND FUNCTIONING TYPEFACE. FRAGEN IS STABLE BUT LIVELY, WITH A GENEROUS SET OF SYMBOLS, PATTERNS, LIGATURES AND ALTERNATES.

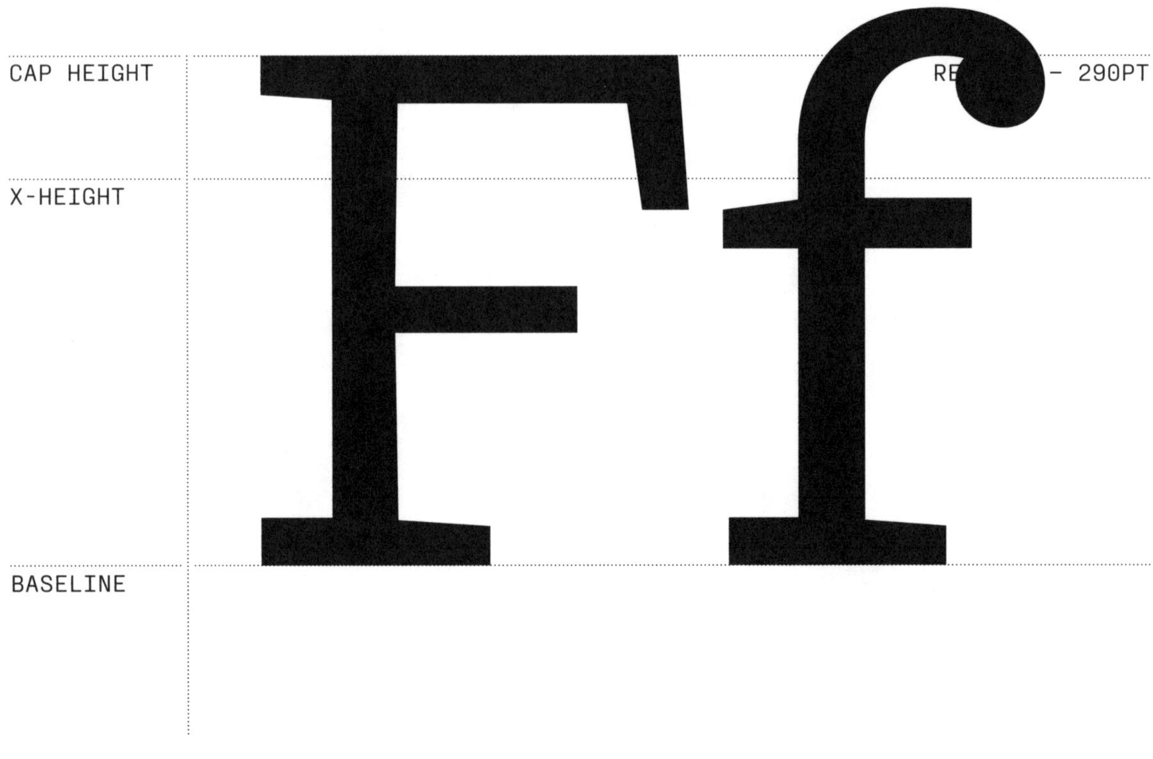

Fragen

THE QUICK BR
IT WOULD BE
ITS A LOVELY
AND THE PUN
PROMISE OF A
THINKING AB
THE LAZY DO
LONG BLACK
THE MOUNTA

#Profiles
»Frühling«
{Treasure}
Swapped*

kilΩ (8
→32% R
¶Jp? N.ñ
@gaş [15]
Quest///w

Eating
soup with my
chopsticks
with my
chopsticks

RULES → ❶ *countable nou*
are instructions that tell
you are allowed to do and
are not allowed to do. "...t
to Rule" ❷ *countable nou*
statement telling peopl
should do in order to ac
or a benefit of some kin
rule is to always drink
❸ *singular noun.* If so
...the normal s

Hi, my name is, *what?*
My name is, *who?*
My name is, *chka-chka,*
Labi Siffre

All** blank **and no
*blank **make** blank*
***a** blank blank* [17]

→ A hotel's a *telly*, a cell p
a *celly*, jealous is *jelly*, yo
box is your belly, to *guerr*
mean to use physical forc
took an L, you took a loss,

TYPEFACE : ABC GAISYR
DESIGNER : DINAMO
LOCATION : BERLIN, GERMANY

PUBLISHED BY : DINAMO
CHRONOLOGY : N/A
RELEASED IN : 2022

LINK : HTTPS://ABCDINAMO.COM/TYPEFACES/GAISYR
STYLES : 3 FAMILIES, 28 STYLES
CREDITS : FABIAN HARB/DINAMO & MICHELANGELO NIGRA (DESIGN), IGINO MARINI (SPACING & KERNING), ROBERT JAMES & RENAN ROSATTI/DINAMO (PRODUCTION)

GAISYR IS A BEAUTIFUL TYPEFACE WITH DINAMO HOUSE-STYLE BUTTERFLY SERIFS. IT TAKES ITS POINT DE DÉPART FROM SKETCHES BY THE EARLY 18TH CENTURY ROYAL TYPOGRAPHER FOR KING LOUIS XIV, JACQUES JAUGEON. A TENSION BETWEEN STRICT GEOMETRY AND LOOPY HAND-HELD GESTURES LIVES ON IN ITS ELEGANT FORMS. JUST CLOSE YOUR EYES AND IMAGINE THE KING SITTING IN HIS GARDEN, MAYBE A BIT SUNBURNED, SURROUNDED BY BUTTERFLIES AND LOW HANGING CITRUS FRUIT, SIPPING ON A (GLASS BOTTLE) OF COKE®. GAISYR IS AVAILABLE IN PROPORTIONAL, MONOSPACED AND SEMI-MONOSPACED STYLES.

CAP HEIGHT

REGULAR – 290PT

X-HEIGHT

Gg

BASELINE

ABC Gaisyr

REGULAR – 40PT

THE QUICK BROWN F
IT WOULD BE THE CH
IT'S A LOVELY DAY IN
AND THE PUNGENT A
PROMISE OF A SUMPT
THINKING ABOUT TH
THE LAZY DOG REMA
LONG BLACK FUR FLU
THE MOUNTAINS ARE

REGULAR – 18PT

The quick brown fox jumps over a lazy dog. He didn't
it would be the cheeky thing to do. After all, he had a re
It's a lovely day in the neighbourhood, with the sun shi
and the pungent aroma of fresh rubbish bins wafting th
promise of a sumptuous meal. The sprightly fox rubs h
thinking about the delicious treasures he's about to dig
the lazy dog remains unperturbed. With her long snout
long black fur fluttering in the breeze, she is in a dream

Abc Gaisyr Abc Gaisyr **Abc Gaisyr**
Abc Gaisyr Abc Gaisyr Abc Gaisyr
&
Abc Gaisyr Abc Gaisyr Abc Gaisyr
Abc Gaisyr Abc Gaisyr Abc Gaisyr

No. 9

1 ONE
2 TWO
3 THREE
4 FOUR
5 FIVE
6 SIX
7 SEVEN
8 EIGHT
9 NINE

TYPEFACE : GAMUTH COLLECTION
DESIGNER : PRODUCTION TYPE
LOCATION : PARIS, FRANCE; SHANGHAI, CHINA

PUBLISHED BY : PRODUCTION TYPE
CHRONOLOGY : 2021 - 2023
RELEASED IN : 2023

LINK : HTTPS://WWW.PRODUCTIONTYPE.COM/COLLECTION/GAMUTH_COLLECTION
STYLES : 24 STYLES, 2 OPTICAL SIZES: TEXT & DISPLAY
CREDITS : MAX ESNÉE (DESIGN)

THE GAMUTH COLLECTION IS CONCEIVED AS A MULTI-FACETED WORK, OF WHICH THE FIRST PANELS ARE TWO OPTICAL SIZES (DISPLAY AND TEXT) OF THE SAME SERIF TYPEFACE. IT BORROWS FROM DUTCH BAROQUE FACES AND THEIR TYPICAL BREADTH: NARROWER THAN USUAL PROPORTIONS, GENEROUS X-HEIGHTS, AND CRISP DETAILING ARE KEY FEATURES OF THE TYPEFACES, AND ADD A DENSE, DEEP TEXTURE TO RUNNING TEXT.

CAP HEIGHT

REGULAR – 290PT

X-HEIGHT

Gg

BASELINE

Gamuth Collection

REGULAR – 45PT

THE QUICK BROWN F
IT WOULD BE THE CH
ITS A LOVELY DAY IN
AND THE PUNGENT A
PROMISE OF A SUMPT
THINKING ABOUT TH
THE LAZY DOG REMA
LONG BLACK FUR FL
THE MOUNTAINS AR

REGULAR – 12PT

The quick brown fox jumps over a lazy dog. He didn't have to, but he thought it would be the cheeky thing to do. After all, he had a reputation to maintain. Its a lovely day in the neighbourhood, with the sun shining, the birds chirping, and the pungent aroma of fresh rubbish bins wafting through the air - the promise of a sumptuous meal. The sprightly fox rubs his paws together in glee, thinking about the delicious treasures he's about to dig into. Still in her spot, the lazy dog remains unperturbed. With her long snout, droopy jowls, and long black fur fluttering in the breeze, she is in a dreamland far away - where the mountains are made of beefy treats, the valleys are filled with tennis balls, and the puddles are just the right temperature. Why be in the rat race?
Its a dogs life, after all.

Attack
Indirect
Scatter
London
Defence
Newton

Feared
Broken
Access
Protect
Glance
Pushed

42

TYPEFACE : GESTURA
DESIGNER : SOCIOTYPE
LOCATION : LONDON, UK

PUBLISHED BY : SOCIOTYPE
CHRONOLOGY : 2019 - 2022
RELEASED IN : 2022

LINK : HTTPS://SOCIO-TYPE.COM/GESTURA
STYLES : 42 STYLES IN TOTAL. 3 SUBFAMILIES: GESTURA TEXT, GESTURA HEADLINE & GESTURA DISPLAY.
7 WEIGHTS FOR EACH SUBFAMILY: THIN, EXTRALIGHT, LIGHT, REGULAR, SEMIBOLD, BOLD & BLACK + ITALICS

GESTURA WAS DESIGNED TO OFFER BOTH THE EFFORTLESS READING EXPERIENCE OF A WORKHORSE SERIF AND THE STRIKING PERSONALITY OF A DISPLAY FACE. WITH AN UNDERLYING CALLIGRAPHIC QUALITY, THE TYPEFACE IS FORMALLY RESTLESS BUT ALWAYS CONTROLLED. ITS CONTRADICTORY CHARACTERISTICS ARE FINELY BALANCED, ADDING UP TO A NATURALLY CONSISTENT WHOLE. AT 42 STYLES AND 3 OPTICAL SIZES WITH AN ABUNDANCE OF ALTERNATE STYLISTIC FEATURES, GESTURA IS A GENUINE DO-IT-ALL SERIF THAT IS JUST AS EFFECTIVE FOR LONG-FORM COPY, STRIKING HEADLINES OR EXPRESSIVE DISPLAY TYPE.

CAP HEIGHT

REGULAR - 290PT

X-HEIGHT

Gg

BASELINE

Gestura

REGULAR – 45PT

THE QUICK BROWN
IT WOULD BE THE
ITS A LOVELY DAY I
AND THE PUNGENT
PROMISE OF A SUM
THINKING ABOUT T
THE LAZY DOG REM
LONG BLACK FUR F
THE MOUNTAINS A

REGULAR – 10PT

The quick brown fox jumps over a lazy dog. He didn't have to, but he thought it would be the cheeky thing to do. After all, he had a reputation to maintain. Its a lovely day in the neighbourhood, with the sun shining, the birds chirping, and the pungent aroma of fresh rubbish bins wafting through the air - the promise of a sumptuous meal. The sprightly fox rubs his paws together in glee, thinking about the delicious treasures he's about to dig into. Still in her spot, the lazy dog remains unperturbed. With her long snout, droopy jowls, and long black fur fluttering in the breeze, she is in a dreamland far away - where the mountains are made of beefy treats, the valleys are filled with tennis balls, and the puddles are just the right temperature. Why be in the rat race?
Its a dogs life, after all.

Gestura Text Thin
Gestura Text Thin Italic
Gestura Text Extralight
Gestura Text Extralight Italic
Gestura Text Light
Gestura Text Light Italic
Gestura Text Regular
Gestura Text Regular Italic
Gestura Text Semibold
Gestura Text Semibold Italic
Gestura Text Bold
Gestura Text Bold Italic
Gestura Text Black
Gestura Text Black Italic

Gestura Headline Thin
Gestura Headline Thin Italic
Gestura Headline Extralight
Gestura Headline Extralight Italic
Gestura Headline Light
Gestura Headline Light Italic
Gestura Headline Regular
Gestura Headline Regular Italic
Gestura Headline Semibold
Gestura Headline Semibold Italic
Gestura Headline Bold
Gestura Headline Bold Italic
Gestura Headline Black
Gestura Headline Black Italic

Gestura Display Thin
Gestura Display Thin Italic
Gestura Display Extralight
Gestura Display Extralight Italic
Gestura Display Light
Gestura Display Light Italic
Gestura Display Regular
Gestura Display Regular Italic
Gestura Display Semibold
Gestura Display Semibold Italic
Gestura Display Bold
Gestura Display Bold Italic
Gestura Display Black
Gestura Display Black Italic

VERSION
1.001

OPTICAL SIZES
3

STYLES
42

GLYPHS
617 (UPRIGHTS)
+ 622 (ITALICS)

GESTURA HEADLINE
Regular (64pt)

23% 73°42'21W
Shrigley *(esque)*
1Ø6×38≠4Ø2*
#jáhnů/fånig?
{1/9} → ST©

Stylistic Set Ø1:
Monolinear Zero, Asterisk + Parentheses

GESTURA DISPLAY
Optical Size → 1 (of) 3

Pointing Index
[Byzantinism]
Counterculture
Victor Laveleye
(Martyrdoms)
“Quite Good”
Swipe Right

TYPEFACE	:	GLASGOW
DESIGNER	:	ALAN MADIĆ
LOCATION	:	PARIS, FRANCE

PUBLISHED BY	:	ALAN MADIĆ
CHRONOLOGY	:	2022 - 2023
RELEASED IN	:	2023

LINK	:	HTTP://WWW.ALANMADIC.COM
STYLES	:	REGULAR, MEDIUM, BOLD, BLACK, REGULAR ITALIC, MEDIUM ITALIC, BOLD ITALIC, BLACK ITALIC

GLASGOW, A TRANSITIONAL TYPEFACE FAMILY, WAS DESIGNED IN FOUR WEIGHTS, WITH CORRESPONDING ITALICS. ITS INTERPRETATION AIMS TO SYNTHESISE AND EXTEND FONTANA, WHICH WAS DESIGNED BY GIOVANNI MARDERSTEIG IN 1936 FOR THE VISUAL IDENTITY OF COLLINS PUBLISHING HOUSE (GLASGOW) - ONE OF THE FIRST MAJOR PUBLISHERS TO HAVE ITS OWN TYPEFACE. DRAWING INSPIRATION FROM ALEXANDER WILSON'S (GLASGOW LETTER FOUNDRY) EARLIER WORK ON TRANSITIONAL TYPEFACES CIRCA 1760, GLASGOW SETS OUT TO RETAIN THE ESSENCE OF FONTANA WHILE CONSIDERING A CONTEMPORARY APPLICATION. SHORTENED ASCENDERS AND DESCENDERS AS WELL AS A COMFORTABLE X-HEIGHT ALLOW IT TO BE FUNCTIONAL IN SMALL TEXT AND TO ASSERT ITS PERSONALITY IN TITLING SCALES.

CAP HEIGHT

REGULAR - 290PT

X-HEIGHT

Gg

BASELINE

Glasgow

REGULAR – 38PT

THE QUICK BROWN FO
IT WOULD BE THE CHE
ITS A LOVELY DAY IN T
AND THE PUNGENT AR
PROMISE OF A SUMPTU
THINKING ABOUT THE

REGULAR – 16PT

The quick brown fox jumps over a lazy dog. He didn't have
it would be the cheeky thing to do. After all, he had a repu
Its a lovely day in the neighbourhood, with the sun shinin
and the pungent aroma of fresh rubbish bins wafting thro
promise of a sumptuous meal. The sprightly fox rubs his p
thinking about the delicious treasures he's about to dig in
the lazy dog remains unperturbed. With her long snout, dr
long black fur fluttering in the breeze, she is in a dreamlar
the mountains are made of beefy treats, the valleys are fill
and the puddles are just the right temperature. Why be in
Its a dogs life, after all.

REGULAR – 8PT

The quick brown fox jumps over a lazy dog. He didn't have to, but he thought it would be the cheeky thing to do. After all, he had a reputation to maintain. Its a lovely day in the neighbourhood, with the sun shining, the birds chirping, and the pungent aroma of fresh rubbish bins wafting through the air - the promise of a sumptuous meal. The sprightly fox rubs his paws together in glee, thinking about the delicious treasures he's about to dig into. Still in her spot, the lazy dog remains unperturbed. With her long snout, droopy jowls, and long black fur fluttering in the breeze, she is in a dreamland far away - where the mountains are made of beefy treats, the valleys are filled with tennis balls, and the puddles are just the right temperature. Why be in the rat race? Its a dogs life, after all.

Hermann Hesse

¡Ludwig Kirchner!

√5(First*)‹folio›

Ww/Shakespeare

The Companion

Rainer Maria Rilke

Chăřlès Måliñ

*(**New-Directions**)*

British[]Library

Tauchnitz &dition

Qi's
käy,
Zhi

TYPEFACE : TT GLOBS
DESIGNER : TYPETYPE.ORG
LOCATION : SAINT PETERSBURG, RUSSIA

PUBLISHED BY : TYPETYPE.ORG
CHRONOLOGY : N/A
RELEASED IN : 2021

LINK : HTTPS://TYPETYPE.ORG/FONTS/TT-GLOBS/
STYLES : 3 STYLES + A VARIABLE FONT

TT GLOBS IS A MODERN SLAB SERIF TYPEFACE WITH WIDE LETTER PROPORTIONS. DUE TO ITS LONG DISPLAY SERIFS AND RATHER NARROW SPACING, WORDS TYPED IN TT GLOBS CONNECT INTO AN ALMOST UNINTERRUPTED DYNAMIC CHAIN, PROVIDING A COHESIVE LOOK. THE RESULT OF WORKING WITH THE TYPEFACE WILL ALWAYS BE A LITTLE DIFFERENT, AND DEPENDING ON THE WORDS YOU CHOOSE, YOU CAN EVEN CREATE YOUR OWN IMAGES.

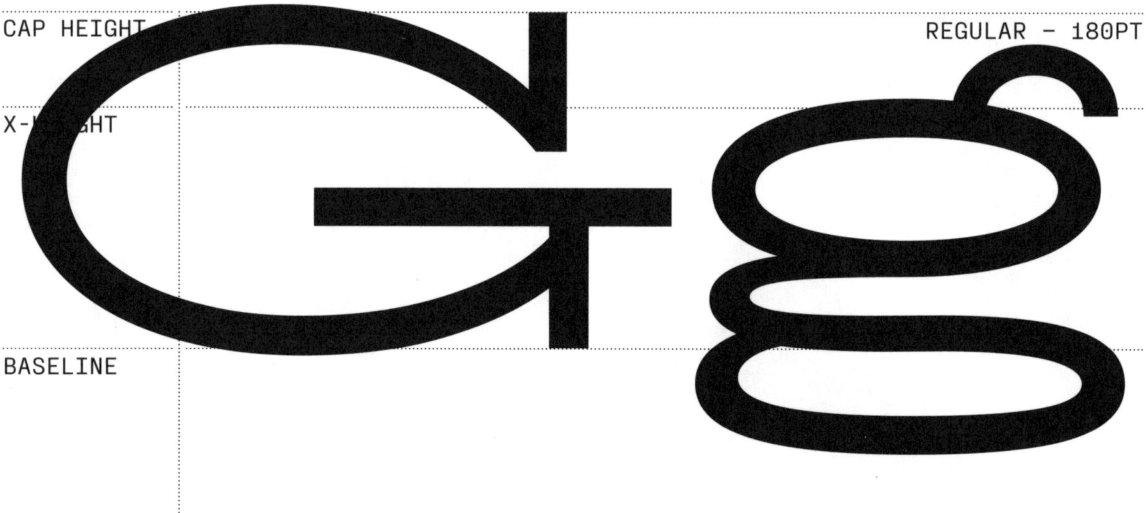

TTGlobs

REGULAR – 48PT

THE QUICK
IT WOULD
IT'S A LOV
AND THE F
PROMISE
THINKING
THE LAZY
LONG BLAC
THE MOUN

REGULAR – 8PT

The quick brown fox jumps over a lazy dog. He didn't have to, bu
it would be the cheeky thing to do. After all, he had a reputatio
It's a lovely day in the neighbourhood, with the sun shining, the
and the pungent aroma of fresh rubbish bins wafting through t
promise of a sumptuous meal. The sprightly fox rubs his paws t
thinking about the delicious treasures he's about to dig into. St
the lazy dog remains unperturbed. With her long snout, droopy
long black fur fluttering in the breeze, she is in a dreamland fa
the mountains are made of beefy treats, the valleys are filled wi
and the puddles are just the right temperature. Why be in the r
It's a dog's life, after all.

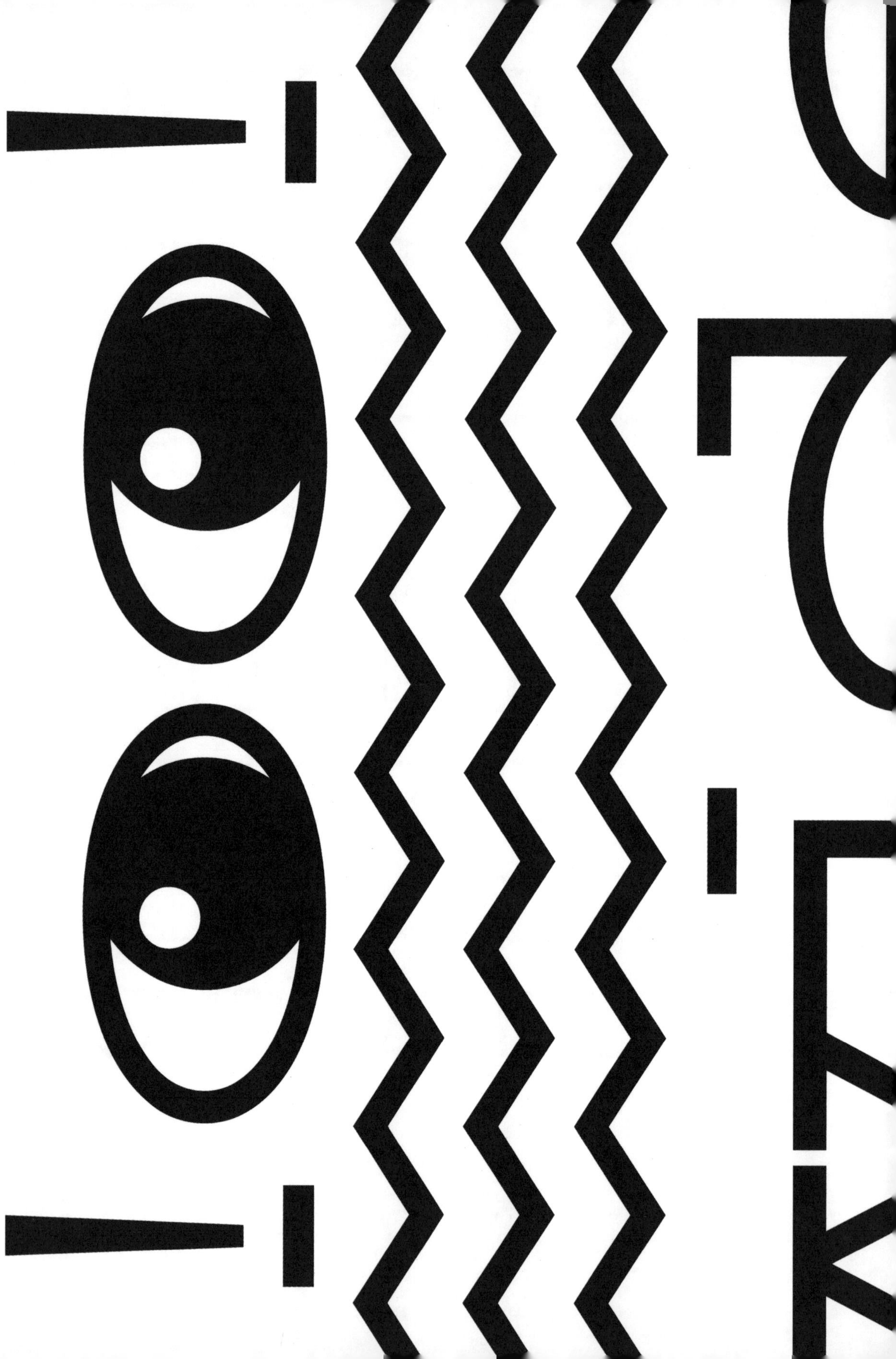

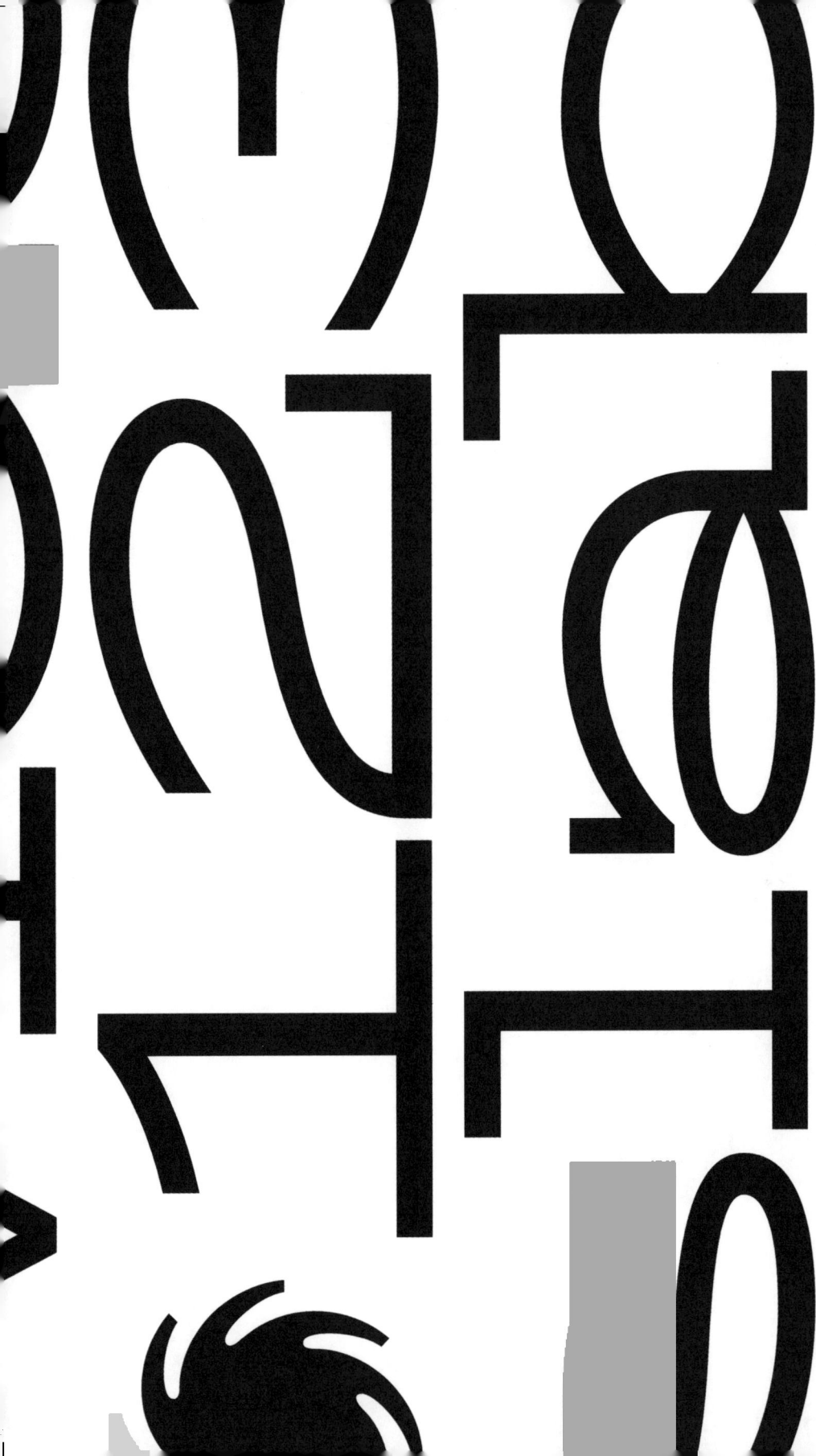

123

slab

TT Globs

TypeType

156

TYPEFACE : GREENSTONE
DESIGNER : SHARP TYPE
COUNTRY : NEW YORK & CALIFORNIA, US

PUBLISHED BY : SHARP TYPE
CHRONOLOGY : 2021
RELEASE : 2021

LINK : HTTPS://SHARPTYPE.CO/TYPEFACES/GREENSTONE/
STYLES : ROMAN, ITALIC

GREENSTONE IS A DISPLAY-ORIENTED SERIF THAT HONES IN ON THE EXPRESSIVE VERNACULAR OF OGG'S MID-CENTURY BOOK JACKET LETTERING AND THE ENGRAVINGS FOUND ON EPITAPHS THROUGHOUT NEW ENGLAND. DESIGNER CONNOR DAVENPORT COMBINES THE PRECISE, CONTROLLED CONSTRUCTION OF THESE INK AND STONE LETTERFORMS WITH UNEXPECTED DRAMATIC FLAIR. THE RESULT IS A DIGITAL HOMAGE TO SACRED TRADITIONS OF HAND LETTERING, ERUDITE AND EXPLORATORY IN EQUAL MEASURE.

CAP HEIGHT

REGULAR - 290PT

X-HEIGHT

BASELINE

Gg

Greenstone

REGULAR - 48PT

THE QUICK BROWN FOX
IT WOULD BE THE CHEE
ITS A LOVELY DAY IN TH
AND THE PUNGENT AR
PROMISE OF A SUMPTU
THINKING ABOUT THE
THE LAZY DOG REMAIN
LONG BLACK FUR FLUT
THE MOUNTAINS ARE M

REGULAR - 12PT

The quick brown fox jumps over a lazy dog. He didn't have to, but he thought it would be the cheeky thing to do. After all, he had a reputation to maintain. Its a lovely day in the neighbourhood, with the sun shining, the birds chirping, and the pungent aroma of fresh rubbish bins wafting through the air - the promise of a sumptuous meal. The sprightly fox rubs his paws together in glee, thinking about the delicious treasures he's about to dig into. Still in her spot, the lazy dog remains unperturbed. With her long snout, droopy jowls, and long black fur fluttering in the breeze, she is in a dreamland far away - where the mountains are made of beefy treats, the valleys are filled with tennis balls, and the puddles are just the right temperature. Why be in the rat race? Its a dogs life, after all.

Discere Faciendo

HH

DOUBLE BUTTE
FORT ROBINSON

Dies Tenebrosa Sicut Nox

A Day As Dark As Night

Abyssus Abyssum Invocat

Deep Calleth Unto Deep

7/8 tt

W G

R © sb

TYPEFACE	:	INFERI
DESIGNER	:	BLAZE TYPE
LOCATION	:	MARSEILLE, FRANCE

PUBLISHED BY	:	BLAZE TYPE
CHRONOLOGY	:	N/A
RELEASED IN	:	2021

LINK	:	HTTPS://BLAZETYPE.EU/TYPEFACES/INFERI
STYLES	:	SERIF, DISPLAY, TEXT, UPRIGHT, ITALIC

INFERI TAKES ITS ROOTS IN GARALDE PRINT-LIKE FONTS. WITH ITS DEFINING FEATURES, LIKE SQUARED EDGES AND PRINT LETTERFORMS, IT COVERS A LARGE PANEL OF USES. IT HAS BEEN DESIGNED IN VARIOUS STYLES AND WEIGHTS, ALLOWING ONE TO HAVE AN EXTENSIVE TYPE-TOOL FOR ANY KIND OF USAGE. WHETHER THE NEED WOULD BE ON BOOK DESIGN, POSTER DESIGN OR EDITORIAL USES, INFERI WILL BE A NICE FIT TO COMPLEX TYPE-SHAPING. IF YOUR GOAL IS TO REACH FOR A PRINTED-TYPE FEELING ON DIGITAL MEDIA (E.G., WEBSITES, APPS), YOU WILL ALSO FIND INFERI TO BE YOUR TOOL OF CHOICE. A WELL-BALANCED FAMILY WITH SQUARED EDGES AND ROUND FINISHES IN THE ROMAN VERSION, THE ITALICS CUT DEEP INTO A MORE MODERN APPROACH. DRAWN WITH A CAREFUL “HAND STYLE” TOUCH, IT PROVIDES A NICE BALANCE FOR COMPLEX LAYOUTS AS ITS PRINT STYLE FORM AND THE OPTICAL GREY BETWEEN ITS ROMAN AND ITALIC VERSIONS ALLOW FOR GREAT LEGIBILITY.

CAP HEIGHT

REGULAR – 290PT

Ii

X-HEIGHT

BASELINE

Inferi

REGULAR – 36PT

THE QUICK BROWN FOX J
IT WOULD BE THE CHEEK
IT'S A LOVELY DAY IN THE
AND THE PUNGENT ARO
PROMISE OF A SUMPTUO
THINKING ABOUT THE D
THE LAZY DOG REMAINS
LONG BLACK FUR FLUTT
THE MOUNTAINS ARE MA
AND THE PUDDLES ARE J

REGULAR – 18PT

The quick brown fox jumps over a lazy dog. He didn't h
it would be the cheeky thing to do. After all, he had a re
It's a lovely day in the neighbourhood, with the sun shi
and the pungent aroma of fresh rubbish bins wafting t
promise of a sumptuous meal. The sprightly fox rubs h
thinking about the delicious treasures he's about to dig
the lazy dog remains unperturbed. With her long snout
long black fur fluttering in the breeze, she is in a dream

might be a Scottish name, taken from a ory about two men on a train. One man ys, *"What's that package up there in the ggage rack?"* And the other answers, ***)h, that's a Devil Trap".*** The first one ks, *"What's a Devil Trap?"* **"Well,"** the other an says, ***"it's an apparatus for trapping Demons at Wallmart."*** The first man says, *"But there are no Demons at* one answers, ***"W trap!"*** So you see actually nothing a **Hitchcock** ever c the term *Devil Tra* anyone can tell, h to describe the lir detective, or suspense story;

Devi

ALIBRATE ROAI

GHTINGS CREV

ALANCED OR

OSHPIT

art," and the other
en, that's no Devil
a Devil trap is
That was as close as
o explaining where
ne from; as far as
le it up. He used it
n of the mystery,

the motivating or primal force behind narrative. Not the motive itself, but the gizmo, situation, or event that lies behi the motive. And a useful term it is. Ove the past **sixty years** writers, particularl mystery writers, have adopted it as the own. *But it deserves a wider appreciati and a greater understanding.* The more examine the idea the more you wi that it describes a **powerful narra** device. found in most, if not all, fic

l trap

IE

S

→ **B-TEAMS** ←

ARE WELCOM

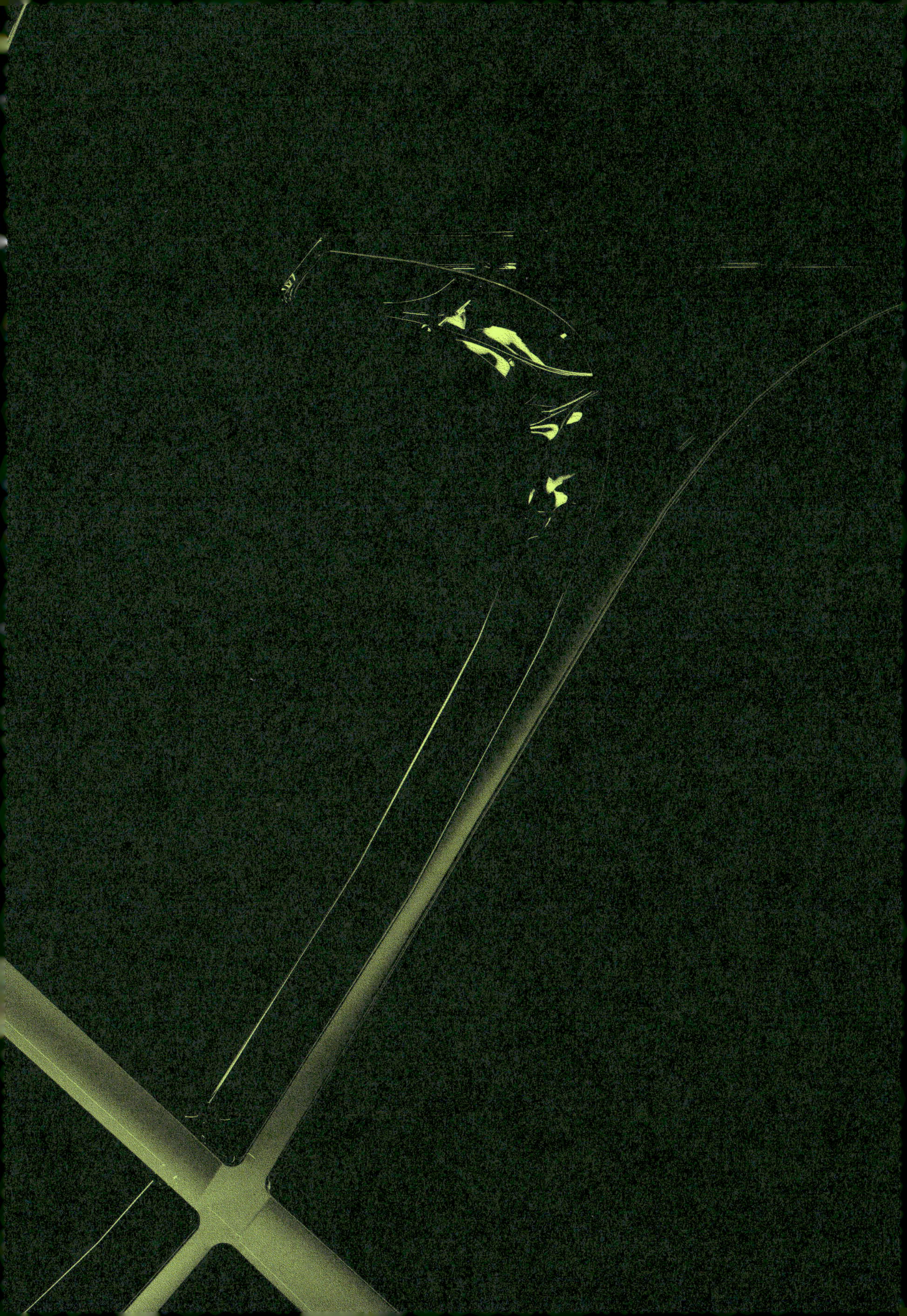

TYPEFACE : INKA
DESIGNER : CARNOKYTYPE
LOCATION : KYSAK, SLOVAKIA

PUBLISHED BY : CARNOKYTYPE
CHRONOLOGY : 2012 - 2015
RELEASED IN : 2015

LINK : HTTPS://CARNOKYTYPE.COM/FONTS/INKA
STYLES : 64 FONTS • 4 WEIGHTS + ITALICS • 4 OPTICAL SIZES (DISPLAY/TITLE/TEXT/SMALL) • 2 FONT VARIANTS (INKA A/INKA B)

INKA IS A MODERN SERIF TYPEFACE WITH WIDE UNIVERSALITY IN FUNCTION, PARTICULARLY EDITORIAL DESIGN (E.G. BOOKS, MAGAZINES). THE TYPEFACE IS BASED ON THE PRINCIPLE OF OPTICAL SIZES DESIGNED FOR THE PARTICULAR USE OF THE SIZE OF TYPESETTING AND CONSISTS OF TWO CONSTRUCTION ALTERNATIVES WITH HIGHER (INKA A) OR LOWER (INKA B) VERTICAL PROPORTIONS. EACH FONT SET (DISPLAY, TITLE, TEXT, AND SMALL) CONSISTS OF FOUR WEIGHTS (REGULAR, MEDIUM, BOLD, AND BLACK), WITH A WIDE CHARACTER SET AND A LOT OF OPENTYPE FEATURES. INKA WAS CREATED WITH LOVE AND NAMED AFTER THE DESIGNER'S PARTNER, INKA.

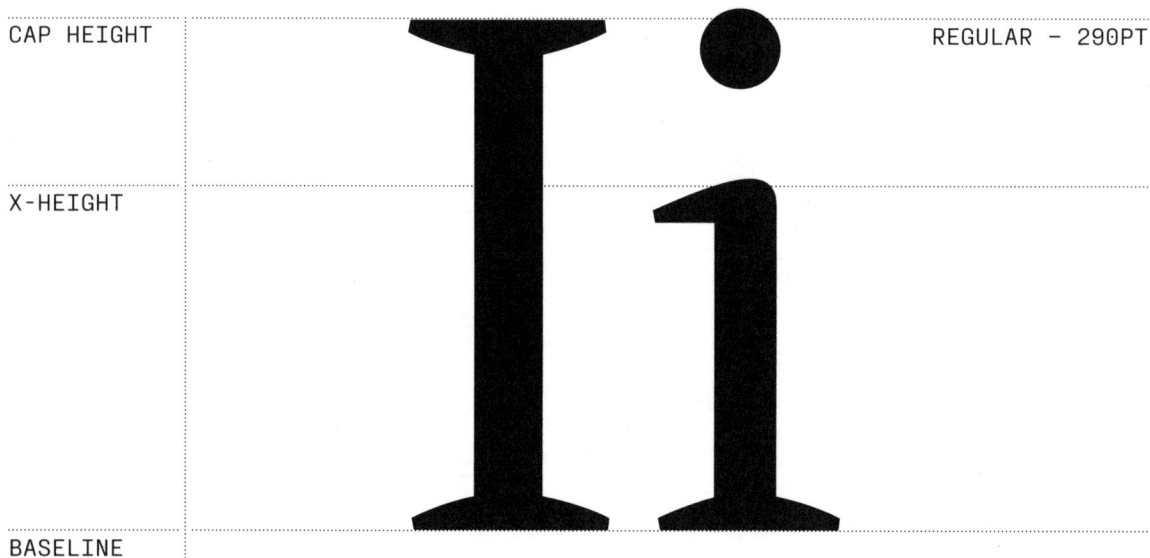

CAP HEIGHT

REGULAR – 290PT

Ii

X-HEIGHT

BASELINE

Inka

REGULAR – 36PT

THE QUICK BROWN FOX J
IT WOULD BE THE CHEEK
IT'S A LOVELY DAY IN THE
AND THE PUNGENT AROM
PROMISE OF A SUMPTUOU
THINKING ABOUT THE DE
THE LAZY DOG REMAINS U
LONG BLACK FUR FLUTTE
THE MOUNTAINS ARE MA
AND THE PUDDLES ARE JU
IT'S A DOG'S LIFE, AFTER A

REGULAR – 12PT

The quick brown fox jumps over a lazy dog. He didn't have to, but he thought it would be the cheeky thing to do. After all, he had a reputation to maintain. It's a lovely day in the neighbourhood, with the sun shining, the birds chirping, and the pungent aroma of fresh rubbish bins wafting through the air - the promise of a sumptuous meal. The sprightly fox rubs his paws together in glee, thinking about the delicious treasures he's about to dig into. Still in her spot, the lazy dog remains unperturbed. With her long snout, droopy jowls, and long black fur fluttering in the breeze, she is in a dreamland far away - where the mountains are made of beefy treats, the valleys are filled with tennis balls, and the puddles are just the right temperature. Why be in the rat race? It's a dog's life, after all.

Súčasná tvorba písma na Slovensku

Nebojím sa konštatovať, že písmotvorbe na Slovensku sa darí viac ako kedykoľvek predtým." Samo Čarnoký

Ak chceme hovoriť o súčasnom písme, musíme sa nutne obzrieť aj do minulosti. Bez poznania kontextu doby a historických súvislostí nemožno hovoriť o dnešku. Aj keď to vyzerá, že história pôvodnej tvorby písma na Slovensku nemá dlhú tradíciu a v porovnaní s mnohými inými krajinami je toto konštatovanie v podstate pravdivé, napriek tomu tu istá tradícia je. Avšak vo všeobecnosti sa o nej veľmi málo vie.

Môj výskum sa zameriava na súčasnú písmarskú tvorbu vytvorenú v slovenskom kontexte, ako

1. Príkladom sú návrhy tlačového písma od Jura Linzbotha.
2. Užitočná v tomto smere j napríklad otvorená facebooková skupina Slo typography, založená J. Filípkom. Pozri *<https://www.facebook.co groups/slovaktypography/*
3. Pozri prílohu dizertačnej práce. Príloha: vzorník písma – Inka, s. 178 – 179.

Inka
TYPEFACE DESIGNED WITH LOVE
THE STORY OF LOVE
Inka → a modern serif typeface was designed with love and is dedicated to my wife Inka
SHE'S
friendly careful
funny playful
kindly intuitive
optimistic
enthusiastic

Inka A

Display →	Regular	→ *Regular Italic*
	Medium	→ *Medium Italic*
	Bold	→ ***Bold Italic***
	Black	→ ***Black Italic***
Title →	Regular	→ *Regular Italic*
	Medium	→ *Medium Italic*
	Bold	→ ***Bold Italic***
	Black	→ ***Black Italic***
Text →	Regular	→ *Regular Italic*
	Medium	→ *Medium Italic*
	Bold	→ ***Bold Italic***
	Black	→ ***Black Italic***
Small →	Regular	→ *Regular Italic*
	Medium	→ *Medium Italic*
	Bold	→ ***Bold Italic***
	Black	→ ***Black Italic***

Inka B

Display →	Regular	→ *Regular Italic*
	Medium	→ *Medium Italic*
	Bold	→ ***Bold Italic***
	Black	→ ***Black Italic***
Title →	Regular	→ *Regular Italic*
	Medium	→ *Medium Italic*
	Bold	→ ***Bold Italic***
	Black	→ ***Black Italic***
Text →	Regular	→ *Regular Italic*
	Medium	→ *Medium Italic*
	Bold	→ ***Bold Italic***
	Black	→ ***Black Italic***
Small →	Regular	→ *Regular Italic*
	Medium	→ *Medium Italic*
	Bold	→ ***Bold Italic***
	Black	→ ***Black Italic***

TYPEFACE	:	ITEMS
DESIGNER	:	SCHICK TOIKKA
LOCATION	:	BERLIN, GERMANY; HELSINKI, FINLAND

PUBLISHED BY	:	SCHICK TOIKKA
CHRONOLOGY	:	2023
RELEASED IN	:	2023

LINK	:	HTTPS://WWW.SCHICK-TOIKKA.COM/ITEMS
STYLES	:	39

ITEMS IS A CONTEMPORARY TYPEFACE THAT TIES IN WITH THE PERVASIVE SERIFS OF THE EARLY DIGITAL PERIOD. RECONCILING FAMILIARITY WITH BEAUTY, IT SEEKS TO OVERCOME THE LIMITATIONS OF THE TIMES FONT AND ITS COMTEMPORARIES. ITS DESIGN IS MORE CONSISTENT, WITH A CONTRAST AXIS AND TOP SERIFS THAT EXHIBIT THE SAME ANGLE ACROSS ALL WEIGHTS. DRAWN WITH A FOCUS ON CAREFULLY MODULATED BLACKS AND SHAPELY WHITES, ITEMS ACHIEVES AN EVEN TYPOGRAPHIC COLOUR. THE LETTER FIT IS TIGHT, LETTING IT SHINE IN DISPLAY SIZES. IT IS INFUSED WITH SLICK DETAILS - LIKE THE SPURRED "G" AS FOUND IN TYPES CUT IN ANTWERP IN THE 1500'S, OR THE JOINS THAT TAPER TO A POINT - THAT MAKE FOR A CRISP LOOK IN TITLES AND HEADLINES. ITS ROBUST BUILD FEATURING A LARGE X-HEIGHT ENSURES A PLEASANT PERFORMANCE IN TEXT SIZES AS WELL - GRANTED THAT THE SPACING IS OPENED UP.

CAP HEIGHT

REGULAR - 290PT

Ii

X-HEIGHT

BASELINE

REGULAR – 48PT

THE QUICK BROWN FO
IT WOULD BE THE CH
IT'S A LOVELY DAY IN T
AND THE PUNGENT A
PROMISE OF A SUMPT
THINKING ABOUT TH
THE LAZY DOG REMA
LONG BLACK FUR FLU

REGULAR – 12PT

The quick brown fox jumps over a lazy dog. He didn't have to, but he thought it would be the cheeky thing to do. After all, he had a reputation to maintain. It's a lovely day in the neighbourhood, with the sun shining, the birds chirping, and the pungent aroma of fresh rubbish bins wafting through the air - the promise of a sumptuous meal. The sprightly fox rubs his paws together in glee, thinking about the delicious treasures he's about to dig into. Still in her spot, the lazy dog remains unperturbed. With her long snout, droopy jowls, and long black fur fluttering in the breeze, she is in a dreamland far away - where the mountains are made of beefy treats, the valleys are filled with tennis balls, and the puddles are just the right temperature. Why be in the rat race? It's a dog's life, after all.

230 Items Medium Rom

YVES KLEIN

230 Items Medium Rom

Nouveau réalisme

230 Items Medium Rom

Pierre Restany

Items Pixel Icons

NY Tokyo
In/Outbox
Podcast
Recycle bin

TYPEFACE : JAZZIER
DESIGNER : DALTON MAAG
LOCATION : LONDON, UK

PUBLISHED BY : DALTON MAAG
CHRONOLOGY : 2021
RELEASED IN : 2021

LINK : HTTPS://WWW.DALTONMAAG.COM/PORTFOLIO/FONT-LIBRARY/JAZZIER.HTML
STYLES : REGULAR

JAZZIER IS A CARICATURE OF AN OLD STYLE SERIF TYPEFACE, PACKED WITH TYPOGRAPHIC SURPRISES AND UNEXPECTED CHARM. IDEAL FOR BOOK COVER DESIGN, POSTERS, MERCHANDISE, AND PACKAGING, IT IS SURE TO CAPTIVATE AND INSPIRE WITH ITS UNIQUE APPROACH AND EXPRESSION.

CAP HEIGHT

REGULAR – 290PT

Jj

X-HEIGHT

BASELINE

Jazzier

REGULAR – 36PT

THE QUICK BROWN
IT WOULD BE THE C
IT'S A LOVELY DAY I
AND THE PUNGENT
PROMISE OF A SUM
THINKING ABOUT T
THE LAZY DOG REM

REGULAR – 18PT

THE QUICK BROWN FOX JUMPS OVER A
IT WOULD BE THE CHEEKY THING TO D
IT'S A LOVELY DAY IN THE NEIGHBOURH
AND THE PUNGENT AROMA OF FRESH R
PROMISE OF A SUMPTUOUS MEAL. THE
THINKING ABOUT THE DELICIOUS TREA
THE LAZY DOG REMAINS UNPERTURBE
LONG BLACK FUR FLUTTERING IN THE B

REGULAR – 8PT

The quick brown fox jumps over a lazy dog. He didn't have to, but he thought it would be the cheeky thing to do. After all, he had a reputation to maintain. It's a lovely day in the neighbourhood, with the sun shining, the birds chirping, and the pungent aroma of fresh rubbish bins wafting through the air - the promise of a sumptuous meal. The sprightly fox rubs his paws together in glee, thinking about the delicious treasures he's about to dig into. Still in her spot, the lazy dog remains unperturbed. With her long snout, droopy jowls, and long black fur fluttering in the breeze, she is in a dreamland far away - where the mountains are made of beefy treats, the valleys are filled with tennis balls, and the puddles are just the right temperature. Why be in the rat race? It's a dog's life, after all.

ABCDEFGHIJKLMNOPQRSTUVWXYZ0123456789abcdefghijklmnopqrstuvw

Jazzier

Sphinx of black quartz, judge my vow.

Proportional Lining
Abc12345678900

Tabular Lining
Abc12345678900

Proportional Oldstyle
Abc12345678900

Tabular Oldstyle
Abc12345678900

£123,689

Proportional Lining

£123,689

Proportional Oldstyle

CZECHIA
Schifftank
PETS
ROTTEN
LOGBOOK

1 2/3

12/34

ES
NEST

DO
UNDONE

A C Œ & 5/8 0 Ť

‡ ⁂ F H J L x

B d $ Ż ❦ Ħ ◊

‽ 4 G I k M ∂

TYPEFACE : JOANE PRO
DESIGNER : W TYPE FOUNDRY
LOCATION : SANTIAGO, CHILE; BARCELONA, SPAIN; LONDON, UK

PUBLISHED BY : W TYPE FOUNDRY
CHRONOLOGY : N/A
RELEASED IN : 2023

LINK : HTTPS://WTYPEFOUNDRY.COM/TYPEFACES/JOANE-PRO
STYLES : XS, S, M, L, XL: THIN, THIN ITALIC, ULTRALIGHT, ULTRALIGHT ITALIC, LIGHT, LIGHT ITALIC, REGULAR, REGULAR ITALIC, MEDIUM, MEDIUM ITALIC, SEMIBOLD, SEMIBOLD ITALIC, BOLD, BOLD ITALIC, ULTRABOLD, ULTRABOLD ITALIC, BLACK, BLACK ITALIC
CREDITS : ALE NAVARRO (DESIGN), DIEGO ARAVENA (QUALITY ASSURANCE)

JOANE PRO IS A NEW TYPEFACE BASED ON JOANE (2018). THIS PROJECT HAS ITS ROOTS IN FRENCH TYPOGRAPHY FROM THE 16TH CENTURY, DUTCH MODELS FROM THE 17TH CENTURY, AND ENGLISH TYPOGRAPHY FROM THE 18TH CENTURY. THE RESULT IS A HIGH-CONTRAST TYPEFACE WITH SHARP FEATURES WHICH PROVIDES AN ORGANIC TEXTURE. IT IS A CONTEMPORARY TYPEFACE WITH 79 STYLES THAT WORK IN DISPLAY AND SMALL SIZES.

CAP HEIGHT

REGULAR - 290PT

X-HEIGHT

Jj

BASELINE

Joane Pro

REGULAR – 48PT

THE QUICK BROWN
IT WOULD BE THE
IT'S A LOVELY DAY
AND THE PUNGENT
PROMISE OF A SUM
THINKING ABOUT T
THE LAZY DOG REM
LONG BLACK FUR F
THE MOUNTAINS A

REGULAR – 8PT

The quick brown fox jumps over a lazy dog. He didn't have to, but he thought it would be the cheeky thing to do. After all, he had a reputation to maintain. It's a lovely day in the neighbourhood, with the sun shining, the birds chirping, and the pungent aroma of fresh rubbish bins wafting through the air - the promise of a sumptuous meal. The sprightly fox rubs his paws together in glee, thinking about the delicious treasures he's about to dig into. Still in her spot, the lazy dog remains unperturbed. With her long snout, droopy jowls, and long black fur fluttering in the breeze, she is in a dreamland far away - where the mountains are made of beefy treats, the valleys are filled with tennis balls, and the puddles are just the right temperature. Why be in the rat race? It's a dog's life, after all.

ABCDEFHIJKLMNOPQ
RSTUVWXY&Z abcdefg
hijklmñopqrstuvwxyz
0123456789 1234567890
.,;:-–—[{("*")}]«»¿!@¡?#$€%

XL Thin *Italic*
XL UltraLight *Italic*
XL Light *Italic*
XL Regular *Italic*
XL Medium *Italic*
XL SemiBold *Italic*
XL Bold *Italic*
XL UltraBold *Italic*
XL Black *Italic*

L Thin *Italic*
L UltraLight *Italic*
L Light *Italic*
L Regular *Italic*
L Medium *Italic*
L SemiBold *Italic*
L Bold *Italic*
L UltraBold *Italic*
L Black *Italic*

M Thin *Italic*
M UltraLight *Italic*
M Light *Italic*
M Regular *Italic*
M Medium *Italic*
M SemiBold *Italic*
M Bold *Italic*
M UltraBold *Italic*
M Black *Italic*

S Thin *Italic*
S Light *Italic*
S Regular *Italic*
S Medium *Italic*
S Bold *Italic*
S Black *Italic*

XS Thin *Italic*
XS Light *Italic*
XS Regular *Italic*
XS Medium *Italic*
XS Bold *Italic*
XS Black *Italic*

THE ***Mediterranean*** BAR

FOOD CONNOISSEURS

Boeuf ***Bourguignon***

'R' DEFAULT ↓ 'A' SS03 ↓ ↓ 'R' SS01 'R' SS02 ↓

HENRI CHARPENTIER

JOANE PRO L SEMIBOLD ITALIC + L

IG @Su

THE BI

Silence of

SAU

ULAR + M LIGHT + XL BLACK ITALIC

daca.xyz

RDMAN

the Lamps

AGES

TYPEFACE : JUGENDREISEN
DESIGNER : PRETTY FACES TYPEFACES
LOCATION : CURITIBA, BRAZIL

PUBLISHED BY : PRETTY FACES TYPEFACES
CHRONOLOGY : 2020
RELEASED IN : 2020

LINK : HTTPS://PRETTYFACESTYPEFACES.COM/JUGENDREISEN
STYLES : LARGE, MEDIUM, SMALL

JUGENDREISEN IS AN OLD STYLE/GARALDE TYPEFACE WITH DESIGN CHOICES INSPIRED BY THE ART NOUVEAU ERA. THE IDEA WAS TO CREATE A TYPEFACE INSPIRED BY THE PERIOD BUT KEEP IT SUBTLE AND UNDERSTATED. IT CARRIES THE WARMTH AND CLASSIC ASPECT TYPICAL OF OLD STYLE TYPEFACES WITH GESTURES AND MOVEMENTS THAT WOULD REMIND YOU OF THE WORK OF DESIGNERS SUCH AS OTTO WEISERT AND HEINRICH KEUNE. SPECIAL CARE WAS PUT SO THAT THESE MOVEMENTS WOULD NOT OVERWHELM THE TYPEFACE, BUT INSTEAD, ADD FLUIDITY, ORIGINALITY AND A GRACEFUL ELEGANCE.

CAP HEIGHT

REGULAR – 290PT

X-HEIGHT

Jj

BASELINE

Jugendreisen

REGULAR – 36PT

THE QUICK BROWN F
IT WOULD BE THE CH
IT'S A LOVELY DAY IN
AND THE PUNGENT A
PROMISE OF A SUMPT
THINKING ABOUT TH
THE LAZY DOG REMA
BLACK FUR FLUTTER
MOUNTAINS ARE MA

REGULAR – 18PT

The quick brown fox jumps over a lazy dog. He c
it would be the cheeky thing to do. After all, he h
It's a lovely day in the neighbourhood, with the s
and the pungent aroma of fresh rubbish bins wa
promise of a sumptuous meal. The sprightly fox
thinking about the delicious treasures he's about
the lazy dog remains unperturbed. With her long
long black fur fluttering in the breeze, she is in
the mountains are made of beefy treats, the valle
and the puddles are just the right temperature. V
It's a dog's life, after all.

LUDWIG M

QYBURN

VERMON

DREIHÄUS

GIVERNY V

MATHILI

OUVELLE
L&M CO.
T TULUM
ERGRUPPE
VERKBUND
ENHÖHE

TYPEFACE : JÄGER
DESIGNER : VIOLAINE & JÉRÉMY
LOCATION : PARIS, FRANCE

PUBLISHED BY : VIOLAINE & JÉRÉMY
CHRONOLOGY : N/A
RELEASED IN : 2020

LINK : HTTPS://VJ-TYPE.COM/15-JAGER
STYLES : MASTER REGULAR, MASTER BOLD, CLASSIC REGULAR, CLASSIC BOLD

JÄGER IS A DISPLAY TYPEFACE, USEFUL FOR HEADLINES OR SHORT TO MEDIUM-LENGTH TEXTS. IT WAS DESIGNED IN 2020 BY JÉRÉMY SCHNEIDER FOR VJ TYPE. THE FONT'S RELEASE FALLS FIVE YEARS AFTER THE FIRST DRAWINGS WERE DEVELOPED FOR AN EXHIBITION AT THE MUSÉES DES ARTS DÉCORATIFS IN PARIS DEDICATED TO CONTEMPORARY ART CRAFTS. A TRIBUTE TO FINE CRAFTSMANSHIP, THE FONT IS VERY DIRECTLY INSPIRED BY TECHNIQUES MASTERED BY CRAFTSMEN IN THEIR WORK, AS SEEN IN THE HOLLOWED-OUT COUNTERFORMS REMINISCENT OF ENGRAVINGS, SCULPTURES OR WORKING WITH CHISELS. THE ANGLES GIVE THE IMPRESSION OF HAVING BEEN CUT IN WOOD, WHILE THE CONTOURS ARE ROUNDED, NEVER SHARP. EACH WEIGHT OFFERS TWO VERSIONS: THE JÄGER MASTER VERSION WHICH IS THE ORIGINAL, MOST ADVANCED, MOST DARING DESIGN, AND THE JÄGER CLASSIC VERSION IN WHICH THE COUNTERFORMS AT THE TOPS OF THE LETTERS HAVE BEEN FILLED IN TO OFFER A SMOOTHER AND MORE VERSATILE OPTION.

CAP HEIGHT

REGULAR – 290PT

Jj

X-HEIGHT

BASELINE

Jäger

THE QUICK BROW

IT WOULD BE THE

IT'S A LOVELY DA

AND THE PUNGEN

PROMISE OF A SU

THINKING ABOUT

THE LAZY DOG RE

LONG BLACK FUR

THE MOUNTAINS A

jã

Eos, A Favorite Greyhound of Prince Albert

1841
Oil on canvas

THE

SURFACE

MOTIFS
FIGURES
PIGMENTS

01

ESTAMPE

SAINT

EUSTACHE

ALBRECHT
DÜRER

1499

1503

Jogari Motifs Y. Klein Figure

2

Motifs
Figure
Pigments

48

TYPEFACE : KERNEVEL
DESIGNER : FORMAGARI
LOCATION : MARSEILLE, FRANCE

PUBLISHED BY : FORMAGARI
CHRONOLOGY : 2020 - 2022
RELEASED IN : 2022

LINK : N/A
STYLES : 8 STYLES, 4 WEIGHTS
REGULAR, ITALIC, BOOK, BOOK ITALIC, BOLD, BOLD ITALIC, BLACK, BLACK ITALIC
CREDITS : LUCAS LE BIHAN (DESIGN)

AN INTERPRETATION OF FREDERIC WILLIAM GOUDY'S UNIVERSITY OF CALIFORNIA OLD STYLE, KERNEVEL IS A CLASSIC-LOOKING TYPEFACE GAZING TOWARDS A MORE DISTANT HORIZON. IN THE REAL WORLD, IT STANDS SOMEWHERE BETWEEN BRITTANY AND CALIFORNIA. ACCORDING TO ITS DESIGNER, IT WAS INSPIRED BY SUMMERS IN BRITTANY: "I WAS FASCINATED BY SAILING SHIPS: LARGE ONES, SMALL ONES, MONOHULLS, MULTIHULLS. I SPENT MY TIME ON THE PONTOONS TO SEE THEM IN REAL LIFE, AND IN MAGAZINES TO COMPARE THEM ON PAPER. THIS INTEREST WAS MAINTAINED BY MY GRANDFATHER WHO TOOK US SAILING ON HIS 36-FOOTER WITH TWO SPREADERS, BETWEEN GROIX, BELLE-ÎLE AND HOUAT. THE DEPARTURE WAS INVARIABLY FROM THE PORT OF KERNEVEL."

CAP HEIGHT REGULAR - 290PT

X-HEIGHT

Kk

BASELINE

Kernevel

THE QUICK BR

IT WOULD BE T

IT'S A LOVELY

AND THE PUN

PROMISE OF A

THINKING AB

THE LAZY DOG

LONG BLACK

THE MOUNTA

❶ From *bodies*
to other *bodies*, ①
CLIMATES, ecosystems
② & technologies,
❸ *all life forms* are
inextricably ④
INTERCONNECTED
⑤ & interdependent.

SCULPTURE,

↻ *DANSE*,

✎ ÉCRITURE,

★ *SCÈNE* ☆

☆ *OUVERTE* ★

← VARIÉTÉS →

TYPEFACE	:	KESSLER
DESIGNER	:	PRODUCTION TYPE
LOCATION	:	PARIS, FRANCE; SHANGHAI, CHINA

PUBLISHED BY	:	PRODUCTION TYPE
CHRONOLOGY	:	2016 - 2019
RELEASED IN	:	2019

LINK	:	HTTPS://WWW.PRODUCTIONTYPE.COM/FAMILY/KESSLER
STYLES	:	6 STYLES; 3 OPTICAL SIZES; ROMAN & ITALIC
CREDITS	:	ALARIC GARNER (DESIGN)

WITH THE RELEASE OF KESSLER, ITS DESIGNER ALARIC GARNIER ACHIEVED A CONTEMPORARY TAKE ON INSCRIPTIONAL SERIFS. QUIRKS MEET PLEASANTRIES THROUGHOUT THE CHARACTER SET, WHILE DELIVERING HIGHLY READABLE, OPTIMISTIC TEXT SETTINGS. CLASSICISM COMES THROUGH IN THE FORMS OF THE LOWERCASE “A” AND “G”, AND TRADITION IS UPHELD IN ITS SLIGHTLY-MORE-CONDENSED ITALIC. HOWEVER, KESSLER IS NEVER DULL; IT TAKES LIBERTIES WITH EVERY “R” AND SPARKLES ACROSS THE PAGE. THERE IS PLENTY OF PERSONALITY IN THE KESSLER DISPLAY, AND ITS TEXT IS SUBSTANTIVE. FOR A FINE SERIF TYPEFACE, IT IS REMARKABLY STURDY, WITH A RICH TYPOGRAPHIC COLOUR THAT ENCOURAGES READING. ITS ITALIC SWOOPS THROUGH LIKE AN AUSTEN PLOT – SMOOTH AND ASSUMING, WITH CHARMING CHARACTER.

CAP HEIGHT

REGULAR – 290PT

X-HEIGHT

Kk

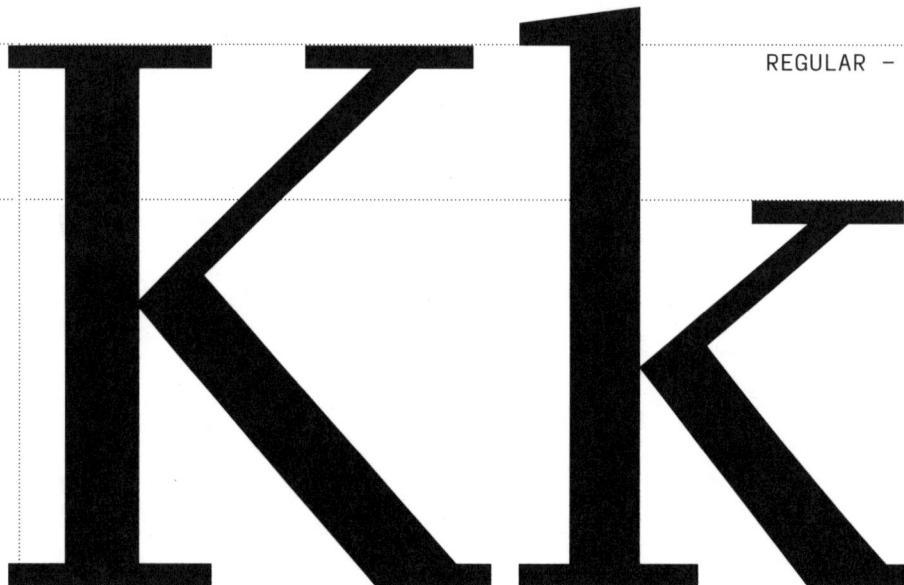

BASELINE

Kessler

REGULAR – 36PT

THE QUICK BROWN FOX J
IT WOULD BE THE CHEEK
IT'S A LOVELY DAY IN THE
AND THE PUNGENT AROM
PROMISE OF A SUMPTUOU
THINKING ABOUT THE DE
THE LAZY DOG REMAINS U
LONG BLACK FUR FLUTTE
THE MOUNTAINS ARE MA
AND THE PUDDLES ARE JU

REGULAR – 18PT

The quick brown fox jumps over a lazy dog. He didn't ha
it would be the cheeky thing to do. After all, he had a re
It's a lovely day in the neighbourhood, with the sun shir
and the pungent aroma of fresh rubbish bins wafting th
promise of a sumptuous meal. The sprightly fox rubs his
thinking about the delicious treasures he's about to dig
the lazy dog remains unperturbed. With her long snout
long black fur fluttering in the breeze, she is in a dreaml

azc
vns
xcr
uoe

54
KESSLER SUPER DISPLAY

TYPEFACE : ABC LAICA
DESIGNER : DINAMO
LOCATION : BERLIN, GERMANY

PUBLISHED BY : DINAMO
CHRONOLOGY : N/A
RELEASED IN : 2019

LINK : HTTPS://ABCDINAMO.COM/TYPEFACES/LAICA
STYLES : 2 FAMILIES, 20 STYLES
CREDITS : ALESSIO D'ELLENA (DESIGN), FRANZISKA WEITGRUBER & MICHELANGELO NIGRA (DESIGN ASSISTANCE), IGINO MARINI (SPACING & KERNING), ROBER JANES, HUGO JOURDAN & RENAN ROSATTI/DINAMO & CHI LONG TRIEU (PRODUCTION)

ABC LAICA IS THE RESULT OF A CRUEL METHODOLOGY: A FORCED COLLABORATION BETWEEN THE BROAD NIB PEN AND THE POINTED NIB PEN, TWO COMMON BUT VERY DIFFERENT DRAWING TOOLS. DESIGNER ALESSIO D'ELLENA SKETCHED EARLY VERSIONS OF THE TYPEFACE BY HAND DURING HIS SPARE TIME AS A STUDENT AT THE ROYAL ACADEMY OF ART IN THE HAGUE, WHICH USUALLY MEANT WHILE SLOUCHING IN UNCOMFORTABLE ARMCHAIRS AT THE AIRPORT OR ON RICKETY TRAMS WINDING THROUGH THE STREETS OF ROME. ABC LAICA'S PATCHWORK OF SHAPES ARE A PLAYFUL RETORT TO THE TRADITION OF CALLIGRAPHY, REFLECTING TODAY'S REALITY OF CHEAP FLIGHTS, CONSTANT HUSTLE, AND REMOTE WORK.

CAP HEIGHT

REGULAR – 290PT

L,1

X-HEIGHT

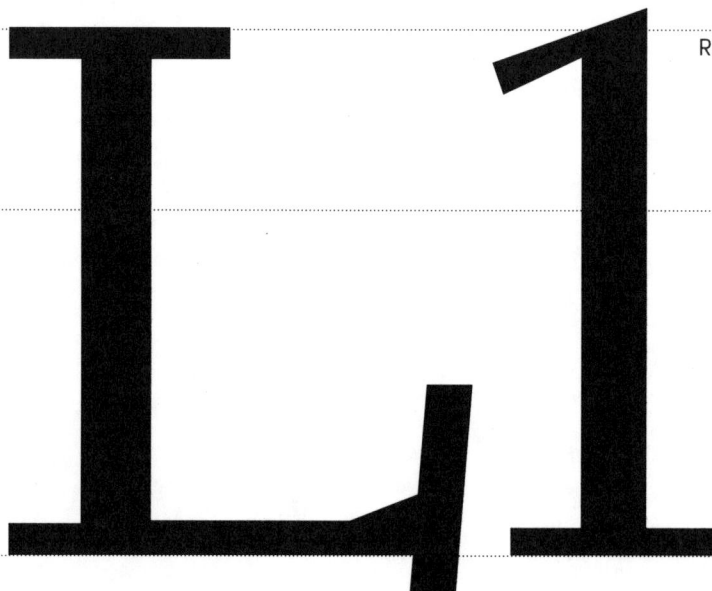

BASELINE

ABC Laica

REGULAR – 46PT

THE QUICK BROW
IT WOULD BE THE
IT'S A LOVELY DAY
AND THE PUNGEN
PROMISE OF A SUM
THINKING ABOUT
THE LAZY DOG RE
LONG BLACK FUR

REGULAR – 18PT

The quick brown fox jumps over a lazy dog. He didn't
it would be the cheeky thing to do. After all, he had a
It's a lovely day in the neighbourhood, with the sun s
and the pungent aroma of fresh rubbish bins wafting
promise of a sumptuous meal. The sprightly fox rubs
thinking about the delicious treasures he's about to
the lazy dog remains unperturbed. With her long sno
long black fur fluttering in the breeze, she is in a dre

‡g.*otf*

*@

02e₩

Laica?!

Type family

oddity

hello

enjoy

thanks

TYPEFACE	:	LARKEN VARIABLE
DESIGNER	:	THE TYPE FOUNDERS
LOCATION	:	UK

PUBLISHED BY	:	TYPE DEPARTMENT
CHRONOLOGY	:	N/A
RELEASED IN	:	N/A

LINK	:	N/A
STYLES	:	14X STYLES

DESIGNED TO REFLECT NATURE, LARKEN IS A CONFIDENT SERIF THAT CREATES A SENSE OF NATURAL SOFTNESS AND EXPRESSIVENESS. CONCEIVED WITH USABILITY IN MIND, LARKEN VARIABLE ALLOWS FOR FLUID DESIGN ACROSS 7 WEIGHTS, ITALICS, AND MAJOR LATIN LANGUAGES, WHILST TRUE ITALICS ADVANCE THE AESTHETICS, BRINGING AN ADDICTIVE, CONTEMPORARY ENERGY TO BUSINESSES AND BRANDS.

CAP HEIGHT

REGULAR – 290PT

X-HEIGHT

Ll

BASELINE

Larken Variable

REGULAR – 48PT

THE QUICK BROWN
IT WOULD BE THE C
IT'S A LOVELY DAY IN
AND THE PUNGENT
PROMISE OF A SUMP
THINKING ABOUT TH
THE LAZY DOG REM
LONG BLACK FUR FL

REGULAR – 12PT

The quick brown fox jumps over a lazy dog. He didn't have to, but he thought it would be the cheeky thing to do. After all, he had a reputation to maintain. It's a lovely day in the neighbourhood, with the sun shining, the birds chirping, and the pungent aroma of fresh rubbish bins wafting through the air – the promise of a sumptuous meal. The sprightly fox rubs his paws together in glee, thinking about the delicious treasures he's about to dig into. Still in her spot, the lazy dog remains unperturbed. With her long snout, droopy jowls, and long black fur fluttering in the breeze, she is in a dreamland far away – where the mountains are made of beefy treats, the valleys are filled with tennis balls, and the puddles are just the right temperature. Why be in the rat race? It's a dog's life, after all.

LAR KEN

52–1967

Jazz Club

〈 NO 4 / 〉

Sinàtra

•@7PM•

BOOGIE!!

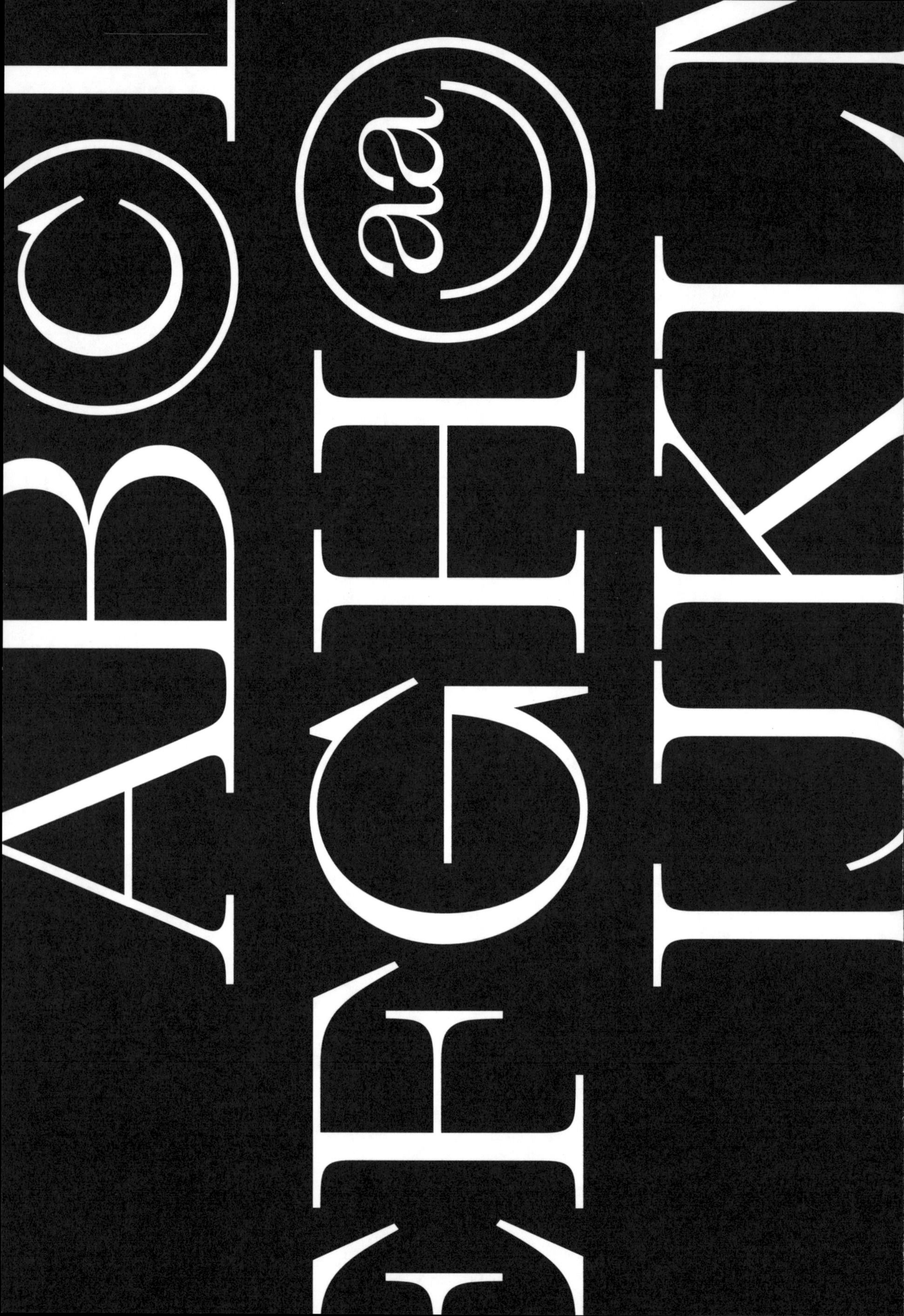

OPQ
®STUV
WXYZ

TYPEFACE : OR LEMMEN
DESIGNER : OR TYPE
LOCATION : REYKJAVÍK, ICELAND; BRUSSELS, BELGIUM

PUBLISHED BY : OR TYPE
CHRONOLOGY : N/A
RELEASED IN : 2018 & 2022

LINK : HTTPS://ORTYPE.IS/SPECIMEN/OR_LEMMEN
STYLES : 30

OR LEMMEN IS INSPIRED BY ANTIQUA, A TYPEFACE DESIGNED BY BELGIAN NEO-IMPRESSIONIST PAINTER GEORGES LEMMEN IN THE EARLY 20TH CENTURY. IT WAS BROUGHT TO THE TEAM'S ATTENTION BY DESIGNER AND TEACHER JEAN-MARC KLINKERT, WHO CAME ACROSS THE TYPEFACE DURING A LETTERPRESS WORKSHOP AT LA CAMBRE IN BRUSSELS. WORKING FROM A SPECIMEN SET IN THE ORIGINAL 10 AND 12 PTS LEAD TYPE, THE SMALL SIZE OF THE PRINT LED TO THE TEAM'S OWN INTERPRETATIONS OF WHAT WOULD BECOME OR LEMMEN. DURING THE PROCESS, A THIN AND LIGHT CUT WAS ALSO IMAGINED AND DEVELOPED ALONGSIDE THE ITALICS.

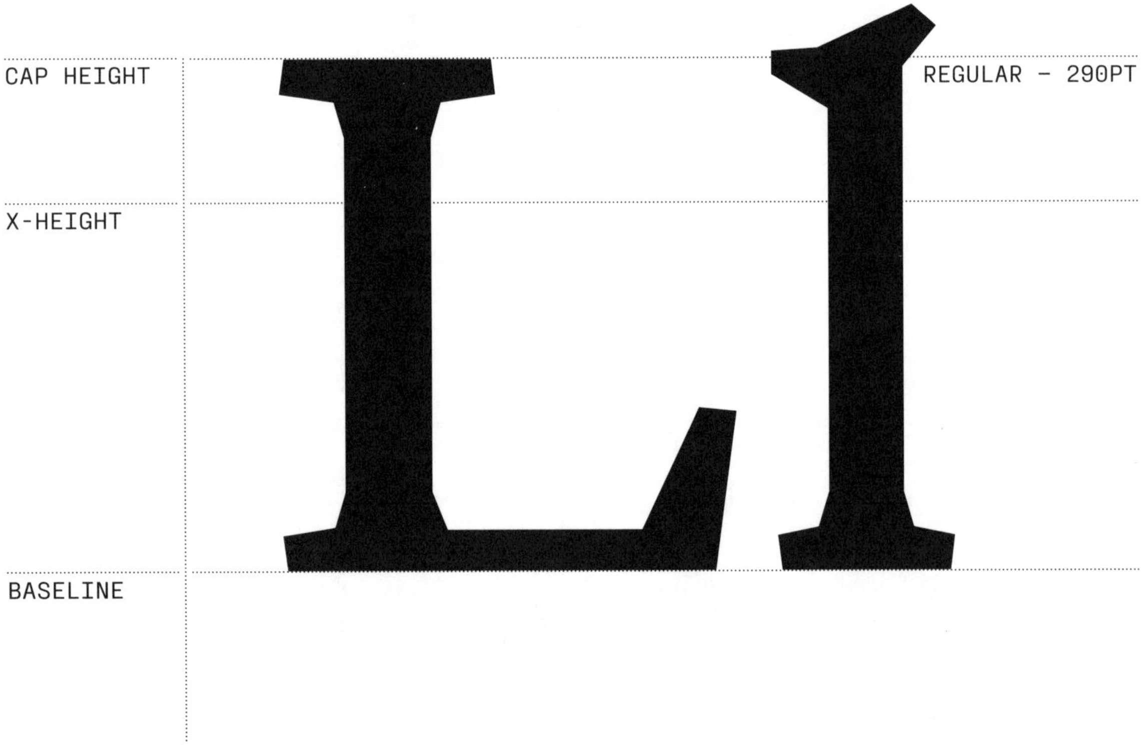

ORLemmen

REGULAR – 48PT

THE QUICK BROW
IT WOULD BE THE
IT'S A LOVELY DAY
AND THE PUNGEN
PROMISE OF A SUN
THINKING ABOUT
THE LAZY DOG RE
LONG BLACK FUR
THE MOUNTAINS A

REGULAR – 8PT

The quick brown fox jumps over a lazy dog. He didn't have to, but he thought it would be the cheeky thing to do. After all, he had a reputation to maintain. It's a lovely day in the neighbourhood, with the sun shining, the birds chirping, and the pungent aroma of fresh rubbish bins wafting through the air - the promise of a sumptuous meal. The sprightly fox rubs his paws together in glee, thinking about the delicious treasures he's about to dig into. Still in her spot, the lazy dog remains unperturbed. With her long snout, droopy jowls, and long black fur fluttering in the breeze, she is in a dreamland far away - where the mountains are made of beefy treats, the valleys are filled with tennis balls, and the puddles are just the right temperature. Why be in the rat race? It's a dog's life, after all.

Georges Lemmen

Beach at Heist, 1891

Oil on wood panel

H 37.5 × W 45.7 cm

Letterpress Set

Brussels to London

2018 → 2023

Family Extension

Neo-impressionist

TYPEFACE : TT LIVRET
DESIGNER : TYPETYPE.ORG
LOCATION : SAINT PETERSBURG, RUSSIA

PUBLISHED BY : TYPETYPE.ORG
CHRONOLOGY : N/A
RELEASED IN : 2022

LINK : HTTPS://TYPETYPE.ORG/FONTS/TT-LIVRET/
STYLES : 32 STYLES + 2 VARIABLE FONTS

TT LIVRET IS AN ELEGANT AND MODERN SERIF TYPE FAMILY WITH A STRONG HISTORICAL CHARACTER. THE FONT EMBODIES THE IDEA OF HIGHLY FUNCTIONAL SERIF TYPEFACES THAT ARE ADVANCED YET EASY TO USE. TT LIVRET CONSISTS OF THREE SUBFAMILIES (DISPLAY, SUBHEAD, AND TEXT), WHICH CAN GIVE YOU ANY LOOK YOU WANT: FROM DECORATIVE TO CALM.

CAP HEIGHT

REGULAR – 290PT

X-HEIGHT

Ll

BASELINE

TT Livret

REGULAR – 36PT

THE QUICK BROWN FOX
IT WOULD BE THE CHEE
IT'S A LOVELY DAY IN TH
AND THE PUNGENT ARO
PROMISE OF A SUMPTUO
THINKING ABOUT THE D

REGULAR – 16PT

The quick brown fox jumps over a lazy dog. He didn't have to,
it would be the cheeky thing to do. After all, he had a reputati
It's a lovely day in the neighbourhood, with the sun shining, t
and the pungent aroma of fresh rubbish bins wafting through
promise of a sumptuous meal. The sprightly fox rubs his paws
thinking about the delicious treasures he's about to dig into. S
the lazy dog remains unperturbed. With her long snout, droop
long black fur fluttering in the breeze, she is in a dreamland f
the mountains are made of beefy treats, the valleys are filled
and the puddles are just the right temperature. Why be in the
It's a dog's life, after all.

REGULAR – 10PT

The quick brown fox jumps over a lazy dog. He didn't have to, but he thought it would be the cheeky thing to do. After all, he had a reputation to maintain. It's a lovely day in the neighbourhood, with the sun shining, the birds chirping, and the pungent aroma of fresh rubbish bins wafting through the air - the promise of a sumptuous meal. The sprightly fox rubs his paws together in glee, thinking about the delicious treasures he's about to dig into. Still in her spot, the lazy dog remains unperturbed. With her long snout, droopy jowls, and long black fur fluttering in the breeze, she is in a dreamland far away - where the mountains are made of beefy treats, the valleys are filled with tennis balls, and the puddles are just the right temperature. Why be in the rat race? It's a dog's life, after all.

ROT DO
UTR TI
EIND HA
DOR EM
GRO MA
ZU

TT Livret

TypeType

LEEUWA
DANTUM
HERTOG
SLOCHT
APPINGE
LOPPERS
HARKST
PIETERB
SCHORT

TYPEFACE : LOUIZE DISPLAY
DESIGNER : 205TF
LOCATION : LYON, FRANCE

PUBLISHED BY : 205TF
CHRONOLOGY : 2011
RELEASED IN : 2011

LINK : HTTPS://WWW.205.TF/LOUIZE
STYLES : ROMAN: REGULAR, MEDIUM, BOLD
ITALIC: REGULAR, MEDIUM, BOLD
CREDITS : MATTHIEU CORTAT (DESIGN)

IN 1846, A LYONNAIS PRINTER, LOUIS PERRIN, COMMISSIONED FOUNDER FRANCISQUE REY TO ENGRAVE A SERIES OF CAPITALS INSPIRED BY MONUMENTAL ROMAN INSCRIPTIONS. HIS “AUGUSTAUX”, ONE OF THE FIRST “REVIVALS” IN THE HISTORY OF TYPOGRAPHY, BECAME RAPIDLY SUCCESSFUL, LAUNCHING THE “RENOUVEAU ELZÉVIRIEN” (OLD-STYLE RENEWAL) MOVEMENT. WITH LOUIZE, MATTHIEU CORTAT PROVIDES A CONTEMPORARY REINTERPRETATION OF THE AUGUSTAUX. IT RETAINS A WISE AND SERENE TONE, THE GREY OF CLEAR TEXT, AND THE SOFT ROUNDNESS OF THE CURVES. LOUIZE DISPLAY IS DISCREET, CALM, AND HARMONIOUS. FOR USE IN TITLES, IT IS AVAILABLE IN A DISPLAY VERSION – A SHARP AND CLEAR VARIANT INSPIRED BY LETTERS ENGRAVED IN STONE.

CAP HEIGHT

REGULAR – 290PT

X-HEIGHT

BASELINE

Ll

Louize Display

THE QUICK BROV

IT WOULD BE TH

IT'S A LOVELY DAY

AND THE PUNGE

PROMISE OF A SU

THINKING ABOU

THE LAZY DOG R

LONG BLACK FUI

THE MOUNTAINS

Elegance
is good taste
& a dash
of daring...

FASHION WEEK FEVER

TYPEFACE : LUCIFER
DESIGNER : NGUYEN GOBBER
LOCATION : VIENNA, AUSTRIA

224

PUBLISHED BY : NGUYEN GOBBER
CHRONOLOGY : 2017 - 2022
RELEASED IN : 2022

LINK : HTTPS://NGUYENGOBBER.COM/TYPEFACES/LUCIFER
STYLES : REGULAR, REGULAR ITALIC, MEDIUM, MEDIUM ITALIC, SEMIBOLD, SEMIBOLD ITALIC, BOLD, BOLD ITALIC + A VARIABLE FONT
CREDITS : PRO HELVETIA & SWISS ART COUNCIL (SUPPORT & FUNDING), SCHRIFTLABOR (DIGITAL PUNCHCUTTING)

LUCIFER FEATURES CONTEMPORARY AESTHETICS WHILE BEING DEEPLY ROOTED IN A LESSER-KNOWN PART OF SWISS DESIGN HISTORY. ITS SHARP, EXPRESSIVE SERIFS AND OVERALL ORGANIC LOOK ARE INSPIRED BY THE HAND-LETTERING OF SWISS DESIGNER ROBERT STÖCKLIN IN HIS POSTER FOR THE SCHWEIZER MUSTERMESSE BASEL IN 1924. THE TYPEFACE'S EXPRESSIVE AESTHETIC EXCELS IN WORDMARKS, HEADLINES, AND POSTER DESIGNS. AT THE SAME TIME, IT IS SUITABLE FOR VARIOUS KINDS OF RUNNING TEXT, WHICH MAKES IT A UNIQUE WORKHORSE TYPE FAMILY. LUCIFER COMES IN EIGHT STYLES OR AS A VARIABLE FONT AND SUPPORTS A WIDE RANGE OF LATIN-BASED SCRIPTS, INCLUDING VIETNAMESE AND PINYIN (MANDARIN CHINESE).

CAP HEIGHT

REGULAR – 290PT

X-HEIGHT

Ll

BASELINE

Lucifer

REGULAR – 36PT

THE QUICK BROWN FOX
IT WOULD BE THE CHEEK
IT'S A LOVELY DAY IN TH
AND THE PUNGENT ARO
PROMISE OF A SUMPTUO
THINKING ABOUT THE D

REGULAR – 14PT

The quick brown fox jumps over a lazy dog. He didn't h
it would be the cheeky thing to do. After all, he had a re
It's a lovely day in the neighbourhood, with the sun shi
and the pungent aroma of fresh rubbish bins wafting t
promise of a sumptuous meal. The sprightly fox rubs h
thinking about the delicious treasures he's about to dig
the lazy dog remains unperturbed. With her long snou
long black fur fluttering in the breeze, she is in a drean
the mountains are made of beefy treats, the valleys are
balls, and the puddles are just the right temperature. W
It's a dog's life, after all.

REGULAR – 8PT

The quick brown fox jumps over a lazy dog. He didn't have to, but he thought it would be the cheeky thing to do. After all, he had a reputation to maintain. It's a lovely day in the neighbourhood, with the sun shining, the birds chirping, and the pungent aroma of fresh rubbish bins wafting through the air – the promise of a sumptuous meal. The sprightly fox rubs his paws together in glee, thinking about the delicious treasures he's about to dig into. Still in her spot, the lazy dog remains unperturbed. With her long snout, droopy jowls, and long black fur fluttering in the breeze, she is in a dreamland far away – where the mountains are made of beefy treats, the valleys are filled with tennis balls, and the puddles are just the right temperature. Why be in the rat race? It's a dog's life, after all.

PLA

im W

FOR

89,5×1

KATE
ELT´
MAT
28 cm

SCHWEIZER
MUSTER-
MESSE
BASEL
Besuchen Sie
die *Mutter* aller
Messen!
17.–27. Mai 1924
**FIERA
CAMPIONARIA
SVIZZERA
BASILEA
Visita la
madre di tutte
le fiere!
17–27 maggio 1924**

FOIRE
SUISSE
D'ECHANTILLONS
BALE
Visitez la
mère de toutes
les foires!
17–27 mai 1924
SWISS
INDUSTRIES
FAIR
BASLE
Visit the
***mother* of all**
faires!
17–27 May 1924

230

TYPEFACE	:	FAIRE LUMA
DESIGNER	:	FAIRE TYPE
LOCATION	:	NEW YORK, US

PUBLISHED BY	:	FAIRE TYPE
CHRONOLOGY	:	2023
RELEASED IN	:	2023

LINK	:	HTTPS://WWW.FAIRETYPE.COM/FONTS/LUMA
STYLES	:	REGULAR, MEDIUM, BOLD, BLACK, REVERSE REGULAR, REVERSE MEDIUM, REVERSE BOLD, REVERSE BLACK

LUMA IS A CONTEMPORARY TYPEFACE WITH ORGANIC ROUND SERIFS AND UNEXPECTED DETAILS. AN EXERCISE IN JUXTAPOSITION, IT WAS BORN FROM THE IDEA OF TRANSFORMING THE SHARP AND MECHANIC SHAPES OF A MONOSPACED TYPEFACE INTO SOMETHING MORE ORGANIC. EVENTUALLY THE ONCE-MONOSPACED TYPEFACE MORPHED INTO THE PROPORTIONAL TYPEFACE YOU SEE HERE, WITH THE ORGANIC SERIFS REMAINING. THE LUMA TYPE FAMILY FEATURES A WEIGHT AXIS AND CUSTOM CONTRAST AXIS THAT CONTROLS THE SIZE OF THE SERIFS AND THE WEIGHT OF THE STEMS. ON THE OTHER END OF THAT CONTRAST AXIS IS LUMA REVERSE, A REVERSE CONTRAST DISPLAY TYPEFACE.

CAP HEIGHT

REGULAR – 290PT

Ll

X-HEIGHT

BASELINE

FAIRE Luma

REGULAR – 48PT

THE QUICK B
IT WOULD BE
IT'S A LOVELY
AND THE PUN
PROMISE OF A
THINKING A
THE LAZY DO

REGULAR – 14PT

The quick brown fox jumps over a lazy dog. He didn't have to, but he thought it would be the cheeky thing to do. After all, he had a reputation to maintain. It's a lovely day in the neighbourhood, with the sun shining, the birds chirping, and the pungent aroma of fresh rubbish bins wafting through the air - the promise of a sumptuous meal. The sprightly fox rubs his paws together in glee, thinking about the delicious treasures he's about to dig into. Still in her spot, the lazy dog remains unperturbed. With her long snout, droopy jowls, and long black fur fluttering in the breeze, she is in a dreamland far away - where the mountains are made of beefy treats, the valleys are filled with tennis balls, and the puddles are just the right temperature. Why be in the rat race? It's a dog's life, after all.

Paradise drongo
Réunion harrier
Drab myzomela
Lesser kiskadee
Dusky sunbird
Marabou stork
Magpie shrike
Arctic redpoll

@&?!

506

Surfbird
Redwing
Mallard
Ibisbill

234

TYPEFACE : MAGNO SERIF
DESIGNER : LUCAS SPOSITO GINI
LOCATION : SÃO PAULO, BRAZIL

PUBLISHED BY : BLACKLETRA TYPE FOUNDRY
CHRONOLOGY : N/A
RELEASED IN : 2022

LINK : HTTPS://BLACKLETRA.COM/TYPEFACES/MAGNO-SERIF
STYLES : THIN, THIN ITALIC, EXTRALIGHT, EXTRALIGHT ITALIC, LIGHT, LIGHT ITALIC, REGULAR, ITALIC, MEDIUM, MEDIUM ITALIC, BOLD, BOLD ITALIC, EXTRABOLD, EXTRABOLD ITALIC, BLACK, BLACK ITALIC

MAGNO BEGAN ITS LIFE WITH A MYSTERIOUS METAL TYPEFACE AS A REFERENCE: A "MEMPHIS" FOUND IN BRAZIL THAT WAS NEVER A REAL MEMPHIS. ALONG THE WAY, THOUGH, THIS CONDENSED FAMILY BECAME A WHOLE NEW THING, FAR FROM A REVIVAL. IT ENDED UP WITH 8 WEIGHTS FOR EVERY VERSION (SERIF AND SANS), PLUS OBLIQUES, A LARGE LATIN CHARACTER SET COVERING OVER 200 LANGUAGES, AND A CONSIDERABLE AMOUNT OF OPENTYPE FEATURES INCLUDING SETS OF NUMBERS, FRACTIONS, SMALL CAPS, SUPERIORS, INFERIORS, ARROWS, QUITE A FEW ALTERNATES, AND EVEN A UNICASE STYLISTIC SET. ITS SPECIAL CARE FOR THE VISUAL MASS AND CONSISTENCY THROUGH THE WIDE RANGE OF WEIGHTS MAKE IT A GOOD DISPLAY OPTION FOR IMPACTFUL MESSAGES.

CAP HEIGHT

REGULAR - 290PT

X-HEIGHT

Mm

BASELINE

Magno Serif

THE QUICK BROWN FOX JUMPS OVE

IT WOULD BE THE CHEEKY THING T

IT'S A LOVELY DAY IN THE NEIGHBO

AND THE PUNGENT AROMA OF FRES

PROMISE OF A SUMPTUOUS MEAL. T

THINKING ABOUT THE DELICIOUS T

THE LAZY DOG REMAINS UNPERTU

LONG BLACK FUR FLUTTERING IN T

THE MOUNTAINS ARE MADE OF BEE

Solidarität
Advertising
Expectativas
Descalificada
Endorsement
Cartographies
Deportaciones
Bekanntenkreis

Understatement
Photographing
Handballeurs
Desenmarañé
Cambalachos
Metropolitan
Dismantling
Suculentas

TYPEFACE : MARBLE ARCH
DESIGNER : DALTON MAAG
LOCATION : LONDON, UK

PUBLISHED BY : DALTON MAAG
CHRONOLOGY : 2023
RELEASED IN : 2023

LINK : HTTPS://WWW.DALTONMAAG.COM/PORTFOLIO/FONT-LIBRARY/MARBLE-ARCH.HTML
STYLES : MULTI-AXIS VARIABLE FONTS + STATIC FONTS IN WEIGHTS & STYLES RANGING FROM CAPTION HAIR TO POSTER BLACK

MARBLE ARCH IS A SERIF TYPEFACE WHICH EMBODIES THE GRANDEUR AND TIMELESS ELEGANCE OF ITS ICONIC LONDON LANDMARK NAMESAKE. BOASTING WEIGHT, ITALIC, AND OPTICAL SIZE AXES IN ITS VARIABLE FONT, IT ADAPTS TO ANY PROJECT FOR CAPTIONS, TEXT, HEADLINES, OR DISPLAY – REGARDLESS OF SCALE.

CAP-HEIGHT

REGULAR – 220PT

Mm

X-HEIGHT

BASELINE

Marble Arch

REGULAR – 36PT

THE QUICK BROWN FO
IT WOULD BE THE CH
IT'S A LOVELY DAY IN
AND THE PUNGENT A
PROMISE OF A SUMPT
THINKING ABOUT TH
THE LAZY DOG REMA

REGULAR – 18PT

The quick brown fox jumps over a lazy dog. He d
it would be the cheeky thing to do. After all, he h
It's a lovely day in the neighbourhood, with the s
and the pungent aroma of fresh rubbish bins wa
promise of a sumptuous meal. The sprightly fox
thinking about the delicious treasures he's abou
the lazy dog remains unperturbed. With her lon
long black fur fluttering in the breeze, she is in a
the mountains are made of beefy treats, the vall

REGULAR – 8PT

The quick brown fox jumps over a lazy dog. He didn't have to, but he thought it would be the cheeky thing to do. After all, he had a reputation to maintain. It's a lovely day in the neighbourhood, with the sun shining, the birds chirping, and the pungent aroma of fresh rubbish bins wafting through the air - the promise of a sumptuous meal. The sprightly fox rubs his paws together in glee, thinking about the delicious treasures he's about to dig into. Still in her spot, the lazy dog remains unperturbed. With her long snout, droopy jowls, and long black fur fluttering in the breeze, she is in a dreamland far away - where the mountains are made of beefy treats, the valleys are filled with tennis balls, and the puddles are just the right temperature. Why be in the rat race? It's a dog's life, after all.

ndance ***Affluence***

gant ***Extravagant***

dor **Marble Arch** *H*

sh Luxurious **Pros**

leasure Delux Sup

Optical Sizes

a	a	a	a	a
Caption	Text	SubHead	Headline	Poster

Marble Arch — Aa *Aa* — Static Weights

Aa *Aa* Aa *Aa*

Aa *Aa* Aa *Aa*

Aa ***Aa*** **Aa** ***Aa***

Aa ***Aa*** **Aa** ***Aa***

27

Poster Black

New

Headline XBold

AW Season

SubHead Bold

It's that time of year again: summer is a distant memory and we're deep in to our winter wardrobes.

Text Regular

Spring/Summer 2023 fashion trends: Ideas for your wardrobe in the season ahead

Caption Regular

The epitome of typographic luxury and grandeur

The pinnacle of adaptability

bring superior readability, legibility, and refinement to any message

Extravagantly luxurious

A rich, indulgent, and captivating serif typeface with high contrast and striking features

Fine-tuned and optimized for the smallest to largest sizes

Express an effortless sophistication

Italics

Elegantly

Hairline Thin Light Regular Medium SemiBold Bold XBold Black

TYPEFACE : ABC MARIST
DESIGNER : DINAMO
LOCATION : BERLIN, GERMANY

PUBLISHED BY : DINAMO
CHRONOLOGY : N/A
RELEASED IN : 2022

LINK : HTTPS://ABCDINAMO.COM/TYPEFACES/MARIST
STYLES : 12 STYLES
CREDITS : SEB MCLAUCHLAN (DESIGN), IGINO MARINI (SPACING & KERNING), ROBERT JANES/DINAMO (PRODUCTION)

MARIST IS A WARM, READER-FRIENDLY FONT WITH PROMINENT SERIFS AND WIDE UPPERCASE PROPORTIONS THAT TAKE THEIR TIME. ITS FORMS ARE INSPIRED BY AFTERNOONS SPENT IN ARCHIVES INVESTIGATING THE LONG HISTORY OF THE OVERLOOKED OLD STYLE, AND MORE SPECIFICALLY, TWO PROMINENT FONTS WITHIN THAT GENRE: JENSON'S ROMAN AND GOLDEN. WHEN FRENCH ENGRAVER NICOLAS JENSON FIRST DEVELOPED HIS ROMAN IN 15TH CENTURY VENICE, THE HIGHLY LEGIBLE TYPEFACE BECAME FAMOUS FOR OUTPERFORMING EVERYTHING ELSE. IN 19TH CENTURY LONDON, WILLIAM MORRIS THEN REINTERPRETED JENSON'S ROMAN FOR HIS GOLDEN TYPE, A CELEBRATION OF CRAFT AESTHETICS FROM THE PAST THAT QUESTIONED SOCIETY'S RELIANCE ON TECHNOLOGY. MARIST PICKS UP SOME OF MORRIS AND JENSON'S THREADS - FINE-TUNING THEIR FORMS FOR CONTEMPORARY EYES AND DIGITAL LIBRARIES.

REGULAR - 260PT

X-HEIGHT

Mm

BASELINE

ABC Marist

THE QUICK BRO
IT WOULD BE T
IT'S A LOVELY D
AND THE PUNG
PROMISE OF A S
THINKING ABO
THE LAZY DOG
LONG BLACK FU
THE MOUNTAI

M A C

R H P

K O T

W Y Z

X N S

M

MARIST

246

TYPEFACE	:	MESSER
DESIGNER	:	INGA PLÖNNIGS
LOCATION	:	BERLIN, GERMANY

PUBLISHED BY	:	FUTURE FONTS
CHRONOLOGY	:	2018
RELEASED IN	:	2018

LINK	:	HTTPS://WWW.FUTUREFONTS.XYZ/INGA-PLONNIGS/MESSER
STYLES	:	LIGHT, LIGHT ITALIC, REGULAR, REGULAR ITALIC, BOLD, BOLD ITALIC, CONDENSED, CONDENSED ITALIC

MESSER STARTED OUT AS A REVIVAL OF WEISS ANTIQUA WHICH WAS ORIGINALLY DESIGNED BY EMIL RUDOLF WEISS IN 1928. ALONG WITH WEISS ANTIQUA'S SIGNATURE CHARACTERS, THE UPSIDE-DOWN "S" AND "S", MESSER ALSO FEATURES SIMILAR DESIGN CHARACTERISTICS IN "Z", "SS", "6" AND "9". COMPARED TO THE ORIGINAL, ITS OVERALL SHAPES HAVE SHARPER EDGES AND THE ITALIC HAS LESS CURLY STROKE ENDINGS. THERE IS ALSO A CONDENSED DISPLAY STYLE THAT FEATURES AN INCREASED CONTRAST TO ENHANCE TYPOGRAPHIC POSSIBILITIES.

Messer

REGULAR – 36PT

THE QUICK BROWN FO
IT WOULD BE THE CHE
IT'S A LOVELY DAY IN T
AND THE PUNGENT AR
PROMISE OF A SUMPTU
THINKING ABOUT THE
THE LAZY DOG REMAIN
LONG BLACK FUR FLUT
THE MOUNTAINS ARE M
AND THE PUDDLES ARE
IT'S A DOG'S LIFE, AFTE

REGULAR – 10PT

The quick brown fox jumps over a lazy dog. He didn't have to, but he thought it would be the cheeky thing to do. After all, he had a reputation to maintain. It's a lovely day in the neighbourhood, with the sun shining, the birds chirping, and the pungent aroma of fresh rubbish bins wafting through the air - the promise of a sumptuous meal. The sprightly fox rubs his paws together in glee, thinking about the delicious treasures he's about to dig into. Still in her spot, the lazy dog remains unperturbed. With her long snout, droopy jowls, and long black fur fluttering in the breeze, she is in a dreamland far away - where the mountains are made of beefy treats, the valleys are filled with tennis balls, and the puddles are just the right temperature. Why be in the rat race? It's a dog's life, after all.

Und der Haifisch, der hat Zähne
Und die trägt er im Gesicht
Und Macheath, der hat ein Messer
Doch das Messer sieht man nicht.

Und es sind des Haifischs Flossen
Rot, wenn dieser Blut vergießt
Mackie Messer trägt 'nen Handschuh
Drauf man keine Untat liest.

An der Themse grünem Wasser
Fallen plötzlich Leute um
Es ist weder Pest noch Cholera
Doch es heißt: Mackie geht um.

An'nem schönen blauen Sonntag
Liegt ein toter Mann am Strand
Und ein Mensch geht um die Ecke
Den man Mackie Messer nennt.

"Fancy gloves, though, wears old Macheath, babe. So there's never a trace of red."

TYPEFACE : COFO METEOR
DESIGNER : CONTRAST FOUNDRY
LOCATION : CALIFORNIA, US

PUBLISHED BY : FUTURE FONTS
CHRONOLOGY : 2021 - 2022
RELEASED IN : 2022

LINK : HTTPS://WWW.FUTUREFONTS.XYZ/CONTRAST-FOUNDRY/COFO-METEOR
STYLES : SEMIBOLD

COFO METEOR IS ELEGANT AND A LITTLE ARROGANT DUE TO ITS EXTRAVAGANT ART DECO FEATURES. ORIGINALLY DESIGNED FOR MOVIE TITLES, IT IS LOOSELY INSPIRED BY A BUNCH OF TYPEFACES: DEVINNE ROMAN, ROMANISCH, LITERATURNAYA, AND EVEN TIMES MODERN. HOWEVER, IT IS NARROW IN PROPORTIONS AND HAS A SLIGHTLY LOWER CONTRAST THAN ITS PREDECESSORS, ALLOWING IT TO WORK ESPECIALLY WELL ON DARK AND COLOURFUL BACKGROUNDS. IF YOU LOOK CLOSER AT THE DETAILS, TERMINALS, AND SERIFS, YOU WILL NOTICE THAT THEY ARE SHARP BUT NOT POINTY — A DETAIL THAT MAKES IT APPEAR WARMER AND FRIENDLIER.

CAP HEIGHT

SEMIBOLD - 290PT

X-HEIGHT

Mm

BASELINE

COFO Meteor

SEMIBOLD - 40PT

THE QUICK BROWN FOX JUMPS OV
IT WOULD BE THE CHEEKY THING T
IT'S A LOVELY DAY IN THE NEIGHBO
AND THE PUNGENT AROMA OF FRE
PROMISE OF A SUMPTUOUS MEAL
THINKING ABOUT THE DELICIOUS T
THE LAZY DOG REMAINS UNPERTU
LONG BLACK FUR FLUTTERING IN T
THE MOUNTAINS ARE MADE OF BE
AND THE PUDDLES ARE JUST THE R

SEMIBOLD - 10PT

The quick brown fox jumps over a lazy dog. He didn't have to, but he thought it would be the cheeky thing to do. After all, he had a reputation to maintain. It's a lovely day in the neighbourhood, with the sun shining, the birds chirping, and the pungent aroma of fresh rubbish bins wafting through the air - the promise of a sumptuous meal. The sprightly fox rubs his paws together in glee, thinking about the delicious treasures he's about to dig into. Still in her spot, the lazy dog remains unperturbed. With her long snout, droopy jowls, and long black fur fluttering in the breeze, she is in a dreamland far away - where the mountains are made of beefy treats, the valleys are filled with tennis balls, and the puddles are just the right temperature. Why be in the rat race? It's a dog's life, after all.

p*#g
a 823

THE VELVET
DARKNESS O
THE CINEMA
HALL?

TYPEFACE : MINOTAUR
DESIGNER : PRODUCTION TYPE
LOCATION : PARIS, FRANCE; SHANGHAI, CHINA

PUBLISHED BY : PRODUCTION TYPE
CHRONOLOGY : 2014 - 2017
RELEASED IN : 2017

LINK : HTTPS://WWW.PRODUCTIONTYPE.COM/COLLECTION/MINOTAUR_COLLECTION
STYLES : 5 FAMILIES; 19 STYLES; 3 WEIGHTS + ROMAN & ITALIC
CREDITS : JEAN-BAPTISTE LEVÉE (DESIGN)

HOW DOES ONE REFERENCE CUBISM IN A TYPEFACE? THE MOST OBVIOUS TACK WOULD BE TO DISASSEMBLE EACH LETTER AND RENDER IT BROKEN AND ABSTRACTED. THIS MIGHT PRODUCE SOMETHING INTERESTING TO LOOK AT, BUT NOT SOMETHING THAT CAN BE USED. MINOTAUR IS MORE PRACTICAL, BUT NO LESS INTERESTING. INITIALLY CREATED FOR A PARIS ART MUSEUM, MINOTAUR SANS AND SERIF IS A FAMILY OF STRAIGHT LINES INSPIRED BY THE CUBIST MOVEMENT. ITS ROOTS ARE VENUS, A LANDMARK GROTESQUE FROM THE ERA THAT GAVE RISE TO CUBISM, AND TWO SERIF MODELS: BRUCE'S SCOTCH ROMAN AND A. V. HERSHEY'S SERIES FOR EARLY VECTOR-BASED COMPUTING. NOT ONLY ARE THE LETTERS' OUTLINES ATYPICAL, BUT THEIR SET NUMBER OF WIDTHS – DERIVED FROM HISTORICAL TECHNICAL LIMITATIONS – PLAY WITH EXPECTATIONS AS WELL.

Minotaur

REGULAR – 36PT

THE QUICK BROWN FOX J
IT WOULD BE THE CHEEK
IT'S A LOVELY DAY IN THE
AND THE PUNGENT AROM
PROMISE OF A SUMPTUO
THINKING ABOUT THE DE
THE LAZY DOG REMAINS

REGULAR – 18PT

The quick brown fox jumps over a lazy dog. He
it would be the cheeky thing to do. After all, he
It's a lovely day in the neighbourhood, with th
and the pungent aroma of fresh rubbish bins
promise of a sumptuous meal. The sprightly f
thinking about the delicious treasures he's ab
the lazy dog remains unperturbed. With her lo
long black fur fluttering in the breeze, she is i

REGULAR – 8PT

The quick brown fox jumps over a lazy dog. He didn't have to, but he thought it would be the cheeky thing to do. After all, he had a reputation to maintain. It's a lovely day in the neighbourhood, with the sun shining, the birds chirping, and the pungent aroma of fresh rubbish bins wafting through the air - the promise of a sumptuous meal. The sprightly fox rubs his paws together in glee, thinking about the delicious treasures he's about to dig into. Still in her spot, the lazy dog remains unperturbed. With her long snout, droopy jowls, and long black fur fluttering in the breeze, she is in a dreamland far away - where the mountains are made of beefy treats, the valleys are filled with tennis balls, and the puddles are just the right temperature. Why be in the rat race? It's a dog's life, after all.

Mythography

Inkanyamba

Reich

Dexamenus

Changeling

Asteropaios

Tlahuelpuchi

Aigikampoi

Lugalbanda

Carbuncle
Bar Juchne
Persisor Perso
Brownie Poseidon
Misi-kinepikw Bodach
Nanom-keea-po-da Labbu
Kabouter Wassan-mon-ganeehla-ak

POLYNICES CULTURE HERO CYLARABES PRESTER JOHN GREEK STAR MYTHS ETHAL CREATION MYTH KING GOLDEMAR MONSTERS OF GREEK MYTHOLOGY EARTH MOTHER METAMORPHOSES Greco-Roman Mosaics Ilus Lugalbanda Geomythology Lycus, son of Poseidon Car Greco-Roman Sculpture Laertes Mythography Legendary Creature Greek God & Goddesses Amyntor

TYPEFACE : MOLEN
DESIGNER : NURRON TYPE
LOCATION : UK

PUBLISHED BY : TYPE DEPARTMENT
CHRONOLOGY : N/A
RELEASED IN : N/A

LINK : HTTPS://TYPE-DEPARTMENT.COM/COLLECTIONS/SANS-SERIF-FONTS/PRODUCTS/MOLEN/
STYLES : 1

MOLEN IS A CHARISMATIC TYPEFACE EQUIPPED WITH AN INTERESTING USE OF CONTRAST THROUGHOUT. IT IS WELL SUITED FOR MAKING A BRAND OR PROJECT STAND OUT THROUGH BOLD TITLES FOR PRODUCT NAMES, MUSIC ARTISTS OR LOGOS.

CAP HEIGHT

REGULAR - 290PT

X-HEIGHT

Mm

BASELINE

Molen

THE QUICK BROWN FO

IT WOULD BE THE CH

IT'S A LOVELY DAY IN

AND THE PUNGENT A

PROMISE OF A SUMPT

THINKING ABOUT THE

THE LAZY DOG REMA

LONG BLACK FUR FLU

THE MOUNTAINS ARE

MOLENO©

«NEXT!»

SULTAN

@KINTO’
€375.89
BOOMING

TYPEFACE : MORION
DESIGNER : THE DESIGNERS FOUNDRY
LOCATION : NEW ZEALAND

PUBLISHED BY : THE DESIGNERS FOUNDRY
CHRONOLOGY : N/A
RELEASED IN : 2017

LINK : HTTPS://THEDESIGNERSFOUNDRY.COM/MORION
STYLES : 12
CREDITS : DAVID EINWALLER (DESIGN)

FIRST RELEASED IN 2017 AS REGULAR AND BOLD THEN RERELEASED 6 YEARS AFTER THE INITIAL SKETCHES TOOK PLACE IN 2020, THE 2.0 VERSION OF MORION NOW HAS 6 WEIGHTS AND MATCHING ITALICS IN THE FAMILY, BUT WITH THE ENTIRE GLYPHSET REVISED, EXTENDED AND RECONSIDERED. THE RERELEASE AIMED TO HAVE MORION PERFORM BETTER IN PRINT AND SMALLER SIZES, YET STILL CARRY THE DISTINCT AESTHETICS OF THE ORIGINAL TWO WEIGHTS. MORION IS A BALANCING ACT BETWEEN TEXT AND DISPLAY TYPE. IT IS CAPABLE AS RUNNING TEXT AT SMALL SIZES YET IS EQUALLY AS STRONG IN LARGE SCALE DISPLAY SETTINGS. SHARP DETAILS AND DYNAMIC CONDENSED ITALICS GIVE IT A CONTEMPORARY, DIGITAL TONE THAT IS EMBEDDED IN A CLASSIC TRANSITIONAL SERIF TYPEFACE.

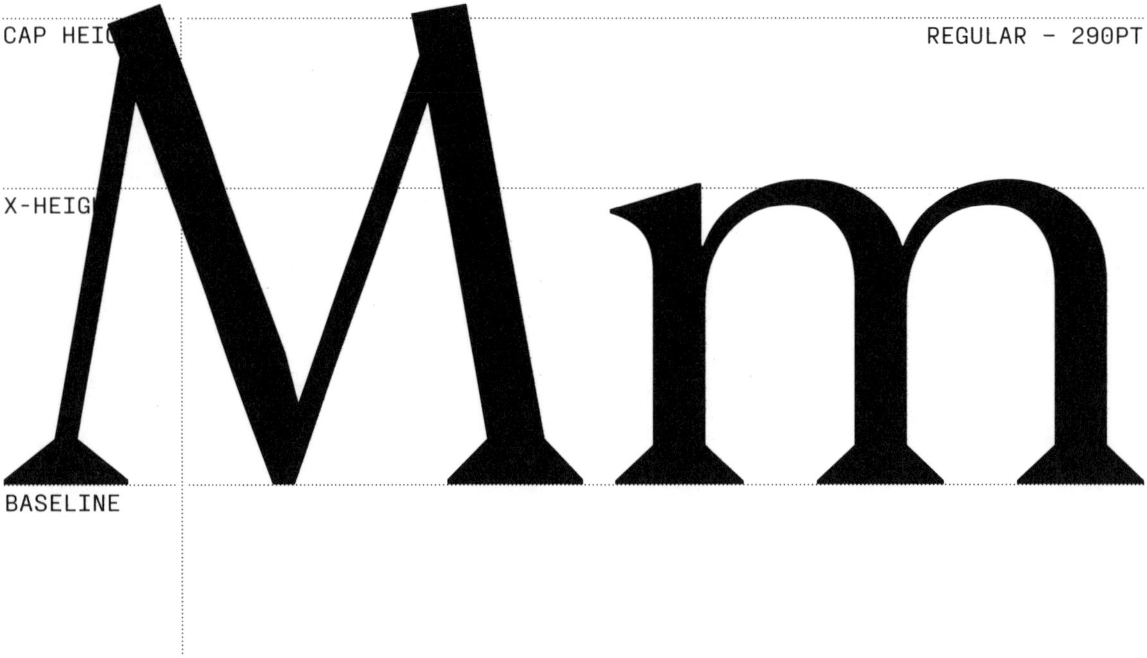

Morion

REGULAR – 48PT

THE QUICK BROWN FOX
IT WOULD BE THE CHEE
IT'S A LOVELY DAY IN TH
AND THE PUNGENT ARC
PROMISE OF A SUMPTUC
THINKING ABOUT THE I
THE LAZY DOG REMAIN
LONG BLACK FUR FLUTT
THE MOUNTAINS ARE M
AND THE PUDDLES ARE

REGULAR – 14PT

The quick brown fox jumps over a lazy dog. He didn't have to, but he thc
it would be the cheeky thing to do. After all, he had a reputation to main
It's a lovely day in the neighbourhood, with the sun shining, the birds chi
and the pungent aroma of fresh rubbish bins wafting through the air - tl
promise of a sumptuous meal. The sprightly fox rubs his paws together i
thinking about the delicious treasures he's about to dig into. Still in her s
the lazy dog remains unperturbed. With her long snout, droopy jowls, a
long black fur fluttering in the breeze, she is in a dreamland far away - w
the mountains are made of beefy treats, the valleys are filled with tennis
and the puddles are just the right temperature. Why be in the rat race?
It's a dog's life, after all.

[Th] Thin Weight

[ThIt] *Thin Italic*

[Ul] Ultralight (2/5)

[UlIt] *Ultralight Italic*

[Lg] Light & Upright

[LgIt] *Light Italic*

[Rg] Regular Color

[RgIt] *Regular Italic*

[Sb] **Semibold**

[Sb] ***Semibold Italic***

[Bd] **Bold (Fett)**

[BdIt] ***Bold Italic***

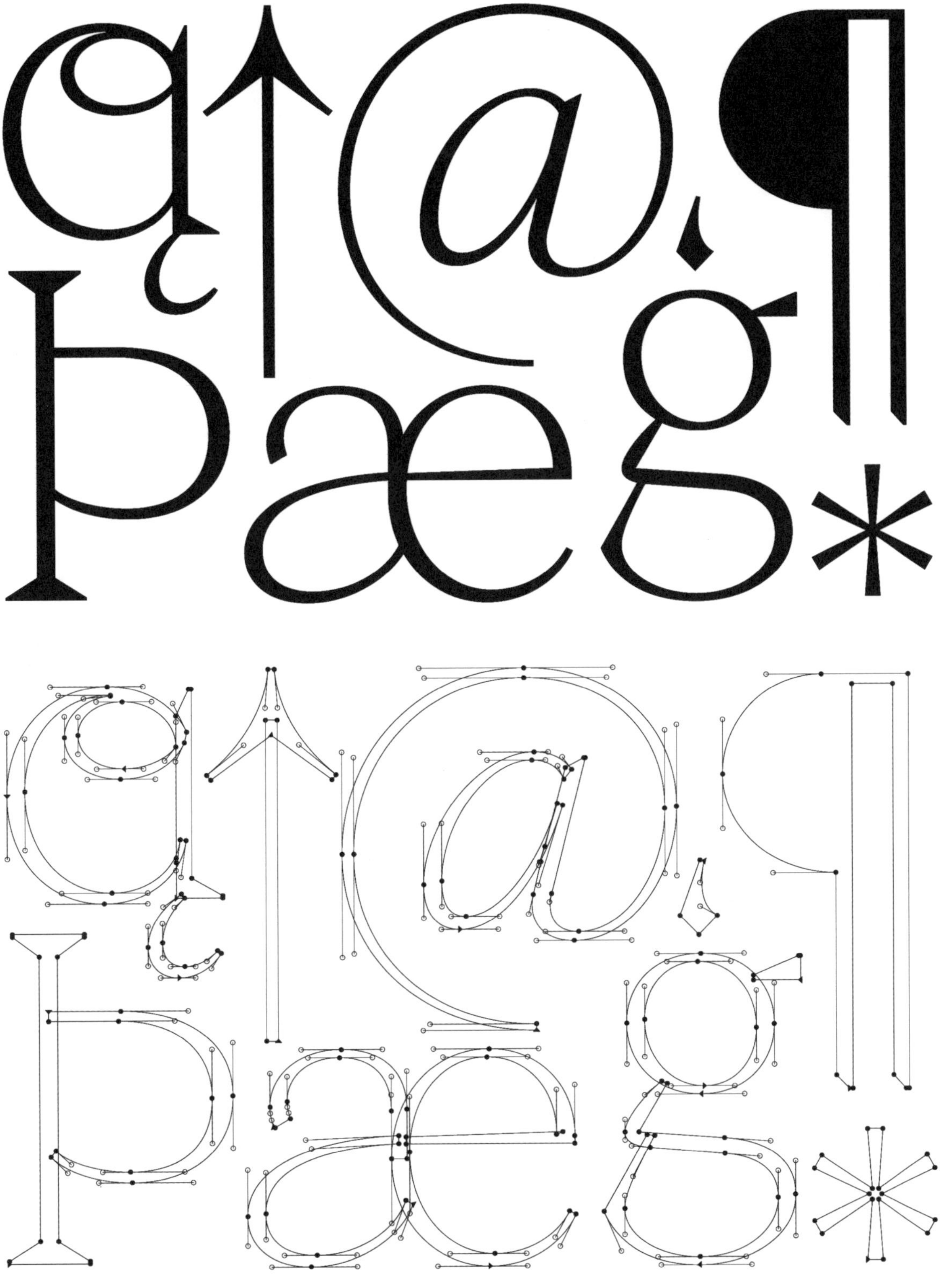

[BdIt] *per* B

[Bd] 72K [

[Bd] &, [

[BdIt] *mo'* [Bc

Blossom→*White* [BdIt]

***Plataăn* GROEN** [SbIt]

Meersch@um [Rg]

!Nerz*Grau?* [LtIt]

Saųmøn [Ul]

ONYX [Th]

For—let us say—a physicist, this is much simpler, since it does not involve the "meaning of text," etc.

{TDF} In your own presentation at the Third Evolution Conference, "'Insight' May Cause Blindness," you remarked: *One of the most important events in our evolution as a designer was our discovery of a specimen by M called The Design of 'As If' (1924)….*

{ABC} According to M, we always work with "fictions," and yet can arrive at practical results, after which the fiction "drops out." One of the countless examples contained in his/her specimen is the "fiction of liberty," which the judge uses only to arrive at a sentence: "The judge concludes that every letterform is free, and, therefore, if he/she has sinned against the laws of typographic legacy, he/she must be punished… But the premise whether a shape is really free, is not examined by the judge… Without the possibility of punishing men, of punishing the designer, no government would be possible. The theoretical fiction of freedom has been invented for practical purpose."

And later: "We have repeatedly insisted above, that the boundary between truth and error is not a rigid one, and we were able ultimately to demonstrate that what we generally call truth, namely a conceptual grid coinciding with the external grid, is merely the most expedient error."

{ABC} Was there a moment or incident that led you to see "content" as constructed?

{TDF} What else led you to identify as a radical constructivist, and how is this related to your shift from an intrapsychic (monadic) to an interactional (systemic) way of conceptualizing problems?

{ABC} I was fascinated with the publications of the S group; their insistence on a circular (rather than linear) causality of specific visual behaviours, and their study of interactional behaviour patterns (rather than individual).

{ABC} No, there was not—it was the outcome of years spent researching and practicing.

{TDF} In an earlier discussion (1997) you quoted L as having precisely said that "An instinct is an explanatory principle." Is insight a parallel explanatory principle? Is there something in addition, that produces the change as it comes into awareness? Is insight an typical epiphenomenon that follows change?

{ABC} I would consider "insight" an explanatory principle in L's sense, except that it is believed to have a magical effect-if applied in design. In our view, the most frequent factor that brings about change in visual lives is what L called a corrective emotional experience, i.e., a chance event that suddenly opens our eyes for a different way out of a specific problem.

{TDF} In your response to P's discussion of your presentation at the Third Evolution Conference, you commented (1997): *Let us briefly mention something that we found very useful in our approach to abandon*

TYPEFACE : NEUMOND
DESIGNER : DALTON MAAG
LOCATION : LONDON, UK

PUBLISHED BY : DALTON MAAG
CHRONOLOGY : 2023
RELEASED IN : 2023

LINK : HTTPS://WWW.DALTONMAAG.COM/PORTFOLIO/FONT-LIBRARY/NEUMOND.HTML
STYLES : VARIABLE FONT WITH A TRACKING AXIS + DENSE & NORMAL STATIC FONTS

NEUMOND IS A CONCEPTUAL TYPEFACE THAT PLAYS WITH THE LIMITS OF LEGIBLE TYPE DESIGN. IT REDUCES SERIF AND LINE WEIGHTS TO THE ABSOLUTE MINIMUM, DELIVERING A GEOMETRIC DISPLAY FONT WHICH IS SHARP AND PRECISE. THE RESULT IS HIGHLY IMPACTFUL AND TRULY ELEGANT.

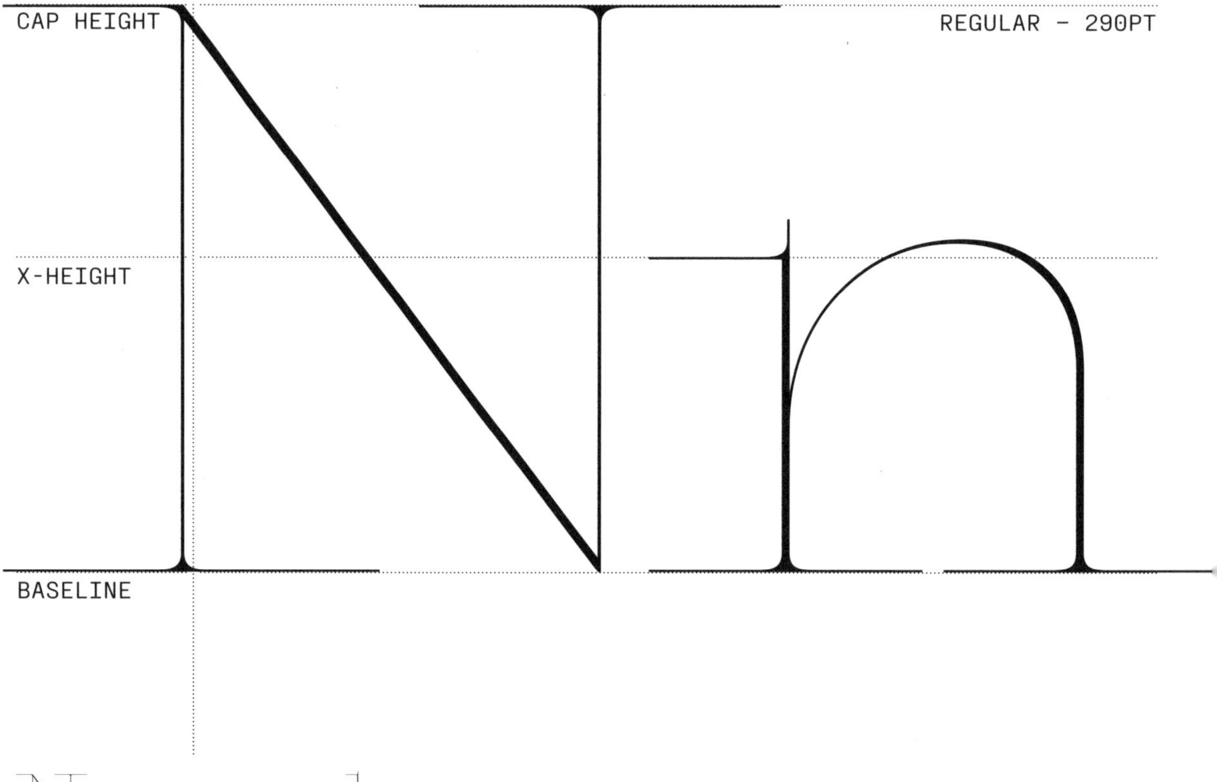

Neumond

REGULAR - 36PT

THE QUICK BROW
IT WOULD BE THE
IT'S A LOVELY DAY
AND THE PUNGEN
PROMISE OF A SU
THINKING ABOUT
THE LAZY DOG RE
LONG BLACK FUR
THE MOUNTAINS A
AND THE PUDDLE

REGULAR - 18PT

The quick brown fox jumps over a lazy dog. He di
it would be the cheeky thing to do. After all, he had
It's a lovely day in the neighbourhood, with the su
and the pungent aroma of fresh rubbish bins waft
promise of a sumptuous meal. The sprightly fox ru
thinking about the delicious treasures he's about t
the lazy dog remains unperturbed. With her long
long black fur fluttering in the breeze, she is in a d

The
moon
and
you

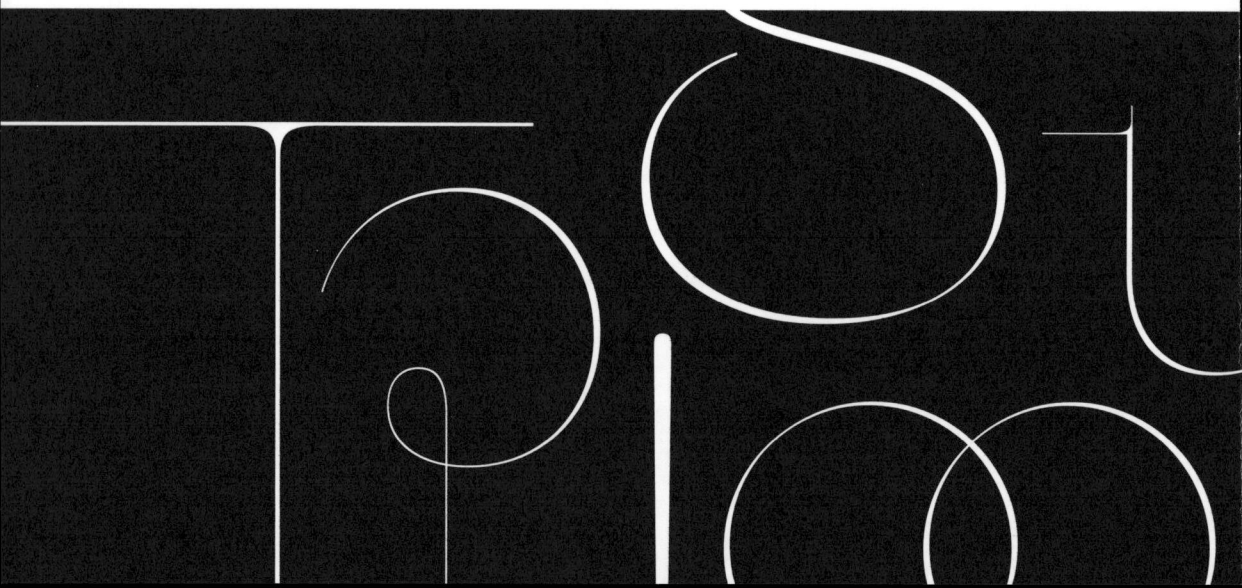

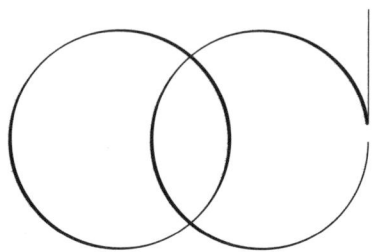

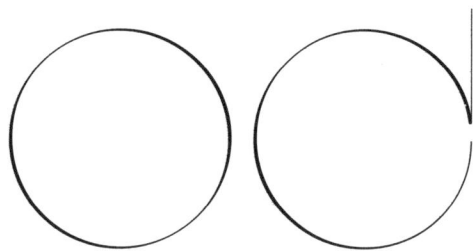

Regular
Dense

COSMOS

Kirkwood Gaps

Space Exploration

Gravitational Constant

Planetary Nebula

typology

15680

15680

§&‡

TYPEFACE	:	NOE
DESIGNER	:	SCHICK TOIKKA
LOCATION	:	BERLIN, GERMANY; HELSINKI, FINLAND

PUBLISHED BY	:	SCHICK TOIKKA
CHRONOLOGY	:	2013 – 2021
RELEASED IN	:	2013 & 2021

LINK	:	HTTPS://WWW.SCHICK-TOIKKA.COM/NOE
STYLES	:	44

WHAT MAKES NOE UNIQUE IS THE AUDACIOUS WAY ITS STROKES END. LARGE, WEDGE-SHAPED SERIFS COME TO A SHARP POINT, AND ARCHES ARE CAPPED WITH PROMINENT BEAKS. HISTORICALLY, SUCH TRIANGULAR SERIFS ARE ASSOCIATED WITH THE "LATIN" GENRE. ALSO KNOWN IN GERMAN AS "ETIENNE" OR "RENAISSANCE", THIS GENRE FIRST BLOSSOMED IN THE 1880'S. IT SHARES THE FORMAL ATTRIBUTES OF OLDER RATIONAL ROMANS, INCLUDING A VERTICAL STRESS AXIS AND A STRONG CONTRAST BETWEEN THICKS AND THINS, BUT IS DISTINGUISHED BY SAID TAPERED SERIFS. NOE ADOPTS THESE CHARACTERISTICS AND REMODELS THEM FOR THE 21ST CENTURY, AS EXEMPLIFIED BY THE LARGE LOWERCASE. THE ACUTE TRIANGULAR TERMINALS ADD A CERTAIN FIERCENESS TO THE USUAL ELEGANCE OF HIGH-CONTRAST SERIF TYPE, WITHOUT DETRACTING FROM ITS POISE AND FINESSE. SLOW, ROUND CURVES ENTER INTO A SEAMLESS DIALOGUE WITH BRISK, SPIKY TERMINALS. THE ITALIC IS ESPECIALLY FLUID, WITH A BLATANTLY CURSIVE CONSTRUCTION AND LONG, TAPERING ENTRY AND EXIT STROKES.

CAP HEIGHT

REGULAR – 290PT

Nn

X-HEIGHT

BASELINE

REGULAR – 36PT

THE QUICK BROWN FOX JU
IT WOULD BE THE CHEEKY
IT'S A LOVELY DAY IN THE N
AND THE PUNGENT AROMA
PROMISE OF A SUMPTUOUS
THINKING ABOUT THE DEL
THE LAZY DOG REMAINS U

REGULAR – 18PT

The quick brown fox jumps over a lazy dog. He didn't have t
it would be the cheeky thing to do. After all, he had a reputa
It's a lovely day in the neighbourhood, with the sun shining,
and the pungent aroma of fresh rubbish bins wafting throu
promise of a sumptuous meal. The sprightly fox rubs his pa
thinking about the delicious treasures he's about to dig into.
the lazy dog remains unperturbed. With her long snout, dro
long black fur fluttering in the breeze, she is in a dreamland

REGULAR – 8PT

The quick brown fox jumps over a lazy dog. He didn't have to, but he thought it would be the cheeky thing to do. After all, he had a reputation to maintain. It's a lovely day in the neighbourhood, with the sun shining, the birds chirping, and the pungent aroma of fresh rubbish bins wafting through the air - the promise of a sumptuous meal. The sprightly fox rubs his paws together in glee, thinking about the delicious treasures he's about to dig into. Still in her spot, the lazy dog remains unperturbed. With her long snout, droopy jowls, and long black fur fluttering in the breeze, she is in a dreamland far away - where the mountains are made of beefy treats, the valleys are filled with tennis balls, and the puddles are just the right temperature. Why be in the rat race? It's a dog's life, after all.

Noe Display · Thin

RÉAUMUR

Yu-Gi-Oh! 5D's

Noe Display · Thin

Levi-Civita

STRANGERS

Noe Display · Thin

A4&B2

Van Xuân

Roma

Itali

Roma

Itali

Roma

Itali

EON

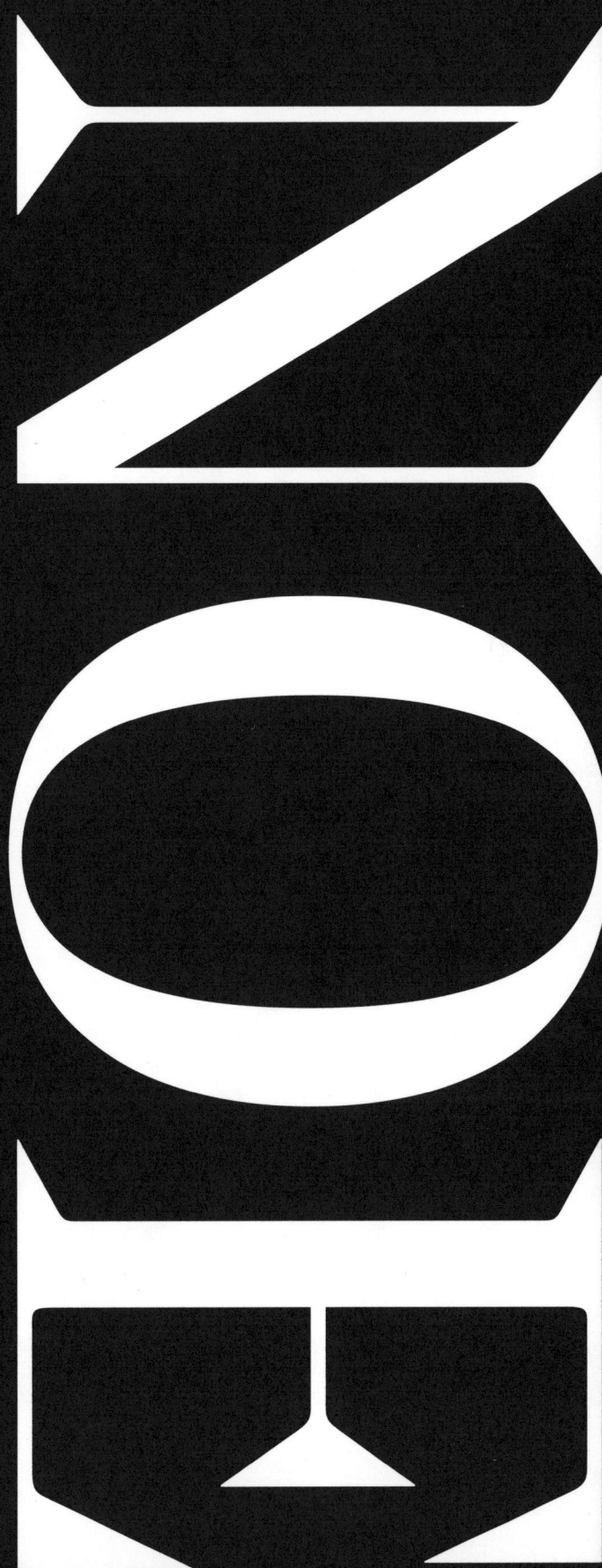

TYPEFACE : NUANCES
DESIGNER : BLAZE TYPE
LOCATION : MARSEILLE, FRANCE

PUBLISHED BY : BLAZE TYPE
CHRONOLOGY : N/A
RELEASED IN : 2022

LINK : HTTPS://BLAZETYPE.EU/TYPEFACES/NUANCES-SERIF
STYLES : SERIF, DISPLAY, CONDENSED, NORMAL, EXTENDED, UPRIGHT, ITALIC

NUANCES IS A VERY RICH SERIF FAMILY, WITH A HIGHLY EXPRESSIVE AND RESOLUTELY MODERN DESIGN. BORN FROM PERSONAL RESEARCH INTO TYPOGRAPHIC DESIGN AND AESTHETIC DETAIL, IT IS A SHARP SERIF WITH STRONG CONTRAST AND ELEGANT CURVES. WITH PARTICULAR ATTENTION PAID TO EACH GLYPH, THIS FONT FAMILY IS MEANT TO BE USED IN LARGE SIZES. IT IS AN EXPRESSIVE TYPEFACE THAT IS TO BE EXPERIENCED, SHOWN, READ AND SEEN THROUGH ITS ELEGANT SHAPES AND CONFIDENT DESIGN.

CAP HEIGHT

EXTRALIGHT – 290PT

X-HEIGHT

Nn

BASELINE

Nuances

EXTRALIGHT - 36PT

THE QUICK BROWN FOX J
IT WOULD BE THE CHEE
IT'S A LOVELY DAY IN TH
AND THE PUNGENT ARO
PROMISE OF A SUMPTUO
THINKING ABOUT THE D
THE LAZY DOG REMAINS

EXTRALIGHT - 18PT

The quick brown fox jumps over a lazy dog. He didn't
it would be the cheeky thing to do. After all, he had a
It's a lovely day in the neighbourhood, with the sun s
and the pungent aroma of fresh rubbish bins wafting
promise of a sumptuous meal. The sprightly fox rubs
thinking about the delicious treasures he's about to d
the lazy dog remains unperturbed. With her long snc
long black fur fluttering in the breeze, she is in a dre

EXTRALIGHT - 8PT

The quick brown fox jumps over a lazy dog. He didn't have to, but he thought it would be the cheeky thing to do. After all, he had a reputation to maintain. It's a lovely day in the neighbourhood, with the sun shining, the birds chirping, and the pungent aroma of fresh rubbish bins wafting through the air - the promise of a sumptuous meal. The sprightly fox rubs his paws together in glee, thinking about the delicious treasures he's about to dig into. Still in her spot, the lazy dog remains unperturbed. With her long snout, droopy jowls, and long black fur fluttering in the breeze, she is in a dreamland far away - where the mountains are made of beefy treats, the valleys are filled with tennis balls, and the puddles are just the right temperature. Why be in the rat race? It's a dog's life, after all.

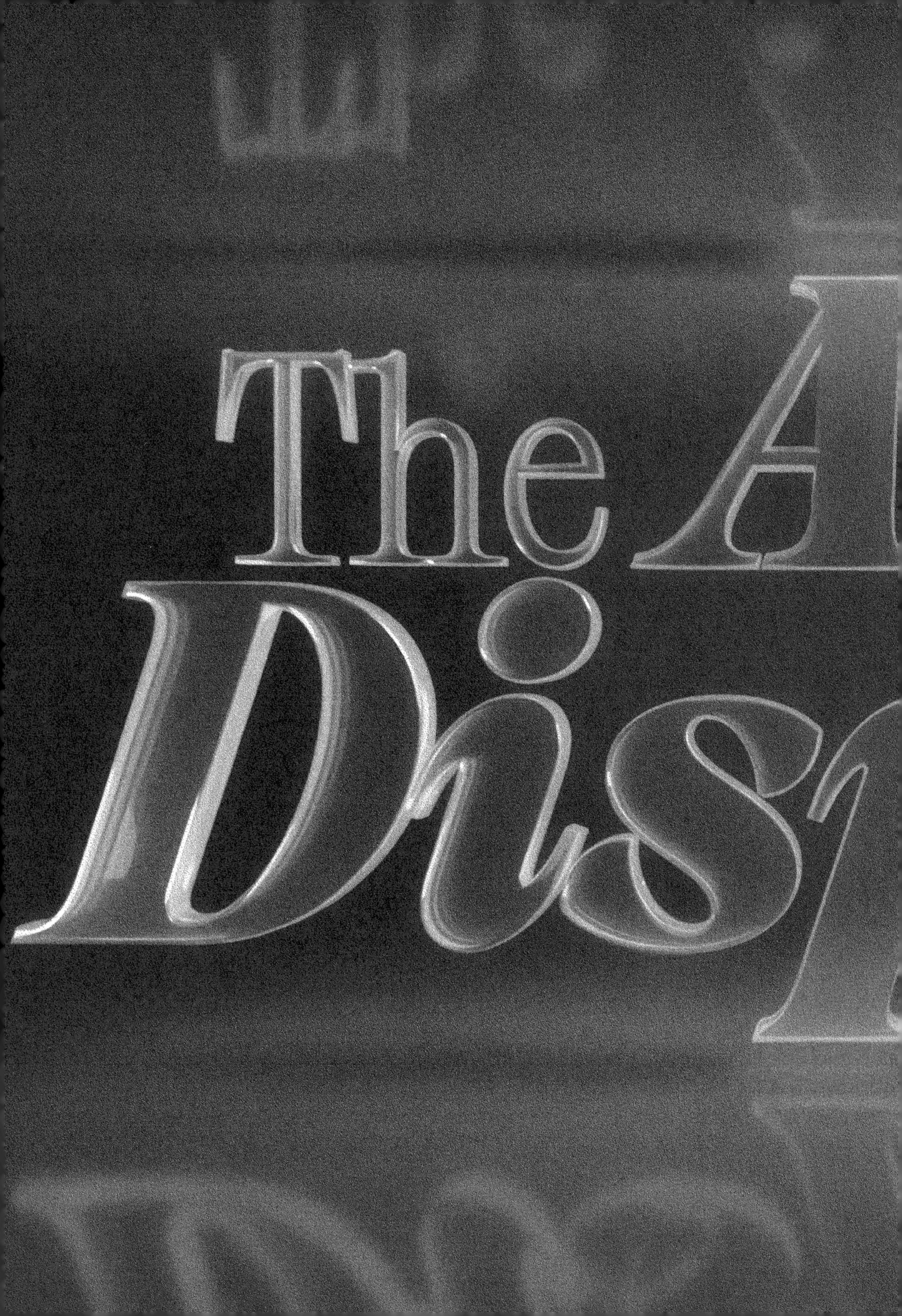
The
Dis

rt of
lay

TYPEFACE : FAIRE OCTAVE
DESIGNER : FAIRE TYPE
LOCATION : NEW YORK, US

PUBLISHED BY : FAIRE TYPE
CHRONOLOGY : 2023
RELEASED IN : 2023

LINK : HTTPS://WWW.FAIRETYPE.COM/FONTS/OCTAVE
STYLES : REGULAR, MEDIUM, BOLD, BLACK

OCTAVE IS A REVIVAL OF AN ELZEVIR-STYLE TYPEFACE ORIGINALLY DESIGNED BY THÉOPHILE BEAUDOIRE. THE REVIVAL IS BASED ON A CUT OF BEAUDOIRE'S ELZEVIR USED IN A BOOK TITLED "HISTOIRE DE LA MUSIQUE EN RUSSIE" BY ALBERT SOUBIES (1898), AND REMAINS FAIRLY FAITHFUL TO THE SOURCE MATERIAL WITH OPTICAL ADJUSTMENTS AND IMPROVEMENTS MADE DURING THE DIGITAL DRAWING PROCESS. THE TYPEFACE FEATURES A TRANSLATION-STYLE CONTRAST, MEANING THE THICKS AND THINS OF THE LETTERS WERE LARGELY DECIDED BY HOW A CALLIGRAPHIC BROAD-NIBBED PEN WOULD CREATE THOSE LETTERS. SMALL SERIFS AND HEAVY-FEELING BOWLS IN LETTERFORMS GIVE THE TYPEFACE A COOL ELEGANCE.

CAP HEIGHT

REGULAR – 290PT

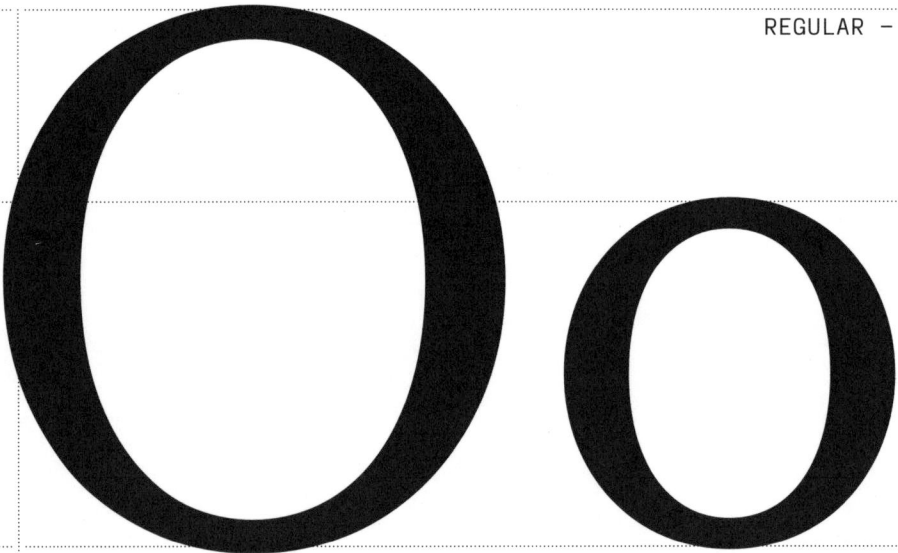

X-HEIGHT

Oo

BASELINE

FAIRE Octave

THE QUICK BR
IT WOULD BE
IT'S A LOVELY
AND THE PUN
PROMISE OF A
THINKING AB
THE LAZY DO
LONG BLACK
THE MOUNTA

Daft Punk • Discovery • 2001

1

One More Time
Aerodynamic
3 Digital Love
Harder 4 Better
Faster Stronger
5 Crescendolls
6
Nightvision
7
Superheroes

Faire Octave • Regular • 2023

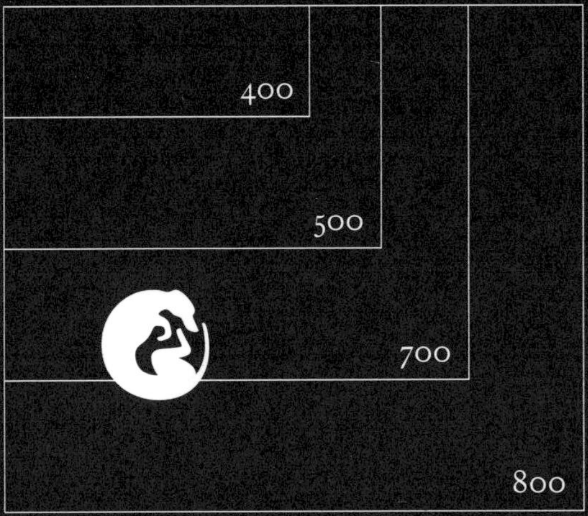

Regular
Medium
Bold
Black

Mon cher Oncle Cary, Tu viens d'entrer dans ton dix-septième lustre; tes grandes facultés intellectuelles sont toujours très vives, je suis heureux de pouvoir te dédier un modeste livre qui traite de choses que tu aimas toute ta vie. Ancien maître imprimeur typographe et amant des Muses, tu comprendras mieux qu'un autre combien a été longue et ardue la tâche que je me suis imposée pour éviter l'écueil où tant de typographes ont échoué depuis si longlemps. Si je suis arrivé au but, c'est grâce à les savantes leçons et c'est un acte de haute justice de faire remoter jusqu'à mon professeur, le peu de mérite que je puis avoir en faisant paraître le premier Manuel de Typographie musicale. Reçois, mon cher Oncle, cette nouvelle preuve de ma constante amitié, Th. BEAUDOIRE. On dit que les Muses ont créé la Musique, et Aristide Quintitien nous apprend que le système des grecs était basé sur le tétracorde (quatre cordes) ou échelle de quatre sons qu'ils répétaient comme nous répétons l'octave. Les grecs notaient la musique à l'aide des lettres de leur alphabet. Vers le Ve siècle, Boéce notait la musique au moyen de lettres différentes de l'alphabet latin; vint ensuite la méthode dite grégorienne dans laquelle on employait: 1° les sept premières lettres majuscules de l'alphabet ABCDEFG pour l'octave grave, l'A représentait le LA grave; 2° les sept premières lettres minuscules pour l'octave des sons médiaux; 3° pour les sons aigus on doublait les minuscules. Un peu plus tard on ajouta une corde à l'octave grave, c'est-à-dire une note correspondante au SOL grave; elle fut représentée par le gamma grec. L'échelle des sons commençant par le gamma prit le nom de "Gamme". Dans chacune de ces gammes la note altérable SI, était représentée par les B, b; on écrivait le SI naturel avec un b carré; quand cette note était plus faible, plus molle, on employait un b rond ; ce sont ces deux lettres qu'on appelle maintenant bécarre (b carré, bémol [b mol]). Après la notation alphabétique vinrent quelques essais de notation noire, mais du VIIe au XIIIe siècle, la plus grande partie des manuscrits en musique religieuse et profane fut notée par les Neumes, espèces de signes sténographiques. On les écrivait au-dessus des paroles à diverse hauteurs conventionnelles. Les sons aigus étaient représentés par l'accent aigu, les sons graves par l'accent grave; plusieurs sons, modulés sur une syllabe, par des ligatures formées avec ces accents.

DISCO

VOYA

IO

HIGH

TOOI

VERY
GER
LIFE
ONG

⓪ ⑧ ⑭

TYPEFACE	:	OGG
DESIGNER	:	SHARP TYPE
COUNTRY	:	NEW YORK & CALIFORNIA, US

PUBLISHED BY	:	SHARP TYPE
CHRONOLOGY	:	2013 - 2019
RELEASE	:	2019

LINK	:	HTTPS://SHARPTYPE.CO/TYPEFACES/OGG-SUPERFAMILY/OGG/
STYLES	:	ROMAN, ITALIC

OGG WAS INSPIRED BY THE HAND LETTERING OF OSCAR OGG, AN AMERICAN BOOK DESIGNER, CALLIGRAPHER, AND AUTHOR. DESIGNED BY LUCAS SHARP, THE TYPEFACE'S ICONIC DESIGN CAPTURES THE UNIQUE COMBINATION OF CALLIGRAPHIC AND TYPOGRAPHIC FORM THAT OSCAR ACHIEVED THROUGH THE USE OF HAND-CARVED PEN NIBS, BRUSHES, AND WHITE-OUT. THE COMPLEMENTARY TEXT FACE INFUSES THE SIGNATURE CALLIGRAPHIC STYLING OF ITS DISPLAY COUNTERPART WITH A MIX OF TRANSITIONAL AND OLD STYLE TEXT FACE MODELS, RESULTING IN A SEAMLESS READING EXPERIENCE. AS A SYSTEM, THE OGG FAMILY MIRRORS THE SINGULAR TYPOGRAPHIC HIERARCHY THAT OSCAR ACHIEVED IN HIS BOOK JACKET LETTERING.

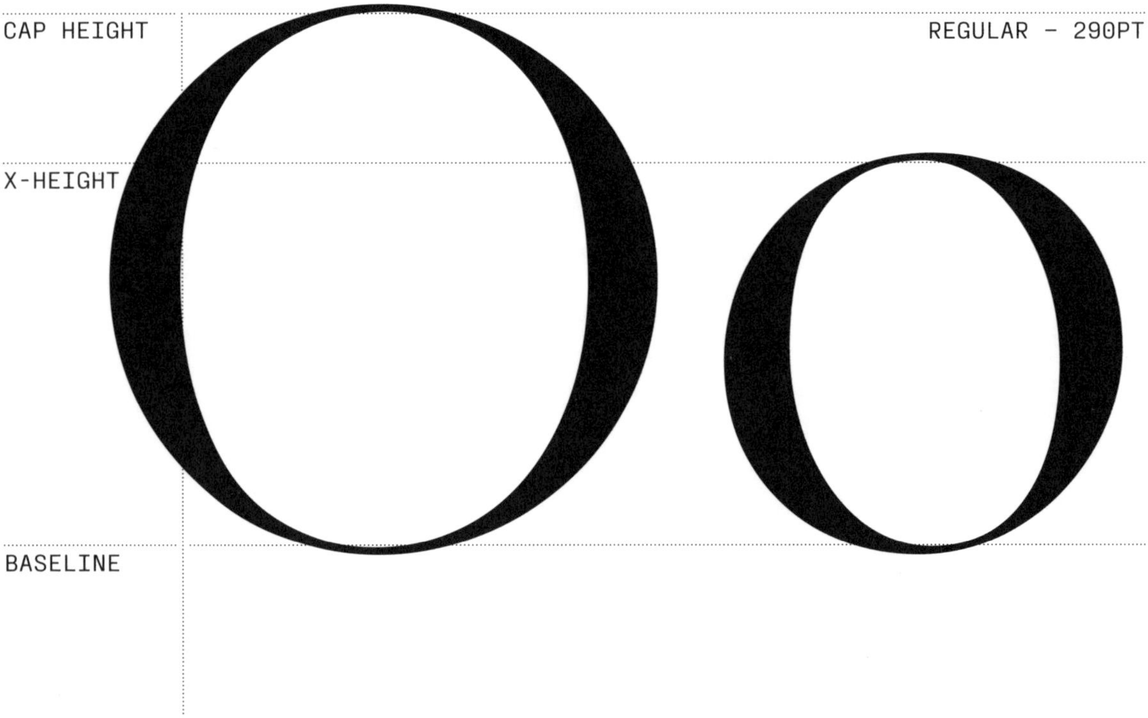

Ogg

REGULAR – 60PT

THE QUICK BRO
IT WOULD BE TH
IT'S A LOVELY D
AND THE PUNG
PROMISE OF A S
THINKING ABOU

REGULAR – 18PT

The quick brown fox jumps over a lazy dog. He didn't ha
it would be the cheeky thing to do. After all, he had a rep
It's a lovely day in the neighbourhood, with the sun shini
and the pungent aroma of fresh rubbish bins wafting thro
promise of a sumptuous meal. The sprightly fox rubs his
thinking about the delicious treasures he's about to dig in
the lazy dog remains unperturbed. With her long snout, c
long black fur fluttering in the breeze, she is in a dreamla
the mountains are made of beefy treats, the valleys are fi
and the puddles are just the right temperature. Why be in

The 26 Letters

Hayakawa

Ermenegildo

Alessandro

Jean Barthet

Dominique

Furstenberg

Balenciaga

Psychedelic

Michalsky

Tranquillityite

Chalconatronite

TYPEFACE	:	ORBIKULAR
DESIGNER	:	COTYPE FOUNDRY
LOCATION	:	LONDON, UK

PUBLISHED BY	:	COTYPE FOUNDRY
CHRONOLOGY	:	N/A
RELEASED IN	:	2021

LINK	:	HTTPS://COTYPEFOUNDRY.COM/OUR-FONTS/ORBIKULAR/
STYLES	:	6 WEIGHTS, 12 STYLES: EXTRALIGHT, LIGHT, REGULAR, SEMIBOLD, BOLD, EXTRABOLD + ITALICS + A VARIABLE FONT
CREDITS	:	MATT WILLEY & CHANTAL JAHCHAN/PENTAGRAM (SPECIMEN BOOK DESIGN)

ORBIKULAR IS A FUNCTIONAL SERIF FAMILY THAT CAN STAND THE TEST OF TIME, WHILST STILL FEELING MODERN AND UNIQUE. EACH LETTERSHAPE HAS BEEN CRAFTED WITH GREAT ATTENTION TO DETAIL IN ORDER TO ENSURE GREAT LEGIBILITY AT LARGE AND SMALL SIZES. SOME CHARACTERISTICS ARE THE USE OF BALL TERMINALS, A HIGH X-HEIGHT, VERTICAL STRESS, AND HIGH CONTRAST. ALTERNATE CHARACTERS, OLD STYLE AND TABULAR NUMERALS, LIGATURES, AS WELL AS VARIOUS SYMBOLS WERE ALSO INCLUDED TO ALLOW THE USER TO EASILY CHANGE THE PERSONALITY OF THE TYPEFACE.

CAP HEIGHT

REGULAR – 290PT

X-HEIGHT

Oo

BASELINE

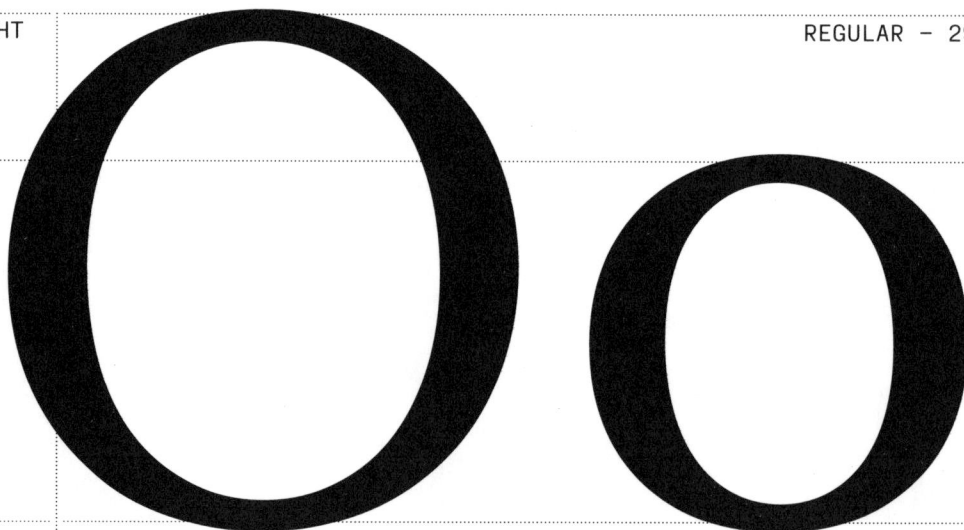

Orbikular

REGULAR – 36PT

THE QUICK BROWN FOX JU
IT WOULD BE THE CHEEKY
IT'S A LOVELY DAY IN THE
AND THE PUNGENT AROM
PROMISE OF A SUMPTUOU
THINKING ABOUT THE DE
THE LAZY DOG REMAINS U

REGULAR – 18PT

The quick brown fox jumps over a lazy dog. He didn't h
it would be the cheeky thing to do. After all, he had a re
It's a lovely day in the neighbourhood, with the sun shi
and the pungent aroma of fresh rubbish bins wafting t
promise of a sumptuous meal. The sprightly fox rubs h
thinking about the delicious treasures he's about to dig
the lazy dog remains unperturbed. With her long snou
long black fur fluttering in the breeze, she is in a drear

REGULAR – 8PT

The quick brown fox jumps over a lazy dog. He didn't have to, but he thought it would be the cheeky thing to do. After all, he had a reputation to maintain. It's a lovely day in the neighbourhood, with the sun shining, the birds chirping, and the pungent aroma of fresh rubbish bins wafting through the air - the promise of a sumptuous meal. The sprightly fox rubs his paws together in glee, thinking about the delicious treasures he's about to dig into. Still in her spot, the lazy dog remains unperturbed. With her long snout, droopy jowls, and long black fur fluttering in the breeze, she is in a dreamland far away - where the mountains are made of beefy treats, the valleys are filled with tennis balls, and the puddles are just the right temperature. Why be in the rat race? It's a dog's life, after all.

RH°D

SAVILL

BLOOM

J.D.HILL

EST° 19

LIVERE

ES LTD

E ROW

& SONS

IARD CO

23 LDN

OOL ST

TYPEFACE : RABBIT HOLE DISPLAY
DESIGNER : BOAFFF
LOCATION : UK

PUBLISHED BY : TYPE DEPARTMENT
CHRONOLOGY : N/A
RELEASED IN : N/A

LINK : HTTPS://TYPE-DEPARTMENT.COM/COLLECTIONS/SERIF-FONTS/PRODUCTS/
STYLES : 1

RABBIT HOLE DISPLAY WAS INSPIRED BY TWISTED CHARACTERS FROM A SECRET WORLD. ITS DESIGNER INVITES USERS TO "STEP INTO A STRANGE WORLD LIKE ALICE IN WONDERLAND AND FALL INTO THE HOLE - IT'S TIME!".

CAP HEIGHT

REGULAR - 290PT

BASELINE

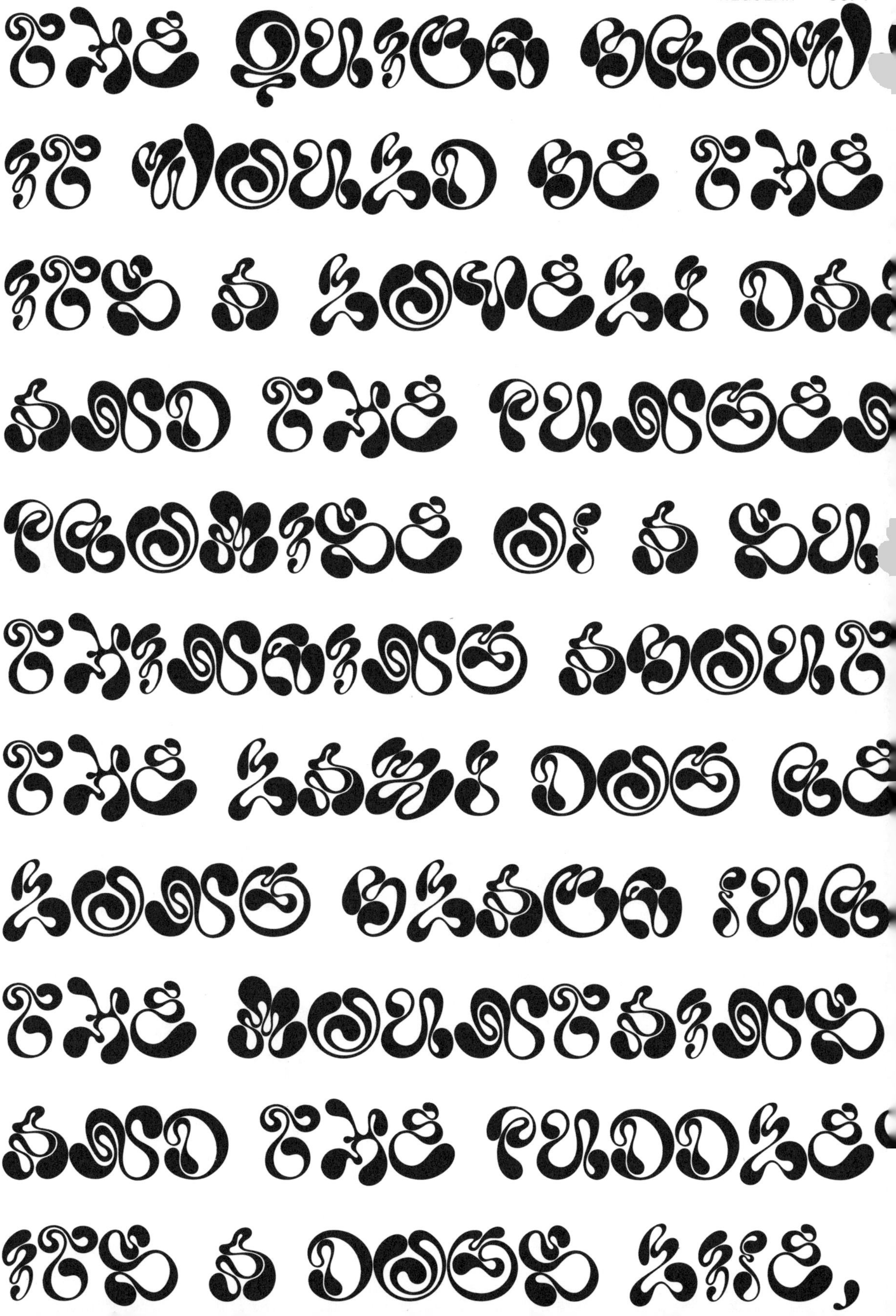

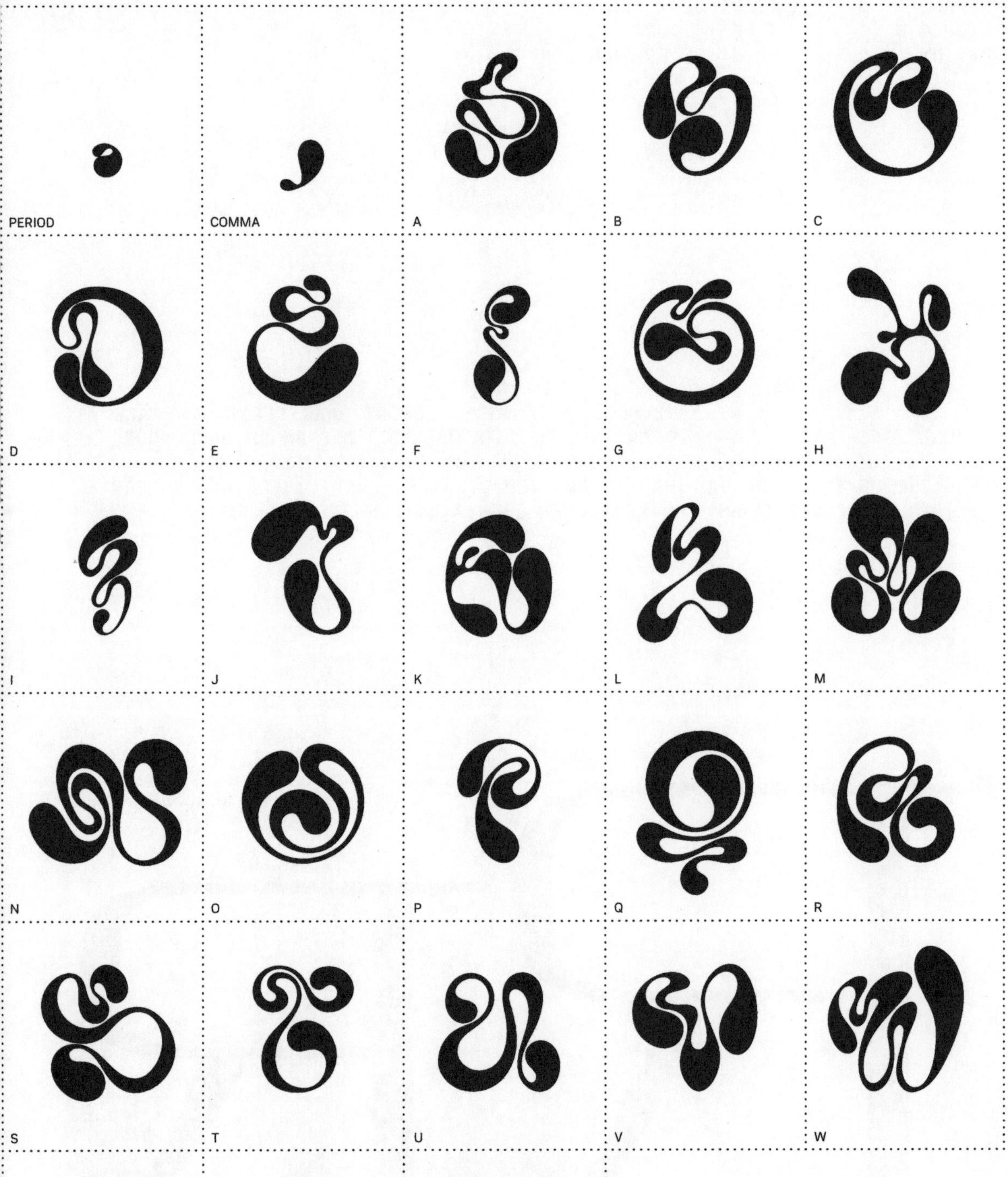
PERIOD
COMMA
A
B
C
D
E
F
G
H
I
J
K
L
M
N
O
P
Q
R
S
T
U
V
W
X
Y
Z

TYPEFACE	:	TT RICORDI TODI
DESIGNER	:	TYPETYPE.ORG
LOCATION	:	SAINT PETERSBURG, RUSSIA

PUBLISHED BY	:	TYPETYPE.ORG
CHRONOLOGY	:	N/A
RELEASED IN	:	2021

LINK	:	HTTPS://TYPETYPE.ORG/FONTS/TT-RICORDI/
STYLES	:	1

TT RICORDI TODI IS A WIDE-PROPORTIONED SERIF TYPEFACE WITH A CLASSIC BASE AND A CONTEMPORARY NATURE. THE PROJECT WAS BASED ON PLAQUES WITH ENGRAVED STREET NAMES FROM THE SMALL ITALIAN TOWN OF TODI. THE TYPEFACE IS CHARACTERISED BY CRISP AND SHARP CHARACTER DETAILS, EMPHASISED IN A MODERN WAY. IT IS EXQUISITE YET SHARP AND SOMETIMES EVEN A LITTLE PRETENTIOUS.

REGULAR – 290PT

TT RICORDI TODI

REGULAR - 40PT

THE QUICK BROWN
IT WOULD BE THE
IT'S A LOVELY DAY
AND THE PUNGENT
PROMISE OF A SUM
THINKING ABOUT T

REGULAR - 16PT

THE QUICK BROWN FOX JUMPS OVER A LAZY DOG. HE
IT WOULD BE THE CHEEKY THING TO DO. AFTER ALL, H
IT'S A LOVELY DAY IN THE NEIGHBOURHOOD, WITH TH
AND THE PUNGENT AROMA OF FRESH RUBBISH BINS W
PROMISE OF A SUMPTUOUS MEAL. THE SPRIGHTLY FO
THINKING ABOUT THE DELICIOUS TREASURES HE'S AI
THE LAZY DOG REMAINS UNPERTURBED. WITH HER L
LONG BLACK FUR FLUTTERING IN THE BREEZE, SHE IS
THE MOUNTAINS ARE MADE OF BEEFY TREATS, THE VA
AND THE PUDDLES ARE JUST THE RIGHT TEMPERATUI
IT'S A DOG'S LIFE, AFTER ALL.

REGULAR - 8PT

THE QUICK BROWN FOX JUMPS OVER A LAZY DOG. HE DIDN'T HAVE TO, BUT HE THOUGHT IT WOULD BE THE CHEEKY THING TO DO. AFTER ALL, HE HAD A REPUTATION TO MAINTAIN. IT'S A LOVELY DAY IN THE NEIGHBOURHOOD, WITH THE SUN SHINING, THE BIRDS CHIRPING, AND THE PUNGENT AROMA OF FRESH RUBBISH BINS WAFTING THROUGH THE AIR - THE PROMISE OF A SUMPTUOUS MEAL. THE SPRIGHTLY FOX RUBS HIS PAWS TOGETHER IN GLEE, THINKING ABOUT THE DELICIOUS TREASURES HE'S ABOUT TO DIG INTO. STILL IN HER SPOT, THE LAZY DOG REMAINS UNPERTURBED. WITH HER LONG SNOUT, DROOPY JOWLS, AND LONG BLACK FUR FLUTTERING IN THE BREEZE, SHE IS IN A DREAMLAND FAR AWAY - WHERE THE MOUNTAINS ARE MADE OF BEEFY TREATS, THE VALLEYS ARE FILLED WITH TENNIS BALLS, AND THE PUDDLES ARE JUST THE RIGHT TEMPERATURE. WHY BE IN THE RAT RACE? IT'S A DOG'S LIFE, AFTER ALL.

•JAZZ•

~~THE

SOUL*

12345

<ABC>

TT Ricordi Todi

TypeType

TYPEFACE	:	COFO ROBERT
DESIGNER	:	CONTRAST FOUNDRY
LOCATION	:	CALIFORNIA, US

PUBLISHED BY	:	CONTRAST FOUNDRY
CHRONOLOGY	:	2012 - 2018
RELEASED IN	:	2018

LINK	:	HTTPS://CONTRASTFOUNDRY.COM/TYPEFACE/COFO-ROBERT
STYLES	:	LIGHT, LIGHT ITALIC, REGULAR, REGULAR ITALIC, BOOK, BOOK ITALIC, MEDIUM, MEDIUM ITALIC, BOLD, BOLD ITALIC, HEAVY, HEAVY ITALIC, BLACK, BLACK ITALIC
CREDITS	:	ANNA KHORASH

COFO ROBERT IS A MODERN TWIST ON A CLASSIC. ITS EXPRESSIVE NATURE AND THE SPIRIT OF THE INDUSTRIAL REVOLUTION ARE MIXED WITH A HINT OF NEW TECHNOLOGY AND A POWERFUL HUMAN TOUCH, TO TURN ROBERT INTO A RATIONAL MULTIFUNCTIONAL TYPE FAMILY WITH AUTHORITATIVE ROMANS AND EXPRESSIVE ITALICS IN 7 WEIGHTS. ROBERT IS ALSO PACKED WITH ALL THE EXTRAS THAT DESIGNERS DREAM OF: SEVERAL SETS OF DECORATIVE NUMBERS, ARROWS, HANDS, BULLETS, AND SMALL CAPS – SUPPLYING EVEN MORE TOOLS FOR CREATIVE FREEDOM AND MAKING THE POSSIBILITIES OF ITS USAGE LIMITLESS.

CAP HEIGHT

REGULAR – 290PT

X-HEIGHT

Rr

BASELINE

COFO Robert

THE QUICK BRO
IT WOULD BE TH
IT'S A LOVELY DA
AND THE PUNGE
PROMISE OF A SU
THINKING ABOU
THE LAZY DOG R
LONG BLACK FU
THE MOUNTAIN

@
R
&
J
§
5
AND

BIG BANG COSMOLOGY

Metric expansion is a key feature of Big Bang cosmology, is modeled mathematically with the *Friedmann-Lemaître-Robertson-Walker* metric and is a generic property of the universe we inhabit. However, the model is valid only on large scales (roughly the scale of galaxy clusters and above), because gravitational attraction binds matter together strongly enough that metric expansion cannot be observed at this time, on a smaller scale. As such, the only galaxies receding from one another as a result of metric expansion are those separated by cosmologically relevant scales larger than the length scales associated with the gravitational collapse that are possible in the age of the universe given the matter density and average expansion rate. Physicists have postulated the existence of dark energy, appearing as a cosmological constant in the simplest gravitational models as a way to explain the acceleration. According to the simplest extrapolation of the currently-favored cosmological model, the Lambda-CDM model, this acceleration becomes more dominant into the future. In June 2016, NASA and ESA scientists reported that the universe was found to be expanding 5% to 9% faster than thought earlier, based on studies using the Hubble Space Telescope

TYPEFACE : ROMEK
DESIGNER : THE DESIGNERS FOUNDRY
LOCATION : NEW ZEALAND

PUBLISHED BY : THE DESIGNERS FOUNDRY
CHRONOLOGY : N/A
RELEASED IN : 2021

LINK : HTTPS://THEDESIGNERSFOUNDRY.COM/ROMEK
STYLES : 28
CREDITS : ANDREA BIGGIO (DESIGN)

ROMEK IS A SERIF TYPEFACE FAMILY WITH SHARP AND ROUNDED VERSIONS, DESIGNED FOR A VAST RANGE OF APPLICATIONS. ITS DESIGN REFERENCES SEVERAL SOURCES, INCLUDING GENZSCH-ANTIQUA (1906), ORLANDO (1920), AND PAGANINI (1928) BY NEBIOLO. ROMEK STARTED AS A DISPLAY TYPEFACE AND EVOLVED INTO A TEXT FONT AFTER MANY REVISIONS. THE FONT CONSISTS OF 7 WEIGHTS IN SHARP AND ROUNDED VERSIONS WITH MATCHING ITALICS. ITS OPENTYPE FEATURES INCLUDE CASE-SENSITIVE FORMS, LIGATURES, OLD STYLE AND TABULAR FIGURES, NUMERATORS, DENOMINATORS, FRACTIONS, ORDINALS, SMALL CAPS AND ROMAN NUMERALS.

CAP HEIGHT

REGULAR – 290PT

X-HEIGHT

Rr

BASELINE

Romek

REGULAR – 55PT

THE QUICK BRO
HAVE TO, BUT H
IT WOULD BE TH
A REPUTATION T
IT'S A LOVELY DA
SHINING, THE B
AND THE PUNGE
THROUGH THE A

REGULAR – 8PT

The quick brown fox jumps over a lazy dog. He didn't have to, but he thought it would be the cheeky thing to do. After all, he had a reputation to maintain. It's a lovely day in the neighbourhood, with the sun shining, the birds chirping, and the pungent aroma of fresh rubbish bins wafting through the air - the promise of a sumptuous meal. The sprightly fox rubs his paws together in glee, thinking about the delicious treasures he's about to dig into. Still in her spot, the lazy dog remains unperturbed. With her long snout, droopy jowls, and long black fur fluttering in the breeze, she is in a dreamland far away - where the mountains are made of beefy treats, the valleys are filled with tennis balls, and the puddles are just the right temperature. Why be in the rat race? It's a dog's life, after all.

Fulvia
Monte
Salaria
Trionfale
Collatina
Portuense
Ardeatina

Supercomputers

Charismatically

Environmentalist

Proportionately

Overrepresented

Microelectronic

Transcendentally

Chronologically

hh

TYPEFACE : SAINTE COLOMBE
DESIGNER : PRODUCTION TYPE
LOCATION : PARIS, FRANCE; SHANGHAI, CHINA

PUBLISHED BY : PRODUCTION TYPE
CHRONOLOGY : 2016 - 2018
RELEASED IN : 2018

LINK : HTTPS://WWW.PRODUCTIONTYPE.COM/FAMILY/SAINTE_COLOMBE
STYLES : 10 STYLES; 5 WEIGHTS; ROMAN & ITALIC
CREDITS : YOANN MINET (DESIGN)

SAINTE COLOMBE IS A NEW SERIF TYPEFACE AVAILABLE IN A RANGE OF FIVE WEIGHTS, FROM EXTRA LIGHT TO BOLD. DECIDEDLY NOT DRIVEN BY GEOMETRY NOR SYMMETRY, IT IS ACTUALLY JUST THE OPPOSITE — EXPRESSIVE, LIKE MUSIC, BUT ALSO WITH A REPRESSED SHELL TRYING TO CONTAIN THAT EXPRESSION. WITH ITS UNIQUE SHARPNESS, FLAGRANT SERIFS, AND OPEN COUNTERS, IT IS NOT AFRAID TO MOVE, AS LONG AS THAT MOVEMENT HAPPENS IN SUBTLE WAYS.

Sainte Colombe

THE QUICK BI
IT WOULD BE
IT'S A LOVELY
AND THE PUN
PROMISE OF A
THINKING AB
THE LAZY DO
LONG BLACK
THE MOUNTA

MYSTICS----
---»MYSTICS
MYSTICS----
---»MYSTICS
MYSTICS----
---»MYSTICS
MYSTICS----
---»MYSTICS
MYSTICS----
---»MYSTICS

Lyrics

Venice

TYPEFACE : FT SAKRAL
DESIGNER : FUERTE TYPE
LOCATION : DUBAI, UAE; COLONIA, URUGUAY

PUBLISHED BY : FUERTE TYPE
CHRONOLOGY : 2022 – 2023
RELEASED IN : 2023

LINK : HTTPS://WWW.FUERTETYPE.COM/TYPEFACES/SAKRAL/
STYLES : TEXT: REGULAR, REGULAR ITALIC, MEDIUM, MEDIUM ITALIC, BOLD, BOLD ITALIC, BLACK, BLACK ITALIC
DISPLAY: REGULAR, REGULAR ITALIC, MEDIUM, MEDIUM ITALIC, BOLD, BOLD ITALIC, BLACK, BLACK ITALIC

SAKRAL INITIALLY FOUND ITS INFLUENCE IN 2018 WHEN FUERTE'S DIRECTOR, FERMÍN GUERRERO, ENCOUNTERED A HAND-PAINTED SIGN WITH VERY DISTINCTIVE LETTER-SHAPES FEATURING HIGHLY ELONGATED SERIFS WITH UNUSUAL PROPORTIONS AND CONTRAST. REFERENCING THIS SIGN, THE STARTING POINT OF THE PROJECT, SAKRAL RETAINS ITS HANDWRITTEN – OR PAINTED, IN THIS CASE – STRUCTURE AND GENERAL FEEL, AND COMBINES IT WITH CONSTRUCTED DETAILS ECHOING THE CONTEXT WHERE THE SIGN WAS LOCATED: ZURICH'S OLD TOWN. MEDIEVAL ARMOURY IMAGERY, SUCH AS KNIGHTS, SWORDS AND SHIELDS, ACTED AS A SOURCE OF INSPIRATION, RESULTING IN A VIBRANT AND IDIOSYNCRATIC TYPEFACE WITH A CONTEMPORARY LOOK AND STRONG VISUAL APPEAL.

CAP HEIGHT

REGULAR – 290PT

X-HEIGHT

Ss

BASELINE

FT Sakral

REGULAR – 48PT

THE QUICK BROWN FOX
IT WOULD BE THE CHE
IT'S A LOVELY DAY IN T
AND THE PUNGENT AR
PROMISE OF A SUMPT
THINKING ABOUT THE
THE LAZY DOG REMAI
LONG BLACK FUR FLUT
THE MOUNTAINS ARE
AND THE PUDDLES AR
IT'S A DOG'S LIFE, AFT

REGULAR – 10PT

The quick brown fox jumps over a lazy dog. He didn't have to, but he thought it would be the cheeky thing to do. After all, he had a reputation to maintain. It's a lovely day in the neighbourhood, with the sun shining, the birds chirping, and the pungent aroma of fresh rubbish bins wafting through the air - the promise of a sumptuous meal. The sprightly fox rubs his paws together in glee, thinking about the delicious treasures he's about to dig into. Still in her spot, the lazy dog remains unperturbed. With her long snout, droopy jowls, and long black fur fluttering in the breeze, she is in a dreamland far away - where the mountains are made of beefy treats, the valleys are filled with tennis balls, and the puddles are just the right temperature. Why be in the rat race? It's a dog's life, after all.

IN THE BEGINNING THERE WAS JACK

1234567+

AS A SECULAR, NON-SECTARIAN, *UNIVERSAL NOTION* OF ART AROSE IN 19TH-CENTURY *WESTERN EUROPE* "ARTISTS"

Antiques, toys, coins, stamps *and Artists' books published with love!*

Display

Aa *Aa*

Aa *Aa*

Aa ***Aa***

Aa ***Aa***

ON HIS BOX JACK BOLDLY DECLARED,

LET THERE BE HOUSE. AND HOUSE *MUSIC* WAS *BORN.*

ND JACK HAD A GROOVE. AND FROM

THE RENAISSANCE SAW AN INCREASE IN *MONUMENTAL SECULAR WORKS*, BUT UNTIL THE PROTESTANT REFORMATION CHRISTIAN ART CONTINUED *TO BE PRODUCED IN GREAT QUANTITIES*. DURING THIS TIME, *AN-*

D E F

1234567+

G H I

Michelangelo Buonarroti painted the Sistine Chapel and carved the famous Pietà, gianlorenzo Bernini created the massive columns in St. Peter's Basilica, and Leonardo da Vinci *painted the Last Supper*. The Reformation had a huge effect Won Christian art,

N

Text

Aa *Aa*

Aa *Aa*

Aa *Aa*

Aa *Aa*

FT

ß a

g h i j k l m n

fb fh ffl fk

o p q r s t u v

The studio was co-founded in 1984 by *brothers* Fernando (1961) and Humberto (1953) *Campana*.

w x y z a ω

THIS GROOVE CAME THE GROOVES OF ALL GROOVES &

WHILE ONE DAY VICIOUSLY THROWIN

TYPEFACE	:	SALTER
DESIGNER	:	SHARP TYPE
LOCATION	:	NEW YORK & CALIFORNIA, US

PUBLISHED BY	:	SHARP TYPE
CHRONOLOGY	:	2021
RELEASED IN	:	2021

LINK	:	HTTPS://SHARPTYPE.CO/TYPEFACES/SALTER/
STYLES	:	ROMAN, ITALIC

SALTER IS A SCRIPT-BASED TYPEFACE INSPIRED BY THE 20TH CENTURY BOOK JACKET CALLIGRAPHY OF OSCAR OGG AND GEORGE SALTER. THE TENSION BETWEEN SALTER'S ANGULAR AND ROUND FEATURES EVOKE THE HARD LINEAR STROKES AND SOFTER ROTATION OF A MASTER CALLIGRAPHER'S PEN – OR IN THIS CASE, TWO OF THEM: ONE CAN ALMOST SEE THE SHARED HAND OF SALTER AND OGG IN THESE UNCANNY LETTERFORMS, WHICH HAVE A DISTINCTLY INKY TEXTURE IN BOTH ROMAN AND ITALIC STYLES THAT IS REMARKABLE GIVEN THEIR DIGITAL PROVENANCE. SALTER IS AT HEART AN INTERGENERATIONAL DIALOGUE AND AN HOMAGE TO THE TIMELESS LEGACY OF TWO LETTERING MASTERS.

CAP HEIGHT

REGULAR – 290PT

Ss

X-HEIGHT

BASELINE

Salter

THE QUICK BI

IT WOULD BE

IT'S A LOVELY

AND THE PUN

PROMISE OF A

THINKING AB

®

—Conch

y Alc

14.5%

Viña.M

aV.C.P*

2°F70′

1883W

oët ∞ ☼

TYPEFACE : SAMZARA
DESIGNER : THE DESIGNERS FOUNDRY
LOCATION : NEW ZEALAND

PUBLISHED BY : THE DESIGNERS FOUNDRY
CHRONOLOGY : N/A
RELEASED IN : 2019

LINK : HTTPS://THEDESIGNERSFOUNDRY.COM/SAMZARA
STYLES : 2
CREDITS : LA BOLDE VITA (DESIGN)

THE INITIAL SKETCHES FOR SAMZARA BEGAN IN 2018, EXPERIMENTING WITH MIXING ELEMENTS AND PRINCIPLES OF VARIOUS TYPE CLASSIFICATIONS. THE FINAL DESIGN IS BASED ON CLASSIC SLAB SERIF FORMS, TRANSLATING OVERALL SHAPES AND THICK BRACKETED SERIFS INTO A SOMEWHAT EXPERIMENTAL DIGITAL ANTIQUA LANGUAGE. UNLIKE MOST SERIF TYPEFACES, SAMZARA'S SERIFS HAVE THE SAME THICKNESS AS THE BODIES, CREATING NEW AND SOMETIMES AWKWARD LETTER SHAPES. THE UPRIGHT ROMAN IS SUPPORTED BY AN ITALIC STYLE; SLANTED AT AN UNUSUAL STRONG ANGLE OF 21°. PLAYFUL FORMS ARE CREATED BY THE VERTICAL SERIFS THAT ARE NOT SLANTING. AS A DISPLAY TYPEFACE, IT IS BEST USED FOR HEADLINES AND QUOTES IN EDITORIALS, POSTERS AND IDENTITIES. COMBINE IT WITH A BOLD GROTESQUE OR AN EXTENDED SANS FOR MAXIMUM IMPACT!

Samzara

REGULAR - 36PT

THE QUICK BROWN
IT WOULD BE THE C
IT'S A LOVELY DAY
AND THE PUNGENT
PROMISE OF A SUM
THINKING ABOUT T
THE LAZY DOG REM

REGULAR - 18PT

The quick brown fox jumps over a lazy d
it would be the cheeky thing to do. After
It's a lovely day in the neighbourhood, wi
and the pungent aroma of fresh rubbish
promise of a sumptuous meal. The sprigh
thinking about the delicious treasures he'
the lazy dog remains unperturbed. With
long black fur fluttering in the breeze, sh

REGULAR - 8PT

The quick brown fox jumps over a lazy dog. He didn't have to, but he thought it would be the cheeky thing to do. After all, he had a reputation to maintain. It's a lovely day in the neighbourhood, with the sun shining, the birds chirping, and the pungent aroma of fresh rubbish bins wafting through the air - the promise of a sumptuous meal. The sprightly fox rubs his paws together in glee, thinking about the delicious treasures he's about to dig into. Still in her spot, the lazy dog remains unperturbed. With her long snout, droopy jowls, and long black fur fluttering in the breeze, she is in a dreamland far away - where the mountains are made of beefy treats, the valleys are filled with tennis balls, and the puddles are just the right temperature. Why be in the rat race? It's a dog's life, after all.

· The SAM

fussy cycle of {*rep*

are *ITAL*

of *SLAN*

the first millenniu

Samsara STU

such as the *SA*

ZARA of a

nted} reincarnation

C 21° exts

TED ce during

BCE. The *»idea«* of

BBORN.

RIFS. TM

Samzara Regular ▪
Samzara Italic •

LA BOLDE VITA

TYPEFACE : GT SECTRA
DESIGNER : GRILLI TYPE
LOCATION : LUCERNE, SWITZERLAND; NEW YORK, US

PUBLISHED BY : GRILLI TYPE
CHRONOLOGY : N/A
RELEASE : 2013

LINK : HTTP://WWW.GRILLITYPE.COM/TYPEFACE/GT-SECTRA
STYLES : 30
CREDITS : DOMINIK HUBER, MARC KAPPELER/MOIRÉ & NOËL LEU/GRILLI TYPE (DESIGN), DOMINIK HUBER & GRILLI TYPE (SCRIPT EXTENSIONS), MARIA DOREULI, VASSILIS GEORGIOU & DONNY TRUONG (CONSULTING)

GT SECTRA IS A CONTEMPORARY SERIF TYPEFACE COMBINING THE CALLIGRAPHY OF THE BROAD NIB PEN WITH THE SHARPNESS OF THE SCALPEL KNIFE. IT IS THIS SHARPNESS THAT DEFINES ITS CONTEMPORARY LOOK. IT WAS ORIGINALLY DESIGNED FOR USE IN THE LONG-FORM JOURNALISM MAGAZINE “REPORTAGEN” AND HAS NOW EXPANDED TO THREE SUBFAMILIES: GT SECTRA, GT SECTRA FINE, AND GT SECTRA DISPLAY. THE FAMILY STANDS OUT FOR ITS HIGH LEGIBILITY WHILE RETAINING A UNIQUE VISUAL CHARACTER.

CAP HEIGHT

REGULAR – 290PT

X-HEIGHT

Ss

BASELINE

GT Sectra

REGULAR – 36PT

THE QUICK BROWN FOX
IT WOULD BE THE CHEE
IT'S A LOVELY DAY IN TH
AND THE PUNGENT ARO
PROMISE OF A SUMPTUC
THINKING ABOUT THE D
THE LAZY DOG REMAINS

REGULAR – 18PT

The quick brown fox jumps over a lazy dog. He didn't ha
it would be the cheeky thing to do. After all, he had a rep
It's a lovely day in the neighbourhood, with the sun shin
and the pungent aroma of fresh rubbish bins wafting thr
promise of a sumptuous meal. The sprightly fox rubs his
thinking about the delicious treasures he's about to dig i
the lazy dog remains unperturbed. With her long snout,
long black fur fluttering in the breeze, she is in a dreaml

REGULAR – 8PT

The quick brown fox jumps over a lazy dog. He didn't have to, but he thought it would be the cheeky thing to do. After all, he had a reputation to maintain. It's a lovely day in the neighbourhood, with the sun shining, the birds chirping, and the pungent aroma of fresh rubbish bins wafting through the air - the promise of a sumptuous meal. The sprightly fox rubs his paws together in glee, thinking about the delicious treasures he's about to dig into. Still in her spot, the lazy dog remains unperturbed. With her long snout, droopy jowls, and long black fur fluttering in the breeze, she is in a dreamland far away - where the mountains are made of beefy treats, the valleys are filled with tennis balls, and the puddles are just the right temperature. Why be in the rat race? It's a dog's life, after all.

GT Sectra

GT Sectra Fine

GT Sectra Display

R

Amazing Bookmark Calligraphy

Z

TYPEFACE : SIGURD
DESIGNER : LEÓN HUGUES
LOCATION : PARIS, FRANCE

PUBLISHED BY : BLAZE TYPE
CHRONOLOGY : 2020 - 2021
RELEASE : 2021

LINK : HTTPS://BLAZETYPE.EU/TYPEFACES/SIGURD
STYLES : 15 STYLES, 5 WEIGHTS, 3 SLANTS
CREDITS : MATTHIEU SALVAGGIO/BLAZE TYPE (COLLABORATION)

THE SIGURD FONT FAMILY WAS INSPIRED BY THE HERO OF THE NIBELUNGEN SAGA, SIEGFRIED. IT AIMS TO BE AN ELEGANT TYPEFACE THAT IS DEEPLY STRONG IN ITS DESIGN CONSTRUCTION, WHICH DRAWS FROM THE SHAPES OF SWORDS AND FEUDAL ARMOURS. ITS DESIGN PROCESS BEGAN FROM AN OLD SCRAP OF LETTERS FOUND IN AN OBSCURE SET OF EDA STORIES. WITH AN EXTREME ITALIC VERSION OF THE WORD "SIGURD" AS THE STARTING POINT, THE TYPEFACE CURRENTLY COMES IN SEVEN WEIGHTS AND TWO SETS OF MATCHING ITALICS WITH DIFFERENT ANGLES FOR A TOTAL OF 21 FONTS. CONTAINING A WIDE SET OF ALTERNATES, SWASHES, AND VARIOUS OPENTYPE FEATURES, SIGURD ALLOWS FOR EXPERIMENTATION AND ENABLES INCREDIBLE TYPE-FOCUSED DESIGNS SUCH AS HEADLINES, LOGOS, ALBUM COVERS, AND POSTERS.

CAP HEIGHT

REGULAR - 290PT

Ss

X-HEIGHT

BASELINE

Sigurd

REGULAR – 40PT

THE QUICK BROWN FOX
IT WOULD BE THE CHEE
IT'S A LOVELY DAY IN TH
AND THE PUNGENT ARO
PROMISE OF A SUMPTU
THINKING ABOUT THE D
THE LAZY DOG REMAIN
LONG BLACK FUR FLUT

REGULAR – 18PT

The quick brown fox jumps over a lazy dog. He didn't have to
it would be the cheeky thing to do. After all, he had a reputat
It's a lovely day in the neighbourhood, with the sun shining, t
and the pungent aroma of fresh rubbish bins wafting throug
promise of a sumptuous meal. The sprightly fox rubs his paw
thinking about the delicious treasures he's about to dig into. S
the lazy dog remains unperturbed. With her long snout, droo
long black fur fluttering in the breeze, she is in a dreamland
the mountains are made of beefy treats, the valleys are filled
and the puddles are just the right temperature. Why be in the
It's a dog's life, after all.

EDDAS

Grief And Tears

MOTTE

Rennzeug Vembrace Manifer

ENARME HELMS GORGETS

Crupper Handles Badded

SEHYNBALDS TABARD

Espalier Gorget Groin

MAIL GREAVE CUIRIE

Tows Surcoat Fence

S @

! a

% T

e

SIGURD

TYPEFACE : SIMULA
DESIGNER : SHARP TYPE
COUNTRY : NEW YORK & CALIFORNIA, US

PUBLISHED BY : SHARP TYPE
CHRONOLOGY : 2019
RELEASE : 2019

LINK : HTTPS://SHARPTYPE.CO/TYPEFACES/SIMULA/
STYLES : ROMAN, ITALIC

SIMULA IS THE DEBUT TYPEFACE OF ARTIST AND DESIGNER JUSTIN SLOANE. POSSESSING NO FORMAL TRAINING IN TYPEFACE DESIGN, JUSTIN'S STRONG SENSE OF TYPOGRAPHIC FORM IS COUPLED WITH AN EFFORTLESS NAÏVETÉ, RESULTING IN A TYPEFACE THAT IS BOTH FUNCTIONAL AND UNEXPECTED. THE RESULT OF 4 YEARS OF DRAWING AND REDRAWING, SIMULA BECAME AN ARTISTIC PRACTICE WITHIN ITSELF: A MECHANICAL RE-INTERPRETATION OF CALLIGRAPHIC FORM THAT FLOUTS CONVENTION WITH EVERY STROKE.

CAP HEIGHT

BOOK – 290PT

X-HEIGHT

Ss

BASELINE

Simula

BOOK – 36PT

THE QUICK BROWN FOX J
IT WOULD BE THE CHEEK
IT'S A LOVELY DAY IN THE
AND THE PUNGENT AROM
PROMISE OF A SUMPTUO
THINKING ABOUT THE DE
THE LAZY DOG REMAINS

BOOK – 18PT

The quick brown fox jumps over a lazy dog. He didn't ha
it would be the cheeky thing to do. After all, he had a rep
It's a lovely day in the neighbourhood, with the sun shini
and the pungent aroma of fresh rubbish bins wafting thr
promise of a sumptuous meal. The sprightly fox rubs his
thinking about the delicious treasures he's about to dig in
the lazy dog remains unperturbed. With her long snout,
long black fur fluttering in the breeze, she is in a dreamla

BOOK – 8PT

The quick brown fox jumps over a lazy dog. He didn't have to, but he thought it would be the cheeky thing to do. After all, he had a reputation to maintain. It's a lovely day in the neighbourhood, with the sun shining, the birds chirping, and the pungent aroma of fresh rubbish bins wafting through the air – the promise of a sumptuous meal. The sprightly fox rubs his paws together in glee, thinking about the delicious treasures he's about to dig into. Still in her spot, the lazy dog remains unperturbed. With her long snout, droopy jowls, and long black fur fluttering in the breeze, she is in a dreamland far away – where the mountains are made of beefy treats, the valleys are filled with tennis balls, and the puddles are just the right temperature. Why be in the rat race?
It's a dog's life, after all.

Æ 9

ffk ø e

£ fh

!!” ⊠

—…

ΣΩ[\]?

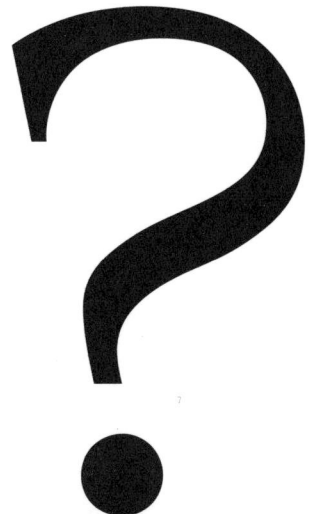

TYPEFACE : SLACK LIGHT
DESIGNER : DUE STUDIO
LOCATION : UK

PUBLISHED BY : TYPE DEPARTMENT
CHRONOLOGY : N/A
RELEASED IN : N/A

LINK : HTTPS://TYPE-DEPARTMENT.COM/COLLECTIONS/SERIF-FONTS/PRODUCTS/SLACK-LIGHT/
STYLES : 1

SLACK LIGHT IS A CONTEMPORARY SERIF TYPEFACE THAT FEATURES TIGHT APERTURES AND AN ELASTIC EFFECT ON THE SERIFS. IT SIMULATES THE MOVEMENT OF SLACKLINE WEBBING WHEN ONE IS WALKING, RUNNING, OR BALANCING ON IT. SLACK LIGHT IS CURVED, ROUND, ELEGANT, AND DECEPTIVELY CLASSICIST WHILE BEING STRAIGHT AND EDGY WITH ITS ALTERNATES. WITH 530+ GLYPHS AND A WIDE RANGE OF STYLISTIC SETS, THE TYPEFACE IS AVAILABLE IN ONE LIGHT WEIGHT.

CAP HEIGHT

LIGHT - 290PT

X-HEIGHT

Ss

BASELINE

Slack Light

LIGHT - 48PT

THE QUICK BROW
IT WOULD BE THE
IT'S A LOVELY DA
AND THE PUNGEN
PROMISE OF A SU
THINKING ABOUT
THE LAZY DOG RE
LONG BLACK FUR
THE MOUNTAINS

LIGHT - 8PT

The quick brown fox jumps over a lazy dog. He didn't have to, but he thought it would be the cheeky thing to do. After all, he had a reputation to maintain. It's a lovely day in the neighbourhood, with the sun shining, the birds chirping, and the pungent aroma of fresh rubbish bins wafting through the air - the promise of a sumptuous meal. The sprightly fox rubs his paws together in glee, thinking about the delicious treasures he's about to dig into. Still in her spot, the lazy dog remains unperturbed. With her long snout, droopy jowls, and long black fur fluttering in the breeze, she is in a dreamland far away - where the mountains are made of beefy treats, the valleys are filled with tennis balls, and the puddles are just the right temperature. Why be in the rat race? It's a dog's life, after all.

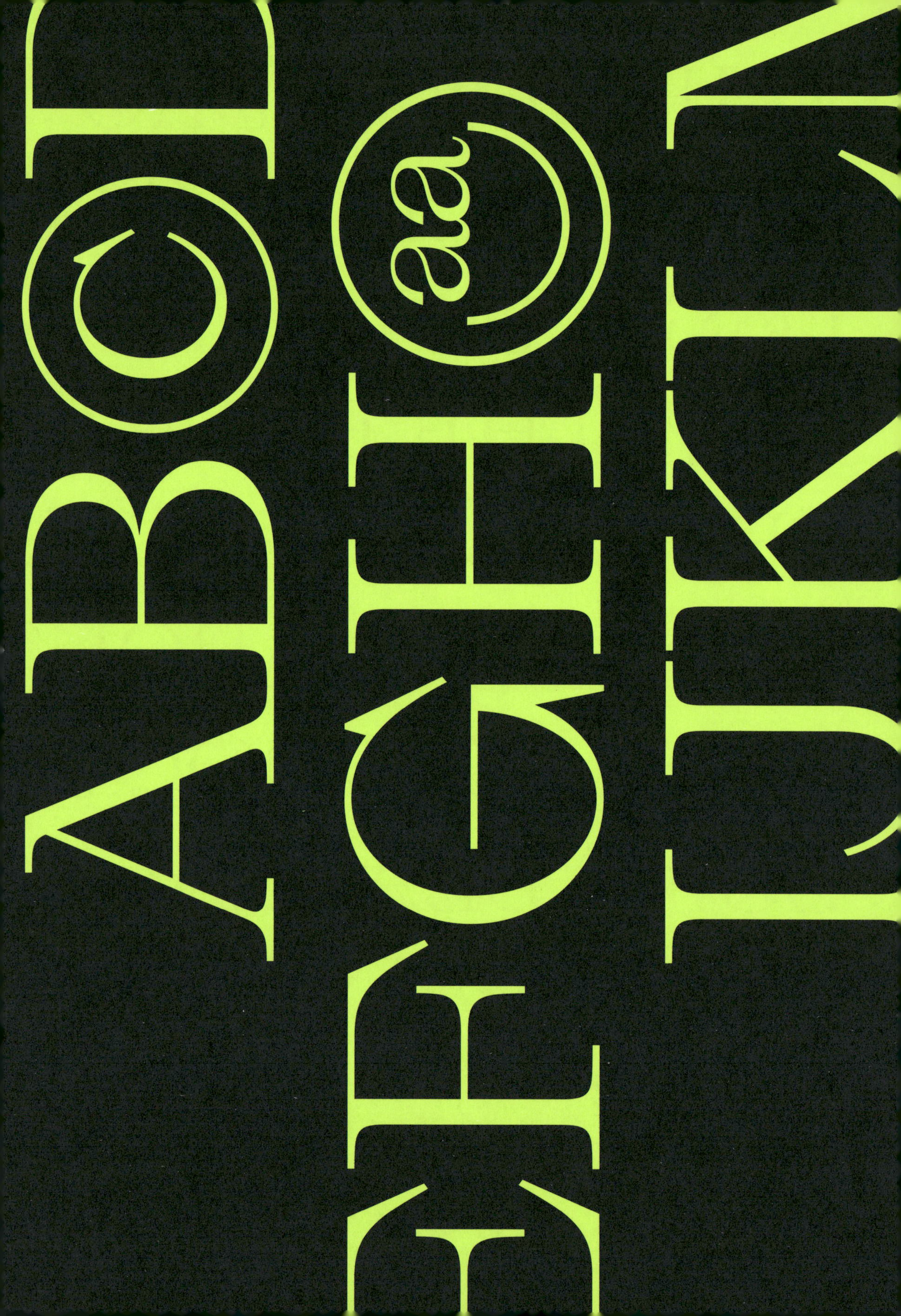

NOPQ
®STUV
WXYZ

TYPEFACE : FAIRE SPRIG
DESIGNER : FAIRE TYPE
LOCATION : NEW YORK, US

PUBLISHED BY : FAIRE TYPE
CHRONOLOGY : 2023
RELEASED IN : 2023

LINK : HTTPS://WWW.FAIRETYPE.COM/FONTS/SPRIG
STYLES : HAIRLINE, THIN, LIGHT, REGULAR, MEDIUM, BOLD, BLACK, SUPER, HAIRLINE ITALIC, THIN ITALIC, LIGHT ITALIC, REGULAR ITALIC, MEDIUM ITALIC, BOLD ITALIC, BLACK ITALIC, SUPER ITALIC

SPRIG IS A CONTEMPORARY SERIF TYPE FAMILY WITH ROUND, FRIENDLY DETAILS. INSPIRED BY EARLY VERSIONS OF CHELTENHAM BY BERTRAM GROSVENOR GOODHUE, IT BEGAN AS A REVIVAL BUT OVER TIME GREW AWAY FROM ITS ROOTS AND INTO A MORE MODERN, GEOMETRIC TYPEFACE. THE TYPE RETAINS ICONIC DETAILS FROM GOODHUE'S CHELTENHAM LIKE THE OPEN COUNTER "G" AND ROUND TEARDROP TERMINALS, BUT HAS UPDATED PROPORTIONS TO INCREASE LEGIBILITY AND USABILITY. A WIDE NUMBER OF OPENTYPE FEATURES PROVIDE ACCESS TO SPECIAL CHARACTERS LIKE SWASH CAPS, LIGATURES, AND ALTERNATE GLYPHS.

CAP HEIGHT

REGULAR – 290PT

X-HEIGHT

Ss

BASELINE

FAIRE Sprig

REGULAR – 48PT

THE QUICK BROWN FOX
IT WOULD BE THE CHEE
IT'S A LOVELY DAY IN TH
AND THE PUNGENT ARO
PROMISE OF A SUMPTUO
THINKING ABOUT THE D
THE LAZY DOG REMAINS
LONG BLACK FUR FLUTT

REGULAR – 10PT

The quick brown fox jumps over a lazy dog. He didn't have to, but he thought it would be the cheeky thing to do. After all, he had a reputation to maintain. It's a lovely day in the neighbourhood, with the sun shining, the birds chirping, and the pungent aroma of fresh rubbish bins wafting through the air - the promise of a sumptuous meal. The sprightly fox rubs his paws together in glee, thinking about the delicious treasures he's about to dig into. Still in her spot, the lazy dog remains unperturbed. With her long snout, droopy jowls, and long black fur fluttering in the breeze, she is in a dreamland far away - where the mountains are made of beefy treats, the valleys are filled with tennis balls, and the puddles are just the right temperature. Why be in the rat race? It's a dog's life, after all.

REGULAR – 8PT

The quick brown fox jumps over a lazy dog. He didn't have to, but he thought it would be the cheeky thing to do. After all, he had a reputation to maintain. It's a lovely day in the neighbourhood, with the sun shining, the birds chirping, and the pungent aroma of fresh rubbish bins wafting through the air - the promise of a sumptuous meal. The sprightly fox rubs his paws together in glee, thinking about the delicious treasures he's about to dig into. Still in her spot, the lazy dog remains unperturbed. With her long snout, droopy jowls, and long black fur fluttering in the breeze, she is in a dreamland far away - where the mountains are made of beefy treats, the valleys are filled with tennis balls, and the puddles are just the right temperature. Why be in the rat race? It's a dog's life, after all.

ct

c_t.ss07

Sprig

ditmas park

italic

23

Hairline *Italic*
Thin *Italic*
Light *Italic*
Regular *Italic*
Medium *Italic*
Bold *Italic*
Black *Italic*
Super *Italic*

Egyptian Mint
Capim Sudão
Thé des bois
Rosmarinus
Macadâmia

W
AT
ER

Sprig Hairline · OpenType Swashes

POWERBOAT
Powerboat
SPARROWHAWK
Sparrowhawk

POWERBOAT
Powerboat
SPARROWHAWK
Sparrowhawk

Sprig Hairline Italic · OpenType Swashes

TYPEFACE : STELLAGE
DESIGNER : SM FOUNDRY
LOCATION : APELDOORN, THE NETHERLANDS

PUBLISHED BY : SM FOUNDRY
CHRONOLOGY : 2018 - 2020
RELEASED IN : 2020

LINK : HTTPS://S-M.NU/TYPEFACES/STELLAGE
STYLES : DISPLAY, REGULAR, ITALIC, CONSTRUCTED, CONSTRUCTED ITALIC

STELLAGE IS A VERSATILE GEOMETRIC SERIF TYPEFACE WITH SQUARE AND TRIANGULAR SERIFS, INSPIRED BY THE VISUAL CULTURE OF POSTMODERN ARCHITECTURE AND DESIGN. YOU COULD IMAGINE EVERY CHARACTER OF STELLAGE AS A LITTLE BUILDING WHERE MODERN AND CLASSICAL SHAPES MEET. THE RESULT IS A SHARP SERIF THAT OFFERS GREAT LEGIBILITY IN SMALL SIZES WITH INTERESTING DETAILS AS A DISPLAY TYPEFACE.

CAP HEIGHT

REGULAR - 290PT

X-HEIGHT

Ss

BASELINE

Stellage

REGULAR - 36PT

THE QUICK BROWN FO
IT WOULD BE THE CH
IT'S A LOVELY DAY IN
AND THE PUNGENT A
PROMISE OF A SUMPT
THINKING ABOUT TH
THE LAZY DOG REMA
LONG BLACK FUR FLU
THE MOUNTAINS ARE
AND THE PUDDLES AR
IT'S A DOG'S LIFE, AFT

REGULAR - 10PT

The quick brown fox jumps over a lazy dog. He didn't have to, but he thought it would be the cheeky thing to do. After all, he had a reputation to maintain. It's a lovely day in the neighbourhood, with the sun shining, the birds chirping, and the pungent aroma of fresh rubbish bins wafting through the air - the promise of a sumptuous meal. The sprightly fox rubs his paws together in glee, thinking about the delicious treasures he's about to dig into. Still in her spot, the lazy dog remains unperturbed. With her long snout, droopy jowls, and long black fur fluttering in the breeze, she is in a dreamland far away - where the mountains are made of beefy treats, the valleys are filled with tennis balls, and the puddles are just the right temperature. Why be in the rat race? It's a dog's life, after all.

Regular, 45 pt / 50 pt.

Aa Bb Cc Dd Ee Ff Gg Hh Ii Jj
Kk Ll Mm Nn Oo Pp Qq Rr Ss Tt
Uu Vv Ww Xx Yy Zz & Æ ß @
0 1 2 3 4 5 6 7 8 9 :;., !?

Italic, 45 pt / 50 pt.

Aa Bb Cc Dd Ee Ff Gg Hh Ii Jj
Kk Ll Mm Nn Oo Pp Qq Rr Ss Tt
Uu Vv Ww Xx Yy Zz & Æ ß @
0 1 2 3 4 5 6 7 8 9 :;., !?

Constructed, 45 pt / 50 pt.

Aa Bb Cc Dd Ee Ff Gg Hh Ii Jj
Kk Ll Mm Nn Oo Pp Qq Rr Ss Tt
Uu Vv Ww Xx Yy Zz & Æ ß @
0 1 2 3 4 5 6 7 8 9 :;., !?

Italic, 45 pt / 50 pt.

Aa Bb Cc Dd Ee Ff Gg Hh Ii Jj
Kk Ll Mm Nn Oo Pp Qq Rr Ss Tt
Uu Vv Ww Xx Yy Zz & Æ ß @
0 1 2 3 4 5 6 7 8 9 :;., !?

der 950

eight 720

ht 486

AM

ne 0

nder -243

Stellage Family Overview

es

STELLAGE

1 Regular 2 *Italic*

3 Constructed 4 *Italic*

5 Display

TYPEFACE : GT SUPER
DESIGNER : GRILLI TYPE
LOCATION : LUCERNE, SWITZERLAND; NEW YORK, US

PUBLISHED BY : GRILLI TYPE
CHRONOLOGY : N/A
RELEASED IN : 2018

LINK : HTTPS://WWW.GT-SUPER.COM/
STYLES : 20
CREDITS : NOËL LEU/GRILLI TYPE, MIRCO SCHIAVONE & RETO MOSER

GT SUPER IS THE RESULT OF AN EXTENSIVE INVESTIGATION INTO DISPLAY SERIF TYPEFACES FROM THE 1970'S AND 1980'S. IT FOCUSES ON THE EXPRESSIVE AND IDIOSYNCRATIC NATURE OF CALLIGRAPHIC MOTIONS, AND CAPTURES THEM IN A WELL-BALANCED SYSTEM OF TEXT AND DISPLAY STYLES.

CAP HEIGHT

REGULAR – 290PT

X-HEIGHT

Ss

BASELINE

GT Super

REGULAR – 36PT

THE QUICK BROWN FOX
IT WOULD BE THE CHE
IT'S A LOVELY DAY IN T
AND THE PUNGENT ARO
PROMISE OF A SUMPTU
THINKING ABOUT THE
THE LAZY DOG REMAIN

REGULAR – 18PT

The quick brown fox jumps over a lazy dog. He didn't
it would be the cheeky thing to do. After all, he had a
It's a lovely day in the neighbourhood, with the sun s
and the pungent aroma of fresh rubbish bins wafting
promise of a sumptuous meal. The sprightly fox rubs
thinking about the delicious treasures he's about to d
the lazy dog remains unperturbed. With her long sno
long black fur fluttering in the breeze, she is in a drea

REGULAR – 8PT

The quick brown fox jumps over a lazy dog. He didn't have to, but he thought it would be the cheeky thing to do. After all, he had a reputation to maintain. It's a lovely day in the neighbourhood, with the sun shining, the birds chirping, and the pungent aroma of fresh rubbish bins wafting through the air - the promise of a sumptuous meal. The sprightly fox rubs his paws together in glee, thinking about the delicious treasures he's about to dig into. Still in her spot, the lazy dog remains unperturbed. With her long snout, droopy jowls, and long black fur fluttering in the breeze, she is in a dreamland far away - where the mountains are made of beefy treats, the valleys are filled with tennis balls, and the puddles are just the right temperature. Why be in the rat race? It's a dog's life, after all.

W

E

er

TYPEFACE : SWEAR
DESIGNER : OH NO TYPE CO.
LOCATION : CALIFORNIA, US

PUBLISHED BY : OH NO TYPE CO.
CHRONOLOGY : N/A
RELEASED IN : 2020

LINK : HTTPS://OHNOTYPE.CO/FONTS/SWEAR
STYLES : 6 WEIGHTS, 4 OPTICAL SIZES (SWEAR TEXT, SWEAR DECK, SWEAR DISPLAY, SWEAR BANNER), 2 ITALICS, TOTALLING 72 STYLES

THE SWEAR FAMILY SPANS FOUR OPTICAL SIZES WITH SIX WEIGHTS IN ROMAN, ITALIC, AND “CILATI” (REVERSE-CONTRAST ITALIC) FOR A TOTAL OF 72 STYLES. ITS DESIGN WAS INSTIGATED BY PRACTICING BRUSH ROTATIONS WITH A FLAT BRUSH, AND INSPIRED BY THE DEFT BRUSH SKILLS OF THE DESIGNERS' FRIENDS VINCENT DE BOER, JULIEN PRIEZ AND GEN RAMIREZ.

CAP HEIGHT

REGULAR – 290PT

X-HEIGHT

Ss

BASELINE

REGULAR – 36PT

THE QUICK BROWN FOX JU
IT WOULD BE THE CHEEK
IT'S A LOVELY DAY IN THE
AND THE PUNGENT AROM
PROMISE OF A SUMPTUOU
THINKING ABOUT THE DE
THE LAZY DOG REMAINS U
LONG BLACK FUR FLUTTE
THE MOUNTAINS ARE MA
AND THE PUDDLES ARE JU
IT'S A DOG'S LIFE, AFTER A

REGULAR – 16PT

The quick brown fox jumps over a lazy dog. He didn't have
it would be the cheeky thing to do. After all, he had a repu
It's a lovely day in the neighbourhood, with the sun shinin
and the pungent aroma of fresh rubbish bins wafting thro
promise of a sumptuous meal. The sprightly fox rubs his
thinking about the delicious treasures he's about to dig in
the lazy dog remains unperturbed. With her long snout, d
long black fur fluttering in the breeze, she is in a dreamla

Helloh
Hi There
Heeey
What's up
Hiiiiii
Hellooooo
Heyyyyy
G'Day
How r yuuu

8 3

97

0 5

124

TYPEFACE	:	TARTUFFO
DESIGNER	:	BOUK RA
LOCATION	:	MONTPELLIER, FRANCE

PUBLISHED BY	:	LIFT TYPE
CHRONOLOGY	:	N/A
RELEASED IN	:	2021

LINK	:	HTTPS://WWW.LIFT-TYPE.FR/SHOP/TYPOGRAPHY/TARTUFFO/
STYLES	:	THIN, LIGHT, REGULAR, MEDIUM, BOLD, THIN ITALIC, LIGHT ITALIC, ITALIC, MEDIUM ITALIC, BOLD ITALIC
CREDITS	:	BOUK RA (DESIGN)

TARTUFFO IS A FRESH TYPEFACE INSPIRED BY MANY CHARACTERS FROM VARIOUS LITERATURE PIECES. ITS NAME COMES FROM A FAMOUS CHARACTER CALLED TARTUFFE FROM "TARTUFFE OR THE IMPERSONATOR" BY THE FRENCH PLAYWRIGHT, ACTOR AND POET, MOLIÈRE. THE FONT WAS ALSO INFLUENCED BY THE "TARTUFO DI PIZZO", WHICH IS A TRADITIONAL ITALIAN DESSERT WITH A CHOCOLATE BASE. TARTUFFO IS AS BAD-LOOKING AND BITTER AS THE HYPOCRITES IN LITERARY WORKS - HOWEVER, IT IS SUCCULENT, FLEXIBLE, AND SWEET - THANKS TO ITS FLUID TEXTURE IN ALL THE DETAILS!

CAP HEIGHT

REGULAR - 290PT

X-HEIGHT

Tt

BASELINE

Tartuffo

REGULAR – 36PT

THE QUICK BROWN FOX JUM
IT WOULD BE THE CHEEKY T
IT'S A LOVELY DAY IN THE N
AND THE PUNGENT AROMA
PROMISE OF A SUMPTUOUS
THINKING ABOUT THE DEL
THE LAZY DOG REMAINS UN
LONG BLACK FUR FLUTTER
THE MOUNTAINS ARE MAD
AND THE PUDDLES ARE JUS
IT'S A DOG'S LIFE, AFTER AL

REGULAR – 10PT

The quick brown fox jumps over a lazy dog. He didn't have to, but he thought it would be the cheeky thing to do. After all, he had a reputation to maintain. It's a lovely day in the neighbourhood, with the sun shining, the birds chirping, and the pungent aroma of fresh rubbish bins wafting through the air - the promise of a sumptuous meal. The sprightly fox rubs his paws together in glee, thinking about the delicious treasures he's about to dig into. Still in her spot, the lazy dog remains unperturbed. With her long snout, droopy jowls, and long black fur fluttering in the breeze, she is in a dreamland far away - where the mountains are made of beefy treats, the valleys are filled with tennis balls, and the puddles are just the right temperature. Why be in the rat race? It's a dog's life, after all.

SUGAR⅔*

±G289 &

{COLORE

§DELI©E

G@TEUX

CROISSAN

PASTRY¶

CANNES»

R}•◊№83®

→SLIC€R≠

#MILK™

T °FRAISE

PRO
MOZ
CURA
REEXQ

NGER
ZARELLA
SSOW
UISHE

TYPEFACE : TECHNIK SERIF
DESIGNER : SAMUEL ČARNOKÝ
LOCATION : SLOVAKIA, KYSAK

PUBLISHED BY : CARNOKYTYPE
CHRONOLOGY : 2012 – 2013
RELEASED IN : 2013

LINK : HTTPS://CARNOKYTYPE.COM/FONTS/TECHNIK_SERIF
STYLES : 4 STYLES • 4 WEIGHTS, 25 / 50 / 100 / 200

TECHNIK SERIF IS A CONSTRUCTED TYPEFACE THAT IS ALMOST STRICTLY DESIGNED FROM BASIC GEOMETRICAL ELEMENTS CONSISTING OF MAINLY CIRCLES, SQUARES, AND DIAGONAL SHAPES. ANOTHER CHARACTERISTIC IS THE CONNECTION OF DIAGONALS, VERTICALS AND DIAGONALS, AS WELL AS SEVERAL CIRCLE SHAPES TOUCHING EACH OTHER AT ONE POINT. THESE FEATURES GIVE THE TYPEFACE AN ORIGINAL LOOK, AND PREVENT THE PROBLEMATIC DARK PLACES IN SOME LETTERS. TECHNIK IS NOT DESIGNED AS A TEXT TYPEFACE; IT IS RECOMMENDED MAINLY FOR DISPLAY TYPOGRAPHY. YOU CAN USE IT WHENEVER YOU NEED THE TECHNICAL ASPECT OF THE CONSTRUCTED TYPEFACES TO LOOK LESS COLD AND MORE FRIENDLY.

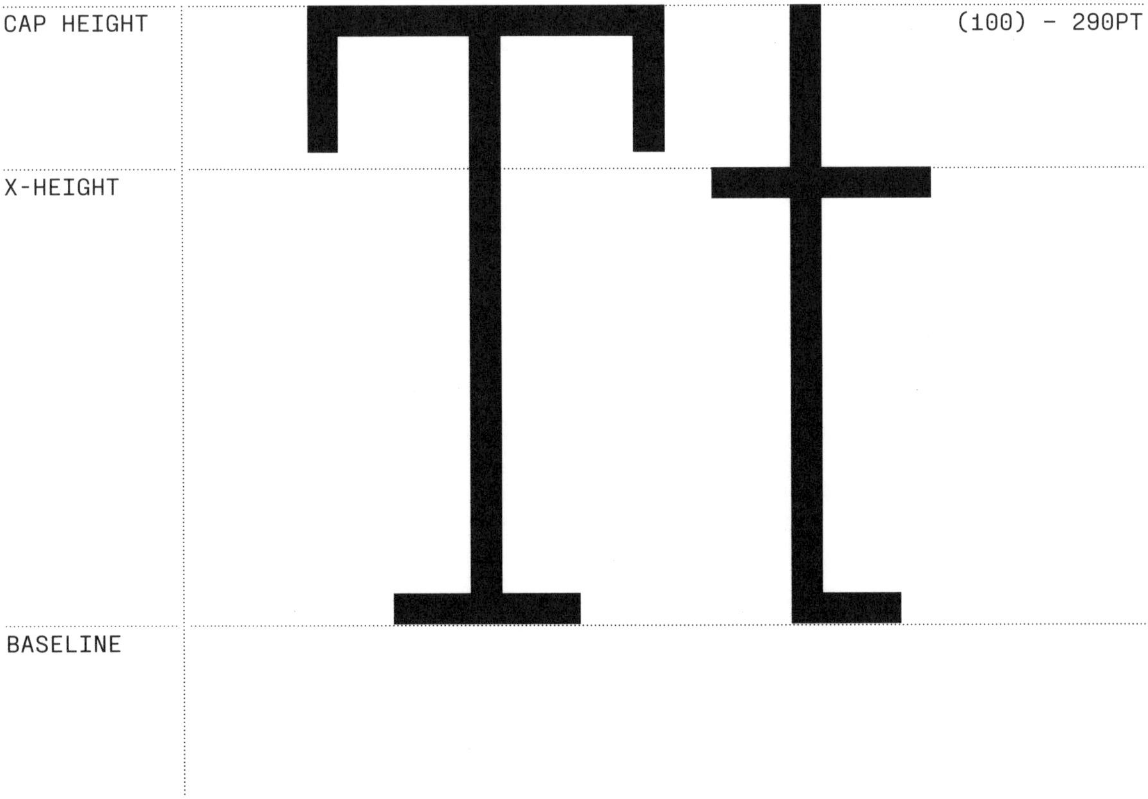

Technik Serif

(100) - 20PT

THE QUICK BROWN FOX JUMPS OVER A LAZY DOG.
IT WOULD BE THE CHEEKY THING TO DO. AFTER AL
IT'S A LOVELY DAY IN THE NEIGHBOURHOOD, WITH
AND THE PUNGENT AROMA OF FRESH RUBBISH BIN
PROMISE OF A SUMPTUOUS MEAL. THE SPRIGHTLY
THINKING ABOUT THE DELICIOUS TREASURES HE'S
THE LAZY DOG REMAINS UNPERTURBED. WITH HE
LONG BLACK FUR FLUTTERING IN THE BREEZE, SHE
THE MOUNTAINS ARE MADE OF BEEFY TREATS, TH
AND THE PUDDLES ARE JUST THE RIGHT TEMPERAT
IT'S A DOG'S LIFE, AFTER ALL.

(100) - 14PT

The quick brown fox jumps over a lazy dog. He didn't have to, but h
it would be the cheeky thing to do. After all, he had a reputation to r
It's a lovely day in the neighbourhood, with the sun shining, the bir
and the pungent aroma of fresh rubbish bins wafting through the a
promise of a sumptuous meal. The sprightly fox rubs his paws toge
thinking about the delicious treasures he's about to dig into. Still in
the lazy dog remains unperturbed. With her long snout, droopy jowl
long black fur fluttering in the breeze, she is in a dreamland far awa
the mountains are made of beefy treats, the valleys are filled with te
and the puddles are just the right temperature. Why be in the rat ra
It's a dog's life, after all.

(100) - 10PT

The quick brown fox jumps over a lazy dog. He didn't have to, but he thought
it would be the cheeky thing to do. After all, he had a reputation to maintain.
It's a lovely day in the neighbourhood, with the sun shining, the birds chirping,
and the pungent aroma of fresh rubbish bins wafting through the air - the
promise of a sumptuous meal. The sprightly fox rubs his paws together in glee,
thinking about the delicious treasures he's about to dig into. Still in her spot,
the lazy dog remains unperturbed. With her long snout, droopy jowls, and
long black fur fluttering in the breeze, she is in a dreamland far away - where
the mountains are made of beefy treats, the valleys are filled with tennis balls,
and the puddles are just the right temperature. Why be in the rat race?
It's a dog's life, after all.

PREDNÁŠKY

TBČK

BAZ
MEG

…LÉRIA

#TABAČKA
KOŠICE

W…RKSHO…

TECHNIK
SERIF
TYPEFACE

K… SÁLA

#MI
ŠTE

CAFÉ & BAR?

Technik

GEOMETRIC

Technik

CONSTRUCTION

Technik

SACRED
GEOMETRY
MYSTERIUM
COSMOGRAPHICUM
TEMENOS

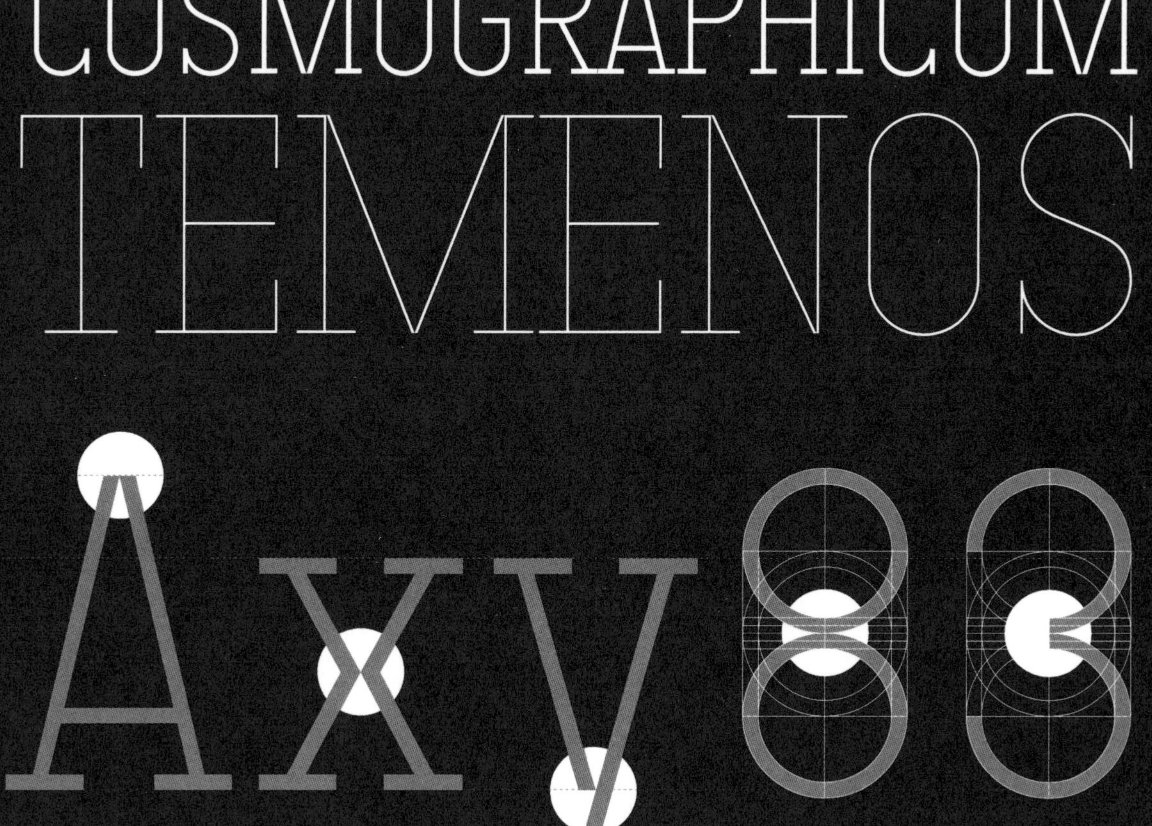

TYPEFACE : TESSERACT
DESIGNER : PRODUCTION TYPE
LOCATION : PARIS, FRANCE; SHANGHAI, CHINA

PUBLISHED BY : PRODUCTION TYPE
CHRONOLOGY : 2015 - 2020
RELEASED IN : 2020

LINK : HTTPS://WWW.PRODUCTIONTYPE.COM/COLLECTION/TESSERACT_COLLECTION
STYLES : 2 FAMILIES (OPTICAL STYLES), 20 STYLES; 5 WEIGHTS; ROMAN & ITALIC
CREDITS : JEAN-BAPTISTE LEVÉE (DESIGN), MARION SENDRAL (CYRILLIC), ILYA RUDERMAN & YURY OSTROMENTSKY (CONSULTING)

CRISP AND SERRATED, TESSERACT IS A STUDY IN MODERNITY AND RESTRAINT. AS THE TYPEFACE PLUNGED INTO CLASSICAL REFERENCES, IT EARNED ITS CONTEMPORANEITY THROUGH WHETTED ENDINGS AND CONSTRAINED CURVES, LENDING A FOCUSED ASPECT TO TEXTS AND TITLES. WITH OPTICAL SIZES FOR TEXT AND A DISPLAY, TESSERACT SHIMMERS ACROSS MEDIA. THE DISPLAY SIZE PLAYS THE WIDE APERTURE AND X-HEIGHT CARD, WITH CHISELLED TERMINALS AND SEE-THROUGH COUNTERSPACE. ITS TEXT SIZE IS QUIETER, WITH A FIRM AND STURDY STRUCTURE FOR IMMERSIVE READING, WHILE THE MATCHING ITALICS DANCE A VIBRANT STACCATO AND COMPLETE THE FAMILY.

CAP HEIGHT

REGULAR – 290PT

Tt

X-HEIGHT

BASELINE

Tesseract

REGULAR – 36PT

THE QUICK BROWN FOX
IT WOULD BE THE CHEE
IT'S A LOVELY DAY IN T
AND THE PUNGENT ARO
PROMISE OF A SUMPTU
THINKING ABOUT THE I
THE LAZY DOG REMAIN
LONG BLACK FUR FLUT
THE MOUNTAINS ARE M
AND THE PUDDLES ARE
IT'S A DOG'S LIFE, AFTE

REGULAR – 10PT

The quick brown fox jumps over a lazy dog. He didn't have to, but he thought it would be the cheeky thing to do. After all, he had a reputation to maintain. It's a lovely day in the neighbourhood, with the sun shining, the birds chirping, and the pungent aroma of fresh rubbish bins wafting through the air - the promise of a sumptuous meal. The sprightly fox rubs his paws together in glee, thinking about the delicious treasures he's about to dig into. Still in her spot, the lazy dog remains unperturbed. With her long snout, droopy jowls, and long black fur fluttering in the breeze, she is in a dreamland far away - where the mountains are made of beefy treats, the valleys are filled with tennis balls, and the puddles are just the right temperature. Why be in the rat race? It's a dog's life, after all.

Mode
Rest
Cr
Serr

rnity
raint
isp
ated

TYPEFACE	:	FT THESAURUS	378
DESIGNER	:	FUERTE TYPE	
LOCATION	:	DUBAI, UAE; COLONIA, URUGUAY	

PUBLISHED BY	:	FUERTE TYPE
CHRONOLOGY	:	2017 - 2022
RELEASED IN	:	2022

LINK	:	HTTPS://WWW.FUERTETYPE.COM/TYPEFACES/THESAURUS/
STYLES	:	TEXT: REGULAR, REGULAR ITALIC, MEDIUM, MEDIUM ITALIC, BOLD, BOLD ITALIC, BLACK, BLACK ITALIC DISPLAY: REGULAR, REGULAR ITALIC, MEDIUM, MEDIUM ITALIC, BOLD, BOLD ITALIC, BLACK, BLACK ITALIC

THESAURUS WAS INSPIRED BY THE TYPOGRAPHIC HISTORY OF THE CITY OF GENEVA, BASED ON THE METAL TYPES THAT ROBERT ESTIENNE BROUGHT FROM PARIS, WHICH WERE USED BY HIS SON, HENRI II ESTIENNE, FOR PRINTING THE FAMOUS "THESAURUS LINGUAE GRAECAE" BOOK IN 1572. THE TYPEFACE BLENDS FEATURES OF THE ORIGINAL METAL TYPES USED BY THE ESTIENNE FAMILY WITH CONTEMPORARY CHARACTERISTICS SUCH AS A LARGE X-HEIGHT, NARROWER FORMS, AND INCREASED MODULATION. UNLIKE THE ORIGINAL TYPES, THESAURUS GREW TO BECOME A SUPER-FAMILY OF 16 FONTS, RESULTING IN A VERSATILE TYPEFACE WITH A RATIONAL FLAVOUR THAT BRIDGES PAST AND PRESENT.

CAP HEIGHT

REGULAR – 290PT

Tt

X-HEIGHT

BASELINE

FT Thesaurus

THE QUICK BROW
TO, BUT HE THOU
IT WOULD BE THE
UTATION TO MAI
IT'S A LOVELY DAY
ING, THE BIRDS C
AND THE PUNGEN
THROUGH THE AI
PROMISE OF A SU

1.Regular
2.Regular Italic
3.Medium
4.Medium Italic
5.Bold
6.Bold Italic
7.Black
8.Black Italic
.....Thesaurus......

Q

TYPEFACE	:	TOBIAS
DESIGNER	:	DISPLAAY TYPE FOUNDRY
LOCATION	:	PRAGUE, CZECH REPUBLIC

PUBLISHED BY	:	DISPLAAY TYPE FOUNDRY
CHRONOLOGY	:	2018 – 2023
RELEASED IN	:	2019

LINK	:	HTTPS://DISPLAAY.NET/TYPEFACE/TOBIAS
STYLES	:	8 WEIGHTS, 16 STYLES + A VARIABLE FONT
CREDITS	:	MARTIN VÁCHA (DESIGN), KRISTÍNA JANDOVÁ (DESIGN ASSISTANCE, SPACING & KERNING)

TOBIAS IS A SERIF TYPEFACE WITH A BAROQUE AND TRANSITIONAL APPEARANCE. ITS WEIGHT STRESS IS DIAGONAL AS PER OLD STYLE OR RENAISSANCE TYPEFACES, WHILE ITS X-HEIGHT IS HIGHER THAN USUAL AND ITS CONNECTION ON STEMS IS NOT SMOOTH (ARCHES ARE PUNCHED INTO STEMS). TOBIAS STANDS NEXT TO ITS BROTHER TEODOR AND SISTER RECKLESS. AS IT ORIGINATES FROM BAROQUE ROOTS, APPROPRIATE TERMINALS ARE MADE OUT OF DROPS AND EARS. THE TYPEFACE ALSO INCLUDES NUMEROUS ALTERNATES WHICH PLAY WITH DIFFERENT DIRECTIONS OF THE SERIFS.

REGULAR – 290PT

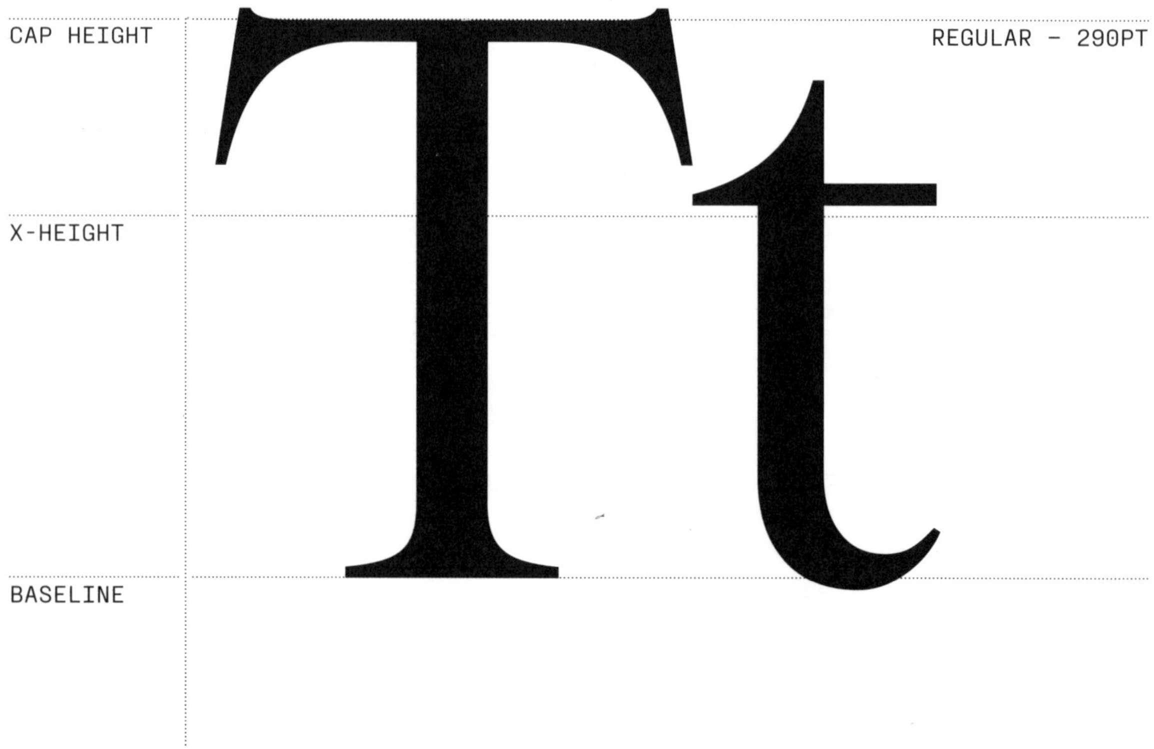

Tobias

THE QUICK BROWN
IT WOULD BE THE
IT'S A LOVELY DAY
AND THE PUNGENT
PROMISE OF A SUM
THINKING ABOUT T
THE LAZY DOG REM
LONG BLACK FUR F
THE MOUNTAINS A
AND THE PUDDLES
IT'S A DOG'S LIFE, A

AäBbCcDdEeFfGgHh
IiJjKkLlMmNnØoPpQqRr
ŞsTtUuVvWwXxYyZz

1234567890
&?!
[(ɑaa, CcGSs, du,
g, grt, KkR, M)]

T
TOB
TOBIAS

AäB

¥ 4 S

k&

bC,

sGg

TT

TYPEFACE : TT TRICKS
DESIGNER : TYPETYPE.ORG
LOCATION : SAINT PETERSBURG, RUSSIA

PUBLISHED BY : TYPETYPE.ORG
CHRONOLOGY : N/A
RELEASED IN : 2018

LINK : HTTPS://TYPETYPE.ORG/FONTS/TT-TRICKS/
STYLES : 12

TT TRICKS IS A MODERN SERIF TYPE FAMILY WITH AN EMPHASISED, BUSINESS-LIKE NATURE. THE ORIGINAL IDEA BEHIND IT WAS TO CREATE A DAILY PLANNER TYPEFACE. THIS LED TO MANY STYLISTIC DECISIONS, LIKE LARGE AND ASYMMETRICAL SERIFS, LOW-CONTRAST STROKES, AND A STENCIL SET. DESPITE THE LARGE NUMBER OF EXPRESSIVE DETAILS, THE TYPEFACE LOOKS GREAT IN BOTH SMALL POINT SIZES AND LARGE TEXT ARRAYS.

CAP HEIGHT

REGULAR - 290PT

Tt

X-HEIGHT

BASELINE

TT Tricks

REGULAR - 40PT

THE QUICK BROWN FO
IT WOULD BE THE CHE
IT'S A LOVELY DAY IN T
AND THE PUNGENT AR
PROMISE OF A SUMPTU
THINKING ABOUT THE

REGULAR - 16PT

The quick brown fox jumps over a lazy dog. He didn't have t
it would be the cheeky thing to do. After all, he had a reputa
It's a lovely day in the neighbourhood, with the sun shining,
and the pungent aroma of fresh rubbish bins wafting throug
promise of a sumptuous meal. The sprightly fox rubs his pa
thinking about the delicious treasures he's about to dig into
the lazy dog remains unperturbed. With her long snout, dro
long black fur fluttering in the breeze, she is in a dreamland
the mountains are made of beefy treats, the valleys are fille
and the puddles are just the right temperature. Why be in th
It's a dog's life, after all.

REGULAR - 8PT

The quick brown fox jumps over a lazy dog. He didn't have to, but he thought it would be the cheeky thing to do. After all, he had a reputation to maintain. It's a lovely day in the neighbourhood, with the sun shining, the birds chirping, and the pungent aroma of fresh rubbish bins wafting through the air - the promise of a sumptuous meal. The sprightly fox rubs his paws together in glee, thinking about the delicious treasures he's about to dig into. Still in her spot, the lazy dog remains unperturbed. With her long snout, droopy jowls, and long black fur fluttering in the breeze, she is in a dreamland far away - where the mountains are made of beefy treats, the valleys are filled with tennis balls, and the puddles are just the right temperature. Why be in the rat race? It's a dog's life, after all.

Æ&ﬆï

†1936

Sgłủ~í

£¾¡ĳø

TT Tricks

TypeType

TYPEFACE	:	KOMETA VICTOR SERIF	392
DESIGNER	:	KOMETA TYPEFACES	
LOCATION	:	BRNO, CZECH REPUBLIC	

PUBLISHED BY	:	KOMETA TYPEFACES
CHRONOLOGY	:	2019 - PRESENT
RELEASED IN	:	2019

LINK	:	HTTPS://WWW.KOMETA.XYZ/TYPEFACES/VICTOR-SERIF/
STYLES	:	HAIRLINE-BLACK + ITALICS, TOTALLING 16 STYLES

VICTOR SERIF, THE FIRST SERIF FACE COMMERCIALLY AVAILABLE BY KOMETA, PAYS HOMAGE TO THE NOW UBIQUITOUS ICON OF NEWSPAPER TYPE THAT CAME TO BE AN INSEPARABLE BACKBONE OF MODERN DESKTOP PUBLISHING. NAMED AFTER VICTOR LARDENT, THE ARTIST TASKED WITH THE CREATION OF TIMES NEW ROMAN, THIS NO-FRILLS TAKE ON THE TRANSITIONAL GENRE WITH SUPPORING LATIN AND CRYLLIC WALKS A THIN LINE OF TYPE EQUALLY POISED BOTH FOR DISPLAY AND TEXT SETTINGS - ALL WHILST MANAGING TO REMAIN MATTER-OF-FACT.

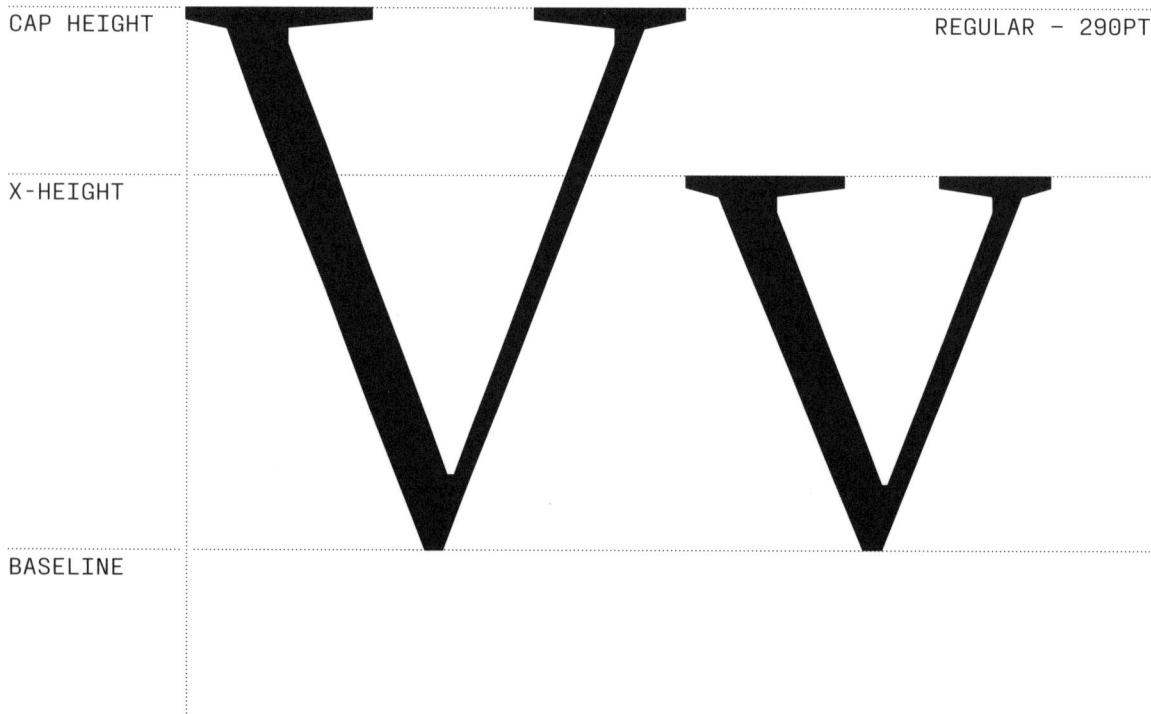

CAP HEIGHT

REGULAR - 290PT

X-HEIGHT

Vv

BASELINE

KOMETA Victor Serif

REGULAR – 36PT

THE QUICK BROWN

IT WOULD BE THE C

IT'S A LOVELY DAY I

AND THE PUNGENT

PROMISE OF A SUM

THINKING ABOUT T

THE LAZY DOG REM

LONG BLACK FUR F

REGULAR – 10PT

The quick brown fox jumps over a lazy dog. He didn't have to, but he thought it would be the cheeky thing to do. After all, he had a reputation to maintain. It's a lovely day in the neighbourhood, with the sun shining, the birds chirping, and the pungent aroma of fresh rubbish bins wafting through the air – the promise of a sumptuous meal. The sprightly fox rubs his paws together in glee, thinking about the delicious treasures he's about to dig into. Still in her spot, the lazy dog remains unperturbed. With her long snout, droopy jowls, and long black fur fluttering in the breeze, she is in a dreamland far away – where the mountains are made of beefy treats, the valleys are filled with tennis balls, and the puddles are just the right temperature. Why be in the rat race? It's a dog's life, after all.

28

Victor Serif Latin

28

(2019)

28

AaBbCcDdEeFfGg
0123456789 etc.

250 180 130 60

Ŗ Ŗ Ŗ Ŗ

T

28

Виктор Сериф Кириллица

28

(2023)

60 130 180 250

я Я Я Я

28

АаБбВвГгДдЕе и прочее...

8 Latin

In the strictest sense, the Victorian era covers the duration of Victoria's reign as Queen of the United Kingdom of Great Britain and Ireland, from her accession on 20 June 1837—after the death of her uncle, William IV—until her death on 22 January 1901, after which she was succeeded by her eldest son, Edward VII. Her reign lasted for 63 years and seven months, a longer period than any of her predecessors. The term 'Victorian' was in contemporaneous usage to describe the era. The era has also been understood in a more extensive sense as a period that possessed sensibilities and

8 Cyrillic

Викторианская эпоха — период правления Виктории, королевы Великобритании и Ирландии, а также императрицы Индии, длившийся с 1837 по 1901 год. Викторианская эпоха представляется неоднородно, поскольку характеризуется стремительными изменениями во многих сферах жизни общества: технологические, демографические сдвиги, изменения политического и социального восприятия. Такие активные и постоянные перемены в сфере экономической и духовной жизни обуславливались

TYPEFACE	:	VISCONTE
DESIGNER	:	ZETAFONTS TYPE FOUNDRY
LOCATION	:	FLORENCE, ITALY

PUBLISHED BY	:	ZETAFONTS TYPE FOUNDRY
CHRONOLOGY	:	2023
RELEASED IN	:	2023

LINK	:	HTTPS://ZETAFONTS.COM/VISCONTE
STYLES	:	1
CREDITS	:	DESINA GRAPHIC DESIGN FESTIVAL (CLIENT)

VISCONTE IS A VARIANT OF THE CALVINO TYPEFACE FAMILY, DEVELOPED AS A BRANDING FONT FOR THE 2023 DESINA GRAPHIC DESIGN FESTIVAL. IT TAKES THE ORIGINAL DESIGN OF THE CALVINO TYPEFACE INTO THE "BRUTAL SERIF" TERRITORY, EXPANDING SPIKY SERIFS AND CREATING UNEXPECTED DISTORTIONS AND CONNECTIONS. ITS NAME IS DERIVED FROM ITALO CALVINO'S FAMOUS NOVEL "IL VISCONTE DIMEZZATO" AND USES THE LOWERCASE LETTER "I" AS A WAY TO EVOKE ITS TITULAR CHARACTER WHO WAS SPLIT INTO TWO BY A CANNONBALL. RAW AND UNAPOLOGETIC, THIS VARIANT HAS ALL THE RUTHLESS FASCINATION OF THE ITALIAN MIDDLE AGES, AND IS WELL SUITED FOR EDITORIAL HEADLINES, POSTERS, BOOK COVERS, AND OTHER ATTENTION-GRABBING DESIGNS.

Visconte

BLACK – 48PT

THE QUICK BROWN
IT WOULD BE THE
IT'S A LOVELY DAY
AND THE PUNGENT
PROMISE OF A SUM
THINKING ABOUT T
THE LAZY DOG RE
LONG BLACK FUR F
THE MOUNTAINS A

BLACK – 8PT

The quick brown fox jumps over a lazy dog. He didn't have to, but he thought it would be the cheeky thing to do. After all, he had a reputation to maintain. It's a lovely day in the neighbourhood, with the sun shining, the birds chirping, and the pungent aroma of fresh rubbish bins wafting through the air - the promise of a sumptuous meal. The sprightly fox rubs his paws together in glee, thinking about the delicious treasures he's about to dig into. Still in her spot, the lazy dog remains unperturbed. With her long snout, droopy jowls, and long black fur fluttering in the breeze, she is in a dreamland far away - where the mountains are made of beefy treats, the valleys are filled with tennis balls, and the puddles are just the right temperature. Why be in the rat race? It's a dog's life, after all.

á Q

c

4 iii

&

E
y
d
g
£

TYPEFACE : F37 WICKLOW
DESIGNER : F37®
LOCATION : MANCHESTER, UK

400

PUBLISHED BY : F37®
CHRONOLOGY : 2020
RELEASED IN : 2020

LINK : HTTPS://F37FOUNDRY.COM/FONTS/F37-WICKLOW
STYLES : 6 WEIGHTS WITH MATCHING OBLIQUES, TOTALLING 12 STYLES

THE STARTING POINT FOR F37 WICKLOW WAS IRISH SCULPTOR MICHAEL BIGGS' INTRICATE LETTER CARVINGS ON THE ARBOUR HILL MEMORIAL IN DUBLIN. BIGGS' "GAELIC ALPHABET" MIXES WONDERFUL GEOMETRIC SHAPES AND F37 WICKLOW REFLECTS THIS BY COMBINING SHARP, TRIANGULAR SERIFS AND DIAMOND TITTLES WITH CIRCULAR FORMS. IT IS A TYPEFACE DRIVEN BY VISUAL CONTRAST.

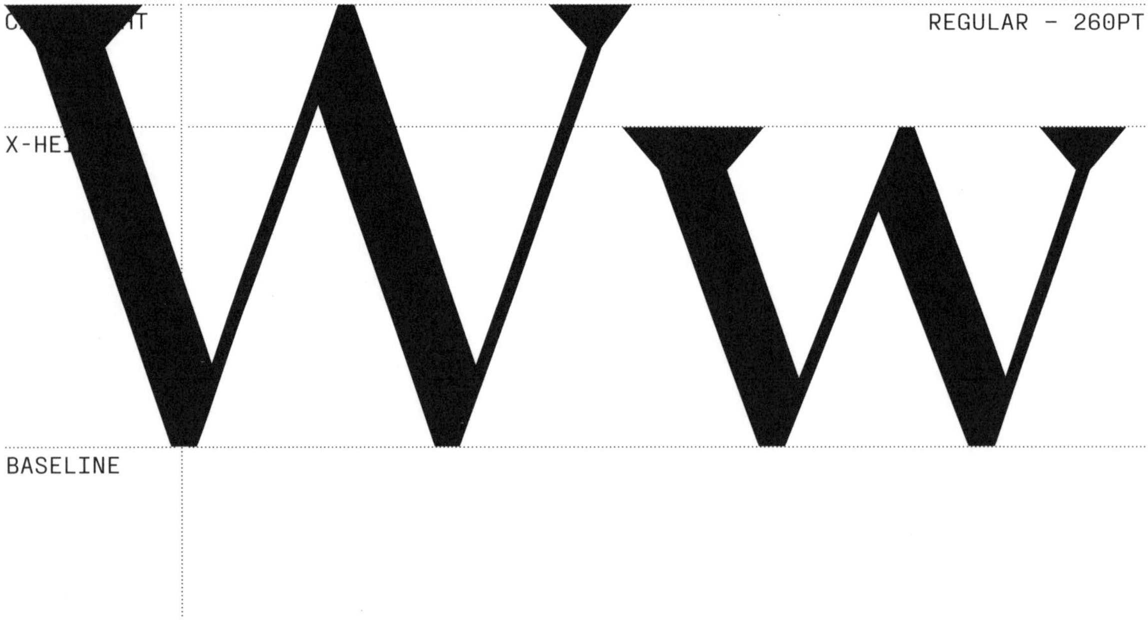

F37Wicklow

REGULAR – 48PT

THE QUICK BROWN F
IT WOULD BE THE CH
IT'S A LOVELY DAY IN T
AND THE PUNGENT A
PROMISE OF A SUMPT
THINKING ABOUT TH

REGULAR – 18PT

The quick brown fox jumps over a lazy dog. He didn't have t
it would be the cheeky thing to do. After all, he had a reputa
It's a lovely day in the neighbourhood, with the sun shining, t
and the pungent aroma of fresh rubbish bins wafting throug
promise of a sumptuous meal. The sprightly fox rubs his paw
thinking about the delicious treasures he's about to dig into.
the lazy dog remains unperturbed. With her long snout, droo
long black fur fluttering in the breeze, she is in a dreamland

REGULAR – 10PT

The quick brown fox jumps over a lazy dog. He didn't have to, but he thought it would be the cheeky thing to do. After all, he had a reputation to maintain. It's a lovely day in the neighbourhood, with the sun shining, the birds chirping, and the pungent aroma of fresh rubbish bins wafting through the air - the promise of a sumptuous meal. The sprightly fox rubs his paws together in glee, thinking about the delicious treasures he's about to dig into. Still in her spot, the lazy dog remains unperturbed. With her long snout, droopy jowls, and long black fur fluttering in the breeze, she is in a dreamland far away - where the mountains are made of beefy treats, the valleys are filled with tennis balls, and the puddles are just the right temperature. Why be in the rat race? It's a dog's life, after all.

Set

Sto

Wicklow light
Wicklow Light Italic

Wicklow Regular
Wicklow Regular Italic

Wicklow Medium
Wicklow Medium Italic

Wicklow Bold
Wicklow Bold Italic

Wicklow Extra Bold
Wicklow Extra Bold Italic

Wicklow Black
Wicklow Black Italic

Wicklow

in

one

TYPEFACE : WULKAN
DESIGNER : THE DESIGNERS FOUNDRY
LOCATION : NEW ZEALAND

PUBLISHED BY : THE DESIGNERS FOUNDRY
CHRONOLOGY : N/A
RELEASED IN : 2019

LINK : HTTPS://THEDESIGNERSFOUNDRY.COM/WULKAN
STYLES : 27
CREDITS : JAN ESTRADA-OSMYCKI (DESIGN)

WULKAN IS A MODERN INTERPRETATION OF OLD STYLE TYPES, DRAWING ITS INSPIRATION, AMONG OTHERS, FROM THE WORKS OF CHARLES HEYER, HERB LUBALIN, AND TOM CARNASE. ITS THIN HAIRLINES AND SHARP, EXAGGERATED ELEMENTS CONTRASTED WITH BALL TERMINALS MAKE FOR A VIBRANT TYPEFACE WELL SUITED FOR LARGE APPLICATIONS. THANKS TO ITS SLIGHTLY COMPRESSED PROPORTIONS AS WELL AS SHORT ASCENDERS AND DESCENDERS, IT CAN BE SET VERY TIGHT FOR A STRONG VISUAL IMPACT. ALTHOUGH IT HAS BEEN A WORK IN PROGRESS SINCE 2019, 24 TEXT STYLES WERE ADDED IN 2022 AND THE DISPLAY STYLES SAW SIGNIFICANT REFINEMENTS.

REGULAR – 240PT

X-HEIG

Ww

BASELINE

Wulkan

REGULAR – 32PT

THE QUICK BROWN FOX JU
IT WOULD BE THE CHEEKY
IT'S A LOVELY DAY IN THE
AND THE PUNGENT AROM
PROMISE OF A SUMPTUOU
THINKING ABOUT THE DE
THE LAZY DOG REMAINS U

REGULAR – 16PT

The quick brown fox jumps over a lazy dog. He didn't have t
it would be the cheeky thing to do. After all, he had a reputa
It's a lovely day in the neighbourhood, with the sun shining,
and the pungent aroma of fresh rubbish bins wafting throug
promise of a sumptuous meal. The sprightly fox rubs his pa
thinking about the delicious treasures he's about to dig into.
the lazy dog remains unperturbed. With her long snout, dro
long black fur fluttering in the breeze, she is in a dreamland
the mountains are made of beefy treats, the valleys are filled
and the puddles are just the right temperature. Why be in th
It's a dog's life, after all.

REGULAR – 8PT

The quick brown fox jumps over a lazy dog. He didn't have to, but he thought it would be the cheeky thing to do. After all, he had a reputation to maintain. It's a lovely day in the neighbourhood, with the sun shining, the birds chirping, and the pungent aroma of fresh rubbish bins wafting through the air - the promise of a sumptuous meal. The sprightly fox rubs his paws together in glee, thinking about the delicious treasures he's about to dig into. Still in her spot, the lazy dog remains unperturbed. With her long snout, droopy jowls, and long black fur fluttering in the breeze, she is in a dreamland far away - where the mountains are made of beefy treats, the valleys are filled with tennis balls, and the puddles are just the right temperature. Why be in the rat race? It's a dog's life, after all.

2 Volcanic Wa

Whispers of the Mountains

In a realm veiled by the mists of antiquity, the land of Anahuac bore witness to the reign of a mighty sovereign, Tlatoani. Amidst his kingdom's tapestry lived a gallant and resolute warrior named Popocatépetl. His visage radiated not only strength but also a valiant spirit that had triumphed over many battles, elevating him to a revered stature among the Tlaxcala tribe.

Upon a serendipitous encounter within the bustling city, Popocatépetl's heart became ensnared by the enchanting presence of a princess named Iztaccíhuatl. This ethereal maiden, the progeny of none other than Tlatoani, was renowned throughout the realm for her peerless grace and captivating beauty. With each stolen glance and whispered word, an unbreakable bond formed, nurturing an affection that blossomed stronger with each passing day.

Popocatépetl, fueled by an ardent desire, beseeched Tlatoani's blessing to unite his fate with that of Iztaccíhuatl. The ruler's consent was granted, yet it bore a solitary condition: Popocatépetl must demonstrate his valor on a distant battlefield, where an imposing adversary awaited conquest. Success in this daunting endeavor would grant him the privilege of claiming Iztaccíhuatl's hand upon his triumphant return.

Undaunted, Popocatépetl embarked on his mission, leaving behind aching hearts and unspoken promises. As he ventured forth, the shadows of envy wove a web of deceit, sowing whispers of Popocatépetl's demise. This nefarious falsehood inflicted immeasurable anguish upon Iztaccíhuatl, who withered beneath the weight of her heart's sorrowful lament.

A
BCD
EFGHIJ
KLMNOP
STUVWX
(123456789;&

IZTACCIHUATL *Elevation* 5,230 m/17,160 ft
Prominence 1,530 m/ 5,020 ft

rriors *Carved In Stone, Ash and Fire*

Returning from his hard-won victory, Popocatépetl was met not with joyous embrace, but with the crushing news of Iztaccíhuatl's untimely passing. Bereft and shattered, his soul fractured by grief's relentless tide, Popocatépetl's world lay in ruins.

Lifting Iztaccíhuatl's lifeless form, Popocatépetl ascended the mountain's solemn heights. There, he kindled a pyre, flames dancing in solemn reflection of his profound sorrow. Pledging an undying vigil, he vowed to safeguard Iztaccíhuatl's eternal slumber, honoring her memory through the eons.

The gods, moved by this testament of boundless devotion, wove their magic into the very fabric of nature. Transfigured into towering monuments of earth and fire, Popocatépetl and Iztaccíhuatl stood united, their love immortalized upon the horizon—two majestic volcanoes, eternal guardians of an enduring love's flame.

R

Z

$?!)

TYPEFACE : ZIN SERIF
DESIGNER : SAMUEL ČARNOKÝ
LOCATION : KYSAK, SLOVAKIA

PUBLISHED BY : CARNOKYTYPE
CHRONOLOGY : 2017 - 2019
RELEASED IN : 2020

LINK : HTTPS://CARNOKYTYPE.COM/FONTS/ZIN_SERIF
STYLES : 30 FONTS • 10 NORMAL + 10 CONDENSED + 10 EXTENDED STYLES • 5 WEIGHTS + ITALICS

ZIN SERIF IS A CONTEMPORARY SERIF TYPEFACE. ONE OF ITS MAIN CHARACTERISTIC FEATURES IS A LARGE X-HEIGHT AND BALANCE BETWEEN THE NEUTRAL CONSTRUCTION OF LETTERS AND DYNAMIC OPEN FORMS. ANOTHER CHARACTERISTIC IS A NARROWER CONNECTION BETWEEN STEMS AND STROKES. THE COMPLETE FONT FAMILY CONSISTS OF THREE WIDTH PROPORTIONS (NORMAL, CONDENSED, AND EXTENDED) IN FIVE WEIGHTS. IT CAN BE USED FOR BOTH TEXT AND DISPLAY TYPESETTING, ESPECIALLY IN MAGAZINE LAYOUTS AND EDITORIAL DESIGN, AS WELL IN ADVERTISING TYPOGRAPHY, SIGNAGE, AND CORPORATE IDENTITIES. ZIN SERIF IS A MEMBER OF THE ZIN SUPERFAMILY, WHICH ALSO INCLUDES SANS, SLAB AND DISPLAY FONTS.

CAP HEIGHT

REGULAR – 290PT

X-HEIGHT

Zz

BASELINE

Zin Serif

REGULAR – 48PT

THE QUICK BROW
IT WOULD BE THE
IT'S A LOVELY DAY
AND THE PUNGEN
PROMISE OF A SU
THINKING ABOUT
THE LAZY DOG RE
LONG BLACK FUR
THE MOUNTAINS

REGULAR – 8PT

The quick brown fox jumps over a lazy dog. He didn't have to, but he thought it would be the cheeky thing to do. After all, he had a reputation to maintain. It's a lovely day in the neighbourhood, with the sun shining, the birds chirping, and the pungent aroma of fresh rubbish bins wafting through the air - the promise of a sumptuous meal. The sprightly fox rubs his paws together in glee, thinking about the delicious treasures he's about to dig into. Still in her spot, the lazy dog remains unperturbed. With her long snout, droopy jowls, and long black fur fluttering in the breeze, she is in a dreamland far away - where the mountains are made of beefy treats, the valleys are filled with tennis balls, and the puddles are just the right temperature. Why be in the rat race?
It's a dog's life, after all.

Zin Serif

a member
of the **Zin** superfamily
by CarnokyType

Gleichmäßigkeit der Färbung

wklęsłolinijne

Předchůdci knihtisku

№4 — Periodikum/2018

Tècniques d'impressió

Risographs have typically had interchangeable color inks and drums allowing for printing in different colors or using spot color in a single print job ● Risograph printers use a soy ink made from vegetable soybean oil ● The Riso MZ serie models have two ink drums, thereby allowing two colors to be printed in one pass ○

Zin Serif

... is a contemporary serif typeface designed for various situations of typographic usage.¶

Each font includes SMALL CAPITALS, old-style & tabular figures (123/123), standard and discretionary ligatures (fi/ffl/ct/st), alternate glyphs (ɑ/g/y/&) and a many of typographic options applied by the OPENTYPE features.■

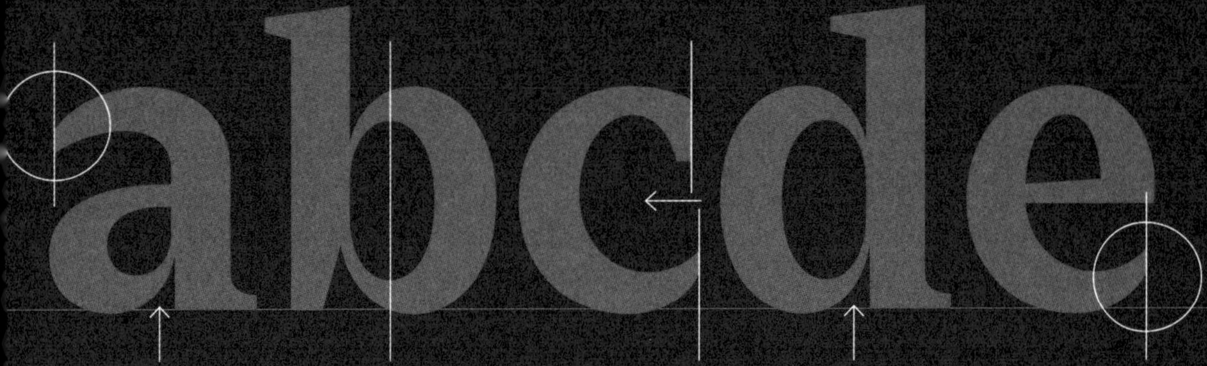

CONDENSED:	**NORMAL:**	**EXTENDED:**
Light	Light	Light
Light Italic	*Light Italic*	*Light Italic*
Regular	Regular	Regular
Regular Italic	*Regular Italic*	*Regular Italic*
Medium	Medium	Medium
Medium Italic	*Medium Italic*	*Medium Italic*
Bold	**Bold**	**Bold**
Bold Italic	***Bold Italic***	***Bold Italic***
Black	**Black**	**Black**
Black Italic	***Black Italic***	***Black Italic***
+	+	+
Demo (Free)	Demo (Free)	Demo (Free)

TYPEFACE : ZNVT23
DESIGNER : ZIN NAGAO / FOZNT
LOCATION : FUKUOKA, JAPAN

PUBLISHED BY : ZIN NAGAO / FOZNT
CHRONOLOGY : 2022
RELEASED IN : 2022

LINK : HTTPS://WWW.FOZNT.COM/ZNVT23
STYLES : NORMAL

ZNVT23 WAS CREATED BY ARRANGING SMALL SQUARES. DESIGNER ZIN NAGAO CONCENTRATED ON ASSEMBLING AND COMPLETING THE SHAPE OF EACH INDIVIDUAL LETTER WITHOUT GIVING MUCH THOUGHT TO THE OVERALL IMAGE. THE UNCOMFORTABLE SHAPES OF THE LETTERS WERE LEFT AS THEY WERE, RESULTING IN A THIN BUT IMPACTFUL TYPEFACE WITH A UNIQUE AIR OF WEIGHT.

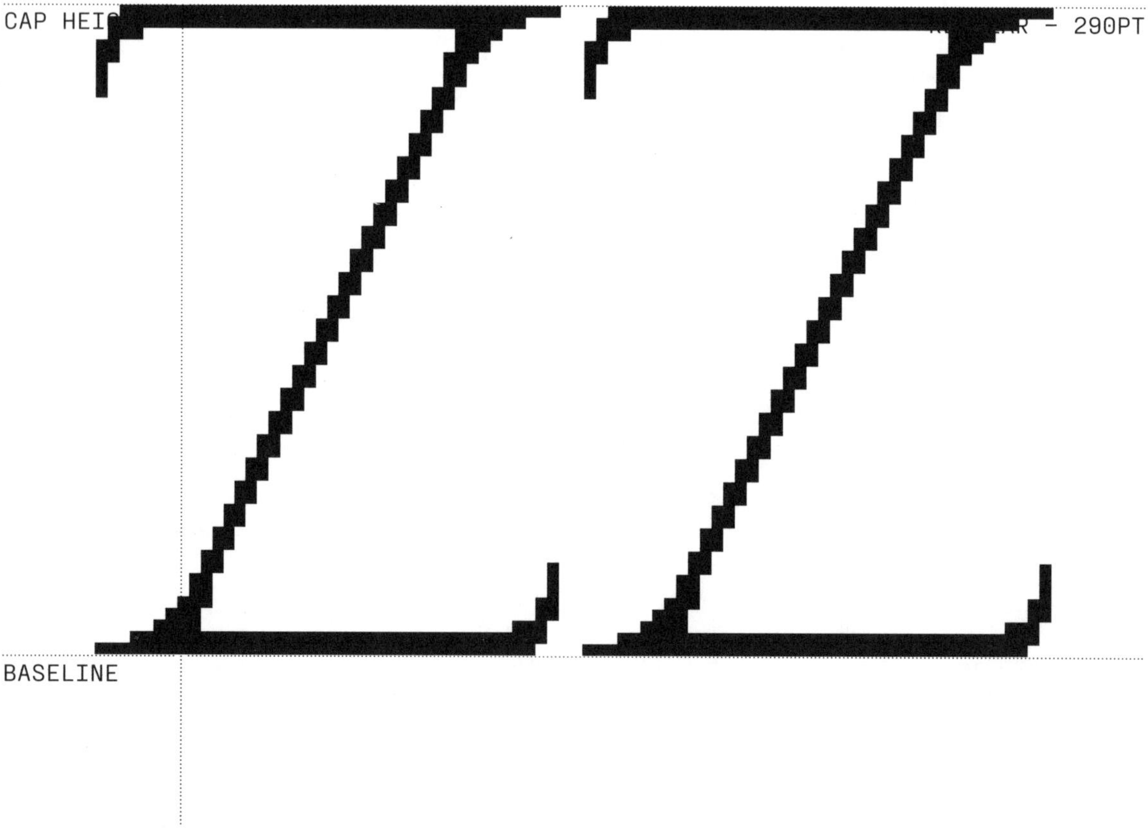

ZNVT23

REGULAR – 40PT

THE QUICK BROWN FOX
IT WOULD BE THE CHEE
IT'S A LOVELY DAY IN T
AND THE PUNGENT ARO
PROMISE OF A SUMPTU
THINKING ABOUT THE

REGULAR – 16PT

THE QUICK BROWN FOX JUMPS OVER A LAZY DOG. HE DIDN
IT WOULD BE THE CHEEKY THING TO DO. AFTER ALL, HE HA
IT'S A LOVELY DAY IN THE NEIGHBOURHOOD, WITH THE SU
AND THE PUNGENT AROMA OF FRESH RUBBISH BINS WAFT
PROMISE OF A SUMPTUOUS MEAL. THE SPRIGHTLY FOX RU
THINKING ABOUT THE DELICIOUS TREASURES HE'S ABOU
THE LAZY DOG REMAINS UNPERTURBED. WITH HER LONG S
LONG BLACK FUR FLUTTERING IN THE BREEZE, SHE IS IN
THE MOUNTAINS ARE MADE OF BEEFY TREATS, THE VALLEY
AND THE PUDDLES ARE JUST THE RIGHT TEMPERATURE. W
IT'S A DOG'S LIFE, AFTER ALL.

REGULAR – 8PT

THE QUICK BROWN FOX JUMPS OVER A LAZY DOG. HE DIDN'T HAVE TO, BUT HE THOUGHT
IT WOULD BE THE CHEEKY THING TO DO. AFTER ALL, HE HAD A REPUTATION TO MAINTAIN.
IT'S A LOVELY DAY IN THE NEIGHBOURHOOD, WITH THE SUN SHINING, THE BIRDS CHIRPING,
AND THE PUNGENT AROMA OF FRESH RUBBISH BINS WAFTING THROUGH THE AIR – THE
PROMISE OF A SUMPTUOUS MEAL. THE SPRIGHTLY FOX RUBS HIS PAWS TOGETHER IN GLEE,
THINKING ABOUT THE DELICIOUS TREASURES HE'S ABOUT TO DIG INTO. STILL IN HER SPOT,
THE LAZY DOG REMAINS UNPERTURBED. WITH HER LONG SNOUT, DROOPY JOWLS, AND
LONG BLACK FUR FLUTTERING IN THE BREEZE, SHE IS IN A DREAMLAND FAR AWAY – WHERE
THE MOUNTAINS ARE MADE OF BEEFY TREATS, THE VALLEYS ARE FILLED WITH TENNIS BALLS,
AND THE PUDDLES ARE JUST THE RIGHT TEMPERATURE. WHY BE IN THE RAT RACE?
IT'S A DOG'S LIFE, AFTER ALL.

AÆBCDEFG
HIJKLMNO
ŒPQRSTUV
23456789

КАССЫ TICKETS
418

КИНОТЕАТР
ХУДОЖЕСТВЕННЫЙ
419

SFFILM
AWARDS
NIGHT
2022

420

SFFILM
AWARDS
NIGHT
2022

SFFILM AWARDS NIGHT 2022

421

SFFILM AWARDS NIGHT 2022

Reframing FASHION

422

New Order 1983
Blue Monday
Label: Factory
NEW ORDER
Released: 1984
Label: Factory
A1 Ceremony
A2 Everything's Gone Green
A3 Temptation
B1 Blue Monday
B2 Confusion
B3 Thieves Like Us

423

GLASGOW
REGULAR, ITALIC
SIZE: 500 PT
LEADING: 400 PT
SPACING: -50
424

BLACK, BLACK ITALIC

SIZE: 500 PT

LEADING: 400 PT
SPACING: –50

Ql's
kaÿ,
Zhv

GLASGOW REGULAR, ITALIC SIZE: 225 PT LEADING: 200 PT SPACING: -20

Tätigkeit

(Museum)

Abstråkt

Universal

Scotland

Excellent!

In 1936 The Monotype Corporation was asked by William Collins to cut a book face for the exclusive use of this firm of printer-publishers. Dr. Giovanni Mardersteig, who founded the Officina Bodoni and has since designed a number of faces including Dante, was called in to advise on the problem. Having decided that a new 20th-century design was in the circumstances inadvisable, he chose to copy a fount cut by Alexander Wilson of the Glasgow Letter Foundry about 1760. In his later types he reflected the influence of Baskerville, and Dr. Mardersteig's adaptation is fairly accurate though he made certain changes, as for example in the slightly reduced height of the capitals. In 1961 the House of Collins allowed the Corporation to make this series available for general use. The chief aim when selecting a type for a book must be to ensure that the book can be easily read, and this at once demands that the type chosen will be a plain one, without any peculiarities in the formation of the letters that may draw the reader's attention to itself. A good book type should be neither too heavy or too light. A heavy type gives too great a contrast between the type and the paper for easy reading, and too light a type makes the page pale and colourless. In *The Officina Bodoni* (1929) Mardersteig described clearly and succinctly the processes by which a book is made at the Officina Bodoni. His account, illustrated with twelve woodcuts by Frans Masereel, was reissued in 1973. This is the text: 'All texts before being set up are thoroughly examined. The best critical edition is chosen, and if it does not agree with the [illegible]ch, a new

In 1936, WM. Collins Sons & co. Ltd. London and Glasgow became the first major publishing house to create its own font.

revised text is established by comparison with the original manuscript or the first edition. When the copy has thus been prepared it is worked through from the typographic point of view from title-page to colophon and got ready, that is: provided with all the necessary directions for the compositor'. 'The compositor picks out each letter from the typecase, which is divided into about a hundred small compartments for upper-case, lower-case, signs of punctuation and spaces, and inserts it in the composing-stick. Before him is the copy, and near him a tray into which he transfers the completed lines from the composing-stick until a page is finished. This page is sometimes bound round with string. Good setting demands careful work, for in hand-press printing it is not so much speed of execution, as evenness of spacing and the avoidance of too frequent divisions of words, which determine the beauty of the page'. The text is read for corrections at least five times. The removal of letters which are defective from casting or from use takes place on the machine before the beginning of the printing and the last reading. Finally the forme is secured with wedges (quoins) and furniture until it forms one solid block as though all the letters had been cast together'. 'The lightly damped sheet is pinned by the pressman to a frame covered with paper or other material, and in printing this frame is folded down on to the forme'. 'Then comes the most troublesome task, the make-ready, which means the removal of unevenness in the impression. The first pull of a sheet, in which the impression is unequal, partly

GLASGOW BLACK ITALIC SIZE: 815 PT LEADING: 600 PT

Q z

428

429

Giovanni Mardersteig was born in Weimar in 1892, became co-editor of Genius, a journal of modern art, in 1919, and set up his printing and publishing enterprise, the Officina Bodoni, at Montagnola in 1922. The Officina was moved to Verona in 1927, and in 1948 he established the Stamperia Valdonega, a mechanised printing works which he continues to control in addition to the hand-press on which, by the end of 1970, more than 150 editions had been printed. Between 1954 and 1965 major exhibitions of the work of Mardersteig were shown in Antwerp, Hamburg, London, Brussels, The Hague, Munich, Verona, Milan, Florence, Venice, Lugano and Berne—and catalogues in the appropriate languages were issued. We owe this wide viewing of books from The Officina Bodoni to Luc Indestege who persuaded Mardersteig to have the first exhibition at Antwerp in 1954. Certainly in England the catalogue for the exhibition held in the British Museum (*Officina Bodoni, Verona: Catalogue of Books printed on the Hand Press, Verona 1954*) was, and still is, the most important record of the Press in which 103 editions were listed. The catalogue reprinted with an Italian text, for a series of exhibitions in Italy in 1962 lists 117 editions, and at the Stamperia Valdonega, where all the catalogues have been printed, an up-to-date record is kept. When Giovanni Mardersteig came to London for the opening of his exhibition in 1954 he was already a well-known visitor but most of his books were not so well known. *The Times Literary Supplement,* commenting on the exhibition, said: "... because most of his books have been produced on the hand-press in strictly limited editions they are not often seen in this country." Two notable exceptions were books printed in the mid 1920's for Elkin Mathews. These were Horace Walpole's *Hieroglyphic Tales* (No. 17, 1926) and Chesterfield's *Poetical Works* (No. 19, 1927). Of this latter book I bought in 1961 a copy for 2 pounds and in 1971 a copy in comparable state for 20 pounds. And the first of Mardersteig's facsimiles of sixteenth century writing books, *The Callligraphic Models of Arrighi* (No. 15, 1926) has an introduction by Stanley Morison and was distributed in London by the bookseller J. and E. Bumpus Ltd. A few copies of this book were available from Bumpus at the end of the 1940's at the original price of 4 pounds but now it is hard to find a copy at any price. As will be seen from the exhibition catalogue, during the second half on the 1920's many books were issued with English texts. This points to Mardersteig's affinity with England long ago established and ever since maintained. In 1927, in the middle of this period of printing many books in English, Mardersteig agreed to print for the Italian Government the complete works of Gabriele d'Annunzio. He moved the press from Montagnola to Verona and set up a printing office inside the factory of Arnoldo Mondadori. The last of the forty-nine volumes was not completed until 1935 when he accepted an invitation to work at the printing house of William Collins in Glasgow. During his year's work there the Fontana typeface was made. After starting the d'Annunzio volumes and before his year at Glasgow Mardersteig took time off in 1932, spent it in London and married Irmi Krayer, the sister of Gustav Krayer, a young artist who was for two years a voluntary worker at the Press with Giovanni Mardersteig. Furthermore, his close association with Stanley Morison was begun in 1925. The five reproductions of writing manuals published between 1926 and 1930 were all edited by Morison whose introductions were printed in English. The association was lifelong and after Morison's death, Giovanni Mardersteig dedicated his *Pietro Bembo on Etna* (No. 150, 1969) to him. Mardersteig's more recent studies of the geometrically constructed roman alphabets of [illegible] Feliciano and France[illegible]th written by him. Th[illegible]ano book, *Alphabetu[illegible]anum* (No. 113, [illegible] rare example[illegible]na Bodoni publis[illegible] in which the text wa[illegible]sult of his [illegible]hes, he was the [illegible]ner of the type and he a[illegible] the p[illegible]ole-page revie[illegible] Charles Mitchell app[illegible] in *The [illegible] Supplement*. Th[illegible] text edition of Felici[illegible] Al[illegible]bet wa[illegible]ibuted by Willia[illegible]ins in 1960 and that of T[illegible]o [illegible]he Bod[illegible]ad in 1971. In England between 1923 and 1954 t[illegible]re two so[illegible] of information on scholarly printing and pu[illegible]g: *The Fleuron,* [illegible] issues between 1923 and 1930; *Signature,* thirty[illegible] issues betw[illegible]5 and 1954. In the wealth of information thes[illegible]ournals provide[illegible] in the last issue of *The Fleuron* is the Offici[illegible]oni mentioned. [illegible]ew of *Andres Brun* (No. 26, 1928) also appear[illegible]is issue. Throughou[illegible]omplete thirty-three issues of *Signat*[illegible]ted by Oliver Simo[illegible]book printed at Officina Bodoni wa[illegible]eviewed, and Mardersteig[illegible]rinter-publisher was never once[illegible]oned. And in Oliver Simo[illegible]tobiography "Hans Marderst[illegible] once referred to as [illegible]r as a printer o[illegible]er-publisher. Two ac[illegible] in English. T[illegible]st, Mardersteig's own book, *The Officina* [illegible] *the operation of a h*[illegible]*ess during the first six years of its work* (No. [illegible]9), and the secon[illegible]edrich Ewald's article, "The O[illegible]cina Bodon[illegible]lished in *The Fl*[illegible], No. VII, 1930, edited by Stanle[illegible] Morison. Th[illegible]re 200 copies [illegible]ardersteig's book in English an[illegible]o copies of *T*[illegible]*ron*. There are[illegible] steig as a[illegible]blisher but[illegible]re is an [illegible]graphi[illegible] the author writes: "At this point we may make a passing reference to the production of Morison's books." But only the Cambridge University Press is named, and no references at all to the books printed by Mardersteig. And in the accompanying list of books, under the heading Calligraphy, although no printers or towns of printing origin are mentioned, the entry for Mercator (No. 33, 1930) has in it the mysterious word "Verona". The tail of the entry reads: "De Sikkel, Antwerp; Pegasus Press, Paris. Verona, 1930." Two articles about Mardersteig, both by Harry Carter, did appear in *Signature*. The first was a note on Collin's Fontana type and the second concerned itself with the design of a new Tauchnitz edition. For the March 1937 issue of *Signature*, Vivian Ridler compiled a list of "printers, printing schools, typographers, publishers" whose work was to be sought after and assembled in the John Johnson collection, a sanctuary of printing at the University Press, Oxford. Included in the list of 180 names were: Cock Robin, Essex House, Fanfrolico, Herrin News Shop, Lane, Printing Schools, various, but there was no mention of our subject and his Press. Whatever the reason for this omission, it shows that the famous Press at Verona was not, in England in 1937, one which readily came to mind even though, in addition to the complete works of d'Annunzio, at least 38 other books were printed and that 17 of them were done in English. Another possible source of information might have been the "Book production notes" regularly contributed to the *London Mercury* by Bernard Newdigate between 1920 and 1937. But in Joseph Thorp's selection we find no reference to the Officina Bodoni and only one reference to the original printer at Parma: "Bodoni more than any one else gave us the 'modern' types which were... rightly banned by Morris for their ugliness..." However, Newdigate, in *The Art of the Book*, 1938, reproduced the title-page of L'Oleandro by Gabriele d'Annunzio (No. 37, 1936) and includes a note on the current activities of Mardersteig. Fontana and Zeno typefaces are shown but the note itself is not too confidence-inspiring in that Bellinzona is named as the first location of the Press although Montagnola is given in all the colophons. About the typefaces from Parma he says: "By favour of the Government of Italy he was able to use the punches cut by Bodoni late in the eighteenth century, and with the types cast from them he printed at a hand-press a magnificent series of books." The "ugliness" of Bodoni types previously referred to seems to have been forgotten: Newdigate certainly did know that types are cast from matrices—not punches—even if he did not know that Mardersteig borrowed matrices from Parma. That concludes my list of English references before the exhibition of 1954 except for Raffaello Bertieri's article on Italian typography in the first issue of *The Dolphin*, 1933, which mentions the existence of a d'Annunzio edition without naming the printer. However, I should say that Hermann Hesse wrote about the Press at Montagnola and about Mardersteig's first publications in the *Neue Zürcher Zeitung* in 1923. This is the article to which Julius Rodenberg referred in his *Deutsche Pressen* in 1925. The German novelist, Hermann Hesse, was a neighbour and friend of Giovanni Mardersteig and his newspaper *feuilleton* is worthy of notice. But first I should like to mention that in 1928 Julius Rodenberg together with Oliver Simon published an illustrated survey of book design in Europe and in the United States since the First World War. In it there is no Officina Bodoni, and when Rodenbergcame to publish his last book *Gröe und Grenzen der Typographie* (Stuttgart, 1959) once more we find no mention of the Officina Bodoni.

To return to Hesse, my search for this newspaper *feuilleton* ended when I received a Xerox copy from Chicago University Library. I had asked for help from the Newberry Library and through James Wells I received this Xerox together with a typed transcription. I had a translation made Wand read Hesse's note for the first time—just forty-seven years after its publication. I have now received a separate printing of the article made by Jacob Hegner, a booklet of sixteen pages done shortly after the *feuilleton* appeared on 4 November 1923. In his article Hesse wrote: "... a few months ago a new printing press came into existence which achieves quality work of the first order." He then mentions the first four published books of the Press which are works by Poliziano, Michelangelo, Goethe and Shelley, and then continues: "The intrinsic value of the achievement lies not in the editorial skill but in the craftsmanship." Of course Mardersteig's editorial skills have since become especially evident in the many books to which he has added notes or introductions. Hesse continued and elaborated his claim for the excellence of his printer-friend's craftsmanship: "The arrangement of the setting, page by page, is the subject of long consultations and countless trials a first trial proof is pulled whereby the minimum pressure is exerted. This trial proof may look perfect to the layman, and possibly there are no mistakes to be seen which may not also be found in any other book." Hermann Hesse made a number of references to Giambattista Bodoni to explain the title *Officina Bodoni* and to describe Mardersteig's inheritance. "This man [G. B. Bodoni] sang, piped, danced and built through the medium of letter forms!" He thought Mardersteig a worthy successor because the value of his work relied "purely on the dignity and the charm of perfect craftsmanship". At this time the sole and exclusive types were of G. B. Bodoni and on this issue Hesse wrote: "... apart of its [the Officina's] merit is due to the alphabets of the old Bodoni." To Hesse, Mardersteig was "a worthy and continuously creative successor" whose ideal was to be expressed in "the honest and successful striving towards perfection". What has happened since 1923 must have astonished even Hermann Hesse. Certainly one aspect of development at Montagnola and at Verona was foretold by Hesse and that is Mardersteig's adherence to "the dignity and charm of perfect craftsmanship" in the design and execution of all his printing and in the design and production of his types. Hesse would have found the greatest delight in a recent and austere facsimile edition of the original Bodoni's *Manuale Tipografico* of 1788 which Mardersteig introduced and published in 1968. Unlike Bodoni's later specimen book, issued by his widow in 1818, this *Manuale* has an abstract purity much in keeping with Mardersteig's own work. It is a specimen book of letters which allows the letters to speak for themselves, not letters in isolation but in their natural arrangement in the making of words and sentences. After 1954 the exhibition catalogue became the chief source of information in English on the work of the Officina Bodoni. This catalogue lists 103 titles. It does not include any volumes of the National Edition of d'Annunzio. The 1954 catalogue, as mentioned above, has been revised and printed in several languages. *Goethes Urworte, Orphisch* (a trial printing of 8 pages) appears in later catalogues before what has earlier been referred to as the first book, Poliziano, *Orphei Tragedia*. The Goethe is described as the first proof of the Press and was included at Luc Indestege's request. A second proof was made but does not appear in any list or catalogue so far discovered. This was Nietzsche, *Zwei Reden Zarathustras*, 1923. My information comes from Robert Elwell, New York. Of the first proof only t[illegible]ed and of the second, only twelve copies. Also in [illegible] setting in [illegible] was made of a prose poem by Maurice d[illegible]in, *Les Bruits de la* [illegible]. Mardersteig did not like this setting. [illegible]nted only four or five [illegible] one of which is owned by James I[illegible]in of New York. Many ye[illegible]r he included this text in *Poèmes en*[illegible] (No. 101, 1954) using his ow[illegible]face, Griffo, in its second state [illegible]ng. Then in 1926 a first spec[illegible]f Bodoni's Cuneo type was made[illegible]ne, *An Excerptfrom a Sentime*[illegible]*rney*. There were twenty-fiv[illegible]s of this small book, boun[illegible]arbled-paper boards with a whi[illegible]r label on the spine. This t[illegible]ears in the 1929 list but not th[illegible]atalogue or any of its revi[illegible]nd the Machiavelli, *La vita di Cast*[illegible]*a Lucca*, which appears [illegible]st book in the 1929 list, Giovan[illegible]ersteig tells me was ne[illegible]. It is described as the first specimen[illegible]oint Bembo type, "[illegible] each on different handmade laid [illegible] papers". T[illegible]e Laurence Sterne (No. 15a, 1926) for a mo[illegible]a pity [illegible] track of this type specimen which has a bear[illegible] of some imp[illegible]e on Giovanni Mardersteig's interest in England or, as he names i[illegible]eroic island. Stanley Morison visited him in Montagnola at C[illegible]astime in 1925 and Mardersteig planned to visit London early in [illegible]e Sterne specimen in Cuneo was printed shortly before the H[illegible] Walpole book for Elkin Mathews referred above. It has the usua[illegible]of colophon with its press-mark and the following words: "[illegible] one of twenty-five copies printed by hand in the month of [illegible] at the Officina Bodoni, Montagnola Switzerland." On [illegible]eding page is a longer notice under the heading "colo[illegible]ardersteig was clearly in a state of disappointment over the postponement of a visit to England due to the General Strike. The message reads: "A journey, it would seem, is at the mercy of political factions; not to sentiment, which is the motive of all good journeys. In a sentiment of admiring affection for the heroic island where I hoped to journey—when railway wheels should move again—this greeting was printed with Giambattista Bodoni's twelve point type 'Cuneo', here used for the first time since his death. H. M." Was this specimen a "greeting" to someone in England whom he was prevented from seeing at an appointed time? Of course the main point revealed in the colophon is the deflection of his intended journey to London by chance circumstances. The end of the Montagnola period was approaching. Mardersteig had already shown a leaning towards anglophilia, and he had met and was being influenced by Morison and Holroyd-Reece, owner of the Pegasus Press in Paris. A visit to London at that time might have provided a very different change from the one which actually took place—namely the printing of the Italian National edition of d'Annunzio at Verona. The Officina Bodoni was firmly established in Via Marsala, Verona, by the time Mardersteig spent two months in London in 1932 and so his return to Verona was assured. Perhaps one reason why the extra "colophon" to Sterne is of special interest lies in its echo of an event in the life of G. B. Bodoni. Bodoni, born at Saluzzo in 1740, worked for eight years in the Vatican at the Propaganda Fide. An interest in the work of John Baskerville had already been aroused and the young Bodoni left Rome in 1766 for England, with the intention of visiting Baskerville at Birmingham. However, malaria forced him to delay the journey and to return home to Saluzzo. Before he could decide to set off again for England he accepted the job of establishing and directing a new Stamperia Ducale at Parma where he remained until his death in 1813. This chance circumstance deflected Bodoni's typographical interest from Baskerville to Pierre-Simon Fournier. It was with Fournier's types that Bodoni began to print and it was on Fournier's designs that Bodoni modelled his first types although the Baskerville influence was always present and even became stronger as Bodoni cut more types. In all, he cut over 25 000 punches and his legacy, now to be found in the Museo Bodoniano, Parma, included over 50 000 matrices. The chance cancellation of his journey to Birmingham may indeed have been momentous. The entire output might have been more closely based upon the work of John Baskerville. The exhibition catalogue, in its present form, does not always give certain details which interest the collector. A number of binding styles have been developed but no information on bindings is given. Giovanni Mardersteig says that the printing is more important, but this does not make the binding unimportant and variant bindings should be noted. Another detail which interests collectors is the numbering of copies. Adriana Ramelli in her Gutenberg Jahrbuch article, 1955, referring to *Primum Pactum Confoederationis Helveticae* (No. 13, 1925), wrote: "This magnificent edition was done for the Society of Swiss Bibliophiles which explains the numbering of the copies which is not to be found in any other work printed at Montagnola. Only later did Mardersteig number copies to help the whim of bibliophiles and also, perhaps above all, to make it possible to follow the adventurous destiny of certain copies." Amongst the writings about the Officina Bodoni, the Ramelli article has some standing but if a definitive catalogue is made it should be mentioned that the Officina Bodoni had this book in preparation for issue

TRANSCENDÊNCIA

430

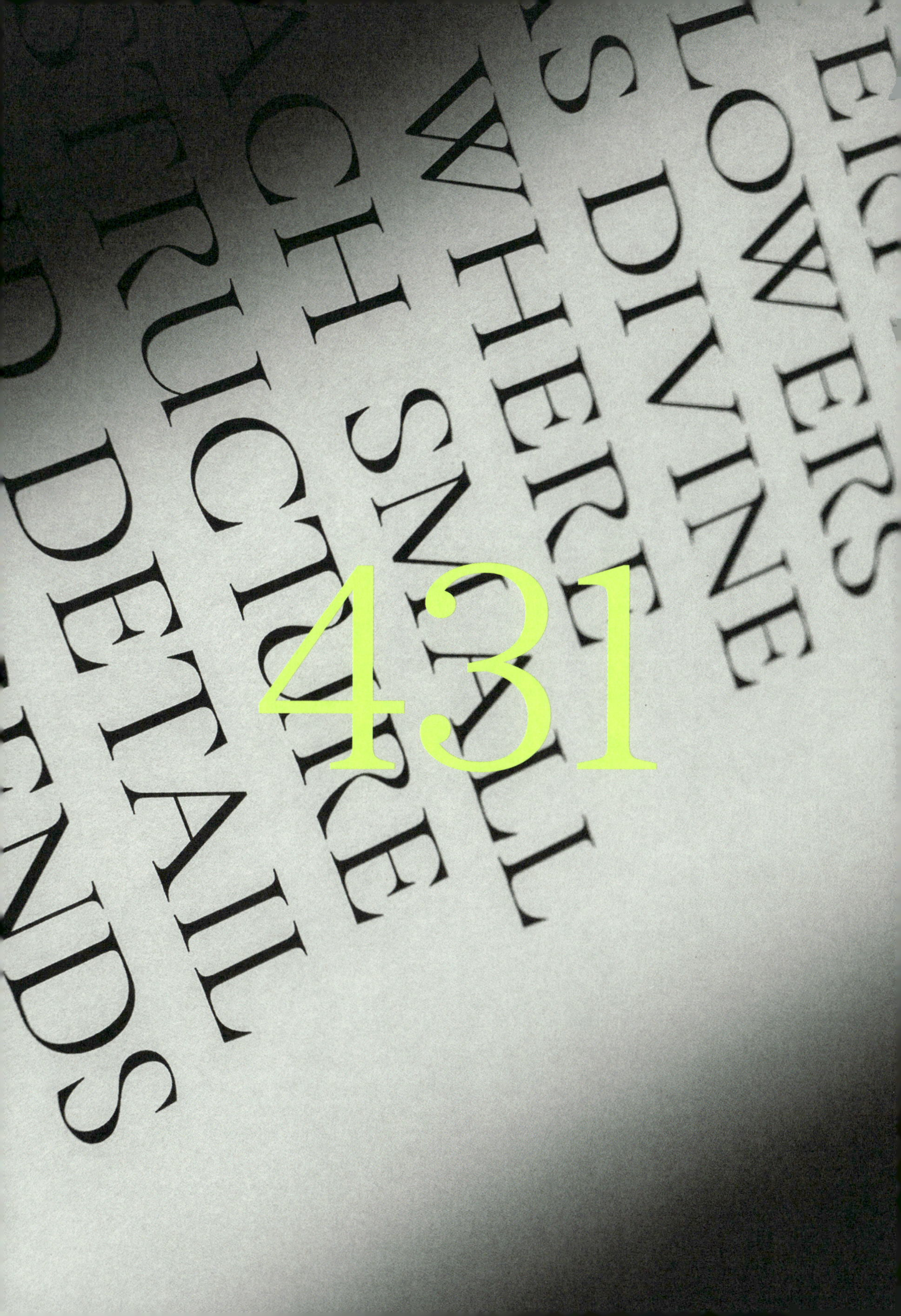

431

432
Orbikular
Type Specimen
Book V.1
Orbikular
Type Specimen
Book V.1

433

434
RHODES LTD
½ SAVILE ROW
VICTORIA RD
KEATS & SON
J.D. FINCH CO
ST ANTHONY
ESTD 1923
NO I HARE CT
Qualification
Qualification
Doyle & Son
Doyle & Son
Rhetorically
Rhetorically
Karyokinesis
Karyokinesis
Pack my box with five dozen liquor jugs
KYOTO
OAXACA DE JUÁREZ
SAN SEBASTIÁN
NEW YORK CITY
BEIRUT
SAN JOSÉ

ROMULUS & REMUS
JACK & JILL ™
ALI & FRAZIER
BED & BREAKFAST
BONNIE & CLYDE
KING & QUEEN®
iné

435

436

437

438

439

440

441

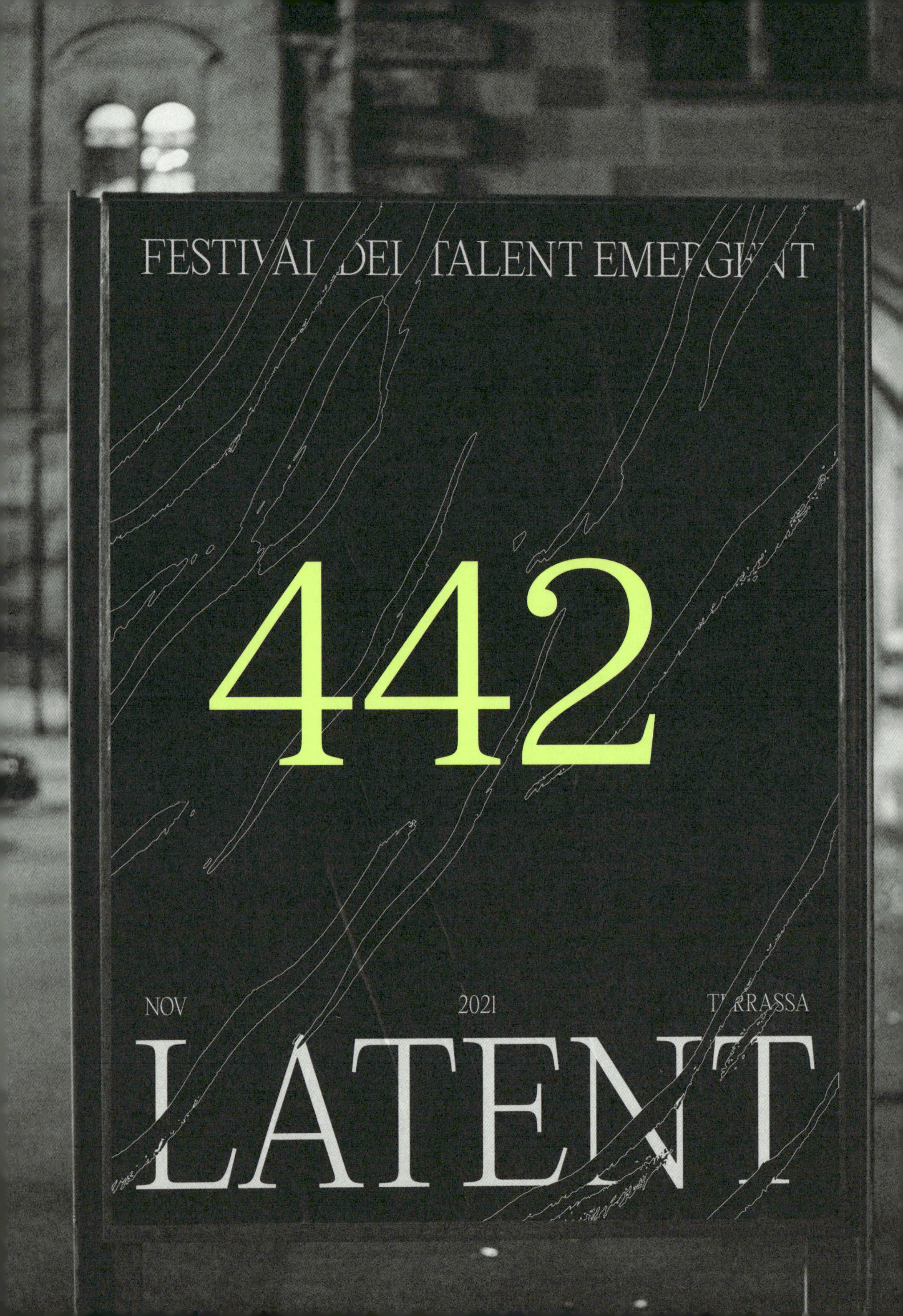
FESTIVAL DEL TALENT EMERGENT
442
NOV
2021
TERRASSA
LATENT

M4
6
NOV
2021
LATE
443
CONRAD ROSET
JAVIER JAÉN
LLUC MASSAGUER
PEP SALA
MARIADIAMANTES
LA ESQUINA
LA RECTORIA

444
LATENT
FESTIVAL DEL TALENT EMERGENT
NOV
2021
TERRASSA

445
LATENT
FESTIVAL DEL TALENT EMERGENT
TERRASSA
NOV
2021

FESTIVAL
OCTOBER 8
DAMROSCH PARK
AT LINCOLN CENTER
TASTE. COOK. SHOP. THINK.
We've cooked up a day of eating, drinking and celebration in the heart of New York City — and saved a seat for you. Ready to dig in to a day like no other? Let's eat!
FEATURING
Ina Garten
Padma Lakshmi
Kim Severenson
Julia Moskin
Yewande Komolafe
FOOD AND DRINK FROM
Terry's Trout Shack
Turkey Titan Gravy Popsicles
Small Expensive Clumps
Did Someone Say Turnips?
Cluckin' and Shuckin'
BUY TICKETS
EXPRESS
RESY
SPONSORED BY

447

The New York Times
FOOD FESTIVAL
OCT 8
Subway
Vending Machines
At This Station
Pay with credit card, ATM/debit card or cash.

The New York Times
FOOD FESTIVAL

YUM
YUM
YUM
449

450

NOM-NOM
NOM-NOM
NOM-NOM
NOM-NOM
NOM-NOM
NOM-NOM
NOM-NOM
NOM-NOM
NOM-NOM
451

452
FINE GRAZING
FINE

FINE GRAZING
453

454

FINE GRAZING
FINE GRAZING
Helen Oltran
+61 431 771 018
hello@finegrazing.com
finegrazing.com

455
FINE

456

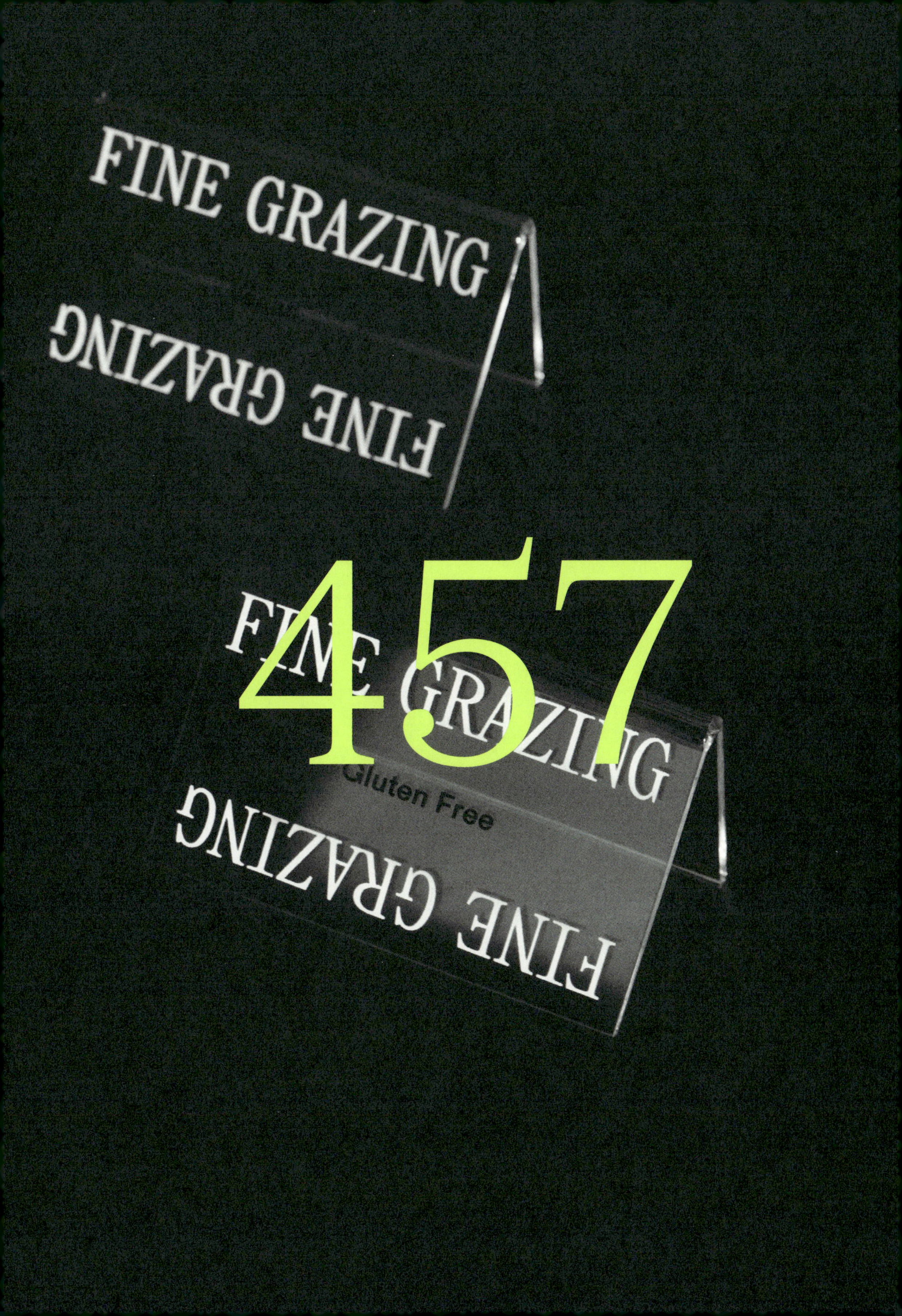
FINE GRAZING
FINE GRAZING
FINE GRAZING
Gluten Free
FINE GRAZING

457

458
THE MOZART

VOUCHER
GUTSCHEIN
VOUCHER
GUTSCHEIN
250
VALUE OF / IM WERT VON
250 EURO
THE MOZART
A MODERN
CLASSIC

460

461

462
THE MOZART
SALZBURG
HOTEL
HOTEL
HOTEL
HOTEL

463

464

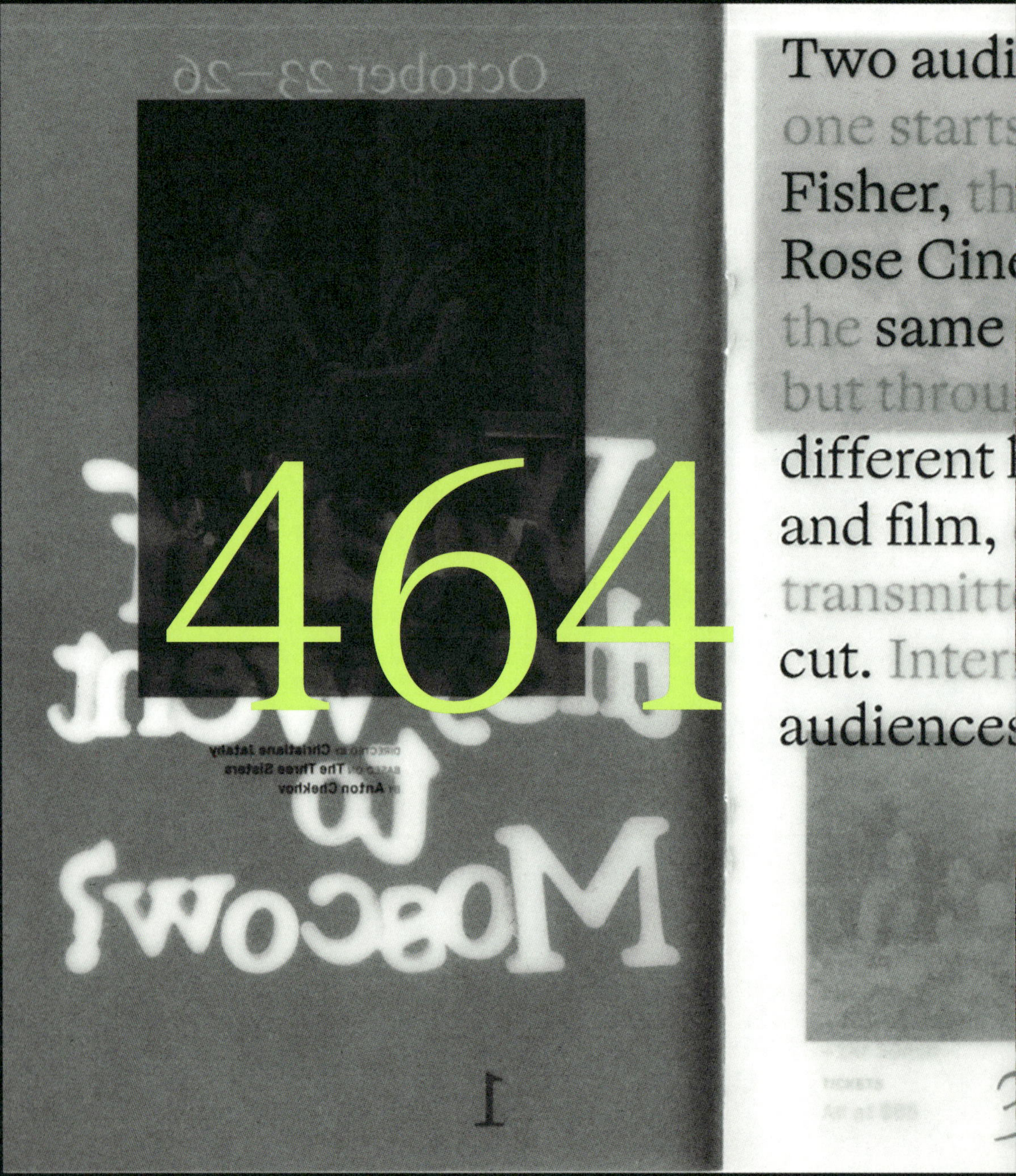

Two audi
one starts
Fisher, th
Rose Cine
the same
but throu
different
and film,
transmitt
cut. Inter
audiences
1

465

October 15–20
Swan Lake/ Loch na hEala
October 18–19
The Second Woman
November 7–9
Bacchae: Prelude to a Purge
November 14–16
The Great Tamer
13

466

Oct 31–Nov 02
Inoah
November 6–14
Bear witness via
a stranger's profound pers
experience in this site-spe
play, which contemplates
afterlife on the internet
and our shifting notions
of connection.
Use
no
Foun
467
December 3–8
Barber
Shop
Chron-
icles
December 12–14
Meow Meow
(With a little help from her friends)
A Very
Meow Me
Holida
Show

SZEKSZÁRDI BIKAVÉR
VÁLOGATÁS 2016
ÚJPEST
FEKETE
2016
BORPINCE

468

469

470

471

474

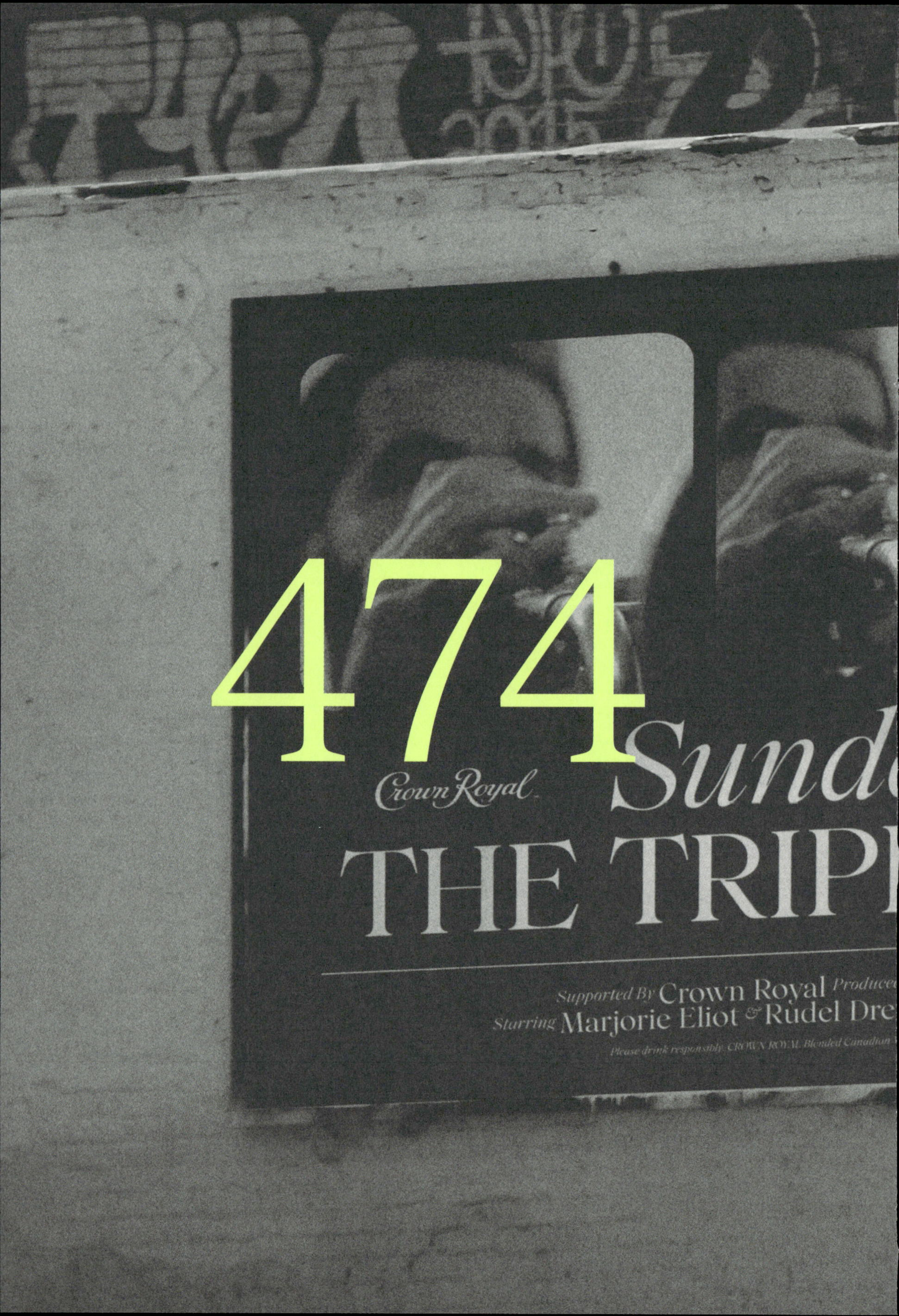
Crown Royal
THE
Supported By Crown Royal
Starring Marjorie Eliot & Rudel

475

ys at
E NICKEL
ept Studios Production
itten and Directed by Jess Colquhoun

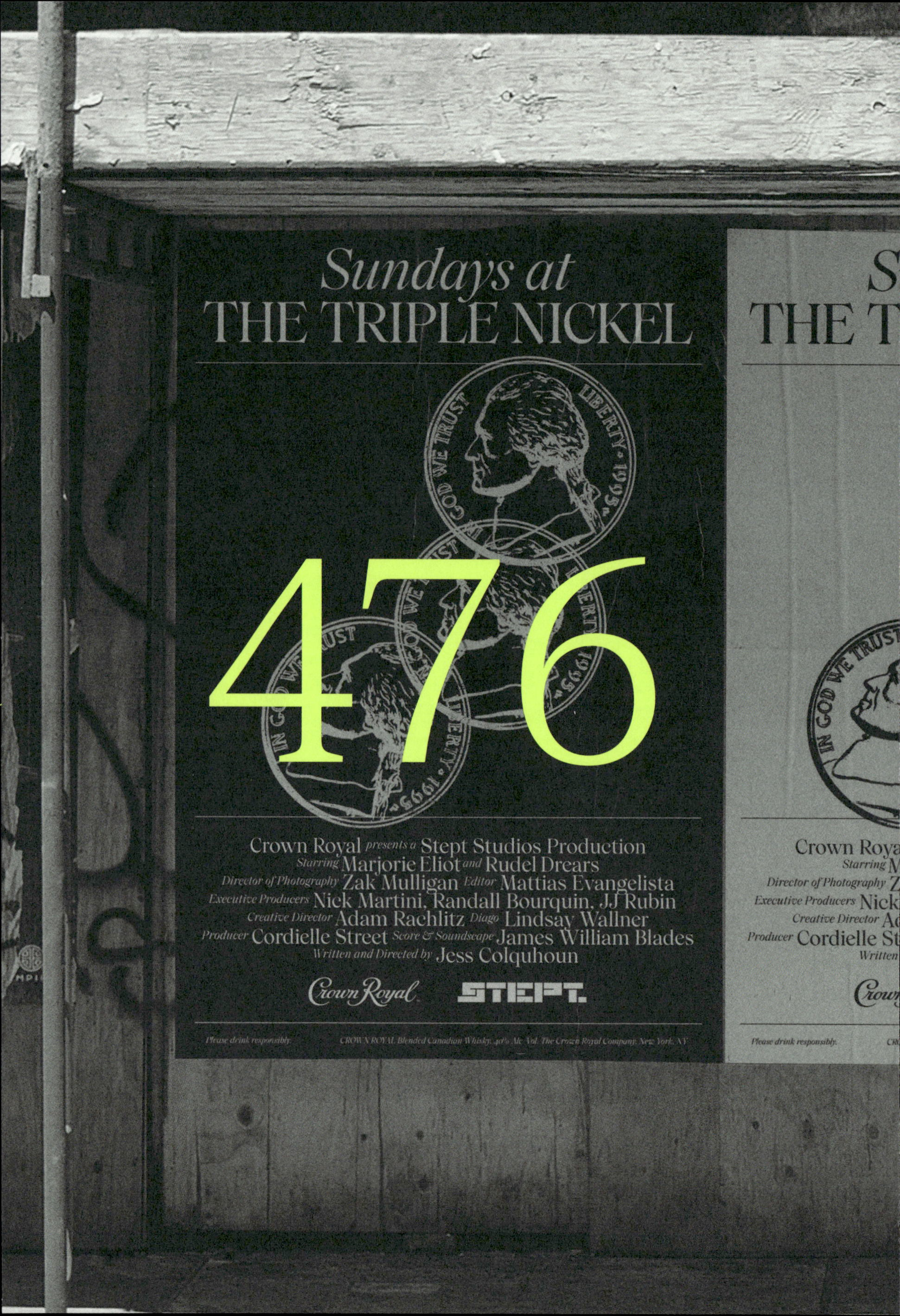
Sundays at
THE TRIPLE NICKEL
IN GOD WE TRUST
LIBERTY
1995
476
Crown Royal presents a Stept Studios Production
Starring Marjorie Eliot and Rudel Drears
Director of Photography Zak Mulligan Editor Mattias Evangelista
Executive Producers Nick Martini, Randall Bourquin, JJ Rubin
Creative Director Adam Rachlitz Diago Lindsay Wallner
Producer Cordielle Street Score & Soundscape James William Blades
Written and Directed by Jess Colquhoun
Crown Royal
STEPT.
Please drink responsibly.
CROWN ROYAL Blended Canadian Whisky. 40% Alc Vol. The Crown Royal Company. New York, NY
Sundays at
THE TRIPLE NICKEL
Crown Royal
Please drink responsibly.

THE TRIPLE NICKEL

477

Crown Royal

Sundays at

478

479

480

481

482

483
Alberto García Alix
VEINTINUEVE TRECE
Txema Salvans
14—16.11.2019
Curto Pepe Vera
Proyecto Islas Canarias
Yolanda Domínguez

484

VEINTINUEVE
TRECE
Encuentro de
Fotografía y
Artes Visuales
de Lanzarote
ALBERTO GARCÍA ALIX
TXEMA SALVANS
YOLANDA DOMÍNGUEZ
PABLO CURTO
PROYECTO ISLAS CANARIAS
PEPE VERA
ANA PALACIOS

Ana Palacios

© Ana Palacios

Ana Palacios es periodista y fotógrafa documental. Tras quince años trabajando en producción de cine internacional con directores con Ridley Scott, Milos Forman o Roman Polanski, en 2010 cambia radicalmente su trayectoria profesional hacia la fotografía documental visibilizando comunidades vulnerables de la mano de ONG como UNICEF, Manos Unidas o África Directo a quien quiera mirar hacia este lado. Su objetivo es difundir la voz de los invisibles desde el optimismo y la esperanza.

Ha publicado tres libros: *Art in Movement* , *Albino* y *Niños esclavos. La puerta de atrás* sobre la reinserción de los niños víctimas de trata en África Occidental que también consta de una exposición y el primer documental que dirige.

Pablo Curto

© Pablo Curto

Trabaja como fotógrafo de moda y director de cine. Solía trabajar como ingeniero industrial, pero lo dejó en 2013. También solía ser alérgico al pescado, pero también lo ha superado.

Ha trabajado para clientes como LOEWE, Pepe Jeans o ZARA y su trabajo editorial ha sido publicado en Vogue Por[illegible] GQ España, El País Sema[illegible] L'Officiel (ES, [illegible] Sunday Telegraph (UK[illegible] nombrar alg[illegible] bién ha participado e[illegible]o-siciones y [illegible]yecc[illegible] en el New York Fash[illegible]ilm Festival [illegible] el MA[illegible] Museum de Roma.

Alberto García Alix

© Alberto García Alix

Fotógrafo, creador audiovisual, escritor y editor. Sus primeras [illegible]posiciones en solitario las realiza en los [illegible]chenta en las galerías Moria[illegible] [illegible]llio Gallery (Londres). Ostenta el Premio Nacio[illegible] Fotografía (1999) y Pre[illegible]brado 'Caballero de la Orden de las Artes y de las L[illegible] de Francia' en 2012. [illegible]tre otros, ha expuesto su trabajo en el Museo Nacional Centro de Arte Reina Sofí[illegible] parisina Maison Eu[illegible]péenne de la Photographie, el Museo Casa de la Fotografía de Moscú, o el Museo [illegible]nal del Prado. Su[illegible]bras se encuentran en grandes colecciones de arte de todo el mundo como la ale[illegible] Deutshe Börse [illegible]s Fondos Nacionales de Arte Contemporáneo de Francia.

485

Perfect Day. © Txema Salvans

My Kingdom. © Txema Salvans

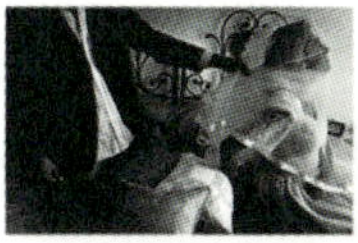

Nice to meet you. © Txema Salvans

The waiting game. © Txema Salvans

Arrecife
TXEMA SALVANS
PABLO CURTO
PEPE VERA
Veintinueve Trece
MÁS INFORMACIÓN Y TICKETS EN
VEINTINUEVETRECE.COM
Veintinueve Trece
14—16.11.2019
CIC
Arrecife
MÁS INFORMACIÓN Y TICKETS EN
VEINTINUEVETRECE.COM

486

Veintinueve Trece
14—16.11.2019
ALBERTO GARCÍA ALIX
TXEMA SALVANS
YOLANDA DOMÍNGUEZ
PABLO CURTO
PROYECTO ISLAS CANARIAS
PEPE VERA
ANA PALACIOS
de Lanzarote
MÁS INFORMACIÓN Y TICKETS EN
VEINTINUEVETRECE.COM
veintinueve trece
ALBERTO GARCÍA ALIX
TXEMA SALVANS
YOLANDA DOMÍNGUEZ
PABLO CURTO
PROYECTO ISLAS CANARIAS
PEPE VERA
ANA PALACIOS
PALOMA RINCÓN

487

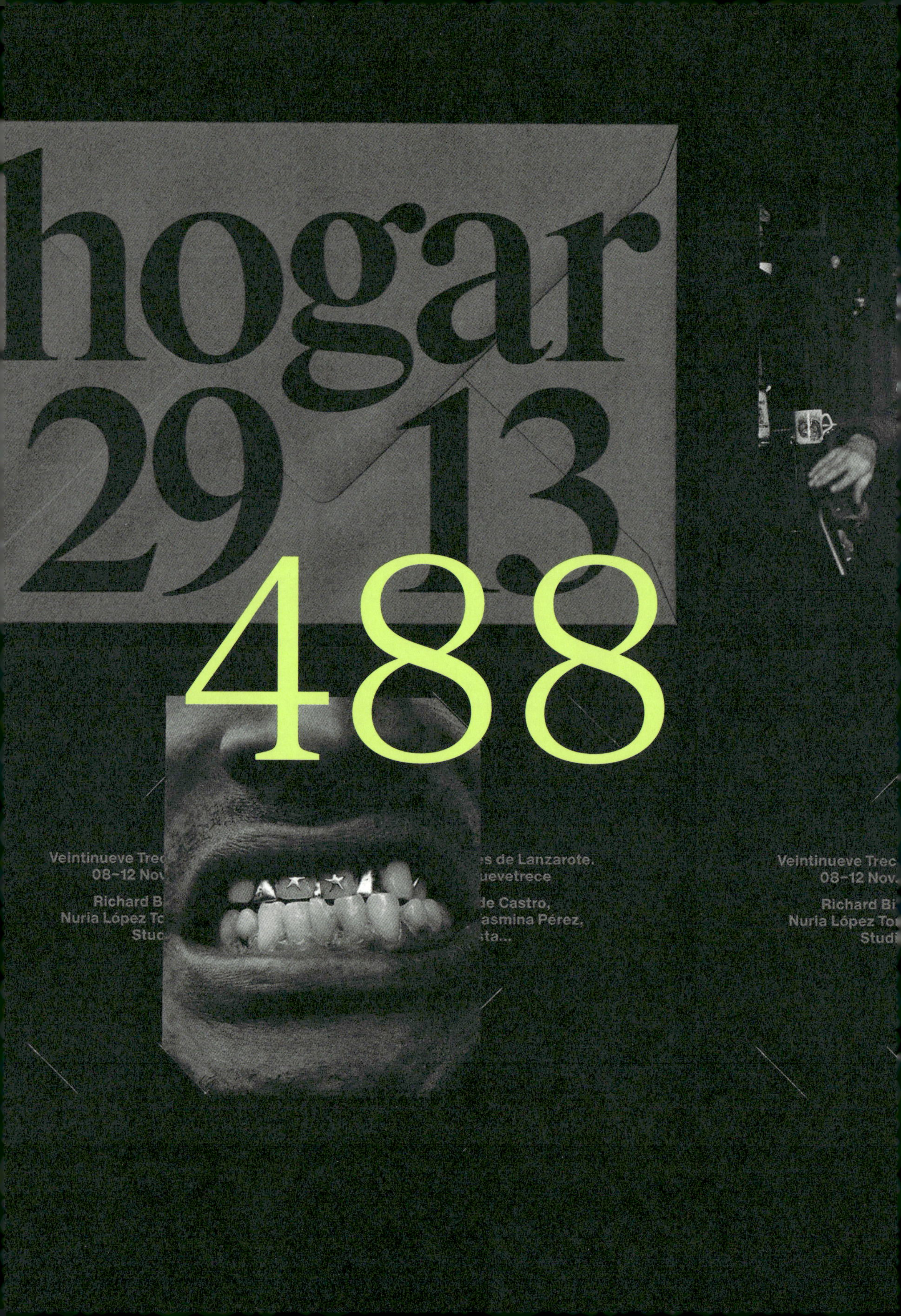
hogar
29 13
488
Veintinueve Trec
08–12 Nov
Richard B
Nuria López To
Stuc
es de Lanzarote.
uevetrece
de Castro,
asmina Pérez,
sta...
Veintinueve Trec
08–12 Nov.
Richard Bi
Nuria López To
Studi

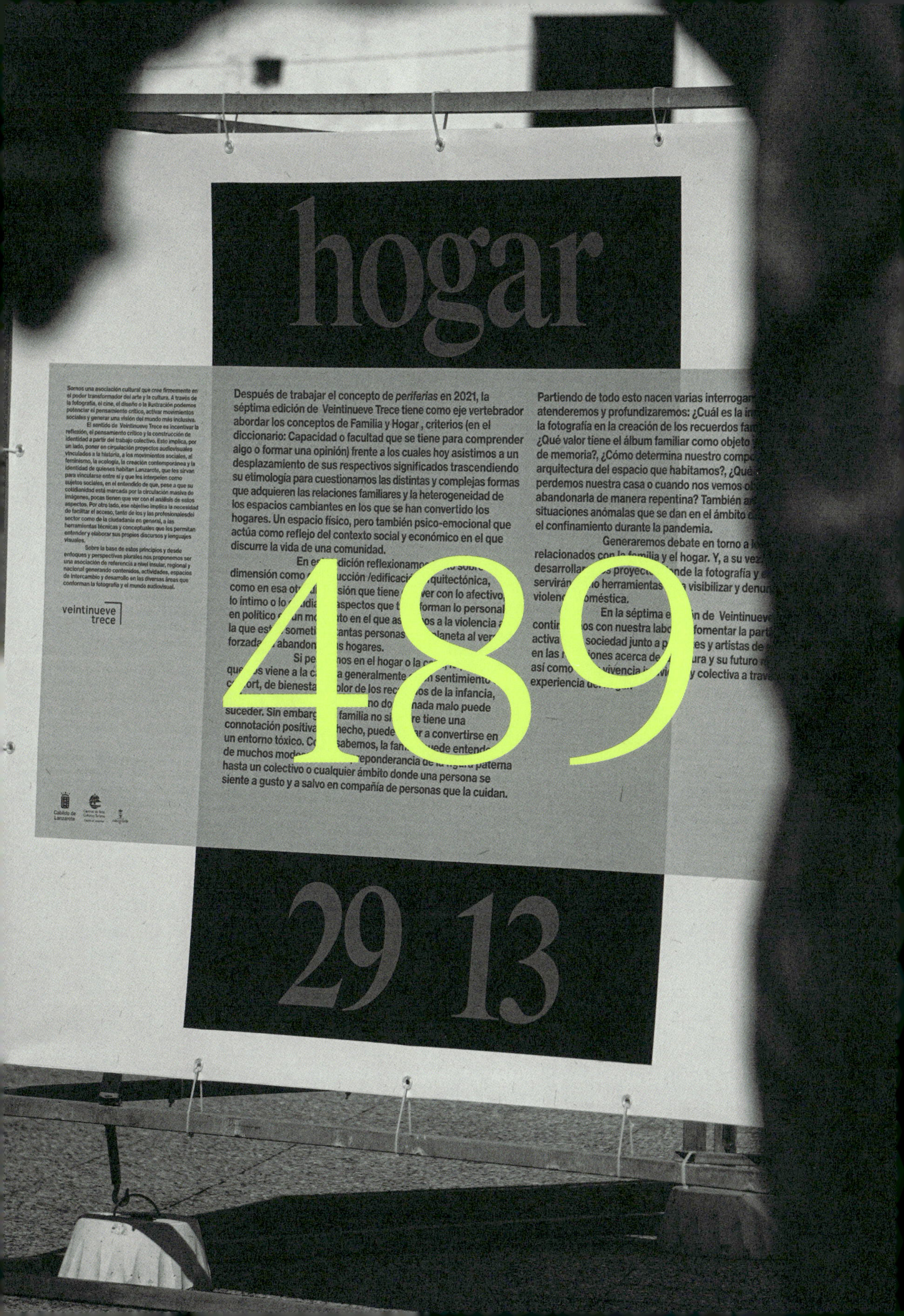
hogar
Después de trabajar el concepto de *periferias* en 2021, la séptima edición de Veintinueve Trece tiene como eje vertebrador abordar los conceptos de Familia y Hogar , criterios (en el diccionario: Capacidad o facultad que se tiene para comprender algo o formar una opinión) frente a los cuales hoy asistimos a un desplazamiento de sus respectivos significados trascendiendo su etimología para cuestionamos las distintas y complejas formas que adquieren las relaciones familiares y la heterogeneidad de los espacios cambiantes en los que se han convertido los hogares. Un espacio físico, pero también psico-emocional que actúa como reflejo del contexto social y económico en el que discurre la vida de una comunidad.
hasta un colectivo o cualquier ámbito donde una persona se siente a gusto y a salvo en compañía de personas que la cuidan.
veintinueve trece
29 13

489

Richard Billingham, Lua Ribeira, Juan Brenner, Estela de Castro,
Nuria López Torres, Rebeka Arce, Albert Salas, Elías Taño, Yasmina Pérez,
Studio Bruma, Saray Ossorio y Néstor Pérez Batista...
hogar
29 13
Juan
Brenner
Veintinueve Trece. 7° Encuentro de Fotografía y Artes Visuales de Lanzarote.
08–12 Nov. 2022 www.veintinuevetrece.com, @veintinuevetrece
Cabildo de Lanzarote
Gobierno de Canarias
cultura recife
Richard
Billingha

490

491

Richard Billingham, Lua Ribeira, Juan Brenner, Estela de Castro,
Nuria López Torres, Rebeka Arce, Albert Salas, Elías Taño, Yasmina Pérez,
Studio Bruma, Saray Ossorio y Néstor Pérez Batista...
hogar
29 13
Estela de Castro
Veintinueve Trece. 7º Encuentro de Fotografía y Artes Visuales de Lanzarote.
08–12 Nov. 2022 www.veintinuevetrece.com, @veintinuevetrece
Cabildo de Lanzarote
Gobierno de Canarias

492

OUTFRONT / JCDecaux
Compound
1395 Coronado Ave
Long Beach, CA 90804
@compoundlbc
compoundlb.com
Saturday, June 27
12—3pm
Anna Sew Hoy
Sculpture Activation

493

494
Bag
Check
Compound
1395 Coronado Avenue
Long Beach, CA 90804
CHAOS to COSMOS
1395 Coronado Ave
Long Beach, CA 90804
Gisela
Fred Eversley
Steve Fawley
Jennifer Guidi
Anthony James
Max Jansons
Seffa Klein
Florence Miller Pierce
Eamon Ore Giron
Helen Pashgian
Fay Ray
Rachel Rose
Anna Sew Hoy
Chrysanne Stathacos
Gail Stoicheff
Tavares Strachan
Alma Woodsey Thomas
Thanks for visiting!
ART AT COMPOU
PROGRAMMING

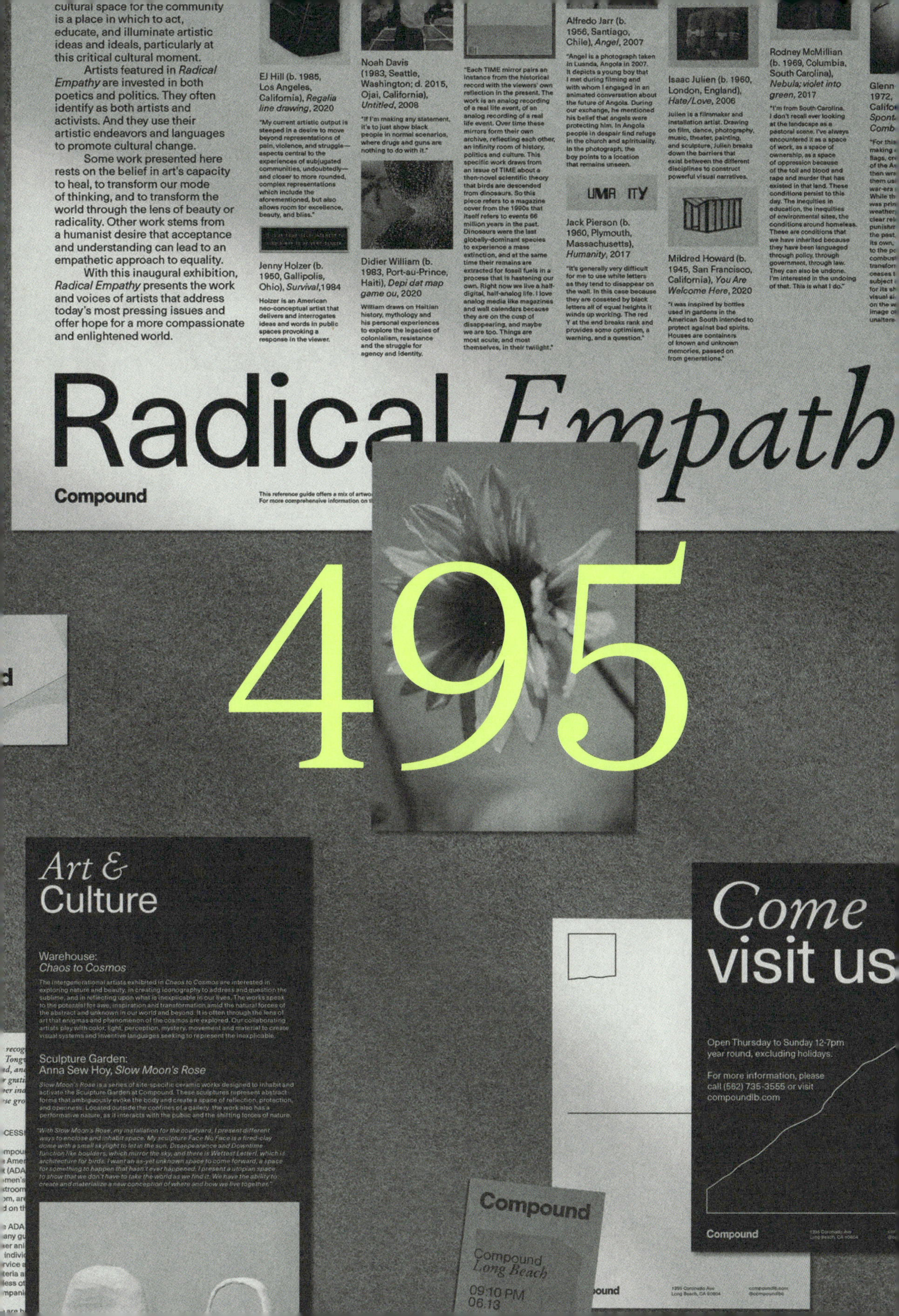
cultural space for the community is a place in which to act, educate, and illuminate artistic ideas and ideals, particularly at this critical cultural moment.
Artists featured in Radical Empathy are invested in both poetics and politics. They often identify as both artists and activists. And they use their artistic endeavors and languages to promote cultural change.
Some work presented here rests on the belief in art's capacity to heal, to transform our mode of thinking, and to transform the world through the lens of beauty or radicality. Other work stems from a humanist desire that acceptance and understanding can lead to an empathetic approach to equality.
With this inaugural exhibition, Radical Empathy presents the work and voices of artists that address today's most pressing issues and offer hope for a more compassionate and enlightened world.
EJ Hill (b. 1985, Los Angeles, California), Regalia line drawing, 2020
"My current artistic output is steeped in a desire to move beyond representations of pain, violence, and struggle—aspects central to the experiences of subjugated communities, undoubtedly—and closer to more rounded, complex representations which include the aforementioned, but also allows room for excellence, beauty, and bliss."
Jenny Holzer (b. 1950, Gallipolis, Ohio), Survival, 1984
Holzer is an American neo-conceptual artist that delivers and interrogates ideas and words in public spaces provoking a response in the viewer.
Noah Davis (1983, Seattle, Washington; d. 2015, Ojai, California), Untitled, 2008
"If I'm making any statement, it's to just show black people in normal scenarios, where drugs and guns are nothing to do with it."
Didier William (b. 1983, Port-au-Prince, Haiti), Depi dat map game ou, 2020
William draws on Haitian history, mythology and his personal experiences to explore the legacies of colonialism, resistance and the struggle for agency and identity.
"Each TIME mirror pairs an instance from the historical record with the viewers' own reflection in the present. The work is an analog recording of a real life event, of an analog recording of a real life event. Over time these mirrors form their own archive, reflecting each other, an infinity room of history, politics and culture. This specific work draws from an issue of TIME about a then-novel scientific theory that birds are descended from dinosaurs. So this piece refers to a magazine cover from the 1990s that itself refers to events 66 million years in the past. Dinosaurs were the last globally-dominant species to experience a mass extinction, and at the same time their remains are extracted for fossil fuels in a process that is hastening our own. Right now we live a half-digital, half-analog life. I love analog media like magazines and wall calendars because they are on the cusp of disappearing, and maybe we are too. Things are most acute, and most themselves, in their twilight."
Alfredo Jarr (b. 1956, Santiago, Chile), Angel, 2007
"Angel is a photograph taken in Luanda, Angola in 2007. It depicts a young boy that I met during filming and with whom I engaged in an animated conversation about the future of Angola. During our exchange, he mentioned his belief that angels were protecting him. In Angola people in despair find refuge in the church and spirituality. In the photograph, the boy points to a location that remains unseen.
UMA ITY
Jack Pierson (b. 1960, Plymouth, Massachusetts), Humanity, 2017
"It's generally very difficult for me to use white letters as they tend to disappear on the wall. In this case because they are cosseted by black letters all of equal heights it winds up working. The red Y at the end breaks rank and provides some optimism, a warning, and a question."
Isaac Julien (b. 1960, London, England), Hate/Love, 2006
Julien is a filmmaker and installation artist. Drawing on film, dance, photography, music, theater, painting, and sculpture, Julien breaks down the barriers that exist between the different disciplines to construct powerful visual narratives.
Mildred Howard (b. 1945, San Francisco, California), You Are Welcome Here, 2020
"I was inspired by bottles used in gardens in the American South intended to protect against bad spirits. Houses are containers of known and unknown memories, passed on from generations."
Rodney McMillian (b. 1969, Columbia, South Carolina), Nebula; violet into green, 2017
"I'm from South Carolina. I don't recall ever looking at the landscape as a pastoral scene. I've always encountered it as a space of work, as a space of ownership, as a space of oppression because of the toil and blood and rape and murder that has existed in that land. These conditions persist to this day. The inequities in education, the inequities of environmental sites, the conditions around homeless. These are conditions that we have inherited because they have been languaged through policy, through government, through law. They can also be undone. I'm interested in the undoing of that. This is what I do."
Radical Empathy
Compound
Art & Culture
Warehouse:
Chaos to Cosmos
The intergenerational artists exhibited in Chaos to Cosmos are interested in exploring nature and beauty, in creating iconography to address and question the sublime, and in reflecting upon what is inexplicable in our lives. The works speak to the potential for awe, inspiration and transformation amid the natural forces of the abstract and unknown in our world and beyond. It is often through the lens of art that enigmas and phenomenon of the cosmos are explored. Our collaborating artists play with color, light, perception, mystery, movement and material to create visual systems and inventive languages seeking to represent the inexplicable.
Sculpture Garden:
Anna Sew Hoy, Slow Moon's Rose
Slow Moon's Rose is a series of site-specific ceramic works designed to inhabit and activate the Sculpture Garden at Compound. These sculptures represent abstract forms that ambiguously evoke the body and create a space of reflection, protection, and openness. Located outside the confines of a gallery, the work also has a performative nature, as it interacts with the public and the shifting forces of nature.
"With Slow Moon's Rose, my installation for the courtyard, I present different ways to enclose and inhabit space. My sculpture Face No Face is a fired-clay dome with a small skylight to let in the sun. Disappearance and Downtime function like boulders, which mirror the sky, and there is Wettest Letter!, which is architecture for birds. I want an as-yet unknown space to come forward, a space for something to happen that hasn't ever happened. I present a utopian space to show that we don't have to take the world as we find it. We have the ability to create and materialize a new conception of where and how we live together."
Come visit us
Open Thursday to Sunday 12-7pm year round, excluding holidays.
For more information, please call (562) 735-3555 or visit compoundlb.com
Compound
Compound
Compound Long Beach
09:10 PM
06.13

495

496

497

45°30'20"N 73°35'20" O
BleuRoyal
Bleu Royal
Gin fait au Québec
Gin made in Quebec
Couleur 100% naturelle
100% natural colour
Gin floral distingué
Floral distinguish gin
45% alc. / vol.
750 mL

498
Bleu Royal
Gin bleu floral
Floral blue gin
Produit du
Québec, Canada
12 x 750 ml
18 kg
1 00 62825 09391 6
BleuRoyal
Distillé par
Distilled by
BluePearl.

499
Bleu
Royal
Gin bleu floral
Floral blue gin
Produit du
Québec, Canada
12 x 750 ml
18 kg
BluePearl.
07/16/2018

500

CI&Sf
60 TIRAGES DE TÊTE
RELIURE HOUDART
Chaire Innovation & Savoir_faire
2012
2017

501

502
60 TIRAGES DE TÊTE
RELIURE HOUDART
Chaire
Innovation &
Savoir_faire
2012
2017

ÉCOLE NATIONALE
SUPÉRIEURE
DES ARTS DÉCORATIFS
PARIS
FONDATION
BETTENCOURT
SCHUELLER
503

504

Cl&Sf
WORKSHOPS INNOVATION & SAVOIR–FAIRE
Chaire Innovation & Savoir—faire
Julie Daut
× Atelier Silicybin
TECHNIQUE DU VERRE
Photographie
Dominique
PERFUMES FACTORY
Cet ensemble de trois coffrets permet d'appréhender le monde des odeurs et apprendre à fabriquer des parfums, seul ou en groupe, chez soi ou au sein d'un atelier olfactif.
Le premier coffret contient le nécessaire pour procéder à une distillation pour la récupération des huiles essentielles, à partir d'agrumes ou de pétales de fleurs.
Le deuxième coffret comprend un orgue de parfumeur contenant des «parfums de base», les résultats des distillations et des flacons vides afin de procéder à la formulation des parfums. Les «parfums de base» évoquent des notions pouvant être combinées afin de «créer» ses propres parfums. Ils sont similaires à des mots et peuvent être additionnés entre eux selon une grammaire à expérimenter pour former des phrases olfactives. L'usager devient ainsi apprenti parfumeur.
Enfin, le troisième coffret contient plusieurs types de diffuseurs.
Techniques et matériaux: verre soufflé, PMMA, ébénisterie, parfumerie, fraisage numérique, découpe laser, frêne, liège
56
57

2013
2014
505
Partenaires
2

506

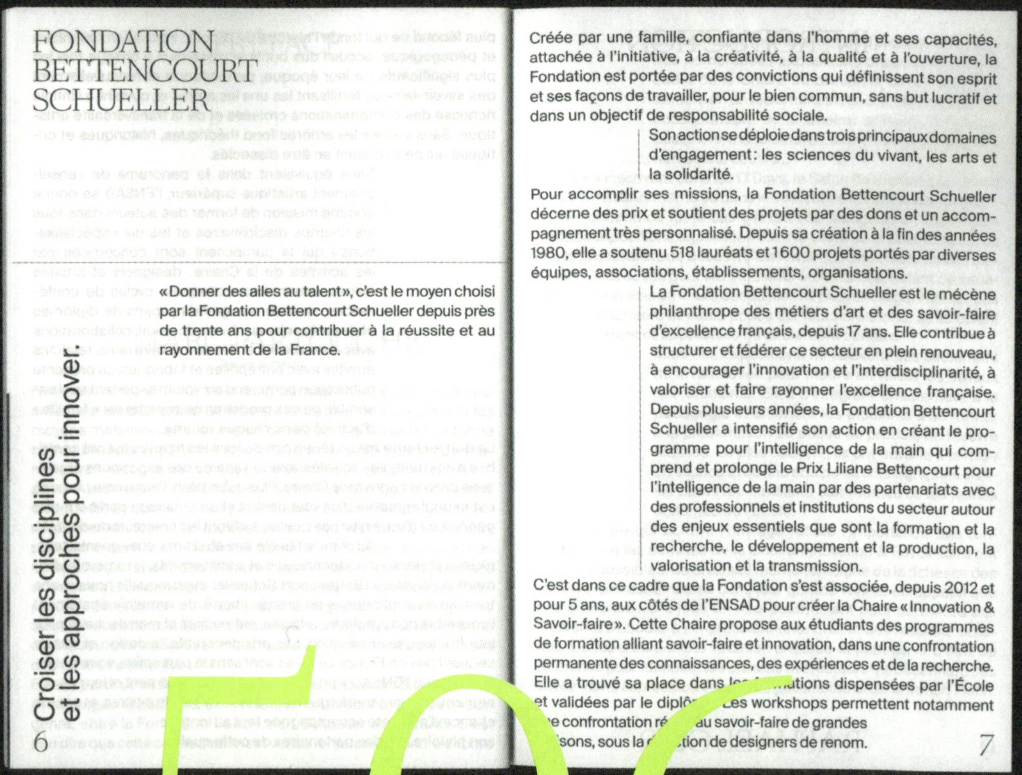
FONDATION BETTENCOURT SCHUELLER
Croiser les disciplines et les approches pour innover.
«Donner des ailes au talent», c'est le moyen choisi par la Fondation Bettencourt Schueller depuis près de trente ans pour contribuer à la réussite et au rayonnement de la France.
6
Créée par une famille, confiante dans l'homme et ses capacités, attachée à l'initiative, à la créativité, à la qualité et à l'ouverture, la Fondation est portée par des convictions qui définissent son esprit et ses façons de travailler, pour le bien commun, sans but lucratif et dans un objectif de responsabilité sociale.
Son action se déploie dans trois principaux domaines d'engagement: les sciences du vivant, les arts et la solidarité.
Pour accomplir ses missions, la Fondation Bettencourt Schueller décerne des prix et soutient des projets par des dons et un accompagnement très personnalisé. Depuis sa création à la fin des années 1980, elle a soutenu 518 lauréats et 1600 projets portés par diverses équipes, associations, établissements, organisations.
La Fondation Bettencourt Schueller est le mécène philanthrope des métiers d'art et des savoir-faire d'excellence français, depuis 17 ans. Elle contribue à structurer et fédérer ce secteur en plein renouveau, à encourager l'innovation et l'interdisciplinarité, à valoriser et faire rayonner l'excellence française. Depuis plusieurs années, la Fondation Bettencourt Schueller a intensifié son action en créant le programme pour l'intelligence de la main qui comprend et prolonge le Prix Liliane Bettencourt pour l'intelligence de la main par des partenariats avec des professionnels et institutions du secteur autour des enjeux essentiels que sont la formation et la recherche, le développement et la production, la valorisation et la transmission.
C'est dans ce cadre que la Fondation s'est associée, depuis 2012 et pour 5 ans, aux côtés de l'ENSAD pour créer la Chaire «Innovation & Savoir-faire». Cette Chaire propose aux étudiants des programmes de formation alliant savoir-faire et innovation, dans une confrontation permanente des connaissances, des expériences et de la recherche.
7

Fontes contemporaines
Photographie
Flora Laudrin
Johanna Benaïnous & Elsa Parra
71

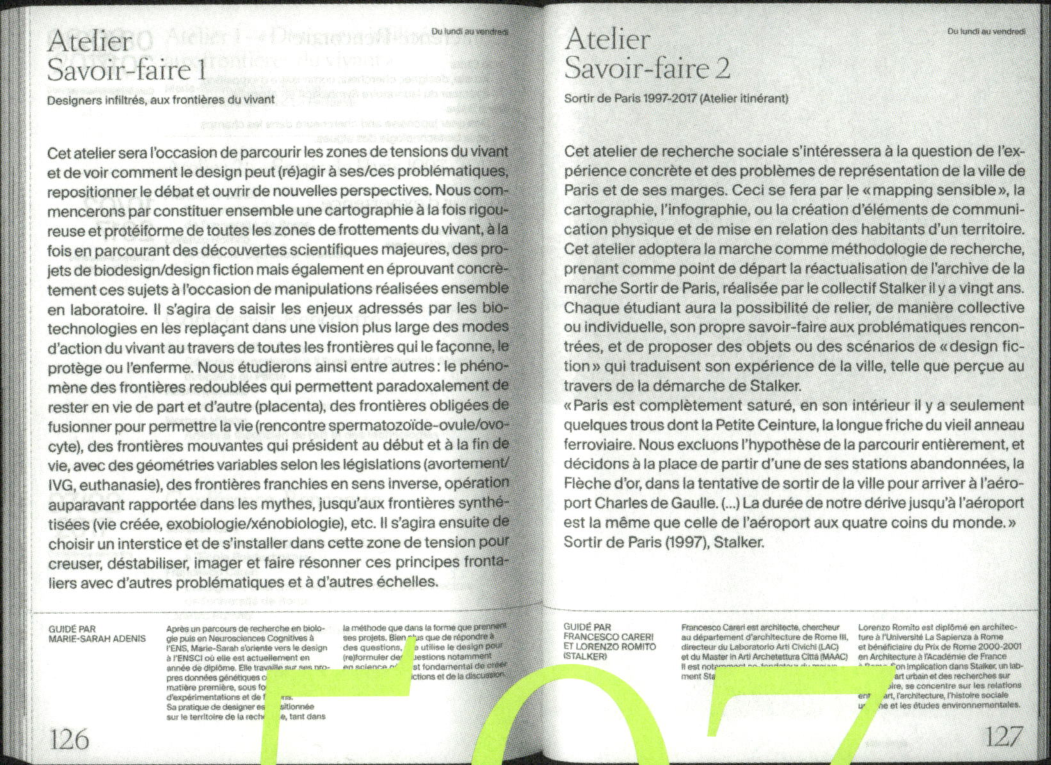

Du lundi au vendredi

Atelier Savoir-faire 1

Designers infiltrés, aux frontières du vivant

Cet atelier sera l'occasion de parcourir les zones de tensions du vivant et de voir comment le design peut (ré)agir à ses/ces problématiques, repositionner le débat et ouvrir de nouvelles perspectives. Nous commencerons par constituer ensemble une cartographie à la fois rigoureuse et protéiforme de toutes les zones de frottements du vivant, à la fois en parcourant des découvertes scientifiques majeures, des projets de biodesign/design fiction mais également en éprouvant concrètement ces sujets à l'occasion de manipulations réalisées ensemble en laboratoire. Il s'agira de saisir les enjeux adressés par les biotechnologies en les replaçant dans une vision plus large des modes d'action du vivant au travers de toutes les frontières qui le façonne, le protège ou l'enferme. Nous étudierons ainsi entre autres : le phénomène des frontières redoublées qui permettent paradoxalement de rester en vie de part et d'autre (placenta), des frontières obligées de fusionner pour permettre la vie (rencontre spermatozoïde-ovule/ovocyte), des frontières mouvantes qui président au début et à la fin de vie, avec des géométries variables selon les législations (avortement/IVG, euthanasie), des frontières franchies en sens inverse, opération auparavant rapportée dans les mythes, jusqu'aux frontières synthétisées (vie créée, exobiologie/xénobiologie), etc. Il s'agira ensuite de choisir un interstice et de s'installer dans cette zone de tension pour creuser, déstabiliser, imager et faire résonner ces principes frontaliers avec d'autres problématiques et à d'autres échelles.

GUIDÉ PAR MARIE-SARAH ADENIS

Après un parcours de recherche en biologie puis en Neurosciences Cognitives à l'ENS, Marie-Sarah s'oriente vers le design à l'ENSCI où elle est actuellement en année de diplôme. Elle travaille sur ses propres données génétiques c[illegible] matière première, sous fo[illegible] d'expérimentations et de f[illegible]. Sa pratique de designer es[illegible]sitionnée sur le territoire de la reche[illegible]e, tant dans la méthode que dans la forme que prennent ses projets. Bien [illegible]us que de répondre à des questions, [illegible]e utilise le design pour (re)formuler de[illegible]uestions notamment en science o[illegible]st fondamental de créer [illegible]ictions et de la discussion.

126

Du lundi au vendredi

Atelier Savoir-faire 2

Sortir de Paris 1997-2017 (Atelier itinérant)

Cet atelier de recherche sociale s'intéressera à la question de l'expérience concrète et des problèmes de représentation de la ville de Paris et de ses marges. Ceci se fera par le « mapping sensible », la cartographie, l'infographie, ou la création d'éléments de communication physique et de mise en relation des habitants d'un territoire. Cet atelier adoptera la marche comme méthodologie de recherche, prenant comme point de départ la réactualisation de l'archive de la marche Sortir de Paris, réalisée par le collectif Stalker il y a vingt ans. Chaque étudiant aura la possibilité de relier, de manière collective ou individuelle, son propre savoir-faire aux problématiques rencontrées, et de proposer des objets ou des scénarios de « design fiction » qui traduisent son expérience de la ville, telle que perçue au travers de la démarche de Stalker.

« Paris est complètement saturé, en son intérieur il y a seulement quelques trous dont la Petite Ceinture, la longue friche du vieil anneau ferroviaire. Nous excluons l'hypothèse de la parcourir entièrement, et décidons à la place de partir d'une de ses stations abandonnées, la Flèche d'or, dans la tentative de sortir de la ville pour arriver à l'aéroport Charles de Gaulle. (...) La durée de notre dérive jusqu'à l'aéroport est la même que celle de l'aéroport aux quatre coins du monde. »
Sortir de Paris (1997), Stalker.

GUIDÉ PAR FRANCESCO CARERI ET LORENZO ROMITO (STALKER)

Francesco Careri est architecte, chercheur au département d'architecture de Rome III, directeur du Laboratorio Arti Civichi (LAC) et du Master in Arti Archetettura Città (MAAC). Il est not[illegible] ment Sta[illegible]

Lorenzo Romito est diplômé en architecture à l'Université La Sapienza à Rome et bénéficiaire du Prix de Rome 2000-2001 en Architecture à l'Académie de France [illegible]on implication dans Stalker, un lab[illegible] art urbain et des recherches sur [illegible]ire, se concentre sur les relations ent[illegible]art, l'architecture, l'histoire sociale ur[illegible]e et les études environnementales.

127

507

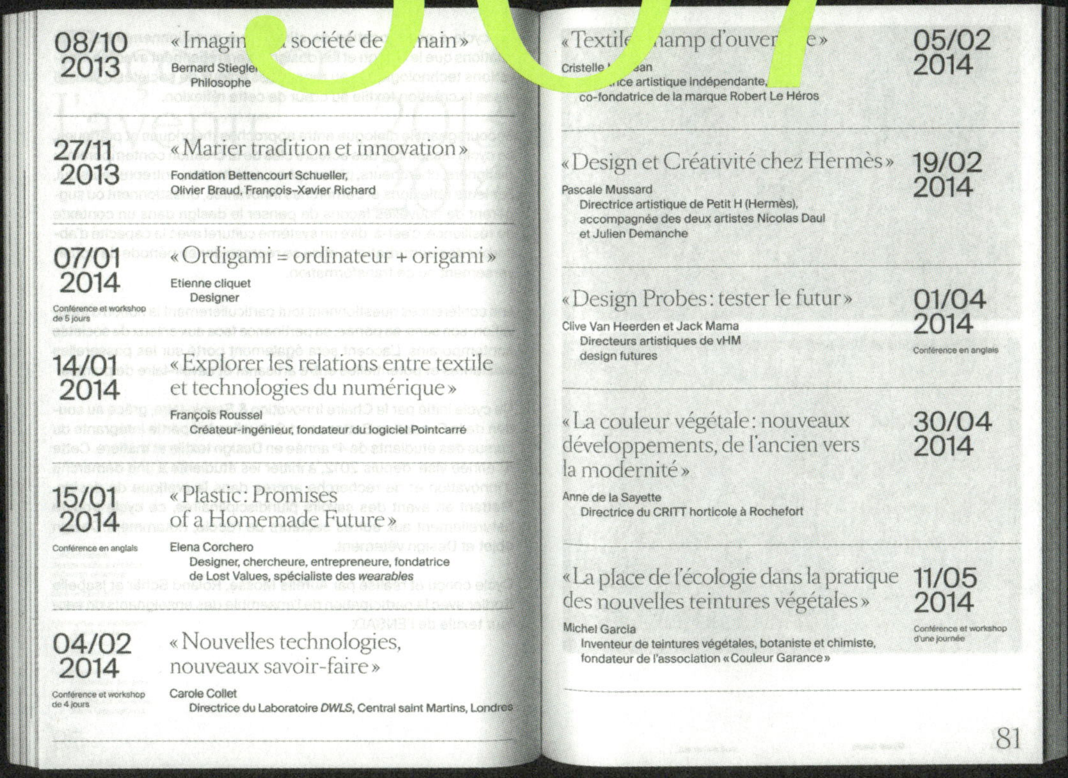

08/10 2013 — « Imagin[illegible] société de [illegible]main »
Bernard Stiegle[illegible]
Philosophe

27/11 2013 — « Marier tradition et innovation »
Fondation Bettencourt Schueller,
Olivier Braud, François-Xavier Richard

07/01 2014 — « Ordigami = ordinateur + origami »
Conférence et workshop de 5 jours
Etienne cliquet
Designer

14/01 2014 — « Explorer les relations entre textile et technologies du numérique »
François Roussel
Créateur-ingénieur, fondateur du logiciel Pointcarré

15/01 2014 — « Plastic: Promises of a Homemade Future »
Conférence en anglais
Elena Corchero
Designer, chercheure, entrepreneure, fondatrice de Lost Values, spécialiste des *wearables*

04/02 2014 — « Nouvelles technologies, nouveaux savoir-faire »
Conférence et workshop de 4 jours
Carole Collet
Directrice du Laboratoire *DWLS*, Central saint Martins, Londres

« Textile[illegible]hamp d'ouver[illegible]e » — 05/02 2014
Cristelle [illegible]ean
[illegible]ce artistique indépendante,
co-fondatrice de la marque Robert Le Héros

« Design et Créativité chez Hermès » — 19/02 2014
Pascale Mussard
Directrice artistique de Petit H (Hermès), accompagnée des deux artistes Nicolas Daul et Julien Demanche

« Design Probes : tester le futur » — 01/04 2014
Conférence en anglais
Clive Van Heerden et Jack Mama
Directeurs artistiques de vHM design futures

« La couleur végétale : nouveaux développements, de l'ancien vers la modernité » — 30/04 2014
Anne de la Sayette
Directrice du CRITT horticole à Rochefort

« La place de l'écologie dans la pratique des nouvelles teintures végétales » — 11/05 2014
Conférence et workshop d'une journée
Michel Garcia
Inventeur de teintures végétales, botaniste et chimiste, fondateur de l'association « Couleur Garance »

81

508

509

510

Clear Channel
PICASSO.
MUSEU PICASSO
EXPOSICIÓ
18.12.2020
4.4.2021
LES CAHIERS
THE SKETCH BOOKS
LOS CUADERNOS
ELS QUADERNS
Ajuntament de Barcelona

511

18.12.2020
4.4.2021
PICASSO.
Museu Picasso
@MUSEUPICASSO
LES
LOS
ELS
Amb la col·laboració de:
CATALUNYA RÀDIO

513

CUIDEM EL MUSEU
I ET CUIDEM A TU
Seguim les directrius de les autoritats.
Desinfectem freqüentment.
Hem reduït l'aforament per garantir la distància de seguretat.
Hem adequat els espais per a fer confortable la visita.
Fem ús de senyalització de prevenció.
Cuidamos
el museo y
te cuidamos a ti
Hemos reducido el aforo para garantizar la distancia de seguridad.
Hemos adecuado los espacios para que la visita resulte confortable.
Recurrimos a señalización de prevención.
Disponemos de dispensadores de hidrogel desinfectante para las manos.
Hemos formado a nuestro personal.
We have reduced capacity to guarantee a safe distance between visitors.
To allow for a comfortable visit we have adapted our spaces.
We use signs to remind visitors what to do.
We have installed hygienic hand sanitiser dispensers.
We have trained our staff.
Museu Picasso

514

515

516
ARXI
POSS

517

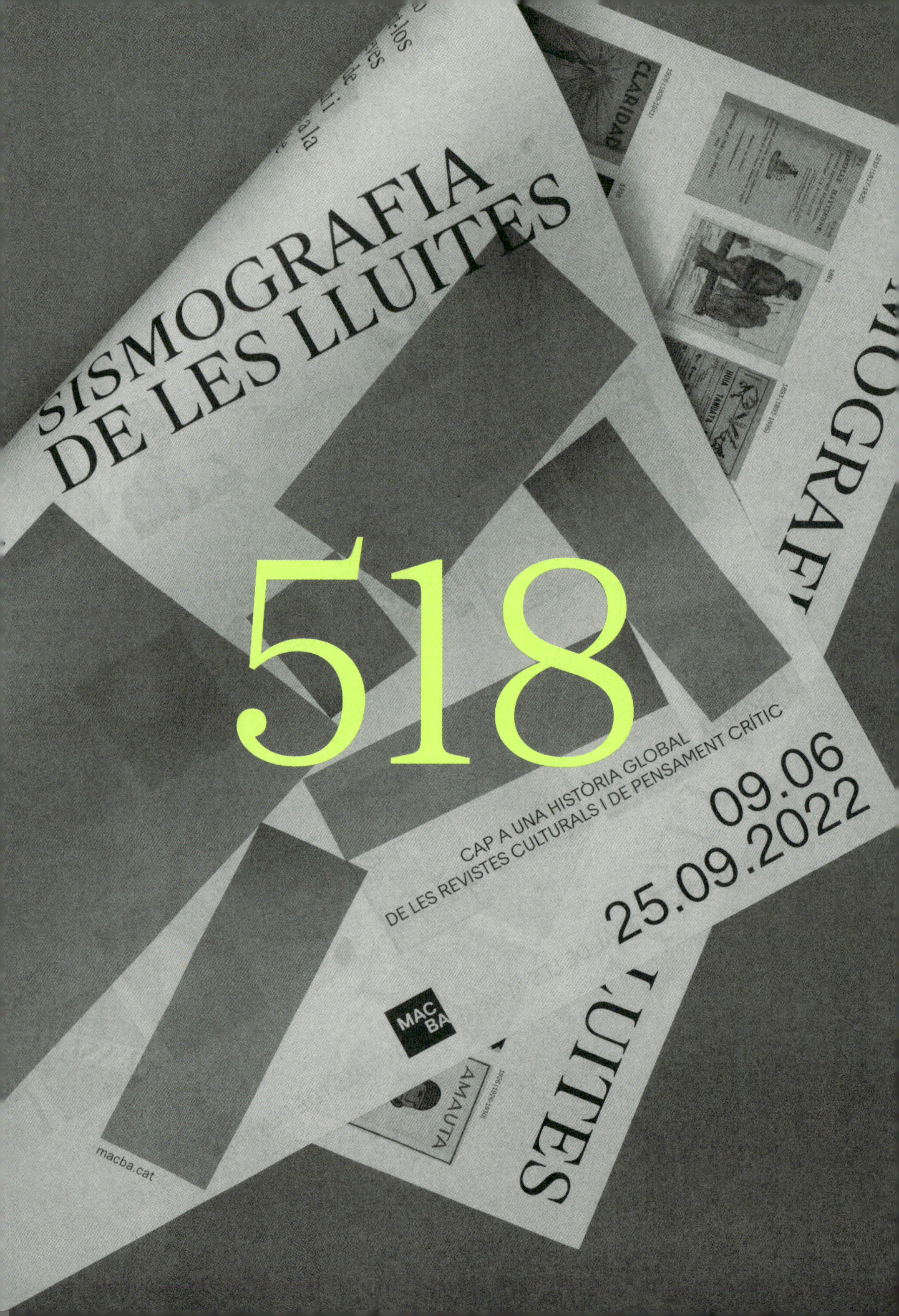
SISMOGRAFIA
DE LES LLUITES
518
CAP A UNA HISTÒRIA GLOBAL
DE LES REVISTES CULTURALS I DE PENSAMENT CRÍTIC
09.06
25.09.2022
MAC
BA
macba.cat
CLARIDAD
AMAUTA
LLUITES

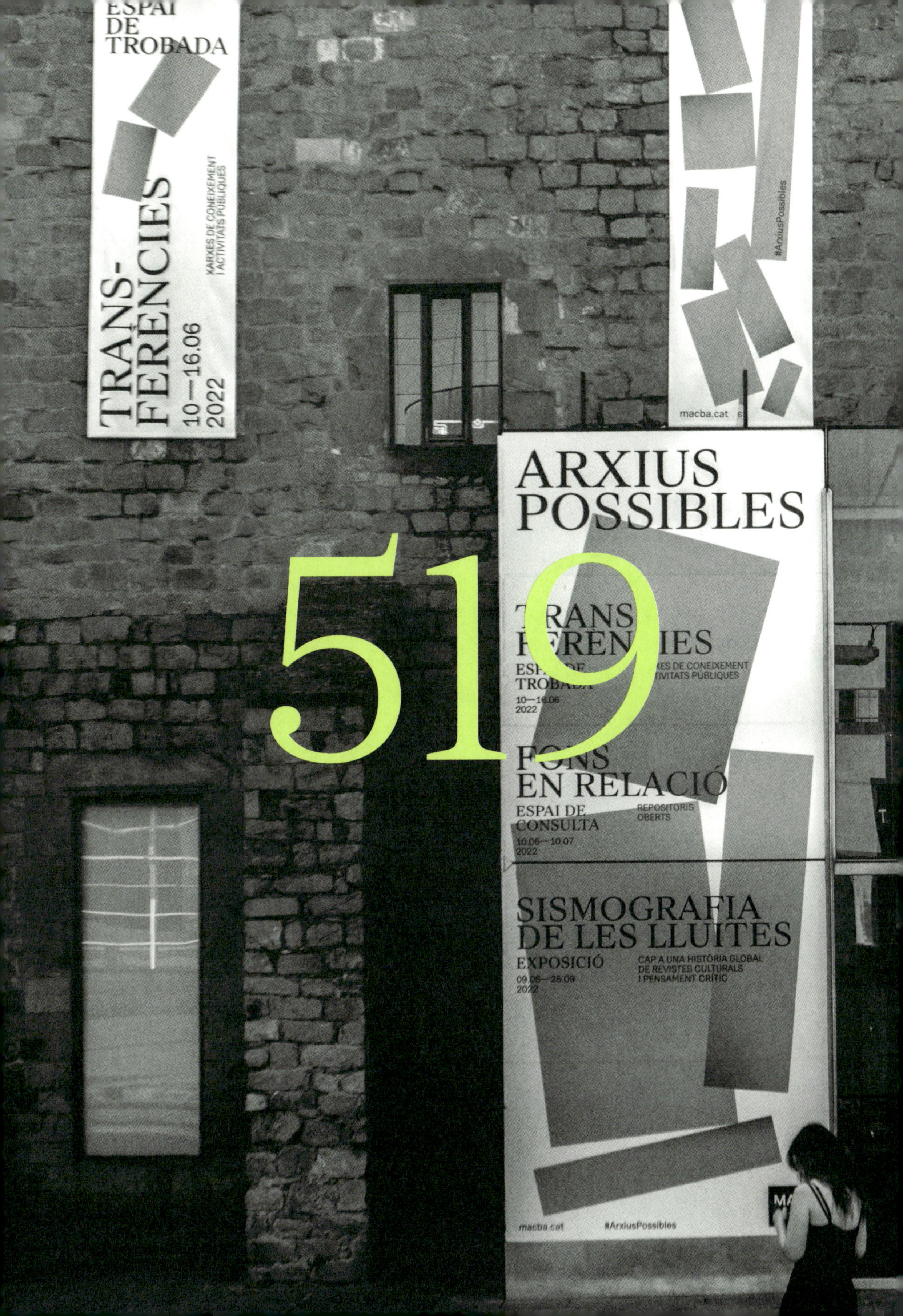
519
ESPAI
DE
TROBADA
TRANS-
FERÈNCIES
XARXES DE CONEIXEMENT
I ACTIVITATS PÚBLIQUES
10—16.06
2022
#ArxiusPossibles
macba.cat
ARXIUS
POSSIBLES
FONS
EN RELACIÓ
ESPAI DE
CONSULTA
REPOSITORIS
OBERTS
10.06—10.07
2022
SISMOGRAFIA
DE LES LLUITES
EXPOSICIÓ
CAP A UNA HISTÒRIA GLOBAL
DE REVISTES CULTURALS
I PENSAMENT CRÍTIC
09.06—25.09
2022
macba.cat
#ArxiusPossibles

COCOA FLAVANOLS CONTAIN 221MILLIGRAMS PER100GRAMS OF CHOCOLATE
每100克巧克力中可可黄烷醇含量221毫克
可可豆产地:委内瑞拉
COCOA BEAN
TYPE: CRIOLLO
ORIGIN: VENEZUELA
可可豆种类:克里奥罗
DARK CHOCOLATE
黑巧克力
CHO
葡萄西柚 NO.05
净含量
25g*4枚入
Net
100g
0TRANS FA
0糖0植脂末
BELG
原产国
GRAPE
葡西柚巧克力
520
BAKING, CRUSHING, BLENDING, GRINDING, REFINING, ACID REMOVAL, TEMPERING CASTING
烘焙 压碎 调配○研磨○精炼○去酸 回火铸形
RELAT HUMIDITY
PERATU
相对湿度≤55% 储存温度≤22°C 溶点温度≥36°C
CHO
本品白砂糖添加量为零
THE AMOUNT OF SUGAR ADDED TO THIS PRODUCT IS ZERO
可可豆里拥有自然界中含量最高的可可黄烷醇
营养成分表 Nutrition information
项目 每100g NRV%
能量 2225kJ 26%
蛋白质 7.1g 12%
脂肪 30.5g 51%
碳水化合物 57.4g 9%
钠 98mg 5%
品牌 CHO
品名 葡萄西柚黑巧克力
产品类型 混合型巧克力制品
配料表 可可液块、可可脂、香草(黑巧克力可可脂含量≥45%;黑巧克力总可可固形物含量≥98%)
净含量 125g
致敏物提示 该产品含有磷脂、乳制品
保质期 12个月
储存条件 避免阳光直射,置阴凉通风处
制造商 某(杭州)食品有限公司
产地 杭州市西湖区某某路22号
地址 杭州市西湖区某某路996号6幢中区3楼
生产许可证号 SC11221011551818
产品标准 GB/T 18181
生产商电话 021-6666 8888
可可黄烷醇有助于人体血管健康保持正常血压
生产日期(年月日)
ABC-abc-1234

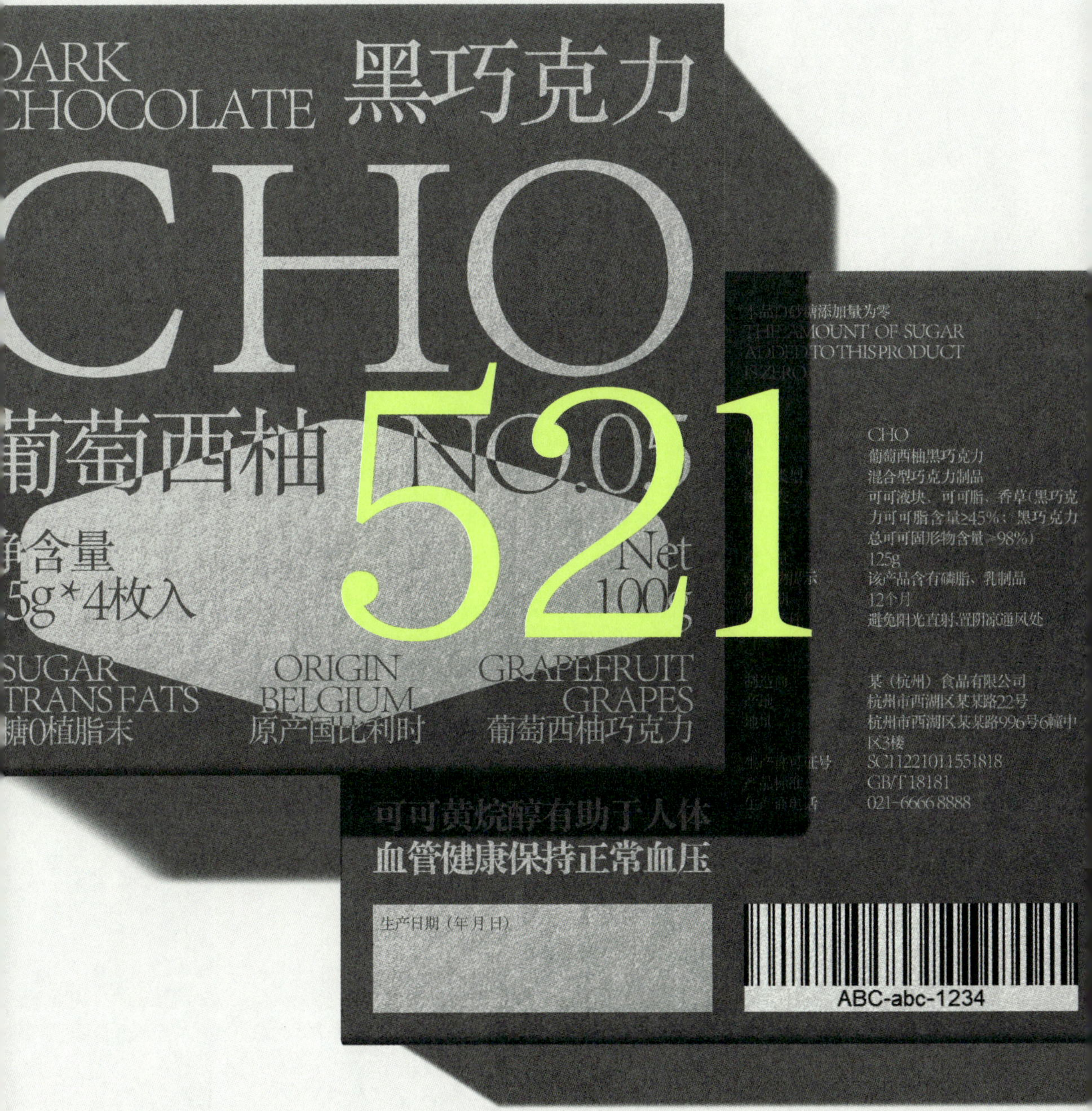
DARK
CHOCOLATE
黑巧克力
CHO
葡萄西柚
NO.05
521
净含量
25g*4枚入
Net
100g
SUGAR
TRANS FATS
糖0植脂末
ORIGIN
BELGIUM
原产国比利时
GRAPEFRUIT
GRAPES
葡萄西柚巧克力
THE AMOUNT OF SUGAR
ADDED TO THIS PRODUCT
IS ZERO
CHO
葡萄西柚黑巧克力
混合型巧克力制品
可可液块、可可脂、香草(黑巧克力可可脂含量≥45%；黑巧克力总可可固形物含量≥98%)
125g
该产品含有磷脂、乳制品
12个月
避免阳光直射,置阴凉通风处
某（杭州）食品有限公司
杭州市西湖区某某路22号
杭州市西湖区某某路996号6幢中区3楼
SC11221011551818
GB/T 18181
021-6666 8888
可可黄烷醇有助于人体
血管健康保持正常血压
生产日期（年月日）
ABC-abc-1234

522
DARK CHOCOLATE 黑巧克力
CHO
葡萄西柚 NO.05
净含量
25g*4枚入
Net
100g
0SUGAR
0TRANS FATS
0糖0植脂末
ORIGIN
BELGIUM
原产国比利时
GRAPEFRUIT
GRAPES
葡萄西柚巧克力

523
DARK
CHOCOLATE
黑巧克力
CHO
葡萄西柚
NO.05
净含量
25g*4枚入
Net
100g
0SUGAR
0TRANS FATS
0糖0植脂末
ORIGIN
BELGIUM
原产国比利时
GRAPEFRUIT
GRAPES
葡萄西柚巧克力

www.
macaoDA.org
©Macau Designers Association
澳門
設計師協會
MDA
Since 1986
Since 1986
©Macau Designers Association
澳門
設計師協會
MDA
Since 1986
Macau Designers
Association

524

525
澳門設計師協會
Macau Designers
Association
MDA
Since 1986

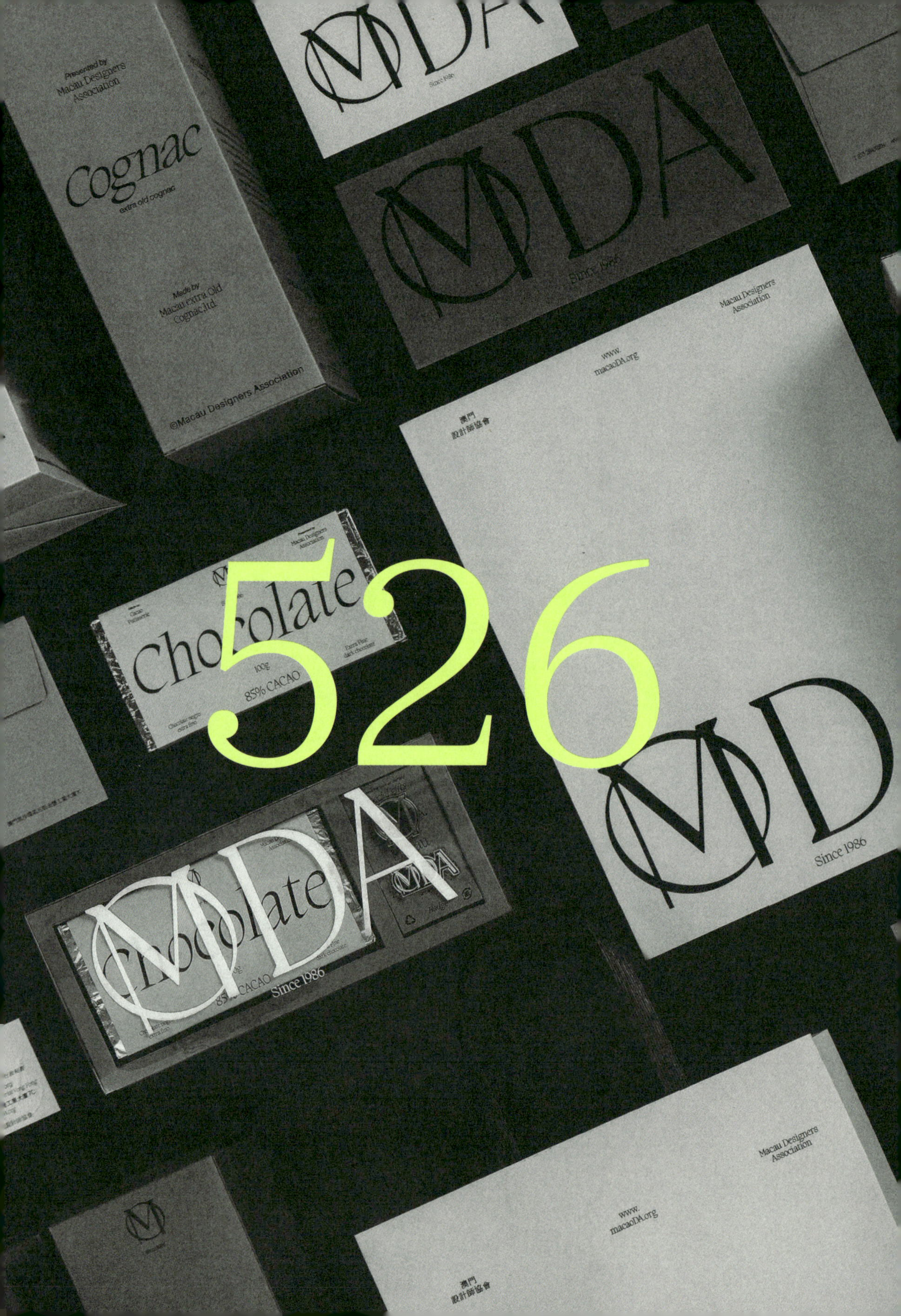
Presented by
Macau Designers
Association
Cognac
extra old cognac
Made by
Macau extra Old
Cognac,ltd.
©Macau Designers Association
MDA
Since 1986
Macau Designers
Association
www.
macaoDA.org
澳門
設計師協會
Chocolate
100g
85% CACAO
Extra Fine
dark chocolate
MD
Since 1986
MDA
Chocolate
85% CACAO
Since 1986
Macau Designers
Association
www.
macaoDA.org
澳門
設計師協會

527

Presented by
Macau Designers
Association
Cognac
extra old cognac
Made by
Macau extra Old
Cognac ltd.
Cognac
MDA
Since 1986
Macau Designers
Association

528
FUTURING

529

BROCK, 16 Rue Jacques Cujas
31000 Toulouse.
Lundi 14h00 à 19h00
Mardi → Samedi 10h30 à 19h00
→ 05.62.27.08.21
(store)
BROCK
Depuis
530

BR
531

CH3. GLYPHS INDEX

TYPEFACE :ADORNO REGULAR P12

a	b	c	d	e	f	G	h	I	J	k	L	m
n	o	p	q	R	s	T	u	v	w	x	y	z
a	b	c	d	e	f	G	h	I	J	k	L	m
n	o	p	q	R	s	T	u	v	w	x	y	z

TYPEFACE :AFFAIRS REGULAR P16

A	B	C	D	E	F	G	H	I	J	K	L	M
N	O	P	Q	R	S	T	U	V	W	X	Y	Z
a	b	c	d	e	f	g	h	i	j	k	l	m
n	o	p	q	r	s	t	u	v	w	x	y	z

TYPEFACE :ALDGATE SERIF REGULAR P20

A	B	C	D	E	F	G	H	I	J	K	L	M
N	O	P	Q	R	S	T	U	V	W	X	Y	Z
a	b	c	d	e	f	g	h	i	j	k	l	m
n	o	p	q	r	s	t	u	v	w	x	y	z

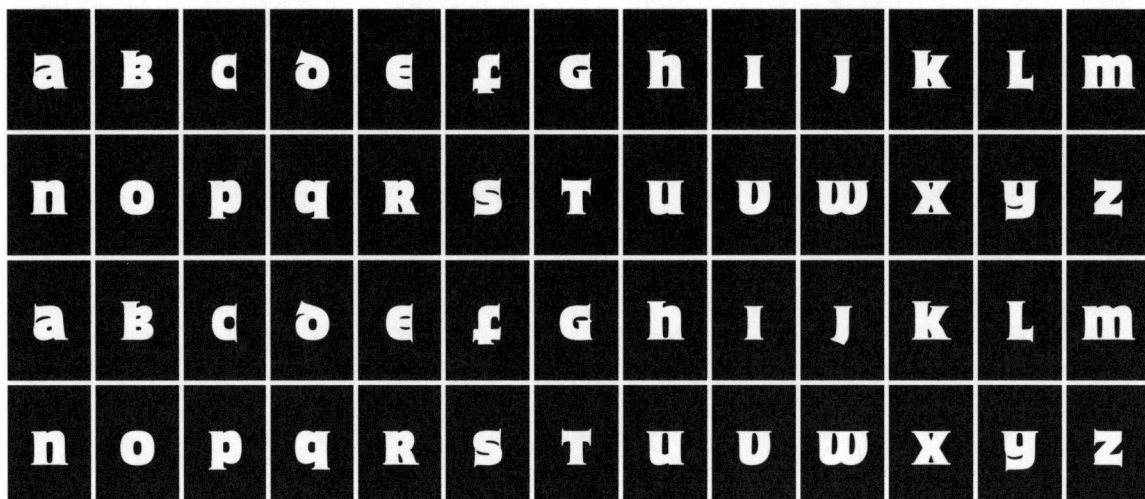

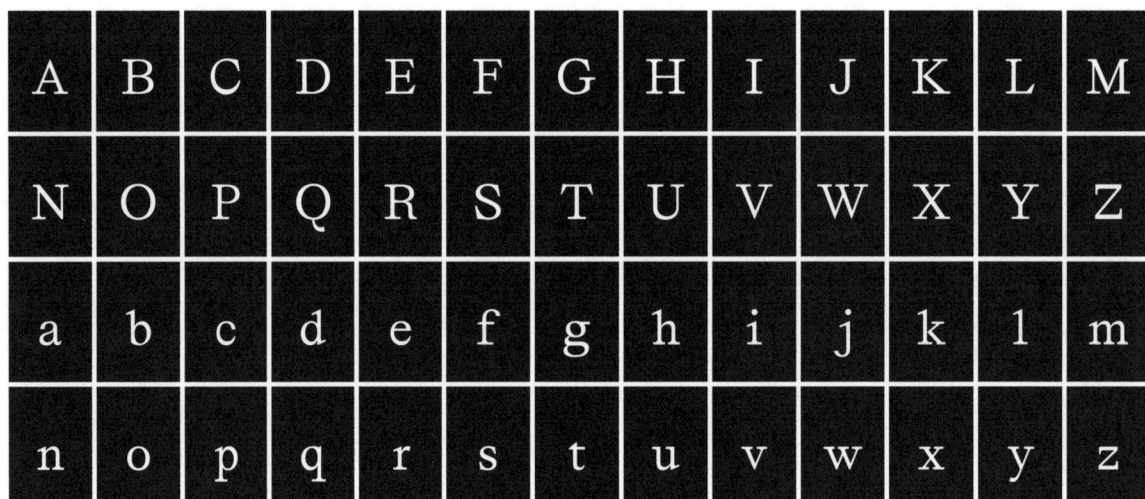

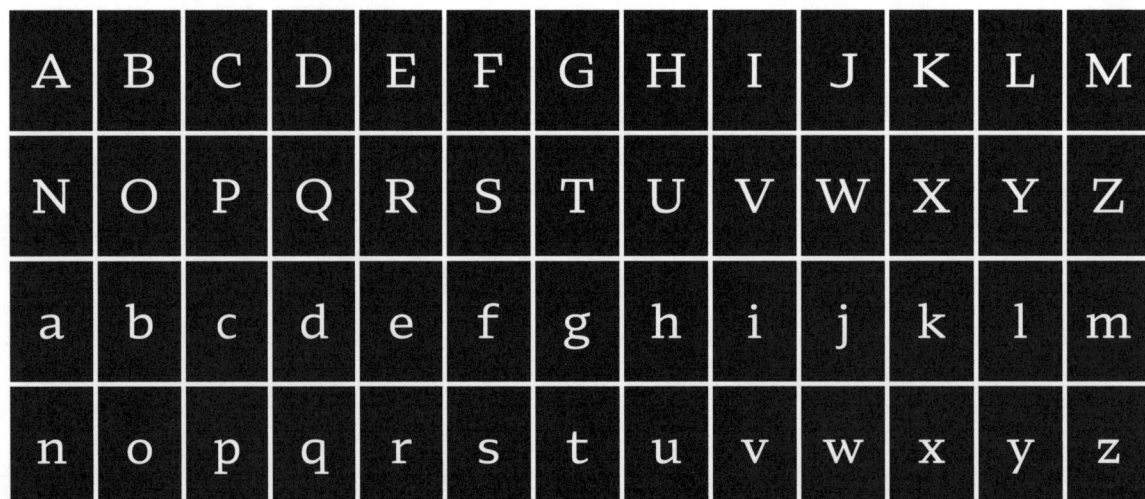

TYPEFACE :ALIZEH REGULAR P24

A	B	C	D	E	F	G	H	I	J	K	L	M
N	O	P	Q	R	S	T	U	V	W	X	Y	Z
a	b	c	d	e	f	g	h	i	j	k	l	m
n	o	p	q	r	s	t	u	v	w	x	y	z

TYPEFACE :GT ALPINA REGULAR P28

A	B	C	D	E	F	G	H	I	J	K	L	M
N	O	P	Q	R	S	T	U	V	W	X	Y	Z
a	b	c	d	e	f	g	h	i	j	k	l	m
n	o	p	q	r	s	t	u	v	w	x	y	z

TYPEFACE :ANTIQUA ROMAN REGULAR P32

A	B	C	D	E	F	G	H	I	J	K	L	M
N	O	P	Q	R	S	T	U	V	W	X	Y	Z
a	b	c	d	e	f	g	h	i	j	k	l	m
n	o	p	q	r	s	t	u	v	w	x	y	z

TYPEFACE :APOC REGULAR P36

A	B	C	D	E	F	G	H	I	J	K	L	M
N	O	P	Q	R	S	T	U	V	W	X	Y	Z
a	b	c	d	e	f	g	h	i	j	k	l	m
n	o	p	q	r	s	t	u	v	w	x	y	z

TYPEFACE :ABC ARIZONA REGULAR P42

A	B	C	D	E	F	G	H	I	J	K	L	M
N	O	P	Q	R	S	T	U	V	W	X	Y	Z
a	b	c	d	e	f	g	h	i	j	k	l	m
n	o	p	q	r	s	t	u	v	w	x	y	z

TYPEFACE :ARTUSI REGULAR P46

A	B	C	D	E	F	G	H	I	J	K	L	M
N	O	P	Q	R	S	T	U	V	W	X	Y	Z
a	b	c	d	e	f	g	h	i	j	k	l	m
n	o	p	q	r	s	t	u	v	w	x	y	z

TYPEFACE :BEASTLY REGULAR P50

A	B	C	D	E	F	G	H	I	J	K	L	M
N	O	P	Q	R	S	T	U	V	W	X	Y	Z
a	b	c	d	e	f	g	h	i	j	k	l	m
n	o	p	q	r	s	t	u	v	w	x	y	z

TYPEFACE :F37 BELLA REGULAR P54

A	B	C	D	E	F	G	H	I	J	K	L	M
N	O	P	Q	R	S	T	U	V	W	X	Y	Z
a	b	c	d	e	f	g	h	i	j	k	l	m
n	o	p	q	r	s	t	u	v	w	x	y	z

TYPEFACE :F37 BOBBY REGULAR P58

A	B	C	D	E	F	G	H	I	J	K	L	M
N	O	P	Q	R	S	T	U	V	W	X	Y	Z
a	b	c	d	e	f	g	h	i	j	k	l	m
n	o	p	q	r	s	t	u	v	w	x	y	z

TYPEFACE :CAKO REGULAR P62

A	B	C	D	E	F	G	H	I	J	K	L	M
N	O	P	Q	R	S	T	U	V	W	X	Y	Z
a	b	c	d	e	f	g	h	i	j	k	l	m
n	o	p	q	r	s	t	u	v	w	x	y	z

TYPEFACE :CANILARI REGULAR P68

A	B	C	D	E	F	G	H	I	J	K	L	M
N	O	P	Q	R	S	T	U	V	W	X	Y	Z
a	b	c	d	e	f	g	h	i	j	k	l	m
n	o	p	q	r	s	t	u	v	w	x	y	z

TYPEFACE :CARDINAL REGULAR P74

A	B	C	D	E	F	G	H	I	J	K	L	M
N	O	P	Q	R	S	T	U	V	W	X	Y	Z
a	b	c	d	e	f	g	h	i	j	k	l	m
n	o	p	q	r	s	t	u	v	w	x	y	z

TYPEFACE :CARDINAL TECH REGULAR P78

A	B	C	D	E	F	G	H	I	J	K	L	M
N	O	P	Q	R	S	T	U	V	W	X	Y	Z
a	b	c	d	e	f	g	h	i	j	k	l	m
n	o	p	q	r	s	t	u	v	w	x	y	z

TYPEFACE :CIGARS REGULAR P82

A	B	C	D	E	F	G	H	I	J	K	L	M
N	O	P	Q	R	S	T	U	V	W	X	Y	Z
a	b	c	d	e	f	g	h	i	j	k	l	m
n	o	p	q	r	s	t	u	v	w	x	y	z

TYPEFACE :COFO CINEMA 1909 REGULAR P86

A	B	C	D	E	F	G	H	I	J	K	L	M
N	O	P	Q	R	S	T	U	V	W	X	Y	Z
A	B	C	D	E	F	G	H	I	J	K	L	M
N	O	P	Q	R	S	T	U	V	W	X	Y	Z

TYPEFACE :CX80 REGULAR P90

A	B	C	D	E	F	G	H	I	J	K	L	M
N	O	P	Q	R	S	T	U	V	W	X	Y	Z
A	B	C	D	E	F	G	H	I	J	K	L	M
N	O	P	Q	R	S	T	U	V	W	X	Y	Z

TYPEFACE :ELIZETH REGULAR P96

A	B	C	D	E	F	G	H	I	J	K	L	M
N	O	P	Q	R	S	T	U	V	W	X	Y	Z
a	b	c	d	e	f	g	h	i	j	k	l	m
n	o	p	q	r	s	t	u	v	w	x	y	z

TYPEFACE :EMILIO REGULAR P100

A	B	C	D	E	F	G	H	I	J	K	L	M
N	O	P	Q	R	S	T	U	V	W	X	Y	Z
a	b	c	d	e	f	g	h	i	j	k	l	m
n	o	p	q	r	s	t	u	v	w	x	y	z

TYPEFACE :ERNST REGULAR P106

A	B	C	D	E	F	G	H	I	J	K	L	M
N	O	P	Q	R	S	T	U	V	W	X	Y	Z
a	b	c	d	e	f	g	h	i	j	k	l	m
n	o	p	q	r	s	t	u	v	w	x	y	z

TYPEFACE :TT ESPINA REGULAR P110

A	B	C	D	E	F	G	H	I	J	K	L	M
N	O	P	Q	R	S	T	U	V	W	X	Y	Z
a	b	c	d	e	f	g	h	i	j	k	l	m
n	o	p	q	r	s	t	u	v	w	x	y	z

TYPEFACE :EXPOSURE REGULAR P114

A	B	C	D	E	F	G	H	I	J	K	L	M
N	O	P	Q	R	S	T	U	V	W	X	Y	Z
a	b	c	d	e	f	g	h	i	j	k	l	m
n	o	p	q	r	s	t	u	v	w	x	y	z

TYPEFACE :FANSAN REGULAR P120

A	B	C	D	E	F	G	H	I	J	K	L	M
N	O	P	Q	R	S	T	U	V	W	X	Y	Z
a	b	c	d	e	f	g	h	i	j	k	l	m
n	o	p	q	r	s	t	u	v	w	x	y	z

TYPEFACE :OHNO FATFACE (12PT) P126

A	B	C	D	E	F	G	H	I	J	K	L	M
N	O	P	Q	R	S	T	U	V	W	X	Y	Z
a	b	c	d	e	f	g	h	i	j	k	l	m
n	o	p	q	r	s	t	u	v	w	x	y	z

TYPEFACE :FRAGEN REGULAR P130

A	B	C	D	E	F	G	H	I	J	K	L	M
N	O	P	Q	R	S	T	U	V	W	X	Y	Z
a	b	c	d	e	f	g	h	i	j	k	l	m
n	o	p	q	r	s	t	u	v	w	x	y	z

TYPEFACE :ABC GAISYR REGULAR P134

A	B	C	D	E	F	G	H	I	J	K	L	M
N	O	P	Q	R	S	T	U	V	W	X	Y	Z
a	b	c	d	e	f	g	h	i	j	k	l	m
n	o	p	q	r	s	t	u	v	w	x	y	z

TYPEFACE :GAMUTH COLLECTION REGULAR P138

A	B	C	D	E	F	G	H	I	J	K	L	M
N	O	P	Q	R	S	T	U	V	W	X	Y	Z
a	b	c	d	e	f	g	h	i	j	k	l	m
n	o	p	q	r	s	t	u	v	w	x	y	z

TYPEFACE :GESTURA REGULAR P142

A	B	C	D	E	F	G	H	I	J	K	L	M
N	O	P	Q	R	S	T	U	V	W	X	Y	Z
a	b	c	d	e	f	g	h	i	j	k	l	m
n	o	p	q	r	s	t	u	v	w	x	y	z

TYPEFACE :GLASGOW REGULAR P148

A	B	C	D	E	F	G	H	I	J	K	L	M
N	O	P	Q	R	S	T	U	V	W	X	Y	Z
a	b	c	d	e	f	g	h	i	j	k	l	m
n	o	p	q	r	s	t	u	v	w	x	y	z

TYPEFACE :TT GLOBS REGULAR P152

A	B	C	D	E	F	G	H	I	J	K	L	M
N	O	P	Q	R	S	T	U	V	W	X	Y	Z
a	b	c	d	e	f	g	h	i	j	k	l	m
n	o	p	q	r	s	t	u	v	w	x	y	z

TYPEFACE :GREENSTONE REGULAR P156

A	B	C	D	E	F	G	H	I	J	K	L	M
N	O	P	Q	R	S	T	U	V	W	X	Y	Z
a	b	c	d	e	f	g	h	i	j	k	l	m
n	o	p	q	r	s	t	u	v	w	x	y	z

TYPEFACE :INFERI REGULAR P160

A	B	C	D	E	F	G	H	I	J	K	L	M
N	O	P	Q	R	S	T	U	V	W	X	Y	Z
a	b	c	d	e	f	g	h	i	j	k	l	m
n	o	p	q	r	s	t	u	v	w	x	y	z

TYPEFACE :INKA REGULAR P166

A	B	C	D	E	F	G	H	I	J	K	L	M
N	O	P	Q	R	S	T	U	V	W	X	Y	Z
a	b	c	d	e	f	g	h	i	j	k	l	m
n	o	p	q	r	s	t	u	v	w	x	y	z

TYPEFACE :ITEMS REGULAR P170

A	B	C	D	E	F	G	H	I	J	K	L	M
N	O	P	Q	R	S	T	U	V	W	X	Y	Z
a	b	c	d	e	f	g	h	i	j	k	l	m
n	o	p	q	r	s	t	u	v	w	x	y	z

TYPEFACE :JAZZIER REGULAR P174

A	B	C	D	E	F	G	H	I	J	K	L	M
N	O	P	Q	R	S	T	U	V	W	X	Y	Z
a	b	c	d	e	f	g	h	i	j	k	l	m
n	o	p	q	r	s	t	u	v	w	x	y	z

TYPEFACE :JOANE PRO REGULAR P178

A	B	C	D	E	F	G	H	I	J	K	L	M
N	O	P	Q	R	S	T	U	V	W	X	Y	Z
a	b	c	d	e	f	g	h	i	j	k	l	m
n	o	p	q	r	s	t	u	v	w	x	y	z

TYPEFACE :JUGENDREISEN REGULAR P184

A	B	C	D	E	F	G	H	I	J	K	L	M
N	O	P	Q	R	S	T	U	V	W	X	Y	Z
a	b	c	d	e	f	g	h	i	j	k	l	m
n	o	p	q	r	s	t	u	v	w	x	y	z

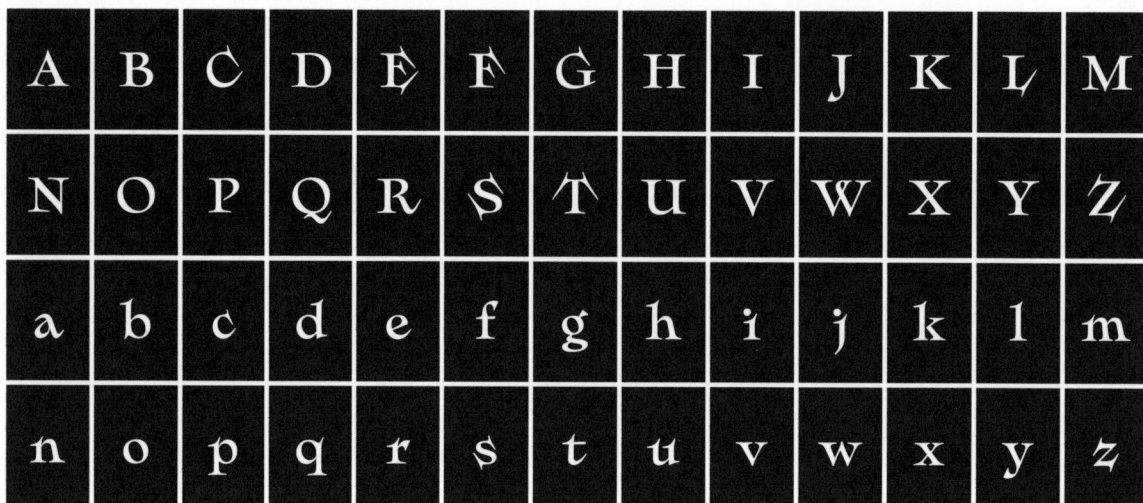

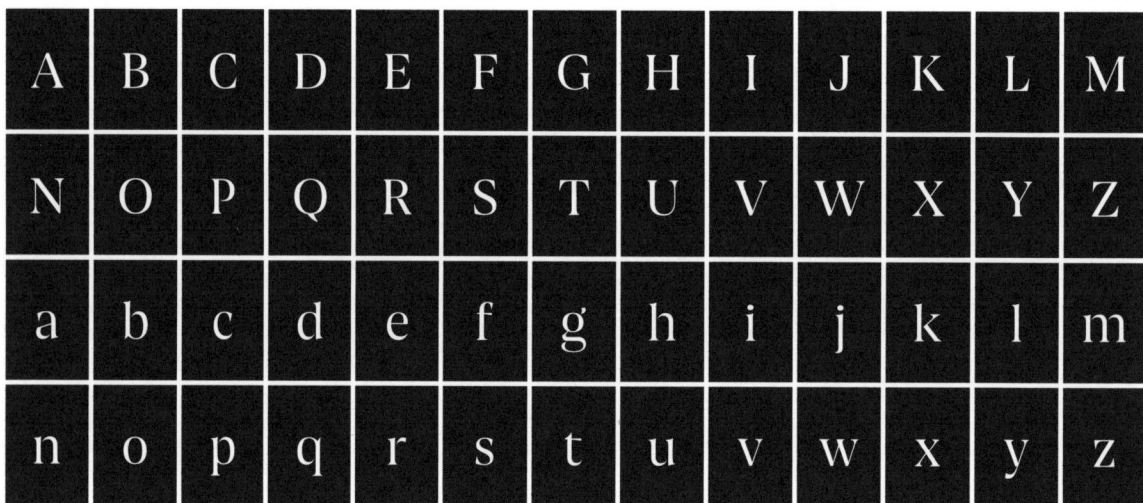

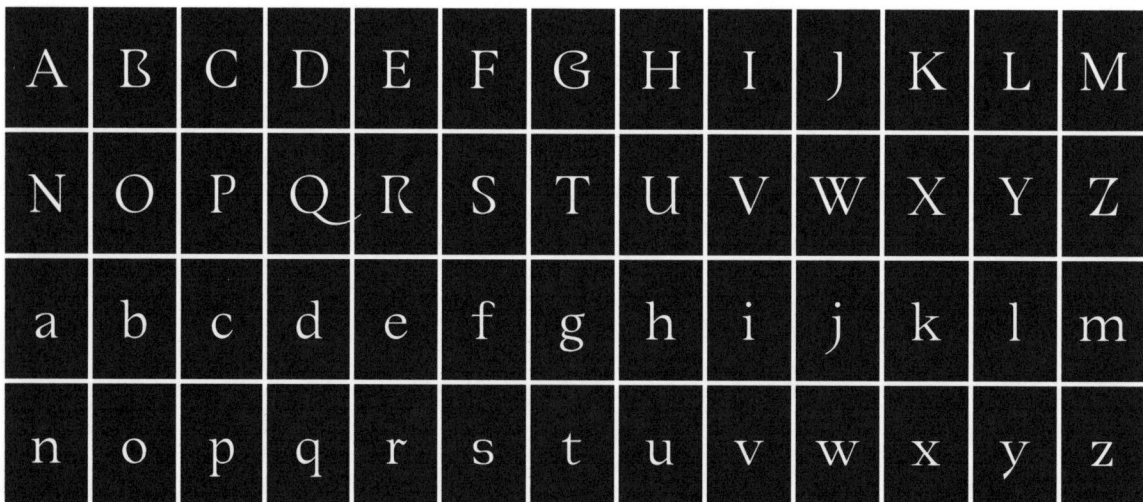

TYPEFACE :JÄGER REGULAR P188

A	B	C	D	E	F	G	H	I	J	K	L	M
N	O	P	Q	R	S	T	U	V	W	X	Y	Z
a	b	c	d	e	f	g	h	i	j	k	l	m
n	o	p	q	r	s	t	u	v	w	x	y	z

TYPEFACE :KERNEVEL REGULAR P194

A	B	C	D	E	F	G	H	I	J	K	L	M
N	O	P	Q	R	S	T	U	V	W	X	Y	Z
a	b	c	d	e	f	g	h	i	j	k	l	m
n	o	p	q	r	s	t	u	v	w	x	y	z

TYPEFACE :KESSLER REGULAR P198

A	B	C	D	E	F	G	H	I	J	K	L	M
N	O	P	Q	R	S	T	U	V	W	X	Y	Z
a	b	c	d	e	f	g	h	i	j	k	l	m
n	o	p	q	r	s	t	u	v	w	x	y	z

TYPEFACE :ABC LAICA REGULAR P202

A	B	C	D	E	F	G	H	I	J	K	L	M
N	O	P	Q	R	S	T	U	V	W	X	Y	Z
a	b	c	d	e	f	g	h	i	j	k	l	m
n	o	p	q	r	s	t	u	v	w	x	y	z

TYPEFACE :LARKEN VARIABLE REGULAR P206

A	B	C	D	E	F	G	H	I	J	K	L	M
N	O	P	Q	R	S	T	U	V	W	X	Y	Z
a	b	c	d	e	f	g	h	i	j	k	l	m
n	o	p	q	r	s	t	u	v	w	x	y	z

TYPEFACE :OR LEMMEN REGULAR P212

A	B	C	D	E	F	G	H	I	J	K	L	M
N	O	P	Q	R	S	T	U	V	W	X	Y	Z
a	b	c	d	e	f	g	h	i	j	k	l	m
n	o	p	q	r	s	t	u	v	w	x	y	z

TYPEFACE :TT LIVRET REGULAR P216

A	B	C	D	E	F	G	H	I	J	K	L	M
N	O	P	Q	R	S	T	U	V	W	X	Y	Z
a	b	c	d	e	f	g	h	i	j	k	l	m
n	o	p	q	r	s	t	u	v	w	x	y	z

TYPEFACE :LOUIZE DISPLAY REGULAR P220

A	B	C	D	E	F	G	H	I	J	K	L	M
N	O	P	Q	R	S	T	U	V	W	X	Y	Z
a	b	c	d	e	f	g	h	i	j	k	l	m
n	o	p	q	r	s	t	u	v	w	x	y	z

TYPEFACE :LUCIFER REGULAR P224

A	B	C	D	E	F	G	H	I	J	K	L	M
N	O	P	Q	R	S	T	U	V	W	X	Y	Z
a	b	c	d	e	f	g	h	i	j	k	l	m
n	o	p	q	r	s	t	u	v	w	x	y	z

TYPEFACE :FAIRE LUMA REGULAR P230

A	B	C	D	E	F	G	H	I	J	K	L	M
N	O	P	Q	R	S	T	U	V	W	X	Y	Z
a	b	c	d	e	f	g	h	i	j	k	l	m
n	o	p	q	r	s	t	u	v	w	x	y	z

TYPEFACE :MAGNO SERIF REGULAR P234

A	B	C	D	E	F	G	H	I	J	K	L	M
N	O	P	Q	R	S	T	U	V	W	X	Y	Z
a	b	c	d	e	f	g	h	i	j	k	l	m
n	o	p	q	r	s	t	u	v	w	x	y	z

TYPEFACE :MARBLE ARCH REGULAR P238

A	B	C	D	E	F	G	H	I	J	K	L	M
N	O	P	Q	R	S	T	U	V	W	X	Y	Z
a	b	c	d	e	f	g	h	i	j	k	l	m
n	o	p	q	r	s	t	u	v	w	x	y	z

TYPEFACE :ABC MARIST REGULAR P242

A	B	C	D	E	F	G	H	I	J	K	L	M
N	O	P	Q	R	S	T	U	V	W	X	Y	Z
a	b	c	d	e	f	g	h	i	j	k	l	m
n	o	p	q	r	s	t	u	v	w	x	y	z

TYPEFACE :MESSER REGULAR P246

A	B	C	D	E	F	G	H	I	J	K	L	M
N	O	P	Q	R	S	T	U	V	W	X	Y	Z
a	b	c	d	e	f	g	h	i	j	k	l	m
n	o	p	q	r	s	t	u	v	w	x	y	z

TYPEFACE :COFO METEOR SEMIBOLD P250

A	B	C	D	E	F	G	H	I	J	K	L	M
N	O	P	Q	R	S	T	U	V	W	X	Y	Z
a	b	c	d	e	f	g	h	i	j	k	l	m
n	o	p	q	r	s	t	u	v	w	x	y	z

TYPEFACE :MINOTAUR REGULAR P254

A	B	C	D	E	F	G	H	I	J	K	L	M
N	O	P	Q	R	S	T	U	V	W	X	Y	Z
a	b	c	d	e	f	g	h	i	j	k	l	m
n	o	p	q	r	s	t	u	v	w	x	y	z

TYPEFACE :MOLEN REGULAR P258

A	B	C	D	E	F	G	H	I	J	K	L	M
N	O	P	Q	R	S	T	U	V	W	X	Y	Z
a	b	c	d	e	f	g	h	i	j	k	l	m
n	o	p	q	r	s	t	u	v	w	x	y	z

TYPEFACE :MORION REGULAR P262

A	B	C	D	E	F	G	H	I	J	K	L	M
N	O	P	Q	R	S	T	U	V	W	X	Y	Z
a	b	c	d	e	f	g	h	i	j	k	l	m
n	o	p	q	r	s	t	u	v	w	x	y	z

TYPEFACE :NEUMOND REGULAR P268

A	B	C	D	E	F	G	H	I	J	K	L	M
N	O	P	Q	R	S	T	U	V	W	X	Y	Z
a	b	c	d	e	f	g	h	i	j	k	l	m
n	o	p	q	r	s	t	u	v	w	x	y	z

TYPEFACE :NOE REGULAR P272

A	B	C	D	E	F	G	H	I	J	K	L	M
N	O	P	Q	R	S	T	U	V	W	X	Y	Z
a	b	c	d	e	f	g	h	i	j	k	l	m
n	o	p	q	r	s	t	u	v	w	x	y	z

TYPEFACE :NUANCES EXTRALIGHT P276

A	B	C	D	E	F	G	H	I	J	K	L	M
N	O	P	Q	R	S	T	U	V	W	X	Y	Z
a	b	c	d	e	f	g	h	i	j	k	l	m
n	o	p	q	r	s	t	u	v	w	x	y	z

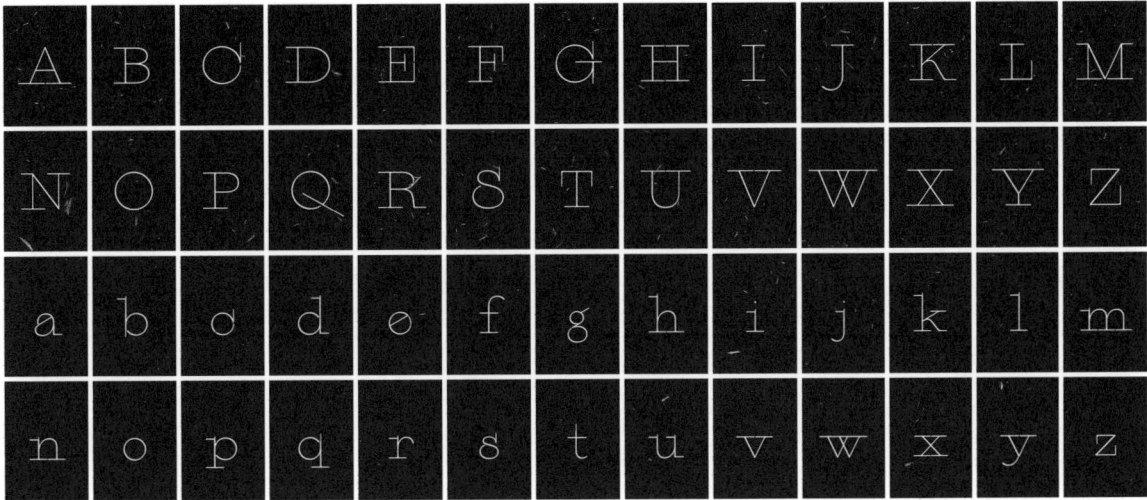

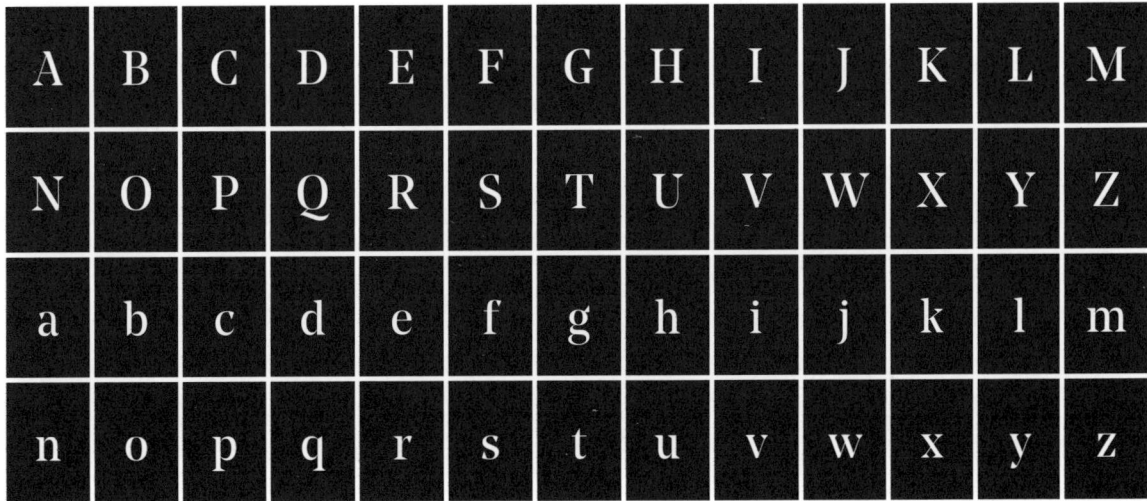

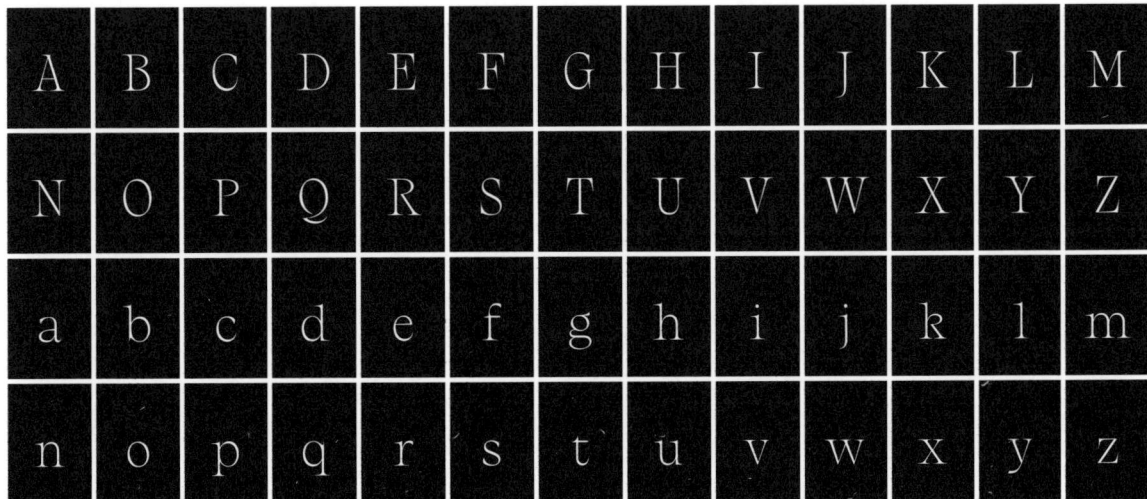

TYPEFACE :FAIRE OCTAVE REGULAR P282

A	B	C	D	E	F	G	H	I	J	K	L	M
N	O	P	Q	R	S	T	U	V	W	X	Y	Z
a	b	c	d	e	f	g	h	i	j	k	l	m
n	o	p	q	r	s	t	u	v	w	x	y	z

TYPEFACE :OGG REGULAR P288

A	B	C	D	E	F	G	H	I	J	K	L	M
N	O	P	Q	R	S	T	U	V	W	X	Y	Z
a	b	c	d	e	f	g	h	i	j	k	l	m
n	o	p	q	r	s	t	u	v	w	x	y	z

TYPEFACE :ORBIKULAR REGULAR P292

A	B	C	D	E	F	G	H	I	J	K	L	M
N	O	P	Q	R	S	T	U	V	W	X	Y	Z
a	b	c	d	e	f	g	h	i	j	k	l	m
n	o	p	q	r	s	t	u	v	w	x	y	z

TYPEFACE :RABBIT HOLE DISPLAY REGULAR P296

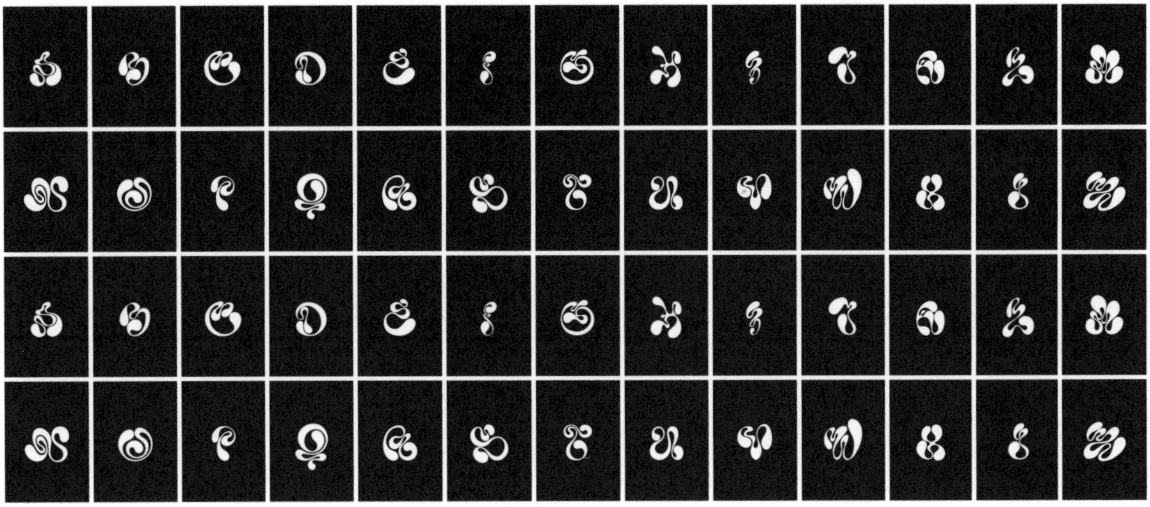

TYPEFACE :TT RICORDI TODI REGULAR P300

A	B	C	D	E	F	G	H	I	J	K	L	M
N	O	P	Q	R	S	T	U	V	W	X	Y	Z
A	B	C	D	E	F	G	H	I	J	K	L	M
N	O	P	Q	R	S	T	U	V	W	X	Y	Z

TYPEFACE :COFO ROBERT REGULAR P304

A	B	C	D	E	F	G	H	I	J	K	L	M
N	O	P	Q	R	S	T	U	V	W	X	Y	Z
a	b	c	d	e	f	g	h	i	j	k	l	m
n	o	p	q	r	s	t	u	v	w	x	y	z

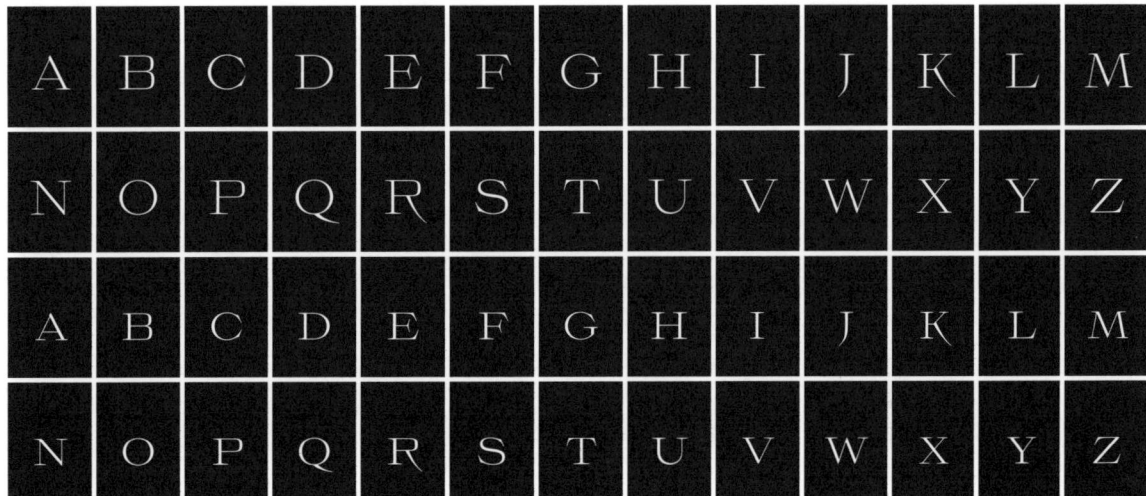

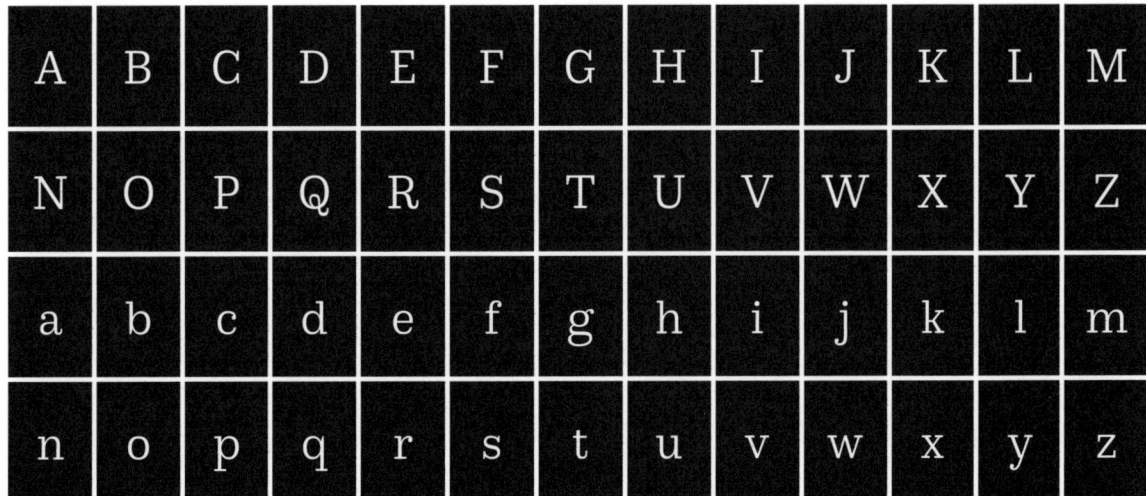

TYPEFACE :ROMEK REGULAR P308

A	B	C	D	E	F	G	H	I	J	K	L	M
N	O	P	Q	R	S	T	U	V	W	X	Y	Z
a	b	c	d	e	f	g	h	i	j	k	l	m
n	o	p	q	r	s	t	u	v	w	x	y	z

TYPEFACE :SAINTE COLOMBE REGULAR P312

A	B	C	D	E	F	G	H	I	J	K	L	M
N	O	P	Q	R	S	T	U	V	W	X	Y	Z
a	b	c	d	e	f	g	h	i	j	k	l	m
n	o	p	q	r	s	t	u	v	w	x	y	z

TYPEFACE :FT SAKRAL REGULAR P316

A	B	C	D	E	F	G	H	I	J	K	L	M
N	O	P	Q	R	S	T	U	V	W	X	Y	Z
a	b	c	d	e	f	g	h	i	j	k	l	m
n	o	p	q	r	s	t	u	v	w	x	y	z

TYPEFACE :SALTER REGULAR P320

A	B	C	D	E	F	G	H	I	J	K	L	M
N	O	P	Q	R	S	T	U	V	W	X	Y	Z
a	b	c	d	e	f	g	h	i	j	k	l	m
n	o	p	q	r	s	t	u	v	w	x	y	z

TYPEFACE :SAMZARA REGULAR P324

A	B	C	D	E	F	G	H	I	J	K	L	M
N	O	P	Q	R	S	T	U	V	W	X	Y	Z
a	b	c	d	e	f	g	h	i	j	k	l	m
n	o	p	q	r	s	t	u	v	w	x	y	z

TYPEFACE :GT SECTRA REGULAR P328

A	B	C	D	E	F	G	H	I	J	K	L	M
N	O	P	Q	R	S	T	U	V	W	X	Y	Z
a	b	c	d	e	f	g	h	i	j	k	l	m
n	o	p	q	r	s	t	u	v	w	x	y	z

TYPEFACE :SIGURD REGULAR P332

A	B	C	D	E	F	G	H	I	J	K	L	M
N	O	P	Q	R	S	T	U	V	W	X	Y	Z
a	b	c	d	e	f	g	h	i	j	k	l	m
n	o	p	q	r	s	t	u	v	w	x	y	z

TYPEFACE :SIMULA BOOK P338

A	B	C	D	E	F	G	H	I	J	K	L	M
N	O	P	Q	R	S	T	U	V	W	X	Y	Z
a	b	c	d	e	f	g	h	i	j	k	l	m
n	o	p	q	r	s	t	u	v	w	x	y	z

TYPEFACE :SLACK LIGHT LIGHT P342

A	B	C	D	E	F	G	H	I	J	K	L	M
N	O	P	Q	R	S	T	U	V	W	X	Y	Z
a	b	c	d	e	f	g	h	i	j	k	l	m
n	o	p	q	r	s	t	u	v	w	x	y	z

TYPEFACE :FAIRE SPRIG REGULAR P346

A	B	C	D	E	F	G	H	I	J	K	L	M
N	O	P	Q	R	S	T	U	V	W	X	Y	Z
a	b	c	d	e	f	g	h	i	j	k	l	m
n	o	p	q	r	s	t	u	v	w	x	y	z

TYPEFACE :STELLAGE REGULAR P352

A	B	C	D	E	F	G	H	I	J	K	L	M
N	O	P	Q	R	S	T	U	V	W	X	Y	Z
a	b	c	d	e	f	g	h	i	j	k	l	m
n	o	p	q	r	s	t	u	v	w	x	y	z

TYPEFACE :GT SUPER REGULAR P356

A	B	C	D	E	F	G	H	I	J	K	L	M
N	O	P	Q	R	S	T	U	V	W	X	Y	Z
a	b	c	d	e	f	g	h	i	j	k	l	m
n	o	p	q	r	s	t	u	v	w	x	y	z

TYPEFACE :SWEAR REGULAR P360

A	B	C	D	E	F	G	H	I	J	K	L	M
N	O	P	Q	R	S	T	U	V	W	X	Y	Z
a	b	c	d	e	f	g	h	i	j	k	l	m
n	o	p	q	r	s	t	u	v	w	x	y	z

TYPEFACE :TARTUFFO REGULAR P364

A	B	C	D	E	F	G	H	I	J	K	L	M
N	O	P	Q	R	S	T	U	V	W	X	Y	Z
a	b	c	d	e	f	g	h	i	j	k	l	m
n	o	p	q	r	s	t	u	v	w	x	y	z

TYPEFACE :TECHNIK SERIF (100) P370

A	B	C	D	E	F	G	H	I	J	K	L	M
N	O	P	Q	R	S	T	U	V	W	X	Y	Z
a	b	c	d	e	f	g	h	i	j	k	l	m
n	o	p	q	r	s	t	u	v	w	x	y	z

TYPEFACE :TESSERACT REGULAR P374

A	B	C	D	E	F	G	H	I	J	K	L	M
N	O	P	Q	R	S	T	U	V	W	X	Y	Z
a	b	c	d	e	f	g	h	i	j	k	l	m
n	o	p	q	r	s	t	u	v	w	x	y	z

TYPEFACE :FT THESAURUS REGULAR P378

A	B	C	D	E	F	G	H	I	J	K	L	M
N	O	P	Q	R	S	T	U	V	W	X	Y	Z
a	b	c	d	e	f	g	h	i	j	k	l	m
n	o	p	q	r	s	t	u	v	w	x	y	z

TYPEFACE :TOBIAS REGULAR P382

A	B	C	D	E	F	G	H	I	J	K	L	M
N	O	P	Q	R	S	T	U	V	W	X	Y	Z
a	b	c	d	e	f	g	h	i	j	k	l	m
n	o	p	q	r	s	t	u	v	w	x	y	z

TYPEFACE :TT TRICKS REGULAR P388

A	B	C	D	E	F	G	H	I	J	K	L	M
N	O	P	Q	R	S	T	U	V	W	X	Y	Z
a	b	c	d	e	f	g	h	i	j	k	l	m
n	o	p	q	r	s	t	u	v	w	x	y	z

TYPEFACE :KOMETA VICTOR SERIF REGULAR P392

A	B	C	D	E	F	G	H	I	J	K	L	M
N	O	P	Q	R	S	T	U	V	W	X	Y	Z
a	b	c	d	e	f	g	h	i	j	k	l	m
n	o	p	q	r	s	t	u	v	w	x	y	z

TYPEFACE :VISCONTE BLACK P396

A	B	C	D	E	F	G	H	I	J	K	L	M
N	O	P	Q	R	S	T	U	V	W	X	Y	Z
a	b	c	d	e	f	g	h	i	j	k	l	m
n	o	p	q	r	s	t	u	v	w	x	y	z

TYPEFACE :F37 WICKLOW REGULAR P400

A	B	C	D	E	F	G	H	I	J	K	L	M
N	O	P	Q	R	S	T	U	V	W	X	Y	Z
a	b	c	d	e	f	g	h	i	j	k	l	m
n	o	p	q	r	s	t	u	v	w	x	y	z

TYPEFACE :WULKAN REGULAR P404

A	B	C	D	E	F	G	H	I	J	K	L	M
N	O	P	Q	R	S	T	U	V	W	X	Y	Z
a	b	c	d	e	f	g	h	i	j	k	l	m
n	o	p	q	r	s	t	u	v	w	x	y	z

TYPEFACE :ZIN SERIF REGULAR P408

A	B	C	D	E	F	G	H	I	J	K	L	M
N	O	P	Q	R	S	T	U	V	W	X	Y	Z
a	b	c	d	e	f	g	h	i	j	k	l	m
n	o	p	q	r	s	t	u	v	w	x	y	z

A	B	C	D	E	F	G	H	I	J	K	L	M
N	O	P	Q	R	S	T	U	V	W	X	Y	Z
A	B	C	D	E	F	G	H	I	J	K	L	M
N	O	P	Q	R	S	T	U	V	W	X	Y	Z

B

CH4.

BIOGRAPHY & PROJECT CREDITS

205TF

205TF IS A TYPE FOUNDRY THAT BRINGS TOGETHER THE WORK OF FRENCH INDEPENDENT TYPEFACE DESIGNERS FROM VARYING CAREER BACKGROUNDS. AS A HUMAN-FOCUSED FOUNDRY, IT SUPPORTS TYPEFACE DESIGNERS BY MAKING THEIR CREATIONS AVAILABLE TO A WIDER AUDIENCE, ALLOWING FOR GREATER RECOGNITION OF THEIR WORK.

PP. 90-95, 114-119, 220-223

FONTS INCLUDED ●
CX80 / EXPOSURE / LOUIZE DISPLAY

ALAN MADIĆ

ALAN MADIĆ RUNS A DESIGN PRACTICE AT THE INTERSECTION OF FASHION, ART, AND CULTURE. WORKING IN BOTH CORPORATE AND CULTURAL FIELDS, HE SHAPES BESPOKE SOLUTIONS THROUGH A MIX OF FUNDAMENTAL AND CONTEMPORARY VISUAL EXPRESSION TECHNIQUES.

PP. 148-151

FONT INCLUDED ●
GLASGOW

PP. 424-429

APPLICATION ●
GLASGOW

BACKBONE BRANDING

BACKBONE BRANDING IS AN INDEPENDENT BRANDING STUDIO IN YEREVAN THAT FUNCTIONS AS A CREATIVE BUSINESS PARTNER TO CLIENTS WHO ARE READY FOR EXTRAORDINARY SOLUTIONS. TO DELIVER EFFECTIVE RESULTS, IT DIGS DEEP INTO A BRAND'S ESSENCE TO UNDERSTAND ITS VALUES AND INGRAIN THEM INTO THE DESIGN PROCESS FOR RELEVANT AND ENGAGING OUTCOMES.

PP. 438-441

APPLICATIONS ●
Φ I L O S O Φ 2020 / FISH CLUB WINE 2017

BAKOOM STUDIO

BAKOOM STUDIO IS A BRANDING AND DESIGN STUDIO WITH A STRONG FOCUS ON CREATING SIGNIFICANT AESTHETIC SOLUTIONS FOR ITS CLIENTS.

PP. 442-445

APPLICATION ●
LATENT 2021

BASE DESIGN

BASE DESIGN IS AN INTERNATIONAL NETWORK OF CREATIVE STUDIOS SPECIALISING IN BRANDING AND COMMUNICATIONS. IT IS A BRAND WITH CULTURAL IMPACT THAT KNOWS HOW TO EARN INFLUENCE, KEEP IT, AND DEFINE AN INDUSTRY THROUGH ITS WORK.

PP. 446-451

APPLICATION ●
THE NEW YORK TIMES: FOOD FESTIVAL 2022

BLACKLETRA TYPE FOUNDRY

BLACKLETRA IS A DIGITAL TYPE FOUNDRY RUN BY BRAZILIAN TYPE DESIGNER DANIEL SABINO, WHO IS CURRENTLY BASED IN SÃO PAULO. ESTABLISHED IN 2012, THE FOUNDRY DEVELOPS CUSTOM AND RETAIL TYPEFACES AS WELL AS LETTERING AND LOGOTYPES. ITS TYPEFACES COMBINE HISTORICAL INTEREST WITH CALLIGRAPHIC INFLUENCES AND SOMETIMES UNUSUAL IDEAS.

PP. 96-99, 234-237

FONTS INCLUDED ●
ELIZETH / MAGNO SERIF

BLAZE TYPE

SINCE 2016, THE INTERNATIONAL TEAM OF EXPERTS AT BLAZE TYPE HAS BEEN WORKING IN CLOSE COLLABORATION TO CREATE STUNNING AND INNOVATIVE FONTS, RESULTING IN A RICH, TIMELESS, AND EVER-EVOLVING CATALOGUE. THE TEAM ALSO PUTS ITS EXPERTISE AT THE SERVICE OF AMBITIOUS BRANDS BY DESIGNING CUSTOM FONTS THAT STAND OUT FROM THE CROWD. COMBINING TYPEFACE DESIGN KNOWLEDGE WITH CONTEMPORARY IDEAS, BLAZE TYPE'S FONTS ARE VALUED FOR THEIR MODERN FEATURES AND AESTHETIC.

PP. 36-41, 160-165, 276-281

FONTS INCLUDED ●
APOC / INFERI / NUANCES

BOTH STUDIO

BOTH IS A BRANDING AND VISUAL COMMUNICATION STUDIO THAT WAS CO-FOUNDED BY SIGIRIYA BROWN AND DAN SMITH IN MELBOURNE. ITS SIMPLE APPROACH IS DRIVEN BY A GENUINE INTEREST IN THE PEOPLE AND COMPANIES WITH WHICH IT CHOOSES TO WORK, LEADING TO THOUGHTFUL AND RELEVANT DESIGN OUTCOMES.

PP. 452-457

APPLICATION ●
FINE GRAZING

BRUCH—IDEE&FORM

BRUCH—IDEE&FORM IS A NATIONALLY AND INTERNATIONALLY AWARDED DESIGN STUDIO BASED IN GRAZ. IT DEVELOPS VISUAL DESIGN CONCEPTS AND APPROPRIATE STRATEGIES FOR THE FIELDS OF BRANDING, EDITORIAL DESIGN, PACKAGING AND SIGNAGE. THROUGH ITS ENDEAVOURS, THE TEAM STRIVES FOR FLEXIBLE SOLUTIONS, NEW APPROACHES, DIFFERENTIATION AND AUTHENTICITY.

PP. 458-463

APPLICATION ●
THE MOZART HOTEL 2019

CARNOKYTYPE

CARNOKYTYPE IS A SMALL KYSAK-BASED TYPE FOUNDRY RUN BY SAMUEL ČARNOKÝ – A LECTURER, TYPOGRAPHER, AND TYPE AND GRAPHIC DESIGNER. FOUNDED IN 2010, CARNOKYTYPE FOCUSES ON PRODUCING HIGH-QUALITY DISPLAY AND TEXT FONTS FOR VARIOUS KINDS OF TYPOGRAPHIC USE.

PP. 166-169, 370-373, 408-411

FONTS INCLUDED ●
INKA / TECHNIK SERIF / ZIN SERIF

CONTRAST FOUNDRY

CONTRAST FOUNDRY (COFO) IS A STUDIO FOCUSED ON DESIGNING LETTERFORMS IN ALL THEIR INCARNATIONS. INITIATED BY A COLLABORATION WITH LIZA RASSKAZOVA, THE STUDIO WAS FOUNDED BY MARIA DOREULI IN 2014. OVER THE YEARS, ITS FULL-TIME TEAM HAS GROWN FROM 2 TO 8 MEMBERS WITH A BACKGROUND IN DESIGN AND SPECIALISATIONS IN FIELDS RANGING FROM MANAGEMENT AND CALLIGRAPHY TO TYPEFACE ENGINEERING.

PP. 86-89, 250-253, 304-307

FONTS INCLUDED ●
COFO CINEMA 1909 / COFO METEOR / COFO ROBERT

PP. 418-421

APPLICATIONS ●
THE KHUDOZHESTVENNY CINEMA IDENTITY / SAN FRANCISCO FILM AWARDS 2022

COTYPE FOUNDRY

COTYPE IS THE LONDON-BASED TYPE FOUNDRY OF MARK BLOOM AND CO. ASIDE FROM DESIGNING CONTEMPORARY TYPEFACES FOR DIGITAL AND PRINTED MEDIUMS, THE TEAM ALSO DESIGNS BESPOKE TYPEFACES AND MODIFICATIONS OF THEIR EXISTING FONT LIBRARY. IT HAS WORKED WITH LEADING DESIGN STUDIOS AND AGENCIES, LICENSING ITS TYPEFACES FOR GLOBAL BRANDS INCLUDING AMAZON, VIRGIN, AND EUROSPORT, TO NAME A FEW.

PP. 292-295

FONT INCLUDED ●
ORBIKULAR

PP. 432-435

APPLICATION ●
ORBIKULAR

DALTON MAAG

DALTON MAAG IS A LONDON-BASED INDEPENDENT TYPEFACE DESIGN STUDIO FOUNDED IN 1991, WITH A PORTFOLIO OF WORK FOR GLOBAL AND LOCAL BRANDS. BEHIND THE WORK AT DALTON MAAG IS AN INTERNATIONAL TEAM OF 50 FONT DEVELOPERS, CREATIVE DIRECTORS, SOFTWARE ENGINEERS, AND SUPPORT STAFF, SPANNING 25 NATIONALITIES AND SPEAKING 14 LANGUAGES.

PP. 20-23, 174-177, 238-241, 268-271

FONTS INCLUDED ●
ALDGATE SERIF / JAZZIER / MARBLE ARCH / NEUMOND

DEV VALLADARES

DEV VALLADARES IS AN INTERDISCIPLINARY DESIGNER AND VISUAL ARTIST FROM MUMBAI, CURRENTLY DESIGNING AT COLLINS, NEW YORK.

PP. 464-467

APPLICATION ●
NEXT WAVE FESTIVAL 2019

DINAMO

DINAMO IS A GERMAN TYPE DESIGN STUDIO THAT PRODUCES RETAIL AND BESPOKE TYPEFACES, DESIGN SOFTWARE, RESEARCH, CONSULTANCY, PHYSICAL OBJECTS, AND EDITIONS. FOUNDED IN BASEL AND BERLIN, IT OPERATES VIA A NETWORK OF SATELLITE MEMBERS ACROSS THE GLOBE, OSCILLATING BETWEEN COMMERCIAL AND CULTURAL PROJECTS OF VARYING SCALES.

PP. 42-45, 134-137, 202-205, 242-245

FONTS INCLUDED ●
ABC ARIZONA / ABC GAISYR / ABC LAICA / ABC MARIST

DISPLAAY TYPE FOUNDRY

INSPIRED BY SPECIFIC MOMENTS OF IMPERFECTION AND SPONTANEOUS IRREGULARITIES, DISPLAAY IS AN INDEPENDENT TYPE FOUNDRY ESTABLISHED IN 2014 AND BASED IN PRAGUE. WITH A DIVERSE TEAM COMPRISING NUMEROUS COLLABORATORS AROUND THE WORLD, THE FOUNDRY FOCUSES ON RETAIL AND CUSTOM TYPEFACES, AIMING TO DEVELOP DISTINCTIVE TYPEFACES UNSEEN IN THE MARKET.

PP. 382-387

FONT INCLUDED ●
TOBIAS

F37®

F37® FOUNDRY & STUDIO IS AN AWARD-WINNING TYPE FOUNDRY AND DESIGN STUDIO THAT SPECIALISES IN FONTS, BRANDING, CREATIVE CODING, AND PUBLISHING. USING THE LATEST TECHNOLOGY, ITS UNIQUE, STREAMLINED, AND FLEXIBLE TEAM CONVEYS SIMPLE IDEAS IN A BEAUTIFULLY-CRAFTED WAY.

PP. 54-61, 400-403

FONTS INCLUDED ●
F37 BELLA / F37 BOBBY / F37 WICKLOW

FAIRE TYPE

FAIRE TYPE IS A NEW INDEPENDENT TYPE FOUNDRY BASED IN BROOKLYN. WORKING AT THE INTERSECTION OF GRAPHIC DESIGN AND TYPE DESIGN, IT CRAFTS FONTS, CUSTOM TYPEFACES, AND BESPOKE LOGOS WITH IMPACT. ITS TYPE CATALOGUE IS A DIVERSE MIX OF TEXT AND DISPLAY FONTS, EXECUTED WITH PRECISION AND A RIGOROUS ATTENTION TO DETAIL.

PP. 230-233, 282-287, 346-351

FONTS INCLUDED ●
FAIRE LUMA / FAIRE OCTAVE / FAIRE SPRIG

FARAWAY DESIGN

FARAWAY DESIGN IS A GROUP OF GRAPHIC, PRODUCT AND MOTION DESIGNERS WITH COPYWRITERS WHO BELIEVE THAT DESIGN IS NOT JUST ABOUT NICE TYPEFACES AND GRAPHICS, BUT THE HARMONY OF WORDS AND SHAPES: THE CONNECTION OF MEANING AND FUNCTION.

PP. 468-469

APPLICATION ●
WINE OF UJPEST 2020

FOLCH STUDIO

FOLCH STUDIO DESIGNS CONCEPTS, BRANDS, NARRATIVES, AND DIGITAL EVENTS THAT REACH AND ENGAGE AUDIENCES ON A NEW PARADIGM.

PP. 470-471

APPLICATION ●
CASA LES PUNXES

FORMAGARI

FORMAGARI IS AN INDEPENDENT TYPE FOUNDRY RUN BY EMMANUEL BESSE IN MARSEILLE, FRANCE. IT AIMS TO PRODUCE QUALITY AND SINGULAR TYPEFACES WHILE HAVING FUN DOING SO.

PP. 194-197

FONT INCLUDED ●
KERNEVEL

FORTH + BACK

FORTH + BACK IS A MULTIDISCIPLINARY DESIGN STUDIO IN LOS ANGELES, FOUNDED BY NIKOLOS KILLIAN AND TANNER WOODBURY. TOGETHER, THEY VIEW THEIR STUDIO AS A PLATFORM TO BREAK GROUND BY ASPIRING TO STAY CURIOUS WHILE SHARING THEIR CURIOSITIES WITH OTHERS.

PP. 472-477, 492-495

APPLICATIONS ●
SUNDAYS AT THE TRIPLE NICKEL 2020 / COMPOUND

FUERTE TYPE

FUERTE IS AN INDEPENDENT TYPE DESIGN STUDIO WITH A UNIQUE INTERNATIONAL FOOTPRINT, SPLIT BETWEEN THE VIBRANT LANDSCAPES OF THE UAE (DUBAI) AND THE GREEN SERENITY OF URUGUAY. IT DEVELOPS RIGOROUSLY CRAFTED TYPEFACES WITH A STRONG GRAPHIC APPEAL TO HELP DESIGNERS CREATE MEMORABLE VISUAL EXPERIENCES. ITS PROJECTS COUPLE THE TECHNICAL AND OPTICAL PRECISION OF TYPE DESIGN WITH CONCEPTS ROOTED IN ITS GRAPHIC DESIGN PRACTICE.

PP. 316-319, 378-381

FONTS INCLUDED ●
FT SAKRAL / FT THESAURUS

GRILLI TYPE

NOËL LEU AND THIERRY BLANCPAIN FOUNDED GRILLI TYPE IN SWITZERLAND IN LATE-2009 AS A COLLABORATIVE AVENUE FOR WORKING WITH OTHER DESIGNERS. TODAY, ITS TEAM OF EIGHT WORKS ACROSS NYC, COPENHAGEN, AND BEYOND. IT OFFERS ORIGINAL RETAIL AND CUSTOM TYPEFACES WITH A CONTEMPORARY AESTHETIC IN THE SWISS TRADITION. THE RELATIONSHIPS THAT IT FORGES WITH OTHER DESIGNERS ARE ESSENTIAL TO ITS MISSION AND INFORMS ITS DESIRE TO PRODUCE USEFUL TYPE.

PP. 28-31, 328-331, 356-359

FONTS INCLUDED ●
GT ALPINA / GT SECTRA / GT SUPER

HEAVYWEIGHT DIGITAL TYPE FOUNDRY

FOUNDED BY FILIP MATEJICEK AND JAN HORCIK IN 2013, HEAVYWEIGHT REFERS TO THE TYPOGRAPHICAL DESCRIPTION OF A VOLUMINOUS FONT STYLE – ITS HEAVY WEIGHT. PRIMARILY, HOWEVER, IT EXPRESSES THE EMPHASIS PUT ON SIMPLICITY, PRECISION OF DETAIL, AND TASTEFUL DESIGN, WHICH CAN BE USED VARIABLY ACROSS GRAPHIC DESIGN APPLICATIONS. BASED ON THIS APPROACH, THE FOUNDRY PRODUCES FONTS THAT ARE USED BY GLOBAL INSTITUTIONS AND SMALL INDEPENDENT START-UPS ALIKE.

PP. 82-85

FONT INCLUDED ●
CIGARS

INGA PLÖNNIGS

INGA PLÖNNIGS IS AN INDEPENDENT TYPE DESIGNER BASED IN BERLIN WHO DIVIDES HER TIME BETWEEN COMMISSIONED WORK FOR INTERNATIONAL CLIENTS AND SELF-INITIATED PROJECTS. HER WORK IS INSPIRED BY HISTORY, NECESSITY AND THE VERNACULAR. FROM LOGOS AND INDIVIDUAL LETTERS TO CUSTOM TYPEFACE FAMILIES, SHE ENJOYS VECTOR-BASED PROJECTS THAT REQUIRE SKILLED HANDS AND A TRAINED EYE.

PP. 246-249

FONT INCLUDED ●
MESSER

JENS NILSSON

JENS NILSSON IS A STOCKHOLM-BASED, AWARD-WINNING GRAPHIC DESIGNER, ART DIRECTOR, AND BRANDING EXPERT WITH OVER 10 YEARS OF INDUSTRY EXPERIENCE. HE IS THE FORMER ART DIRECTOR AT THE SNASK DESIGN AGENCY AND A 2004 HYPER ISLAND ALUMNUS.

PP. 478-481

APPLICATION ●
PACKHELP 2021

KOMETA TYPEFACES

KOMETA TYPEFACES IS A SMALL AND NIMBLE DESIGN STUDIO BASED IN BRNO, PRODUCING HIGH-QUALITY RETAIL AND CUSTOM TYPEFACES THAT MELD TONGUE-IN-CHEEK CONCEPTUALISM WITH A CONTEMPORARY FINISH.

PP. 392-395

FONT INCLUDED ●
KOMETA VICTOR SERIF

LÉON HUGUES

LÉON IS A FRENCH AND BRITISH, PARIS-BASED TYPE DESIGNER WHO FREELANCES IN VARIOUS FOUNDRIES AROUND THE WORLD, COLLABORATING ON NEW TYPEFACES AND ENGINEERING CUSTOM FONTS. FROM OBSESSING WITH CONNECTED SCRIPT FONTS AND ITALICS TO LEARNING ABOUT SOUTHEAST ASIAN SCRIPTS, HE BELIEVES THAT DIVERSIFYING HIS PRACTICE ALLOWS HIM TO LEARN AND DISCOVER NEW WAYS OF DOING TYPOGRAPHY.

PP. 106-109, 332-337

FONTS INCLUDED ●
ERNST / SIGURD

LEÓN ROMERO

LEÓN ROMERO IS A BARCELONA-BASED STUDIO FOUNDED BY JORGE LEÓN AND MIKEL ROMERO. THE STUDIO TAKES A COLLABORATIVE APPROACH TO CREATIVE DIRECTION AND GRAPHIC DESIGN TO PRODUCE BOLD, FUNCTIONAL SOLUTIONS FOR CULTURE AND COMMERCE. DRIVEN BY TYPOGRAPHY, ITS SERVICES INCLUDE VISUAL IDENTITIES, GRAPHIC CAMPAIGNS, EDITORIAL AND WEB DESIGN, PACKAGING, AND ART DIRECTION.

PP. 482-491

APPLICATIONS ●
VEINTINUEVE TRECE, A SMALL BUT MIGHTY PHOTO FESTIVAL IN A REMOTE ISLAND 2019 / VEINTINUEVE TRECE, AN OUTSIDER PHOTOGRAPHY FESTIVAL BROUGHT HOME 2022

LIFT TYPE

LIFT TYPE IS A MONTPELLIER-BASED DIGITAL TYPE FOUNDRY FOUNDED IN 2014 BY ROMAIN OUDIN. IT OFFERS RETAIL AND CUSTOM FONTS, AS WELL AS LIMITED EDITION TYPEFACES FOR SPECIFIC EVENTS EACH YEAR.

PP. 364-369

FONT INCLUDED ●
TARTUFFO

NARROW TYPE

FOUNDED BY TYPE AND GRAPHIC DESIGNER ANDREJ SEVCIK, NARROW TYPE IS A TYPE FOUNDRY THAT CREATES CONTEMPORARY, HIGH-QUALITY FONTS WITH PERSONALITY. TO THE STUDIO, AESTHETICS AND UNIQUENESS ARE JUST AS IMPORTANT AS CRAFTSMANSHIP AND FUNCTIONALITY.

PP. 100-105

FONT INCLUDED ●
EMILIO

PP. 422-423

APPLICATION ●
EMILIO

NGUYEN GOBBER

NGUYEN GOBBER IS THE COLLABORATIVE DESIGN PRACTICE OF HOANG NGUYEN AND DAVID GOBBER THAT HELPS CLIENTS FROM CULTURAL AND ACADEMIC FIELDS BY CREATING DISTINCTIVE VISUAL IDENTITIES AND EDITORIAL DESIGNS. THEY ALSO DESIGN EXPRESSIVE DISPLAY TYPEFACES, WHICH ARE USED AND TRUSTED BY GOOGLE, THE METROPOLITAN MUSEUM OF ART, SOUNDCLOUD, WETRANSFER, VICE MEDIA GROUP, AND TOMORROW X TODAY.

PP. 224-229

FONT INCLUDED ●
LUCIFER

OFFICE OF DEMANDE SPÉCIALE

DEMANDE SPÉCIALE IS A MONTRÉAL-BASED GRAPHIC DESIGN STUDIO WHOSE SPECIALITY LIES IN BUILDING BRAND IDENTITIES. BASED ON EXCHANGE AND COLLABORATION, IT OFFERS CONTEMPORARY SOLUTIONS FOCUSED ON THE ARTS, CULTURE, AND EXPERIMENTATION.

PP. 496-499

APPLICATION ●
BLEUROYAL GIN 2018

OH NO TYPE CO.

JAMES EDMONDSON STARTED OH NO IN 2015, WITH A BACKGROUND IN LETTERING AND A DEEP APPRECIATION FOR LIVELY TYPEFACES THAT ARE UNIQUELY BEAUTIFUL AND FUN TO READ. ITS GOAL HAS ALWAYS BEEN TO CREATE QUALITY WORK THAT HIGHLIGHTS UNDER-APPRECIATED GENRES AND RESPECTS HISTORY WITHOUT REINVENTING THE WHEEL. IT VALUES ORGANIC OVER GEOMETRIC, LIVELY OVER PERFECT, AND GOOD SPACING ABOVE ALL ELSE.

PP. 50-53, 126-129, 360-363

FONTS INCLUDED ●
BEASTLY / OHNO FATFACE / SWEAR

OR TYPE

OR TYPE IS AN ICELANDIC/DANISH TYPE FOUNDRY FOUNDED IN 2013 TO PUBLISH TYPEFACES DESIGNED BY GUNMAD (GUÐMUNDUR ÚLFARSSON & MADS FREUND BRUNSE). IT AIMS TO CHALLENGE THE CONVENTIONS FOUND IN TYPOGRAPHIC TRADITIONS AND CONTEMPORARY VALUES. WORKING WITH VERNACULAR REFERENCES AND INTRINSIC IDEAS, ITS TYPEFACES ARE DESIGNED TO HAVE THEIR OWN REASON FOR BEING RATHER THAN FILLING A GAP IN THE FONT MARKET. THROUGH ITS GROWING LIBRARY OF ALPHABETS, NEW IDEAS COME, AND ALREADY EXISTING TYPEFACES ARE BROUGHT UP TO CREATE A FRESH TAKE ON PREVIOUS IDEAS.

PP. 212-215

FONT INCLUDED ●
OR LEMMEN

PRETTY FACES TYPEFACES

PRETTY FACES TYPEFACES FOCUSES ON CAREFULLY-CRAFTED TYPEFACES THAT ARE BEAUTIFUL AND ATTENTIVE TO BOTH TYPOGRAPHIC TRADITION AND CONTEMPORARY CULTURE, ULTIMATELY AIMING TO EVOKE AN EMOTIONAL RESPONSE IN THE READER.

PP. 184-187

FONT INCLUDED ●
JUGENDREISEN

PP. 430-431

APPLICATION ●
JUGENDREISEN

PRODUCTION TYPE

BASED IN PARIS AND SHANGHAI, PRODUCTION TYPE IS A DIGITAL TYPE DESIGN AGENCY THAT CREATES UNIQUE AND INNOVATIVE TYPEFACES BY BLENDING TRADITIONAL AND CONTEMPORARY DESIGN ELEMENTS. ITS FONTS ARE CHARACTERISED BY ELEGANCE, PRECISION, AND ADAPTABILITY, CATERING TO A WIDE RANGE OF DESIGN NEEDS WHILE MAINTAINING A COHESIVE STYLE.

PP. 74-81, 138-141, 198-201, 254-257, 312-315, 374-377

FONTS INCLUDED ●
CARDINAL / CARDINAL TECH / GAMUTH COLLECTION / KESSLER / MINOTAUR / SAINTE COLOMBE / TESSERACT

QUATRIÈME ÉTAGE

QUATRIÈME ÉTAGE IS THE COLLABORATIVE DESIGN PRACTICE OF TOULOUSE-BASED OPHÉLIE RAYNAUD AND PARIS-BASED VALENTIN PORTE. TOGETHER THEY OFFER CREATIVE AND ART DIRECTION, VISUAL IDENTITY, GRAPHIC DESIGN, AND WEBSITE DESIGN SERVICES. QUATRIÈME ÉTAGE IS ALSO KNOWN TO EXPERIMENT AND INSPIRE THROUGH SELF-INITIATED VISUAL DESIGN PROJECTS.

PP. 530-531

APPLICATION ●
BROCK IDENTITY

RIMASÙU

FOUNDED BY MAXIME MATIAS IN 2016, RIMASÙU IS A CREATIVE STUDIO BASED IN PARIS. IT OPERATES ON THE UNDERLYING APPROACH THAT CONSIDERS THE IMAGE AS A VECTOR OF TRANSMISSION AND SENSATION. COLLABORATING WITH INSTITUTIONS FROM CULTURE, FASHION, AND ART, IT BELIEVES IN A VISION OF PLURAL DESIGN, WHERE THE SKILLS AND KNOWLEDGE OF MANY LEAD TO RELEVANT SHAPES.

PP. 500-507

APPLICATION ●
CHAIRE INNOVATION & SAVOIR-FAIRE 2018

SCHICK TOIKKA

SCHICK TOIKKA IS AN INDEPENDENT TYPE FOUNDRY ESTABLISHED IN 2010 BY FLORIAN SCHICK AND LAURI TOIKKA. LOCATED IN BERLIN AND HELSINKI, IT CREATES HIGH-QUALITY RETAIL FONTS AND CUSTOM TYPEFACES. ITS CLIENTS INCLUDE APPLE, DESIGNMUSEUM HELSINKI, GRAFIA, CHANTELLE, ESQUIRE, ELLE, AND GOOGLE, TO NAME A FEW.

PP. 170-173, 272-275

FONTS INCLUDED ●
ITEMS / NOE

SERGIO LASKIN AGENCY

SERGIO LASKIN AGENCY PROVIDES BRANDING AND MARKETING SERVICES FOR INDUSTRIES SUCH AS FOOD, REAL ESTATE, AND MORE. IT PARTNERS WITH CLIENTS AND ELEVATES THEIR BRAND VALUE WITH THOUGHTFULLY-DESIGNED EXPERIENCES. SINCE FORMING IN 2001, THE AGENCY HAS REMAINED AT THE FOREFRONT OF TECHNOLOGY AND IMPLEMENTS TAILORED SOLUTIONS WITH INTENTIONAL OUTCOMES.

PP. 508-509

APPLICATION ●
FARM KITCHEN 2020

SHARP TYPE

SHARP TYPE IS AN AWARD-WINNING GLOBAL TYPE DESIGN STUDIO THAT OFFERS HIGH QUALITY TYPEFACES FOR RETAIL LICENSING AND CUSTOM CLIENT PROJECTS. EVEN AS THE FOUNDRY EXPANDS ITS FOCUS INTO THE WORLD OF MULTI-SCRIPT LOCALISATIONS, ITS GROWING LIBRARY CONTINUES TO BE UNDERPINNED BY THE CONVERGENCE OF CLASSICAL ERUDITION, CONTEMPORARY ADAPTABILITY, AND PIONEERING AESTHETICS.

PP. 156-159, 288-291, 320-323, 338-341

FONTS INCLUDED ●
GREENSTONE / OGG / SALTER / SIMULA

SM FOUNDRY

INITIATED BY OPEN STUDIO, SM IS AN APELDOORN-BASED DIGITAL TYPE FOUNDRY THAT DESIGNS AND DISTRIBUTES MODERN RETAIL AND CUSTOM FONTS THAT FACILITATE CLEAR AND DISTINCTIVE COMMUNICATION. AT SM FOUNDRY, FONTS ARE PRODUCED WITH FUNCTIONAL AND AESTHETIC CONSIDERATION, RESULTING IN A LIBRARY OF VERSATILE TYPEFACES. IT ALSO OFFERS BESPOKE DESIGN SOLUTIONS INCLUDING LOGOTYPES, CUSTOM FONTS, CUSTOM CHARACTERS, FONT FAMILY EXPANSIONS, AND COMPLETE CUSTOM TYPEFACES.

PP. 16-19, 352-355

FONTS INCLUDED ●
AFFAIRS / STELLAGE

SOCIOTYPE

JOE LEADBEATER IS A LONDON-BASED TYPE DESIGNER WHO HAS BEEN HONING HIS CRAFT FOR CLOSE TO A DECADE. HIS TYPEFACES HAVE BEEN USED BY THE LIKES OF VIRGIN, EXPEDIA, AND STOCKX. HE IS ALSO A CO-FOUNDER OF SOCIOTYPE: A PART INDEPENDENT TYPE FOUNDRY AND PART SELF-PUBLISHER OF THE SOCIOTYPE JOURNAL.

PP. 142-147

FONT INCLUDED ●
GESTURA

STUDIO SLY

STUDIO SLY IS A BOUTIQUE DESIGN STUDIO IN MELBOURNE WITH A FOCUS ON BRANDING. LED BY INDEPENDENT DESIGNER LAUREN FINKS, IT EXPLORES BRAND AND BESPOKE DESIGN, AS WELL AS THE USE OF UNUSUAL MATERIALS AND EXPERIENCES.

PP. 528-529

APPLICATION ●
FUTURING 2023

THE DESIGNERS FOUNDRY

THE DESIGNERS FOUNDRY WAS ESTABLISHED IN 2012 AND HOSTS A CURATED RANGE OF TYPEFACES FROM DESIGNERS ALL OVER THE GLOBE. IT ALSO DESIGNS CUSTOM TYPEFACES.

PP. 130-133, 262-267, 308-311, 324-327, 404-407

FONTS INCLUDED ●
FRAGEN / MORION / ROMEK / SAMZARA / WULKAN

THEYTYPE

THEYTYPE IS AN AUTONOMOUS, CROSS-BORDER FOUNDRY FOR TYPEFACE DESIGN AND FONT PRODUCTION. FOUNDED BY SARAH AUCHES AND ALLEN'S CRUZ IN 2022, IT SPECIALISES IN HIGH QUALITY FONTS AND IS IN THE CONTINUAL PROCESS OF CREATING A SPACE THAT ALLOWS FOR BOTH AMBITION AND CHALLENGES BUT IS GROUNDED IN EXPERIMENTATION AND JOY. IT STRIVES TO FACILITATE A MORE ETHICAL, ACCESSIBLE CREATION OF THE VISUAL LANGUAGE.

PP. 24-27

FONT INCLUDED ●
ALIZEH

TODOJUNTO & ARA ESTUDIO

TODOJUNTO IS A DESIGN AND COMMUNICATION STUDIO BASED IN BARCELONA. TODOJUNTO WORKS WITH LOCAL AND INTERNATIONAL EDUCATIONAL AND CULTURAL INSTITUTIONS, AND ALSO FREQUENTLY COLLABORATES WITH BARCELONA-BASED ARA ESTUDIO, A GRAPHIC DESIGN AND VISUAL COMMUNICATION STUDIO FOCUSED ON BRANDING, EXHIBITION DESIGN, EDITORIAL AND SOCIAL MEDIA GRAPHICS.

PP. 510-519

APPLICATIONS ●
PICASSO. THE SKETCHBOOKS 2021 / ARXIUS POSSIBLES (POSSIBLE ARCHIVES) 2022

TWOPTWO DESIGN

TWOPTWO IS A DESIGN AND INNOVATION STUDIO THAT STRIVES TO MAKE COMPLEXITY SIMPLE AND SIMPLICITY MORE MOVING, BELIEVING THAT THE ESSENCE OF A BRAND IS THE CONNECTION AND TRANSMISSION OF EMOTIONS. IT ALSO BELIEVES THAT COMMUNICATION IS THE MOST CRITICAL POINT OF GRAPHIC DESIGN.

PP. 520-523

APPLICATION ●
CHO CHOCOLATE 2022

TYPE DEPARTMENT

TYPE DEPARTMENT IS THE INDEPENDENT MARKETPLACE OF TYPE01 – A CREATIVE MEDIA PLATFORM, PRINTED MAGAZINE, AND STUDIO EXPLORING THE WONDERFUL WORLD OF TYPE THROUGH CULTURE. FORMED IN MARCH 2020 AS AN EXTENSION OF TYPE01'S PASSION FOR CHAMPIONING TYPOGRAPHIC CREATIVITY, IT SERVES AS AN ONLINE PLATFORM WHERE CREATIVES FROM ALL ENDS OF THE INDUSTRY CAN HOST THEIR FONTS AND DISTRIBUTE LICENSES.

PP. 206-211, 258-261, 296-299, 342-345

FONTS INCLUDED ●
LARKEN VARIABLE / MOLEN / RABBIT HOLE DISPLAY / SLACK LIGHT

TYPETYPE.ORG

TYPETYPE IS A TYPE FOUNDRY THAT HAS SPENT THE LAST DECADE MASTERING ITS CRAFT OF CREATING TYPEFACES. ITS CORE VALUES LIE IN STRIVING FOR EXCELLENCE AND CONSTANT SELF-IMPROVEMENT, AS WELL AS BEING DEDICATED TO THE CRAFT. THE STUDIO'S MISSION IS TO CREATE AND SHARE WELL-DESIGNED, HIGHLY FUNCTIONAL, VERSATILE TYPEFACES WHILE REMAINING VISIONARIES AND PASSIONATE ARTISTS.

PP. 110-113, 152-155, 216-219, 300-303, 388-391

FONTS INCLUDED ●
TT ESPINA / TT GLOBS / TT LIVRET / TT RICORDI TODI / TT TRICKS

UNTITLED MACAO

UNTITLED MACAO SPECIALISES IN VISUAL COMMUNICATION, GRAPHIC IDENTITIES, AND BRANDING – DEDICATING ITSELF TO TAILORING AND REFINING DESIGNS FOR ITS CLIENTS. BESIDES FREQUENTLY BEING INVITED TO PARTICIPATE IN VARIOUS EXHIBITIONS, THE AWARD-WINNING STUDIO'S WORK HAS ALSO BEEN FEATURED IN MANY DESIGN PUBLICATIONS.

PP. 524-527

APPLICATION ●
MACAU DESIGNERS ASSOCIATION REBRANDING 2021

VIOLAINE & JÉRÉMY

VJ-TYPE IS AN INDEPENDENT TYPE FOUNDRY BASED IN PARIS, BORN FROM VIOLAINE & JÉRÉMY'S CREATIVE STUDIO WHERE DRAWING CUSTOM FONTS FOR PROJECTS BECAME A HABIT. THE TEAM DESIGNS FONTS LIKE IT WOULD DESIGN EVERYTHING ELSE: WITH ITS OWN ARTISTIC GESTURES AND SENSIBILITIES. ITS FOCUS LIES IN CREATING STRONG, PECULIAR, AND APPEALING FONTS.

PP. 62-67, 188-193

FONTS INCLUDED ●
CAKO / JÄGER

W TYPE FOUNDRY

W TYPE FOUNDRY FIRST TOOK SHAPE IN 2016, AND HAS SINCE WORKED COLLECTIVELY TO PUBLISH TYPEFACES AND OCCASIONALLY MERCHANDISE CO-DESIGNED WITH COLLABORATORS. ITS CATALOGUE OFFERS DESIGNERS, USERS, AND BRANDS A WIDE VARIETY OF TYPEFACES SPANNING SUPER DISPLAY FONTS, EMOJIS, SANS SERIF TYPE, TEXT, AND EXPERIMENTAL FONTS. IT ALSO OFFERS CUSTOM TYPOGRAPHY AND CONSULTATIONS.

PP. 12-15, 68-73, 120-125, 178-183

FONTS INCLUDED ●
ADORNO / CANILARI / FANSAN / JOANE PRO

YUAN CHEN JIANG

YUANCHEN JIANG IS A MULTIDISCIPLINARY DESIGNER WORKING IN GRAPHIC DESIGN, DIGITAL ART, MOTION, BRANDING, AND STORYTELLING. HE HOLDS A BA FROM THE CHINA CENTRAL ACADEMY OF FINE ART AND AN MFA FROM THE YALE UNIVERSITY SCHOOL OF ART.

PP. 32-35

FONT INCLUDED ●
ANTIQUA ROMAN

ZETAFONTS TYPE FOUNDRY

ZETAFONTS IS AN INDEPENDENT TYPE FOUNDRY BASED IN FLORENCE, ESTABLISHED IN 2001 BY FRANCESCO CANOVARO, DEBORA MANETTI AND COSIMO LORENZO PANCINI. OVER THE YEARS, IT HAS BEEN PRODUCING A PORTFOLIO OF HIGH-QUALITY TYPE FAMILIES, INCLUDING LANGUAGE AND SYMBOL EXTENSIONS FOR DIGITAL AND PHYSICAL APPLICATIONS. IT ALSO OFFERS CUSTOM TYPE DESIGN SERVICES AND BRANDING CONSULTATIONS TO SELECTED CLIENTS WORLDWIDE.

PP. 46-49, 396-399

FONTS INCLUDED ●
ARTUSI / VISCONTE

ZIN NAGAO / FOZNT

FUKUOKA-BASED ZIN NAGAO IS A DESIGNER SPECIALISING IN TYPEFACE DESIGN, GRAPHIC DESIGN, AND MOTION GRAPHICS. DRIVEN BY HIS INTEREST IN FINDING NEW EXPRESSIONS, ZIN WORKS ON EXPERIMENTAL TYPEFACE DESIGNS AND GRAPHICS BASED ON THE CHARACTERS IN HIS EXPERIMENTAL TYPEFACE PROJECT FOZNT, IN HOPES OF CONVEYING THE JOY OF TYPE.

PP. 412-415

FONT INCLUDED ●
ZNVT23

PP. 436-437

APPLICATION ●
ZNVT23

PROJECT CREDITS

PP. 418 - 419
PROJECT: THE KHUDOZHESTVENNY CINEMA IDENTITY
ART DIRECTION: ANNA KULACHEK
TYPEFACE: COFO CINEMA 1909
TYPOGRAPHER: CONTRAST FOUNDRY

PP. 420 - 421
PROJECT: SAN FRANCISCO FILM AWARDS 2022
DESIGN: CAMILLE JEN-MEI GWISE
TYPEFACE: COFO METEOR
TYPOGRAPHER: CONTRAST FOUNDRY

PP. 422 - 423
PROJECT: EMILIO
DESIGN: NARROW TYPE
IMAGE: PEXELS.COM
TYPEFACE: EMILIO
TYPOGRAPHER: NARROW TYPE

PP. 424 - 429
PROJECT: GLASGOW
DESIGN: ALAN MADIĆ
TYPEFACE: GLASGOW
TYPOGRAPHER: ALAN MADIĆ

PP. 430 - 431
PROJECT: JUGENDREISEN
DESIGN: PRETTY FACES TYPEFACES
TYPEFACE: JUGENDREISEN
TYPOGRAPHER: PRETTY FACES TYPEFACES

PP. 432 - 435
PROJECT: ORBIKULAR
DESIGN: MATT WILLEY & CHANTAL JAHCHAN / PENTAGRAM DESIGN
TYPEFACE: ORBIKULAR
TYPOGRAPHER: COTYPE FOUNDRY

PP. 436 - 437
PROJECT: ZNVT23
DESIGN: ZIN NAGAO / FOZNT
TYPEFACE: ZNVT23
TYPOGRAPHER: ZIN NAGAO / FOZNT

PP. 438 - 439 Φ I L O S O Φ 2020
PROJECT:
DESIGN: BACKBONE BRANDING
TYPEFACE: CUSTOM FONT
TYPOGRAPHER: N/A

PP. 440 - 441
PROJECT: FISH CLUB WINE 2017
DESIGN: BACKBONE BRANDING
TYPEFACE: CUSTOM FONT
TYPOGRAPHER: N/A

PP. 442 - 445
PROJECT: LATENT 2021
DESIGN: BAKOOM STUDIO
MOTION: GIMMEWINGS STUDIO
TYPEFACE: EDITORIAL NEW
TYPOGRAPHER: PANGRAM PANGRAM

PP. 446 - 451
PROJECT: THE NEW YORK TIMES – FOOD FESTIVAL 2022
DESIGN: BASE DESIGN
PHOTO: ANISHA SISODA
MOTION DESIGN: NOL HONIG
SPECIAL CREDIT: THE NEW YORK TIMES TEAM
TYPEFACES: NYT CHELTENHAM, NYT FRANKLIN
TYPOGRAPHERS: CARTER & CONE, HOEFLER & CO.

PP. 452 - 457
PROJECT: FINE GRAZING
DESIGN: BOTH STUDIO
PHOTO: SHELLEY HORAN
PRINTING: PRINT LOVE
TYPEFACES: PANAMA, MARIA
TYPOGRAPHERS: THE TEMPORARY STATE, PHIL BABER

PP. 458 - 463
PROJECT: THE MOZART HOTEL 2019
DESIGN: BRUCH—IDEE&FORM
LETTERPRESS: INFINITIVE FACTORY
TYPEFACES: ANTIQUA – AMEN, GROTESK – GERSTNER PROGRAMM
TYPOGRAPHERS: HUNGER UMLAUT, FORGOTTEN SHAPES

PP. 464 - 467
PROJECT: NEXT WAVE FESTIVAL 2019
DESIGN: DEV VALLADARES
MENTORSHIP: JENNIFER COLE PHILLIPS
PHOTO ASSISTANCE: TYLER GRIMES
SPECIAL CREDIT: MARYLAND INSTITUTE OF ART (MICA)
TYPEFACES: OGG, PX GROTESK
TYPOGRAPHERS: SHARP TYPE, OPTIMO

PP. 468 - 469
PROJECT: WINE OF UJPEST 2020
DESIGN: FARAWAY DESIGN
ILLUSTRATION: ALIZ STOCKER
TYPEFACE: N/A
TYPOGRAPHER: N/A

PP. 470 - 471
PROJECT: CASA LES PUNXES
DESIGN: FOLCH STUDIO
ILLUSTRATION: JOSEP PUY
INTERIOR DESIGN: CIRCULAR STUDIO
PHOTO: ARAMIS LEÓN
TYPEFACE: EDITORIAL NEW
TYPOGRAPHER: PANGRAM PANGRAM

PP. 472 - 477
PROJECT: SUNDAYS AT THE TRIPLE NICKEL 2020
DESIGN: FORTH + BACK
TYPEFACE: WULKAN DISPLAY
TYPOGRAPHER: THE DESIGNERS FOUNDRY

PP. 478 - 481
PROJECT: PACKHELP 2021
DESIGN: JENS NILSSON
PHOTOGRAPHY: GOLDEN RETRIEVER
TYPEFACE: OHNO FATFACE
TYPOGRAPHER: OH NO TYPE CO.

PP. 482 - 487
PROJECT: VEINTINUEVE TRECE, A SMALL BUT MIGHTY PHOTO FESTIVAL IN A REMOTE ISLAND 2019
DESIGN: LEÓN ROMERO
MOTION GRAPHICS: DANI ÁVILA
TYPEFACES: WAYFINDER CF, GT AMERICA
TYPOGRAPHERS: CONNARY FAGEN, GRILLI TYPE

PP. 488 - 491
PROJECT: VEINTINUEVE TRECE, AN OUTSIDER PHOTOGRAPHY FESTIVAL BROUGHT HOME 2022
DESIGN: LEÓN ROMERO
MOTION GRAPHICS: DANI ÁVILA
TYPEFACES: RHYMES, ANTIQUE LEGACY
TYPOGRAPHERS: MAXITYPE, OPTIMO

PP. 492 - 495
PROJECT: COMPOUND
DESIGN: FORTH + BACK
TYPEFACES: COMPOUND DISPLAY (CUSTOMISED NEUE HAAS UNICA), STEMPEL GARAMOND
TYPOGRAPHERS: MONOTYPE, FONTSHOP

PP. 496 - 499
PROJECT: BLEUROYAL GIN 2018
DESIGN: OFFICE OF DEMANDE SPÉCIALE
PHOTO: OFFICE OF DEMANDE SPÉCIALE & NATHAN LANG
TYPEFACES: MACKAY, RALEWAY
TYPOGRAPHERS: RENÉ BIEDER, GOOGLE

PP. 500 - 507
PROJECT: CHAIRE INNOVATION & SAVOIR-FAIRE 2018
DESIGN: RIMASÙU
PUBLISHING: LES PRESSES DU RÉEL
BINDING: RELIURE HOUDART PARIS (LIMITED EDITION)
TYPEFACES: SANG BLEU SERIF, SUISSE INT'L
TYPOGRAPHER: SWISS TYPEFACES FOUNDRY

PP. 508 - 509
PROJECT: FARM KITCHEN 2020
DESIGN: SERGIO LASKIN AGENCY
TYPEFACE: N/A
TYPOGRAPHER: N/A

PP. 510 - 515
PROJECT: PICASSO. THE SKETCHBOOKS 2021
DESIGN: TODOJUNTO & ARA ESTUDIO
TYPEFACES: MIGRA, KLARHEIT
TYPOGRAPHERS: PANGRAM PANGRAM, EXTRASET

PP. 516 - 519
PROJECT: ARXIUS POSSIBLES (POSSIBLE ARCHIVES) 2022
DESIGN: TODOJUNTO & ARA ESTUDIO
TYPEFACES: SUISSE WORKS, DU NORD
TYPOGRAPHERS: SWISS TYPEFACES FOUNDRY, PLAYTYPE

PP. 520 - 523
PROJECT: CHO CHOCOLATE 2022
DESIGN: TWOPTWO DESIGN
TYPEFACES: SONG SIMPLIFIED (CHINESE), ADOBE SONG (ENGLISH)
TYPOGRAPHERS: ADOBE, GOOGLE

PP. 524 - 527
PROJECT: MACAU DESIGNERS ASSOCIATION REBRANDING 2021
DESIGN: UNTITLED MACAO
CREATIVE DIRECTION: CHAO SIO LEONG, AU CHON HIN
PHOTO: REX CHANG
TYPEFACE: N/A
TYPOGRAPHER: N/A

PP. 528 - 529
PROJECT: FUTURING 2023
DESIGN: STUDIO SLY
PHOTO: MARK LOBO
TYPEFACES: ABC GAISYR SEMI MONO, ACUMIN VARIABLE SEMI CONDENSED
TYPOGRAPHERS: DINAMO, ADOBE

PP. 530 - 531
PROJECT: BROCK IDENTITY
DESIGN: QUATRIÈME ÉTAGE
TYPEFACES: ES FACE, FRAGMENT MONO, HELVETICA NOW
TYPOGRAPHERS: EXTRASET, WEI HUANG GITHUB, MONOTYPE

ACKNOWLEDGEMENTS

WE WOULD LIKE TO SPECIALLY THANK ALL THE DESIGNERS AND TYPE FOUNDRIES WHO ARE FEATURED IN THIS BOOK FOR THEIR SIGNIFICANT CONTRIBUTION TOWARDS ITS COMPILATION. WE WOULD ALSO LIKE TO EXPRESS OUR DEEPEST GRATITUDE TO OUR PRODUCERS FOR THEIR INVALUABLE ADVICE AND ASSISTANCE THROUGHOUT THIS PROJECT, AS WELL AS THE MANY PROFESSIONALS IN THE CREATIVE INDUSTRY WHO WERE GENEROUS WITH THEIR INSIGHTS, FEEDBACK, AND TIME. TO THOSE WHOSE INPUT WAS NOT SPECIFICALLY CREDITED OR MENTIONED HERE, WE ALSO TRULY APPRECIATE YOUR SUPPORT.

FUTURE EDITIONS

IF YOU WISH TO PARTICIPATE IN VICTION:ARY'S FUTURE PROJECTS AND PUBLICATIONS, PLEASE SEND YOUR PORTFOLIO TO: WE@VICTIONARY.COM